Exam Skills
Geography

Third Edition

Electives and Options
6 and 7

Higher Level
Leaving Certificate

Also Covers LC 2015

Sue Honan

MENTOR BOOKS

Mentor Books Ltd.
43 Furze Road,
Sandyford Industrial Estate,
Dublin 18.
Republic of Ireland

Tel. +353 1 295 2112/3   Fax. +353 1 295 2114
e-mail: admin@mentorbooks.ie
www.mentorbooks.ie

All rights reserved

Edited by:	Treasa O'Mahony
Book Design & Typesetting:	Mary Byrne
Cover Design:	Mary Byrne
Illustrations:	Michael Phillips

The Publishers have made every effort to trace and acknowledge the holders of copyright for material used in this book. In the event of any copyright holder having been omitted, the Publishers will come to a suitable arrangement at the first opportunity.

ISBN: 978-1-909417-41-0
© Sue Honan 2015

Acknowledgements

I would like to thank the following people for their contributions to this book:
Danny McCarthy, Treasa O'Mahony and Mary Byrne at Mentor Books; Dr Tom Hunt at Mullingar Community College; illustrator Michael Phillips; Sue Mulholland and Jean Duffy for their advice and support; the many teachers who gave such helpful contributions to discussions on the marking scheme and answers, in particular, my colleagues Anne Mulligan and Anita White at St. Mary's College, Dundalk.

I could not have produced this book without the input of students who have actually studied for and sat the Leaving Certificate Geography exam especially the students of St. Mary's College, Dundalk.

Thank you to my family for their support and patience.

Sue Honan

CONTENTS

Guidelines 5

> The Exam Paper 5
> What is an SRP? 6
> How to get Full Marks when drawing Graphs. 6
> Fundamental Map and Photo Skills 8

Section 1

Core – Physical Geography 12
  1. Plate Tectonics 13
  2. Volcanoes and Earthquakes 25
  3. Folding and Faulting 34
  4. Rock Types and Landscapes 37
  5. Weathering 46
  6. Human Interaction with the Rock Cycle 51
     - Mining 51
     - Quarrying 52
     - Oil/gas exploration 53
     - Geothermal energy 54
  7. Surface Processes - Rivers/ Ice/ Sea/Mass Movement .. 55
  8. Map Skills 66
  9. Human Interaction with Surface Processes 67
  10. Isostatic Processes 71

Section 2

Core – Regional Geography 73
  11. Types of Regions 74
      (A) Physical / Geomorphological Regions 74
      (B) Cultural Regions 77
      (C) Urban Regions 81
      (D) Socio-economic Regions 86
  12. Irish Regions: The Border Midlands West and Greater Dublin Area ... 89
  13. EU Regions: The Paris Basin and the Mezzogiorno; Human Processes in European Regions 102
  14. The Influence of the EU 113
  15. Non-EU Regions - Brazil, India, South-West USA 116
  16. The dynamics of regions – Human Processes in Ireland, EU and Non-EU Regions 128

Section 3

Electives ... 135

A. Patterns and Processes in Economic Activities (Elective 4)
- **17.** Industrial Location ... 136
- **18.** Developed Economies ... 137
- **19.** Globalisation, Colonialism and MNCs ... 141
- **20.** Local and Global Interests ... 146
- **21.** Ordnance Survey Map Interpretation and Photo Skills ... 149
- **22.** Ireland and the EU ... 154
- **23.** The Economic and Environmental Impact of Economic Activities ... 157
- **24.** Sustainable Development ... 160

B. Patterns and Processes in the Human Environment (Elective 5)
- **25.** Population/OS Map Interpretation/Overpopulation ... 162
- **26.** Migration ... 170
- **27.** Settlement: OS Map and Aerial Photo Interpretation ... 176
- **28.** Urban Land Use and Functions ... 181
- **29.** Central Place Theory ... 188
- **30.** Urban Problems and Planning Strategies ... 193

Section 4

Options ... 200

The Marking Scheme ... 200

Global Interdependence – Option 6 ... 202
- **31.** Development ... 202
- **32.** Interdependence: The Impact of Economic Activities ... 206
- **33.** Trade, Aid, Debt and Landownership ... 215
- **34.** Sustainable Development, NGOs and Empowerment ... 227

Geoecology – Option 7 ... 234
- **35.** Soils ... 234
- **36.** Human Influence on Soils/Soil Erosion ... 248
- **37.** Biomes ... 252
- **38.** Human Influence on Biomes ... 265

Guidelines

The Leaving Certificate Geography paper at Higher Level is divided into three sections. You have 2 hours 50 minutes to complete 5 questions.

The Exam Paper

PART 1
This section consists of 12 short questions each worth 8 marks. You must answer 10 questions. You should take 20 minutes to do this section. The questions are generally based on graphs, tables, diagrams, maps, photos and information you have learned. Questions will cover all areas of the syllabus.

PART 2: Section 1 - Core, Physical and Regional
This section examines core material from the physical and regional geography sections of the course. You are expected to answer one question from each of the physical and regional sections. Each question is divided into three parts: A, B and C. Each question is worth 80 marks. You should spend 35 minutes on each full question. Each part may examine a different part of the course so do not expect a full question on any one topic.

Part A is usually worth 20 marks and should be easy to complete. It may include OS map interpretation, reading a table, drawing a sketch, recognising a landform or interpreting other graphical information. You should spend 5 to 7 minutes on Part A.

Parts B and C are longer and worth 30 marks each. They require discussion or examination of a topic in 12 to 15 Significant Relevant Points or SRPs. SRPs are explained on page 6. Each SRP is worth 2 marks. You will be expected to answer questions on OS maps and photographs in the physical questions. You should spend 12 to 15 minutes each on Parts B and C.

PART 2: Section 2 - Electives
This is the Electives section. This is divided into two sections: (1) Patterns and Processes in Economic Activities and (2) Patterns and Processes in the Human Environment. **You must do ONE question from ONE elective.** Allow 35 minutes for this question. These are also multipart questions with a similar marking system to Section 2. Map and photograph interpretation are an important skill in the Electives. Timing and the number of SRPs required is the same as in Section 2.

PART 3: Options
This is the Options section. **You must do ONE question on your chosen option topic.** Allow 40 minutes for this question. The option topics are: Global Interdependence; Geoecology; Culture and Identity; and the Atmosphere-Ocean Environment. Option answers are written in essay format and are worth 80 marks. You are expected to provide 24 SRPs as well as naming discussion points (aspects) and examples. It is best to discuss 3 or 4 aspects of the question theme in detail.

Overall coherence marks apply in the Option question. Overall coherence is explained at the start of Section 4 in this book. Since 2014 overall coherence accounts for 25% of each option question. Practise and prepare your answers for this section.

The Geographical Investigation

The geographical investigation is NOT examined in the written exam that you sit in June. You will complete a Geographical Investigation on a topic set by the State Examination Commission during the year (i.e. before you sit the Leaving Certificate exam).

What is an SRP?

The examiner will look for Significant Relevant Points {SRPs} in your answers. Each SRP is worth 2 marks. In most of your answers to the B and C parts of a question you should plan to provide between 12 and 15 SRPs.

An SRP is considered to be:
- A comprehensive statement (maybe a short paragraph).
- A geographical term.
- A statistic.*
- A couple of relevant sentences making a point.
- A relevant diagram, map or chart.**
- Extra annotations on a diagram referring to information that is not in the body of your answer.
- A concise explanation of a geographical term.
- Two brief pieces of related information.
- A statistic plus some short explanatory information.

* You cannot fill your answer with statistics as the number of SRPs allowed for these will be limited.
** You should always draw a diagram in the physical geography section where relevant.

How to get Full Marks when drawing Graphs

In Part A of the Core Physical and Regional questions and in the Electives' questions you may be asked to draw a graph. There are some simple steps you can follow to ensure you get the full 20 marks for these questions.

A few simple skills can make all the difference.
- Use graph paper. There are usually 2 marks for this.
- Title the graph. There are 2 marks for this.
- Label the vertical and horizontal axes and show the scale properly on each axis. There are 2 marks for this.
- Mark all the points required clearly on the graph. There are 2 marks for each point correctly plotted.
- Use a ruler to draw your axes and a protractor to draw a pie chart.
- Do not scribble in any bars or sectors of the graph. If you have time at the end, shade in using pale block colours. Use a key if needed.
- Use the graph paper properly. Draw axes on the graph lines.

- There may be 2 marks for your overall presentation: **BE TIDY!**
- If the data shows change over time, draw a trend graph.
- If there is no change over time, draw a bar graph.

Example:
Examine the table below which shows the population of Connacht by county (2006).

County	Population
Galway	232,000
Mayo	124,000
Roscommon	59,000
Sligo	61,000
Leitrim	29,000

Source: www.cso.ie

Using graph paper, draw a suitable graph to illustrate this data. **[20 marks]**

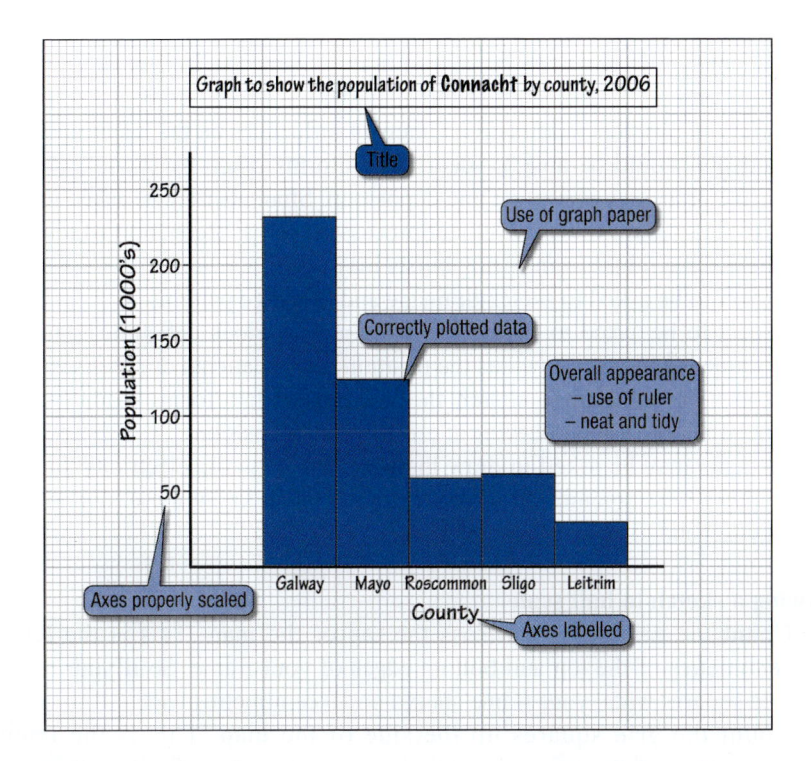

Remember!
The examiner has a template to show how the graph should look. Yours should be the same, i.e. correctly and neatly drawn.

Fundamental Map and Photo Skills

> **NOTE:** While working on the OS map and aerial photo questions supplied in this book, it is advisable to have a copy of **Leaving Certificate Past Exam Papers** to hand. They contain OS maps and aerial photographs referred to in some questions and answers in this book.

1. Map Work Skills

Map skills are an important part of the Leaving Certificate Geography syllabus. OS maps can be examined in the Core and Electives sections of the exam paper. They can be examined as short 20-mark questions or in longer 30-mark questions. Be prepared to get a variety of questions on OS maps. Use past exam papers to prepare for the exam as it is not difficult to get full marks but it is easy to lose marks if you do not pay attention to detail. **Use the guidelines below to prepare for OS map questions.**

- The maps are shown at a scale of 1:50,000. This means that 2 centimetres on the map (one grid square) is equivalent to a distance of 1 kilometre of land.
- All grid references used must be six-figure grid references.
- Students are expected to be able to draw sketches to **half scale** (i.e. half the length and half the breadth of the map extract) and could be asked to show a variety of physical landforms and human influences on the landscape.
- Students should be able to identify landforms made by fluvial, glacial and marine processes of erosion and deposition. Students may be asked to identify possible sites for mass movement processes such as steep, north-facing slopes where scree might form or bog bursts may occur.
- Expect to be asked to sketch drainage and drainage patterns.
- Expect to be asked to sketch the position of various antiquities and modern settlement patterns as well as the position of recreational or other services.
- Expect to be asked to sketch the location of landforms made by fluvial, glacial and marine processes of erosion and deposition.
- Students may be asked to draw the transport network, electricity supply grid or other infrastructure on a map extract. Get to know these symbols on the Key/Legend to save time in the exam.

Drawing a sketch to half scale
(1) Count the grid squares across the top of the map. This is the length in centimetres of the top and bottom edges of your frame. So if your map is 10 grid squares wide, your frame should be 10 centimetres wide.
(2) Count the grid squares up the side of the map. This is the length in centimetres of the left and right edges of your frame. So if your map is 13 grid squares high, the side of your frame should be 13 centimetres long.
(3) Use a ruler to draw the frame to the size you have just calculated.
(4) Write the scale of your sketch on the base of the map. It will always be 1:100,000. Drawing to half scale doubles the Representative Fraction so 1:50,000 becomes 1:100,000. Another way of writing this is 1 cm = 1 km.

(5) Put a title on your sketch.
(6) With a pencil lightly divide your frame and map area into nine equal sections. (Or divide it into sections by drawing diagonals depending on the method your teacher showed you.)
(7) Always mark in the coastline.
(8) If there is a large lake or major river sketch these as well – they may help position the other items you have been asked to draw.
(9) Draw the items required. Make sure they are in the correct location and not too big or small. Use the guide lines you have drawn to help place the items on your sketch.
(10) Roads and railways should be shown as single lines.
(11) You can use map symbols from the map key to represent items such as golf courses or caravan parks.
(12) If asked to show forestry, enclose areas of forestry in a boundary line as shown on the map.
(13) Antiquities can be shown as a dot with a name beside it or in the key.
(14) Shade in or colour lightly; do not scribble or be untidy.
(15) Use a key to name the items.

To give a six-figure grid reference
(a) Look for the sub-zone letter, e.g. S. This is a blue capital letter on the map. There may be several so make sure to check it is the correct letter for the item/location you are looking at.
(b) Read the numbers across the top of the map from left to right, e.g. 135. This is the **easting** number.
(c) Then read the numbers up the side of the map from bottom to top, e.g. 890. This is the **northing** number.

To help you remember the order, think of the word **LEN.**
    Letter: S
    Easting: 135
    Northing: 890

If you can't remember which number is which (easting or northing) just think column number before row number and remember that C is before R in the alphabet.

2. Aerial Photo
Aerial photo interpretation and sketching is most likely to be examined in the Electives and Core Physical sections of the Leaving Certificate exam paper. Photographs can be examined as a short 20-mark or a longer 30-mark question.

You are most likely to be given an oblique photo but you should be prepared to get a vertical photo. Make sure you know the location referencing systems for both (see page 10).

Location reference system for oblique photos:

LEFT BACKGROUND	CENTRE BACKGROUND	RIGHT BACKGROUND
LEFT CENTREGROUND	CENTREGROUND	RIGHT CENTREGROUND
LEFT FOREGROUND	CENTRE FOREGROUND	RIGHT FOREGROUND

Location reference system for vertical photos:

(Vertical photos usually have a north arrow printed on them. Assuming that the north arrow points to the top of the photo the following system is used.)

NORTH WEST	NORTH	NORTH EAST
WEST	CENTRE	EAST
SOUTH WEST	SOUTH	SOUTH EAST

If the north arrow is not pointing to the top of the photo, you must still use compass directions (e.g. south west or north east).

Use the guidelines below to prepare yourself for aerial photograph questions.
- **(1)** If asked to draw a sketch half the length and half the breadth of the photo, use a ruler to measure the length in centimetres of the top edge of the **photo**. Divide this number by 2. This is the length of the top and bottom edges of your frame. Then measure the length in centimetres of the side of the photo and divide by 2. This is the length of the left and right sides of your frame.
- **(2)** If you are not asked to draw a sketch half the length and half the breadth, make sure to draw the frame the **same shape** and orientation (portrait or landscape) as the photo.
- **(3)** Use a pencil to lightly divide the photo and your sketch frame into nine equal sections. Use these boxes to help position the items requested correctly.
- **(4)** Be able to identify different land uses in a photograph.
- **(5)** Be prepared to mark in areas of different land use and functions on your sketch.
- **(6)** Be prepared to mark in physical landforms such as beaches or rivers on your sketch.
- **(7)** Be prepared to choose suitable locations for new developments such as schools, industry or recreational facilities.
- **(8)** Roads and rivers should be marked with a double line. Do not draw them too large.
- **(9)** You should never use OS map symbols to mark the location of an item. Draw the **outline** of the item, **not** a picture of it.

Urban functions and land use on photographs
Remember **RICEPOTS!** This is a mnemonic to help you remember the different urban functions.

RICEPOTS stands for:
Religion/recreation/residential
Industrial
Commercial
Educational
Port
Open spaces
Transport/Tourism
Services

Do not confuse urban functions with urban land use.
Remember that 'function' means 'what it does' and 'land use' means 'what is built'. For example, if the urban function is education, the land use will be a school. You will get marks for stating the function, the land use and where it is on the photo.

SECTION 1

CORE - Physical Geography

→ This section has three questions. You must do **ONE** question.
→ Each question is divided into three parts: A, B and C.
→ At Higher Level each question is worth 80 marks. Part A is usually worth 20 marks and Parts B and C are usually worth 30 marks each.
→ You have 35 minutes to do each full question.
→ **Make sure to pick the question for which you can do all three parts!**
→ Do not spend more than 5 to 7 minutes on Part A of any question. Allow 12 to 15 minutes each for Parts B and C.
→ Expect diagrams, photos and a map in this section.

NOTE

The detail required in any answer is determined by:
• the context and the manner in which the question is asked
• the number of marks assigned to the question.
Requirements and mark allocations may vary from year to year.

Contents

1. Plate Tectonics 13
2. Volcanoes and Earthquakes 25
3. Folding and Faulting 34
4. Rock Types and Landscapes 37
5. Weathering 46
6. Human Interaction with the Rock Cycle 51
   - Mining 51
   - Quarrying 52
   - Oil/gas exploration 53
   - Geothermal Energy 54
7. Surface Processes - Rivers/ Ice/ Sea/Mass Movement 55
8. Map Skills 66
9. Human Interaction with Surface Processes 67
10. Isostatic Processes 71

Chapter 1
Plate Tectonics

Tectonic Activity

Q **Tectonic Activity – Irish Landscape Development: 2015 Question 1C**
Examine the influence of tectonic activity on the development of the Irish landscape. [30 marks]

Marking scheme:
Identify tectonic activity: 2 marks
Examination: 14 x SRPs (14 x 2 marks = 28)

What You Need To Do:
- Describe and explain destructive plate boundaries and the evidence for them in Ireland, e.g. fold mountains of Munster.
- Describe and explain constructive plate boundaries and the evidence for them in Ireland, e.g. lava plateau of the Giant's Causeway.
- Draw a well-labelled diagram.
- Give an example of each.

Answer

A The earth's crust/lithosphere is split into large slabs called plates. The plates sit on partly melted rock in the upper mantle. The plates move because heat from the earth's core generates huge, slow-moving convection currents in the upper mantle. These convection currents drag the plates along with them causing them to collide and separate forming destructive and constructive plate boundaries. The collision and separation of plates is also called tectonic activity and results in surface landforms such as fold mountains, lava plateaux and volcanoes – all of which are found in the Irish landscape.

Fold mountains in Ireland

Plate collision has influenced the Irish landscape. When mantle convection currents cause tectonic plates to collide, rock layers are folded as they are placed under great pressure for a long period of time. If the rocks are folded and uplifted, fold mountains form and this is called orogeny. The Irish landscape has been affected by two orogenies. The oldest is the Caledonian Orogeny. This occurred about 450 million years ago during the Cambrian Period. Ancient tectonic plates collided and formed fold mountain ranges with a north-east – south-west trend. In Ireland, the granite and quartzite remnants of these mountains occur in Wicklow, Galway and Donegal, e.g. the Wicklow Mountains.

Later, about 350 million years ago during the Carboniferous Period, more plate collision happened. During this time, known as the Armórican Orogeny, fold mountains with an east-west trend formed as ancient plates collided. Munster was affected by this mountain building. Ireland's highest mountain range, the Magillicuddy's Reeks, is located here.

Formation of fold mountain

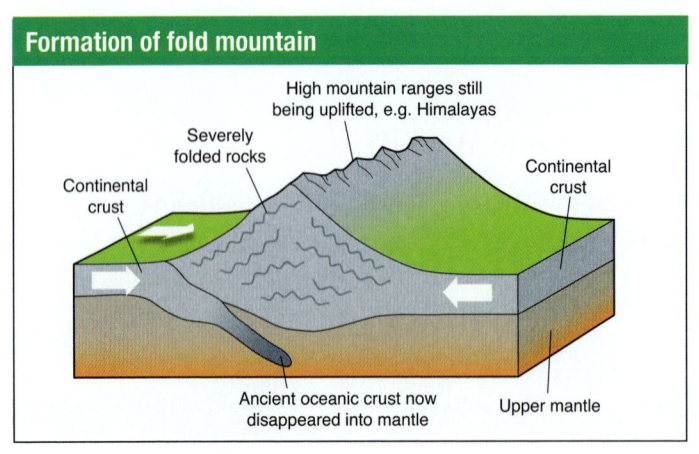

Lava Plateau in Ireland

Plate separation has influenced the Irish landscape. When mantle convection currents cause tectonic plates to separate, the earth's crust splits, normal faults form and large valleys called rift valleys form. Pressure on the mantle below is reduced and basic magma (less than 55% silica content) easily makes its way to the surface along fissures on the floor of the rift valleys. Over time and many thousands of eruptions, lava flows build up into high, flat-topped upland areas made of basalt rock. This process occurred in Ireland 60 million years ago during the Tertiary Period. The Giant's Causeway is a large basalt plateau that formed as the Eurasian plate began to separate from the North American plate.

Diagram to show the formation of a basalt plateau

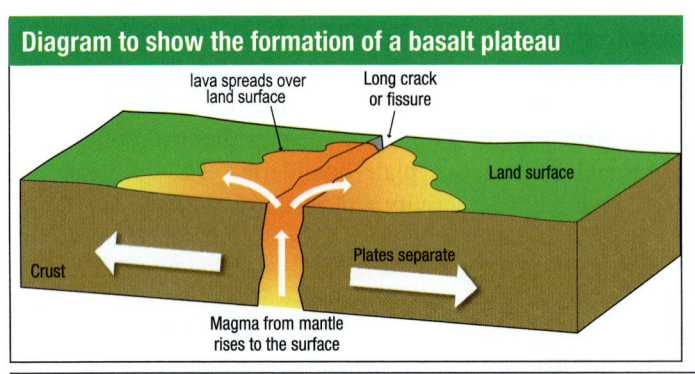

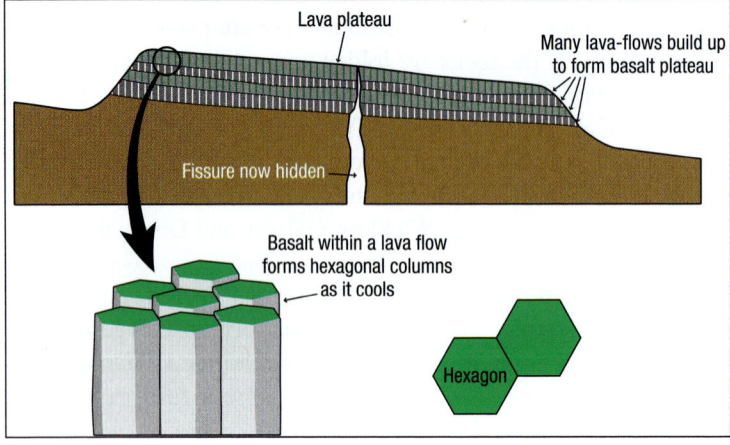

Plate Boundaries

> **Destructive Plate Boundaries: 2014 Question 3B**
> Describe and explain destructive plate boundaries.
> [30 marks]
>
> **Marking scheme:**
> Examination: 15 x SRPs (15 x 2 marks = 30)

> **What You Need To Do:**
> – Describe the three situations where plates are destroyed, giving examples.
> – Draw at least one labelled diagram.

Answer

Destructive plate boundaries.

The earth's crust/lithosphere is split into large slabs called tectonic plates that 'float' on the partly melted rock in the upper mantle. The plates move because heat from the earth's core generates huge slow moving convection currents in the upper mantle. These convection currents drag the plates along with them causing them to collide and separate forming destructive and constructive plate boundaries. In this answer, I will describe and explain destructive plate boundaries.

Destructive plate boundaries occur in three situations:

1. Where oceanic and continental plates collide, e.g. the Nazca Plate colliding with the South American Plate.

Oceanic plates are made of heavy dense silicon and magnesium rich rock, e.g. Basalt. Continental plates are made of lighter aluminum rich rock, e.g. Granite. When an oceanic plate collides with a continental plate, the heavier oceanic plate slides down into the mantle and is destroyed and recycled. This process is called subduction. During subduction, the oceanic crust melts, and the magma moves up through the continental crust above to form explosive volcanic mountain ranges, e.g. the Andes.

Deep trenches form at the boundary of the colliding plates e.g. The Peru-Chile Trench is over 8km deep. Deep earthquakes are associated with these trenches.

As the oceanic crust slides into the mantle, the sediments carried on the sea floor are scraped off and folded up against the continental plate forming fold mountains. These sediments form unique geologic areas called Terranes, e.g. The western edge of the Rocky Mountains.

Oceanic-continental plate collision

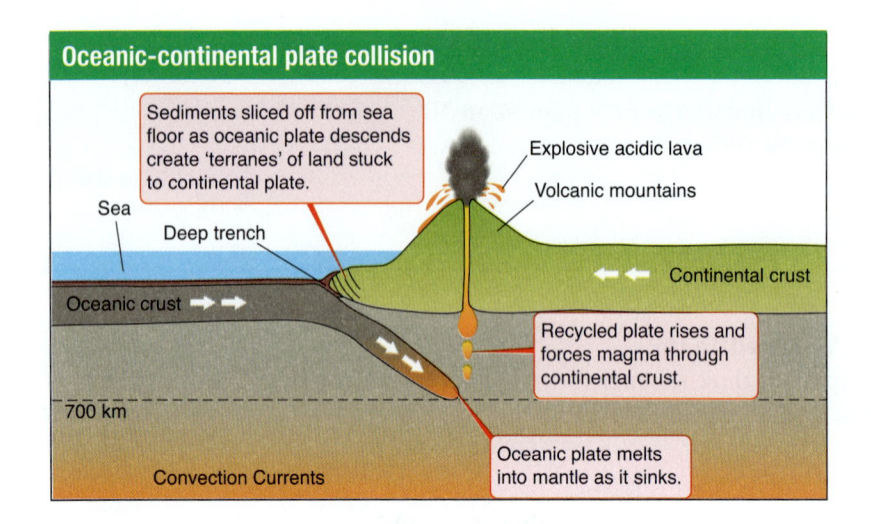

- Sediments sliced off from sea floor as oceanic plate descends create 'terranes' of land stuck to continental plate.
- Explosive acidic lava
- Volcanic mountains
- Sea
- Deep trench
- Continental crust
- Oceanic crust
- Recycled plate rises and forces magma through continental crust.
- 700 km
- Convection Currents
- Oceanic plate melts into mantle as it sinks.

2. Destructive plate boundaries occur where two continental plates collide, e.g. the Indian Plate colliding with the Eurasian Plate.

50 million years ago during the Alpine Orogeny (mountain building), the Indian plate began to collide with the Eurasian plate. Neither plate sinks into the mantle, as they are both less dense than the mantle material below. Both plates are destroyed by folding and uplifted to form fold mountains such as the Himalayas. Fold mountains are often composed of sedimentary rocks that formed on the seabed and today, fossils of marine creatures are found thousands of metres above sea level. Colliding continental plates tend to move sideways and upwards causing devastating shallow earthquakes at the plate boundary, e.g. Pakistan 2005.

Two continents collide

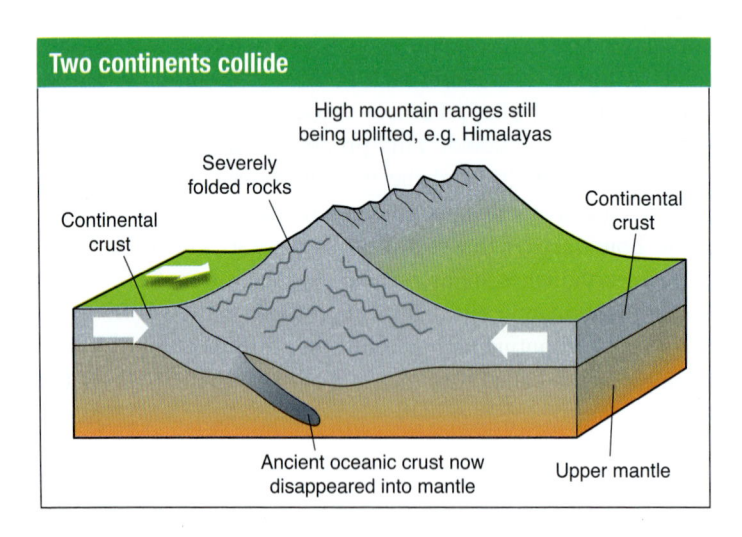

- High mountain ranges still being uplifted, e.g. Himalayas
- Severely folded rocks
- Continental crust
- Continental crust
- Ancient oceanic crust now disappeared into mantle
- Upper mantle

3. Where two oceanic plates collide, e.g. the Pacific Plate colliding with the Philippine Plate, volcanic island arcs form.

An island arc is a curved line of volcanic islands that form at the subduction zone between colliding oceanic plates. Although both plates are oceanic, usually one is heavier, or is moving faster, and it will sink into the mantle below. The plate is melted and the magma rises to form under water volcanoes. They eventually appear above the surface of the sea. The Philippine islands, Japan and the Aleutian Islands were formed in this way. A deep trench marks the subduction zone. Trenches formed at island arcs are some of the deepest parts of the ocean. The Marianas Trench in the Pacific Ocean forms where the fast moving Pacific plate collides with the slower moving Philippines plate. The Marianas Trench is over 11km deep.

> **Plate boundaries: 2009 Question 1B**
> Explain with reference to examples you have studied how plate tectonics helps us to understand the forces at work along crustal plate boundaries.
> **[30 marks]**
>
> **Marking scheme:**
> Name two forces: 2 marks + 2 marks
> Name examples of different boundaries: 2 marks + 2 marks
> Discussion: 11 x SRPs (11 x 2 marks = 22)

> **What You Need To Do:**
> - Briefly outline the theory of plate tectonics.
> - Name two forces that occur at plate boundaries: **destructive/collision** and **constructive/separation** forces.
> - Name an example of two plates involved in collision.
> - Name an example of two plates involved in separation.
> - Explain how crust is destroyed and created at the boundaries you have named.
> - Draw a diagram of a destructive and a constructive plate boundary.

Answer

Two of the **forces** at work along crustal plate boundaries are (a) **collision** and (b) **separation**.

Plate tectonic theory describes how the earth's crust/lithosphere is split into large slabs called plates. The plates move because heat from the earth's core causes the upper mantle to flow in huge slow-moving convection currents. These convection currents drag the plates along with them causing them to collide and separate, forming destructive and constructive plate boundaries.

Force (a): Collision/Destruction

Destructive plate boundaries occur in three situations: **(1)** where oceanic and continental plates collide (e.g. the Pacific Plate colliding with the South American Plate), **(2)** where two continental plates collide (e.g. the Indian Plate colliding with the

Eurasian Plate) and **(3)** where two oceanic plates collide (e.g. the Pacific Plate colliding with the Philippine Plate).

When plates collide, the heavier oceanic plate slides down into the mantle and is destroyed and recycled. This process is called subduction. Subduction causes the formation of explosive volcanic mountains on land (e.g. the Andes) or volcanic island arcs in the sea (e.g. Japan). Deep ocean trenches form at the boundary of the colliding plates (e.g. the Marianas Trench is 11 km deep). In the case of two continents colliding (e.g. the Indian and Eurasian plates), neither will sink as they are less dense than the mantle material below. Both will be destroyed by folding and uplifted to form fold mountains such as the Himalayas. Shallow earthquakes often occur at the boundary of the colliding continental plates.

Force (b): Construction/Separation

Constructive plate boundaries are places where new crust is formed. This occurs where two plates move away from each other, e.g. the Eurasian plate is separating from the North American Plate. Two mantle convection currents flow away from each other. This splits the lithosphere above and drags plates apart, forming a rift valley. Magma from the mantle is able to force its way up through the rift valley and flow out onto the seabed. The magma cools and solidifies into igneous basalt rock. This forms new ocean floor. This process is called sea-floor spreading. As the lava cools on the surface it forms large chains of undersea volcanic mountains called mid-ocean ridges. Sometimes these mountains appear above the water as volcanic islands. Iceland is an example. Unlike at destructive plate boundaries, the volcanoes at constructive plate boundaries are less explosive. This is because the magma contains less silica. As a result, it is very fluid which allows gases to escape. Sea-floor spreading also occus at the East Pacific Rise where the crust moves apart by 11 cm per year. The Mid Atlantic Ridge separates by 2-4 cm per year.

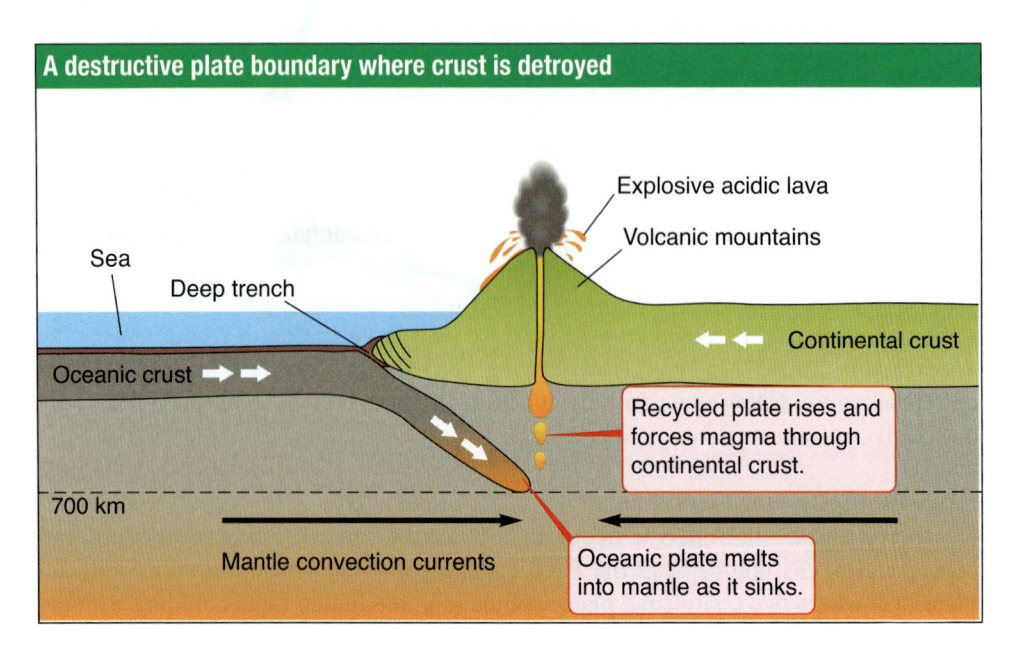

A destructive plate boundary where crust is detroyed

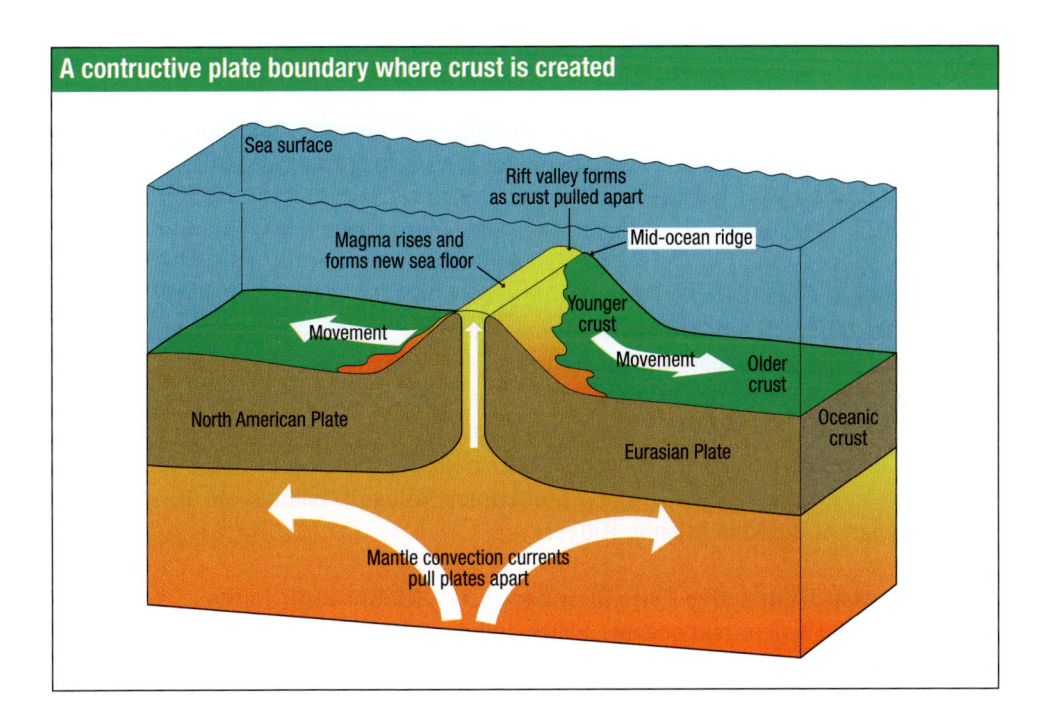

A contructive plate boundary where crust is created

Diagram labels: Sea surface; Rift valley forms as crust pulled apart; Magma rises and forms new sea floor; Mid-ocean ridge; Movement; Younger crust; Movement; Older crust; North American Plate; Eurasian Plate; Oceanic crust; Mantle convection currents pull plates apart

Plate Tectonics and Volcanic Activity

Q

Plate Tectonics and Volcanoes: 2008 Question 2B
Explain how the study of plate tectonics has helped us to understand the global distribution of volcanoes. **[30 marks]**

Marking scheme:
Global examples: 2 marks + 2 marks
Examination of plate tectonics: 13 x SRPs (13 x 2 marks = 26)

What You Need To Do:
- State that volcanic activity occurs in very specific locations across the world and these locations are linked to the operation of the tectonic cycle.
- Explain briefly the tectonic cycle.
- Name the types of locations where volcanoes occur.
- Link these locations to the operation of the tectonic cycle.
- Give an example of volcanoes at each type of plate boundary and at hotspots.
- Draw a labelled diagram to show the tectonic cycle.

A

Answer

Plate tectonic theory describes how the earth's crust/lithosphere is split into large slabs called plates. The plates move because heat from the earth's core causes the upper mantle to flow in huge slow-moving convection currents in the upper mantle. These convection currents drag the plates along with them causing them to collide and separate, forming destructive and constructive plate boundaries.

Volcanoes occur where tectonic plates collide and separate. Volcanoes also occur where a fountain or **plume** of hot mantle material rises to the surface in the middle of a plate. These are called hotspots. These locations are linked to the operation of the tectonic cycle. The tectonic cycle is the constant destruction and generation of crust.

1. Volcanoes at Constructive Plate Boundaries, e.g. Mount Hekla, Iceland
Most constructive boundaries are found under the ocean. At constructive plate boundaries, mantle currents pull the earth's plates apart, e.g. the Eurasian plate is pulled away from the North American plate. The separation of plates forms a long split in the crust called a rift valley. Magma rises from the mantle to fill the gap created by the rift. The magma reaches the surface and cools, forming a long ridge of volcanic mountains called mid-ocean ridges. Sometimes volcanic islands are formed, e.g. Iceland is part of the Mid-Atlantic Ridge.

2. Volcanoes at Destructive Plate Boundaries, e.g. Mount Fuji, Japan
Volcanoes occur where two oceanic plates collide, e.g. the Pacific plate collides with the Philippine plate. Here one plate sinks beneath the other and is absorbed back into the mantle. This process is called subduction. The melted oceanic crust is less dense than the mantle and the recycled material rises through cracks in the crust until it reaches the surface through a vent to form volcanic island arcs. These are curved chains of volcanic islands which mark the subduction zone. The magma at these destructive plate boundaries is very acidic and tends to form steep-sided volcanic cones, e.g. Mount Pinatubo in the Philippine Islands.

3. Volcanoes at hotspots, e.g. the Hawaiian Islands of the Pacific
Sometimes magma from the mantle is able to reach the surface of the earth in the middle of a plate. This location is called a hotspot. Hotspots occur because a large fountain or plume of magma rises to the surface and forces its way through the crust to form volcanoes.

Mantle plumes generally contain very basic magma (less than 55% silica) which is not very gaseous and can flow for many kilometres. The volcanic mountains that result are gently sloping and have very wide bases (shield volcanoes). As the plates move over the mantle plume, new volcanoes form. The existing ones gradually become less active and eventually extinct as the plate moves away from the plume. This has happened in the Hawaiian Islands. The youngest island (Maui) contains active volcanoes which are currently over the hotspot and the old volcanic islands are extinct as they are no longer over the hotspot because the plate has moved away from it.

Tectonic cycle and the location of volcanoes

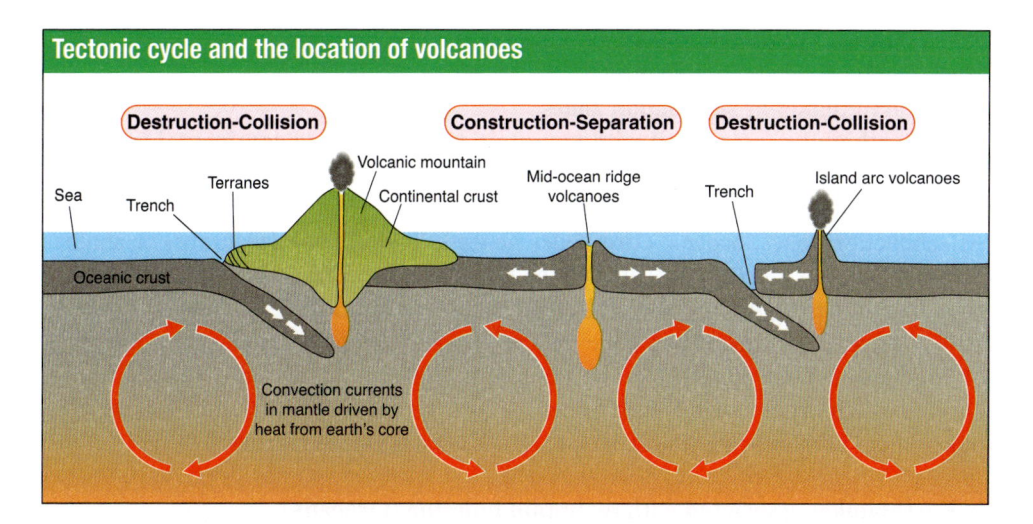

Plate Tectonics and the Occurrence of Earthquakes

Q

Plate Tectonics and Earthquakes: 2012 Question 1C
Explain with reference to examples you have studied how the theory of plate tectonics helps to explain the distribution of earthquakes around the world.

[30 marks]

Marking scheme:
Global Examples of earthquakes: 2 marks + 2 marks
Discussion 13 x SRPs (13 x 2 marks = 26 marks)

What You Need To Do:
- Make the point that earthquakes are associated with the edges of tectonic plates.
- Make the point that different plate boundaries cause different types of quakes (shallow, deep, strong, weak).
- Briefly describe the different types of plate boundaries and describe the types of quakes that occur and why.
- Give an example of an earthquake that has occurred at each type of plate boundary.

Answer

A Earthquakes are caused by movement of the world's tectonic plates. Most earthquakes occur at plate boundaries so a study of these boundaries can help us understand the depth, location and magnitude (on the Richter Scale) of earthquakes.

The theory of plate tectonics explains how the earth's crust is split into huge slabs of rock called tectonic plates. The plates are moved by slow-moving convection currents in the mantle below. The convection currents cause the plates to collide, separate and slide past each other at plate boundaries. There are three types of plate boundaries in the earth's crust and each is associated with earthquakes.

1. Earthquakes at destructive plate boundaries
These can be divided into **two** groups:
- **a. Earthquakes at subduction zones**
- **b. Earthquakes associated with mountain building due to continental collision**

a. Earthquakes at subduction zones
At subduction zones, oceanic crust slides beneath lighter continental crust or another oceanic plate, e.g. the Pacific Plate and the Eurasian plate. The descending plate moves in sudden bursts triggering powerful earthquakes (e.g. the Japanese Tsunami quake in 2011). Because the descending plate may reach great depths before it melts, the focus of subduction zone quakes may be deep (e.g. 300 kilometres below the surface). Quakes which occur at subduction zones are also very powerful, often measuring 8 or more on the Richter Scale (the 2010 Japanese Tsunami Quake registered 9·0).

b. Earthquakes associated with mountain building (Orogeny)
Earthquakes also occur where two continental plates collide and fold mountains are formed, e.g. the Himalayas formed where the Indian Plate and the Eurasian Plate collide and this area experiences earthquake activity.

As the plates collide land is uplifted and shallow quakes occur whose focus is less than 70 kilometres below the surface. These quakes may not rate highly on the Richter Scale but because they are shallow much damage is done. The 2008 Sichuan Quake in China registered 8·0 (very strong for this region), devastated huge areas and left millions homeless. Its focus was only 19 kilometres below the surface.

2. Earthquakes associated with conservative plate boundaries/transform faults
When two tectonic plates slide past each other, a conservative plate boundary is formed. This is seen along the boundary between the North American Plate and the Pacific Plate. Sometimes they lock against each other, and at other times they slide smoothly past each other. When the plates are locked together, pressure may build up for centuries and then suddenly release causing earthquakes. These quakes can be very powerful due to the great amounts of energy released and the shallow depth of the foci. The Haiti 2010 quake occurred at this type of boundary between the North American and Caribbean plates.

3. Earthquakes associated with constructive plate boundaries
Here magma reaches the earth's surface as two plates separate, e.g. at the mid-ocean ridge between the North American and Eurasian plates. The vibration of rising magma and bursting gas bubbles within the magma chamber causes frequent shallow quakes which are not very powerful and rarely cause much damage.

Plate Tectonics and the Occurrence of Fold Mountains

Q

Folding: 2010 Question 2B
Explain how the study of plate tectonics has helped us to understand the global distribution of Fold Mountains. [30 marks]

Marking scheme:
Refer to global distribution: 2 marks + 2 marks
Name 2 fold mountains: 2 marks + 2 marks
Examination of plate tectonics: 11 x SRPs (11 x 2 marks = 22)

What You Need To Do:
- Briefly state the theory of plate tectonics.
- Name two fold mountain ranges.
- Discuss how plate collision causes fold mountains to be formed making sure to name two different examples of plate collision leading to fold mountains.
- Draw and label a diagram.

A

Answer

Examples of fold mountains: The Himalaya Mountains of India and the Andes Mountains of South America.

The theory of plate tectonics describes how the earth's crust/lithosphere is split into large slabs called plates which move around the surface of the earth. The plates move because heat from the earth's core causes magma to flow in huge, slow-moving convection currents in the upper mantle. These mantle convection currents drag the plates along with them, causing them to collide. Where plates collide at convergent/destructive plate boundaries, fold mountains are formed. Fold mountains occur at two types of convergent/destructive plate boundary: subduction zones and where two continental plates collide.

1. Fold mountains at subduction zones

Convection currents in the mantle cause an oceanic plate to collide with a continental plate. This occurs where the Nazca plate collides with the South American plate.

The heavier oceanic crust slides beneath the lighter continental crust. As the plates collide, the sea-floor sediments carried by the oceanic crust are piled against the continental crust. The huge pressure caused by plate collision slowly compresses the sediments and uplifts them. At the same time the rocks of the continental crust are also folded and uplifted. Over millions of years high mountains of folded rock are formed. Fold mountains formed in this way may also have volcanic mountains within them. This is because as the oceanic crust is subducted below the continental crust, it melts and is recycled, e.g. the Andes fold mountains have active volcanoes such as Cotapaxi within them.

The formation of fold mountains at subduction zones

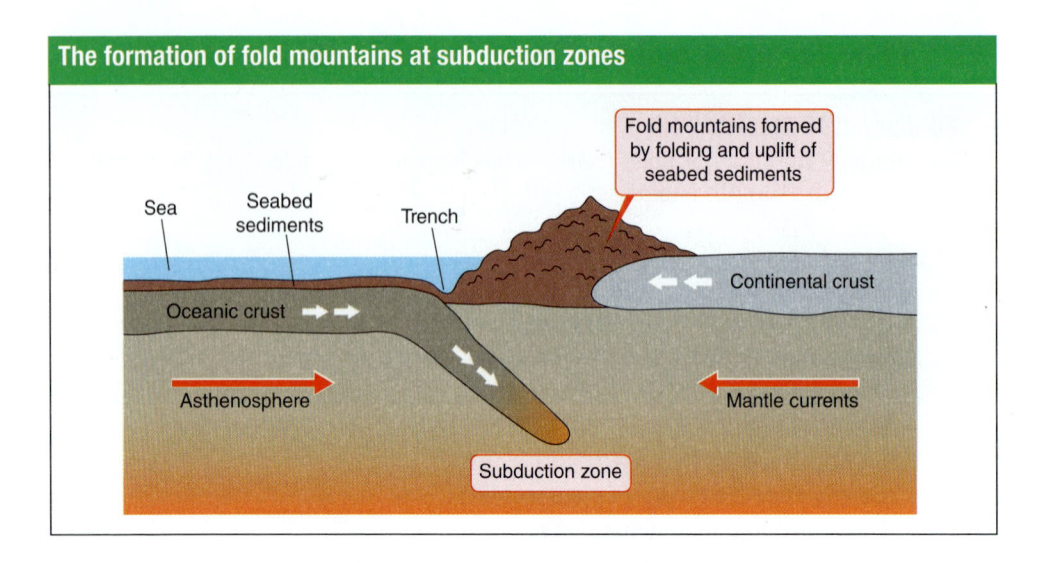

2. Fold mountains where two continental plates collide

Fold mountains form where two continental plates collide. This occurs where the Indian plate collides with the Eurasian plate, thus forming the Himalaya Mountains. Neither plate sinks into the mantle. Both continental plates resist sinking because they are made of rocks rich in silicon and aluminium (sial) that are much less dense than the mantle material below. The slow collision causes the rock on both plates to fold and be uplifted. The Himalaya Mountains are being uplifted at a rate of one cm per year.

Nearly all fold mountains are made of sedimentary rocks such as limestone. The fossils they contain are today three to four kilometres above sea level. The youngest and highest fold mountains are Alpine in age having formed during the last 50 million years, e.g. Mount Everest is 8,848 m high. In Ireland, the fold mountains of the Munster Ridge and Valley province were formed by continental plate collision 350 million years ago during the Armorican phase of mountain building. Today sandstone anticlines form the mountain ridges and limestone-covered valleys form the fold synclines.

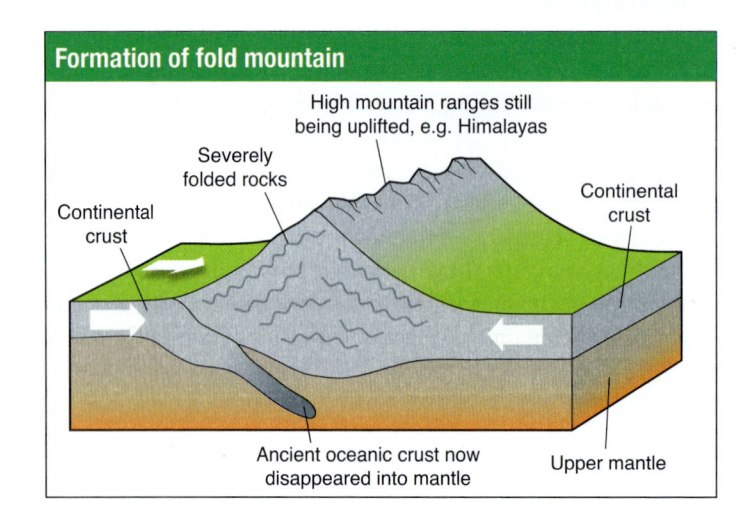

Formation of fold mountain

Chapter 2

Volcanoes and Earthquakes

The Positive Effects of Volcanoes

Q

Volcanoes: 2011 Question 1B
Discuss the positive impacts of volcanic activity. [30 marks]

Marking scheme:
Identify two positive impacts: 2 marks + 2 marks
Discussion: 13 x SRPs (13 x 2 marks = 26)

What You Need To Do:
- Name two positive impacts of volcanic activity.
- Discuss each impact in 5/6 SRPs.
- Give an example of each positive impact.

A

Answer

Volcanic activity around the world has several positive impacts. There are two major benefits of volcanic activity.
1. Tourism
2. Geothermal energy

1. Tourism

Volcanic activity is a major tourist attraction in many countries around the world such as Iceland, Italy and New Zealand. Volcanism creates landscapes that are very dramatic and these attract thousands of visitors every year. For example, about 200,000 people climb Mount Fuji in Japan each year to view the crater.

Volcanic areas also provide hot springs and hot mud pools which attract people to bathe in them because of the benefits to their skin or for fun. This activity is common in Turkey and Iceland.

Geysers are fountains of extremely hot water that erupt from the ground in volcanic regions. They attract thousands of visitors and are popular because they erupt so dramatically and at regular intervals of 30 minutes or so. Old Faithful in Yellowstone National Park, USA erupts every 30 – 120 minutes. Each year 2.6 million people come to see it, generating income for the local economy.

The economic benefits of volcano tourism include increased income for the local area and foreign currency exchange income for the national government. In Iceland each year the arrival of half a million visitors is worth over 700 million Euro to the economy. Many volcanic tourist attractions have tourist services such as coffee shops, souvenir shops and restaurants located nearby. Local people are employed as guides and drivers for visitors. These activities employ people and their wages spread through the local economy (multiplier effect). Visitors to the region also buy other services such as accommodation and transport and this contributes to the national economy of the country.

2. Geothermal energy

Geothermal energy production uses heat from hot igneous rocks to heat water and generate steam which can be used to make electricity. Several countries, especially Iceland and New Zealand, use geothermal energy.

Geothermal energy uses the rock cycle to provide heat and power. Iceland is located on the Mid Atlantic Ridge. Here the Eurasian plate is moving apart from the North American plate. Hot magma from the mantle rises to fill the rift between the plates. Hot igneous rock heats the rainwater that seeps into the ground to a temperature of over 200°C.

The hot water can be captured by drilling two km down into the hot rocks above the magma. The water is then carried by insulated pipes directly to homes and industries to supply hot water and central heating. The energy is also used to heat greenhouses for vegetable production. Iceland uses geothermal energy to make electricity. At present 26% of electricity in Iceland is generated using geothermal energy. The country has five geothermal power plants. Heating from this source of energy provides hot water and heating for 89% of Iceland's housing. It is such a cheap source of heat that some footpaths in Iceland's capital (Reykjavik) are heated.

Geothermal energy reduces the need for fossil fuels and helps reduce harmful greenhouse gas emissions. Iceland also plans to sell its geothermal electricity to Europe through undersea cables measuring 1,170 km in length that will be connected to the UK.

In Iceland geothermal energy is also a tourist attraction. One power plant just south of Reykjavik uses mineral-rich water from the power station to fill up a nearby lake known as the Blue Lagoon. This has become one of Iceland's most famous tourist destinations and has a spa complex beside the lagoon where the water is kept at 40°C for bathers. Over half a million people visit Iceland's geothermal attractions each year.

Volcanic Landforms

Formation of Volcanic Landforms: 2006 Question 3C
Examine the processes that have led to the formation of any **two** volcanic landforms. [30 marks]

Marking scheme:
Name landforms: 2 marks
Discuss processes: 7 x SRPs [for each of two landforms] (7 x 2 marks = 14; 14 x 2 = 28)

What You Need To Do:
- Name two different types of volcanic landform.
- Give an example of each.
- Describe how they are formed.
- Make sure to describe the processes that formed them.

> **NOTE**
> In this answer the processes leading to the formation of **two** extrusive/volcanic landforms are provided for your information (shield volcanoes and basalt plateaux) **as well as** an intrusive volcanic landform (batholiths).

A

Answer

Landform 1(a) : Volcanic Cones - Shield Volcanoes
Example: Mauna Loa, Hawaii

Volcanoes are extrusive volcanic landforms which are found on the earth's surface. Volcanic cones form when magma rises from the mantle and forces its way through a weakness (vent) in the crust and reaches the surface. Magma rises because it is hot and less dense than the cooler rocks above. As the magma rises, gas bubbles in it expand and help the magma force its way through any cracks in the crust above. Once the magma reaches the surface, the sudden release of pressure causes a volcanic eruption to occur and a volcanic cone begins to form.

The shape of the volcano depends on the type of lava erupting from it. Shield volcanoes form when basic lava, which contains less than 55% silica, erupts from the vent. Basic lava is very runny and can flow for many kilometres before it solidifies into basalt rock. Shield volcanoes are built up slowly from the addition of thousands of lava flows that spread over great distances and then cool into thin, gently-sloping sheets of lava.

As a result of this process, shield volcanoes tend to have gently-sloping cones with a wide base. From the air they are circular in shape with the vent in the centre. This resembles a warrior shield and so they are known as shield volcanoes.

Shield volcanoes are common at hotspots where magma forces its way to the surface in the middle of a tectonic plate, e.g. the Hawaiian Islands.

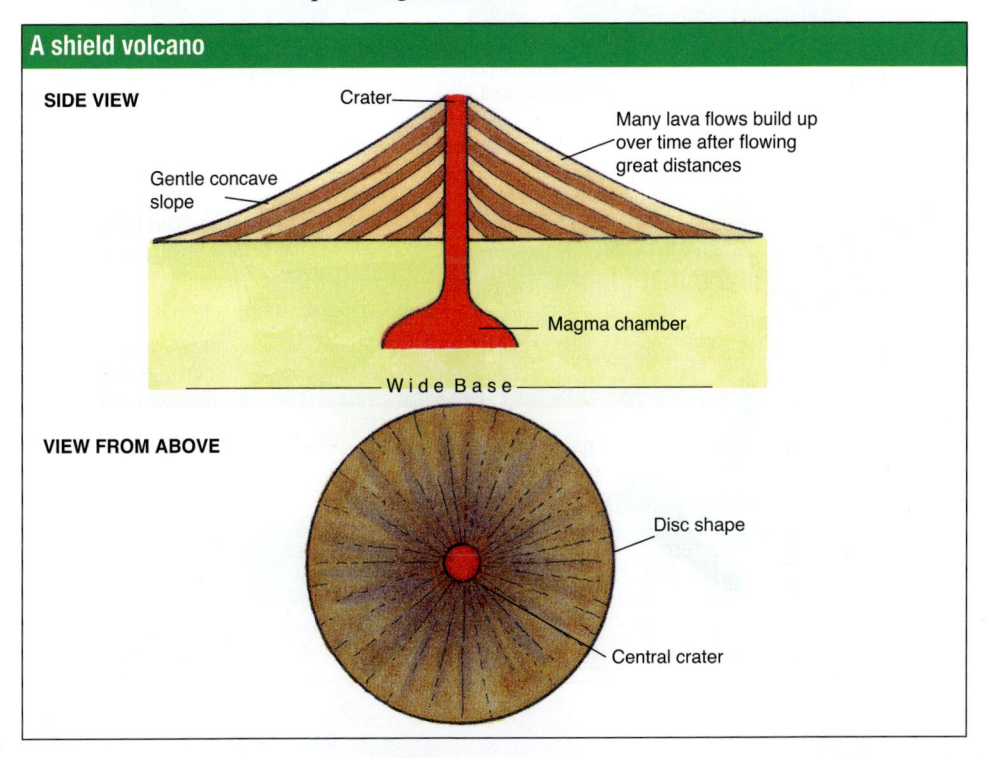

A shield volcano

SIDE VIEW
- Crater
- Many lava flows build up over time after flowing great distances
- Gentle concave slope
- Magma chamber
- Wide Base

VIEW FROM ABOVE
- Disc shape
- Central crater

OR

Landform 1(b): Basalt plateaux
Example: The Giant's Causeway, County Antrim

Basalt plateaux are flat-topped upland areas made of basalt rock. They are made when fissure eruptions occur at constructive plate boundaries. Here two tectonic plates are moving apart. Basic magma containing less than 55% silica flows out onto the landscape through long narrow cracks in the land surface called fissures. Over time the lava from many thousands of fissure eruptions builds the land up into a high basalt plateau. The basalt in the plateau can form distinctive landscapes because of the way it cools during the formation of the plateau. Distinctive polygonal basalt columns can form when thick lava flows cool. These basalt columns form because as the lava cools it contracts slightly and a polygonal-shaped column forms. The columns may be from 3- to 12-sided but in the Giant's Causeway most have 6 sides (hexagonal). In Ireland a distinctive basalt plateau landscape formed 90 to 60 million years ago when plate movement led to large fissure eruptions in the Antrim area.

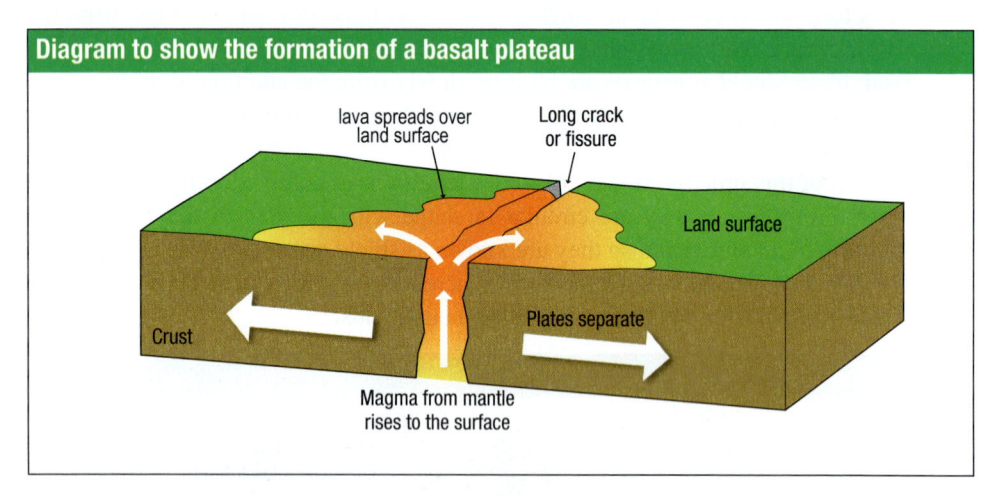

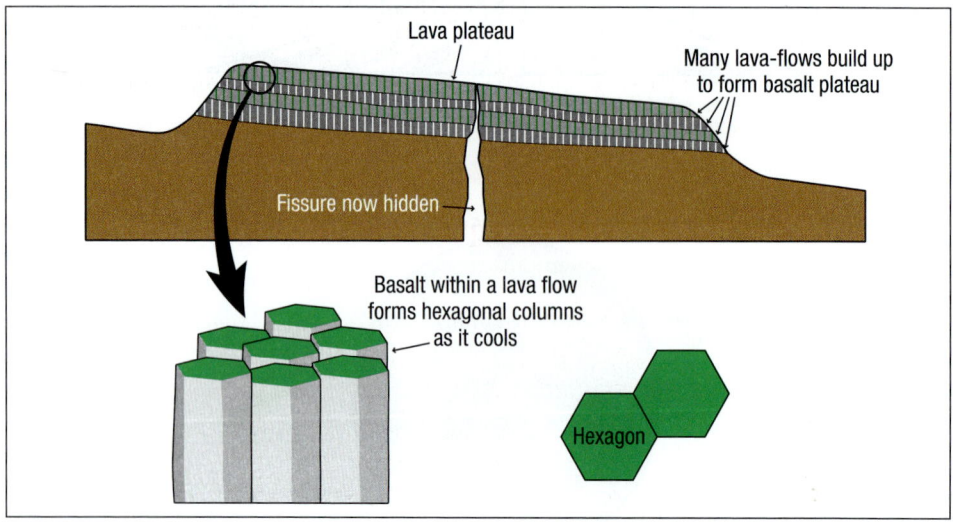

Diagram to show the formation of a basalt plateau

Landform 2: Batholith
Example: the Leinster Batholith

Batholiths are intrusive plutonic volcanic landforms that form deep under the earth's surface. A batholith is a large mass of igneous rock that forms when magma deep in the earth cools slowly to form granite rock.

Batholiths may be made of several masses of magma that rose from the mantle and merged together. The magma was injected underneath rocks that were folded during the collision of plates. As it moved, the rising magma heated and melted the surrounding rocks, changing them into metamorphic rock. The magma does not reach the surface but slows down and eventually stops, often 5 to 30 kilometres below the surface. It then takes thousands of years to cool into a huge mass of granite. Batholiths are visible today because the processes of weathering and erosion have removed the overlying rocks and exposed the once deeply buried granite.

Batholiths are usually surrounded by a zone or **aureole** of metamorphic rocks that were formed as the magma heated and melted the overlying rock.

In Ireland, the Wicklow Mountains are part of a large batholith stretching over 100 kilometres from North Wicklow to Wexford. It formed during the Caledonian folding that occurred 400 million years ago. The core of the batholith is granite and the edges contain metamorphic rocks such as schist and quartzite.

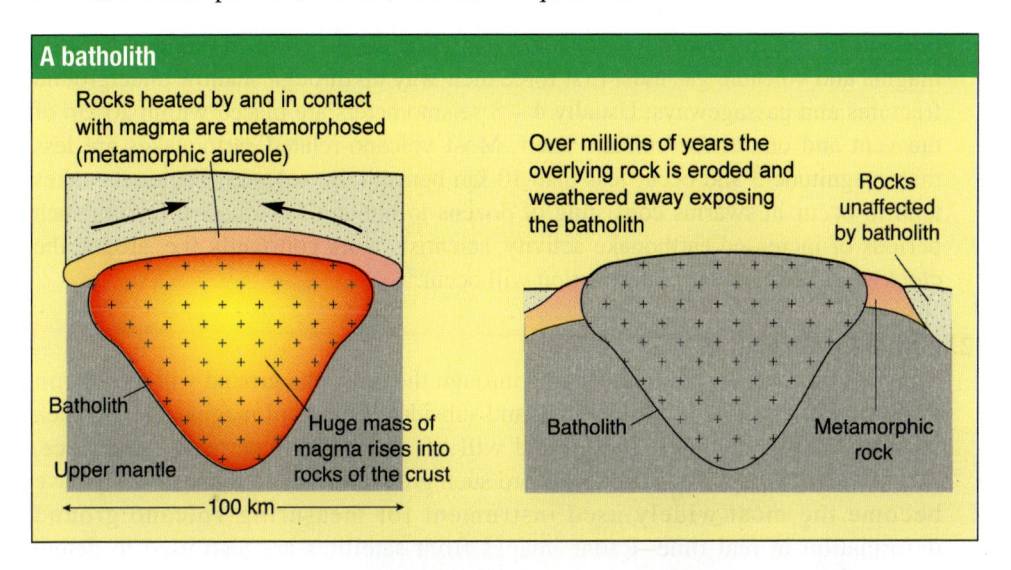

A batholith

Rocks heated by and in contact with magma are metamorphosed (metamorphic aureole)

Over millions of years the overlying rock is eroded and weathered away exposing the batholith

Rocks unaffected by batholith

Batholith

Upper mantle

Huge mass of magma rises into rocks of the crust

100 km

Batholith

Metamorphic rock

Earthquakes

Monitoring and Predicting Earthquakes: 2013 Question 3C
Explain how the occurrence of earthquakes and volcanoes may be monitored and predicted. [30 marks]

Marking scheme:
Explanation: 15 x SRPs (15 x 2 marks = 30)

> **What You Need To Do:**
> - Make sure to discuss both earthquakes and volcanoes.
> - Discuss how volcanoes are monitored and predictable.
> - Discuss that earthquakes cannot reliably be predicted but possible locations are known and some are monitored. Effort is on prevention of damage once a quake occurs.

A
Answer

In this answer, I will discuss how volcanoes and earthquakes may be monitored and predicted.

Monitoring and predicting volcanoes

Volcano scientists monitor hundreds of active volcanoes around the world in order to predict when they will erupt. Typical warning signs that a volcano will erupt are: increased earthquake activity, increased emissions of carbon dioxide and sulphur dioxide gases and ground deformation. Warnings are given and people are evacuated from high-risk locations. Methods used to predict volcanic eruptions are listed below:

1. **Networks of seismometers**

   Earthquake activity beneath a volcano usually increases before an eruption because magma and volcanic gas must first force their way up through shallow underground fractures and passageways. Usually 4 – 8 seismometers are placed within 20 km of the vent and one at the volcano itself. Most volcano-related earthquakes are less than magnitude 3 and occur less than 10 km beneath the volcano. The earthquakes tend to occur in swarms consisting of dozens to hundreds of quakes. During such periods of increased earthquake activity, scientists work constantly (i.e. around the clock) to determine when an eruption will occur.

2. **Ground deformation**

   When rising magma forces its way up through the crust, the ground will usually tilt away from the centre of uplift. If the land subsides because of magma sinking back into the magma chamber, the ground will tilt toward the centre of subsidence. Electronic tiltmeters continuously record such ground tilts on volcanoes. They have become the most widely used instrument for measuring volcano ground deformation in real time. Radar images from satellites are also used to detect ground deformation over larger areas than tiltmeters. When a volcano is close to erupting, the speed and amount of ground deformation increases.

3. **Gas analysis**

   The rate at which a volcano releases gases into the air is related to the volume of magma within its magma chamber. By measuring changes in the emission rate of certain key gases, especially sulfur dioxide and carbon dioxide, scientists can work out when a volcano is likely to erupt. Direct sampling of gas requires that scientists visit a hot fumarole (small cracks on the side of a volcano) or an active crater. Automatic chemical sensors send measurements by radio to volcano observatories.

The remote location of these sampling sites, the hazardous fumes, frequent bad weather and the potential for sudden eruptions can make regular gas sampling dangerous and sometimes impossible.

All of the above prediction methods were successfully used to predict eruptions at Mount St. Helens in America and Mount Etna in Italy as well as others around the world. Both volcanoes have 24-hour monitoring systems.

Monitoring and predicting earthquakes

In contrast to volcanologists (scientists who study volcanoes), seismologists (scientists who study earthquakes) cannot reliably predict when an earthquake will occur. While the exact location of an active volcano is easy to find, the exact location of an earthquake focus is impossible to see before an event. All scientists can do is to identify high risk areas, ensure buildings are built to withstand earthquakes and educate people about how to react when an earthquake occurs.

Earthquakes are associated with fault lines at plate boundaries, e.g. the San Andreas Fault, America. The following methods are used to collect data that could help to predict when and where a quake will occur:

1. Laser beams are used to detect plate movement.
2. A seismometer is used to pick up the vibrations in the earth's crust. An increase in vibrations may indicate a possible earthquake.
3. Radon gas escapes from cracks in the earth's crust. Levels of radon gas can be monitored. A sudden increase may suggest an earthquake.
4. Levels of oil and water in wells may change as the ground is squeezed or stretched during plate movement. Any changes in well levels can show where an earthquake might occur.

Many towns and cities run public awareness programmes to educate people on what to do during a quake and how to prepare for them. New roads/buildings are built to withstand earthquakes by using flexible materials and foundations. Earthquake drills are held in schools and offices. Some factories and power stations have their own seismometers which shut down sensitive electronic equipment used in manufacturing processes if an earthquake occurs. When the Japanese tsunami occurred in 2011, car factories were closed for months afterwards, not because they were damaged but because they could not restart their sensitive machines due to the high number of powerful aftershocks. Tsunami warning systems are in place in the Pacific and Indian Oceans. These are set off when seismometers on the sea bed sense an undersea quake and send tsunami warnings by satellite/radio/TV/text message to people on land.

Q

Effects of Earthquakes: 2008 Question 3C
Examine with reference to actual examples, the measurement and effects of earthquakes. **[30 marks]**

Marking scheme:
Identify measurement: 2 marks
Identify effects: 2 marks + 2 marks
Name examples: 2 marks + 2 marks
Discussion: 10 x 2 SRPs (10 x 2 marks = 20)

What You Need To Do:
- Name methods of measuring quakes.
- Discuss how earthquakes are measured in 5 SRPs – Richter and Modified Mercalli Scale.
- Describe two effects of earthquakes (in 5 SRPs).
- Name two examples.

A

Answer

Measurement of earthquakes

Earthquakes are measured using two methods, the Richter Scale and the Modified Mercalli Scale. The Richter Scale uses instruments called seismometers to measure the amount of energy released (its magnitude) by an earthquake. The Richter Scale is open-ended but the greatest earthquake yet measured was the Great Chilean Quake in 1960 which measured 9·5 on the Richter Scale.

Earthquakes measuring less than 3 on the Richter Scale cannot be felt by people and are detected by instruments only. The Richter Scale is an objective scientific measurement of an earthquake and is used by scientists across the world. Each quake has one reading on the Richter Scale.

The Modified Mercalli Scale does not use instruments. It describes the effects or intensity of an earthquake based on human observations and experiences of the earthquake. It records effects on people, the natural world and manmade structures. The Modified Mercalli Scales runs from I to XII, with I describing a weak earthquake and XII describing one that causes almost complete destruction.

People can report their observations and experiences online to the United States Geological Survey which makes chloropleth maps showing the various intensities experienced across a region. There are several readings for each quake using the Modified Mercalli Scale.

Effects of earthquakes

The effects of earthquakes can be either immediate (short term) or long term. Short-term effects include death and tsunamis as well as the destruction of buildings, roads, bridges, water and power supplies. There may be many refugees and homeless people. These effects are usually reported in the media in the days after a quake has occurred. Long-term effects may include poverty, refugees, long-term homelessness (in China in 2008 over 11 million were made homeless) and psychological trauma as whole generations of people are killed. This occurred after the 2008 Chinese earthquake when many parents lost their only child in collapsed school buildings. Other long-terms effects include economic recession as once wealthy areas have to pay for the rebuilding of infrastructure such as schools, roads and power systems.

The economy of Japan was severely affected by a devastating quake and tsunami in 2011. The destruction of social infrastructure, housing and manufacturing plants will cost the Japanese economy about €162 billion and reduce the economic growth of the country. Global car manufacturing was delayed by nearly nine months as factories manufacturing electronic car parts were damaged and had to stop production. A less common long-term effect occurred after this quake: the tsunami damaged nuclear power stations leading to power shortages and the long-term evacuation of people from the areas affected by radiation released by damaged nuclear reactors.

Liquefiction occurs where settlements are built on deep, loosely-consolidated soils or reclaimed land, rather than on solid bedrock. The ground turns to liquid due to the intense shaking during an earthquake. Buildings sink into the ground e.g Mexico City

Chapter 3
Folding and Faulting

Structures of Deformation

Q

Landform development: 2015 Question 3B
Explain how **one** of the following influences the development of landforms:
- Folding
- Faulting [30 marks]

Marking scheme:
Identify landform: 2 marks
Explanation: 14 x 2 SRPs (14 x 2 marks = 28)

What You Need To Do:
Answer 1: Folding
- Name a landform caused by folding, e.g. fold mountains.
- Explain the formation of fold mountains.
- Give an example.
- Draw a labelled diagram of a fold mountain.

Answer 2: Faulting
- Name landforms caused by faulting, e.g. rift valleys and block mountains.
- Explain the formation of rift valleys and block mountains.
- Draw a well-labelled diagram of a rift valley and a block mountain.

Answer 1: Folding

A

Landform caused by folding: Fold mountains
Examples: the Munster Ridge and Valley Province, Ireland and the Himalaya Mountains, Asia

Folding of rocks occurs when they are compressed or squeezed. Rock can be folded because at depth it is subjected to great heat and pressure which makes the rock flexible and so it can bend without breaking. This compression occurs due to movement and collision of the earth's tectonic plates. As a result of plate collision, the rocks are folded and uplifted and fold mountains are formed. This process is also called orogeny.

In Ireland the landscape of Munster is made of fold mountains. About 350 million years ago old red sandstone rock was formed. It was later covered with carboniferous limestone rock. About 300 million years ago these rocks were compressed during the Armorican Fold Mountain building period. The compression came from the north and south and so the folds have an east-west trend. The limestone was easily eroded from the fold anticlines (up-folded rock) exposing the sandstone beneath. The anticlines are seen today as sandstone mountain ridges such as the MacGillycuddy's Reeks and the Comeragh Mountains. Limestone is preserved in the fold synclines (down-folded rock) which are seen in the large east-west trending valleys such as the Blackwater Valley.

Globally, 3 stages of folding (orogeny) have impacted on landscape development. The oldest is the Caledonian Orogeny which occured 400 million years ago. The trends of these folds are north-east/south-west. They occur in Ireland, e.g. the Wicklow Mountains. The Armorican orogeny occurred 300 million years ago. It formed in Munster and the folds trend east/west. The youngest fold mountains are Alpine. This folding occured 50 million years ago. This trends east/west and is not found in Ireland.

Different types of folds affect the landscape, e.g. symmetric, overfolds and monoclines. Folds can be seen in Loughshinny, Co. Dublin.

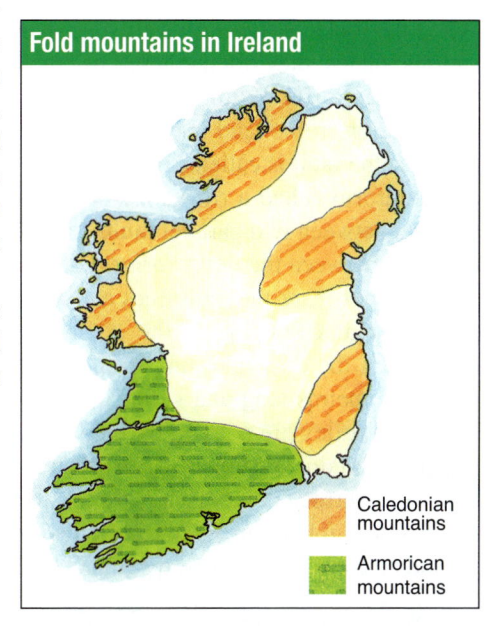

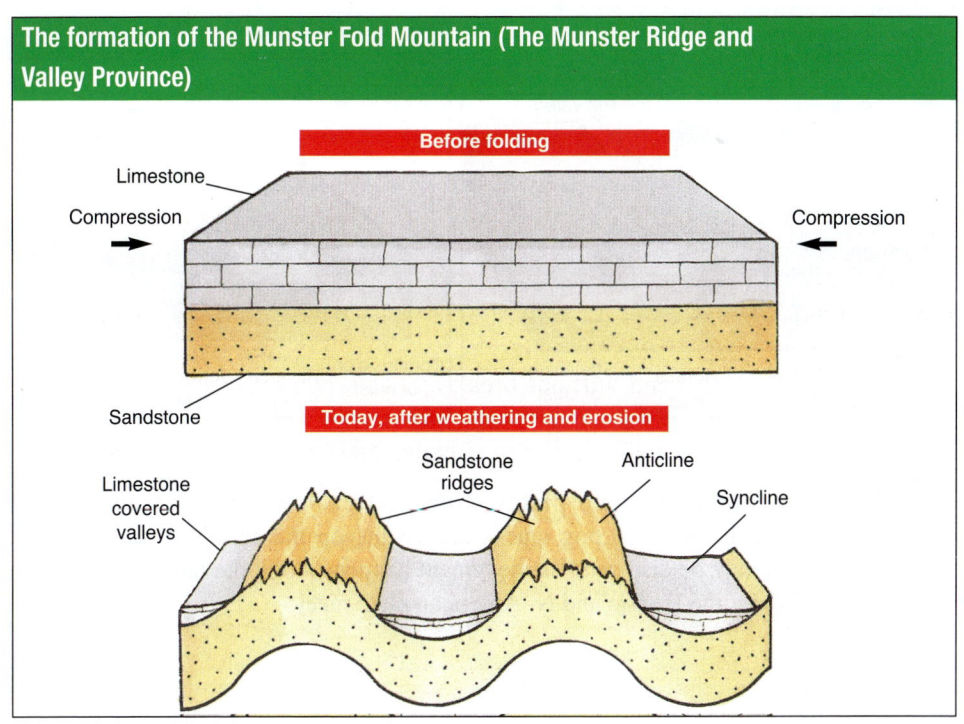

Fold mountains in Ireland

- Caledonian mountains
- Armorican mountains

The formation of the Munster Fold Mountain (The Munster Ridge and Valley Province)

Before folding

Limestone
Compression
Sandstone
Compression

Today, after weathering and erosion

Limestone covered valleys
Sandstone ridges
Anticline
Syncline

Answer 2: Faulting

Landforms caused by faulting:
(a) Rift valleys, e.g. African Rift Valley
(b) Block mountains, e.g. The Ox Mountains, Co. Mayo
(c) Fault lines, e.g. San Andreas Fault, USA

When the rocks of the earth's crust are pulled apart or compressed by the movement of tectonic plates, they often crack. The cracks that form are called faults.

Reverse faults occur when the land along a fault is moved upwards during compression. If the land is being stretched, land may sink downwards along a fault. In this case the fault is called a normal fault.

A landform called a rift valley or graben forms when stretching of the crust causes the land between two parallel faults to sink. The faults in a rift valley are normal faults. The land between the faults forms a flat-floored valley with steep slopes on each side.

The slopes mark the fault lines and are called fault scarps. In the African Rift Valley stretching and faulting of the crust is occurring as a hotspot of magma is rising underneath the crust, pushing it up and stretching it. The African Rift Valley is over 5,000 kilometres long and varies in width from 30 to 100 kilometres wide. The edges of the rift valley are marked by fault scarps which run from Ethiopia to Mozambique. Block mountains or 'horsts' form when the earth's crust is compressed. Reverse faults form and further compression forces the land upwards between the reverse faults. Steep-sided upland areas called 'fault-block' mountains are made. The edges of the upland area are fault scarps, e.g. the Ox Mountains of County Mayo.

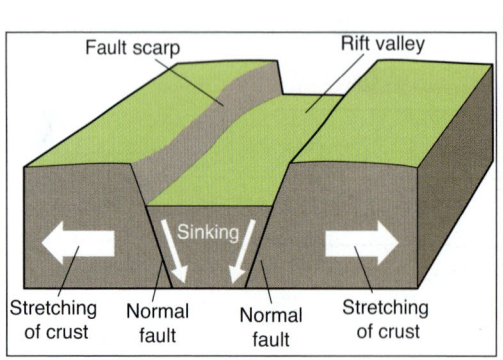

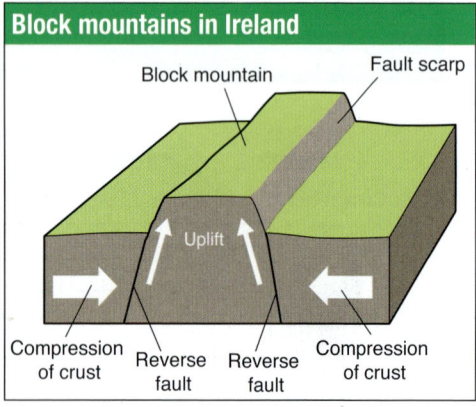

Fault lines occur where two plates slide past each other at a transform or conservative plate boundary. Long cracks are visible on the earth's surface. Rivers, roads and fences may be displaced as movement happens along the fault, e.g. The San Andreas fault where the Pacific and N. American plate meet.

Chapter 4

Rock Types and Landscapes

The Formation of Rocks

Q

Sedimentary Rocks: 2009 Question 2B
Examine, with reference to examples from Ireland, the formation of sedimentary rocks. **[30 marks]**

Marking scheme:
Name two sedimentary rocks: 2 marks + 2 marks
Name two associated Irish locations: 2 marks + 2 marks
Examination: 11 x SRPs (11 x 2 marks = 22)

What You Need To Do:
- Name two sedimentary rocks.
- Name a location where each rock type you mentioned is found.
- Discuss how sedimentary rocks form referring to organic and inorganic sedimentary rocks.
- Draw a labelled diagram to show the formation of sedimentary rock.

A

Answer

The formation of sedimentary rocks
Two sedimentary rocks:
(a) Limestone
Example: The Burren, County Clare
(b) Sandstone
Example: Caha Mountains, County Cork

Sedimentary rocks are made from the build-up (accumulation) of layers of rock particles/sediments in rivers, lakes and seas. Because sedimentary rocks are made from the build-up of sediment, they contain layers called strata. The junction between each layer is known as a bedding plane.

Sediment is turned into rock by the process of lithification. During this process, the great weight of the layers of sediment compacts the grains of rock together. Under pressure, minerals such as calcite and silica leak from the grains and stick them together to form solid rock. Sedimentary rocks may be organic, inorganic or chemical depending on how they have formed.

Organic sedimentary rocks are made from remains of dead plants and animals on the sea floor. During lithification the great weight of sediment causes calcite from shells and skeletons to cement the grains together forming solid rock. Limestone and chalk are formed in this way.

Inorganic sedimentary rocks form when particles of igneous, metamorphic or other sedimentary rocks build up under water and are cemented together by silica. Sandstone and mudstone rock form in this way. Irish sandstone formed 400 to 350 million years ago when Ireland lay 30° south of the equator. At this time and latitude Ireland experienced very dry desert conditions. Huge rivers flowed across this dry landscape carrying the sediments that eventually formed the Old Red Sandstone which is now found in the Cork and Kerry mountains.

Some sedimentary rocks such as sandstone are porous. This means they have spaces between the grains which can hold water, oil and gas. Other sedimentary rocks are pervious. This means that they do not contain pores so water, oil and gas pass through the joints and bedding planes instead, e.g. limestone.

Chemically formed sedimentary rocks are made by the evaporation of seawater from enclosed seas or lakes. When seawater evaporates, the dissolved substances it contains such as gypsum and salt are left behind as solid rock. These rocks are also called evaporites.

Chemically formed rocks are deposited in a definite order during evaporation of seawater: gypsum is deposited when 37% of the water has evaporated, rock salt when 93% of the water has gone. Rock salt was formed in this way and is found in Carrickfergus, County Antrim. Gypsum is found in Kingscourt, County Cavan.

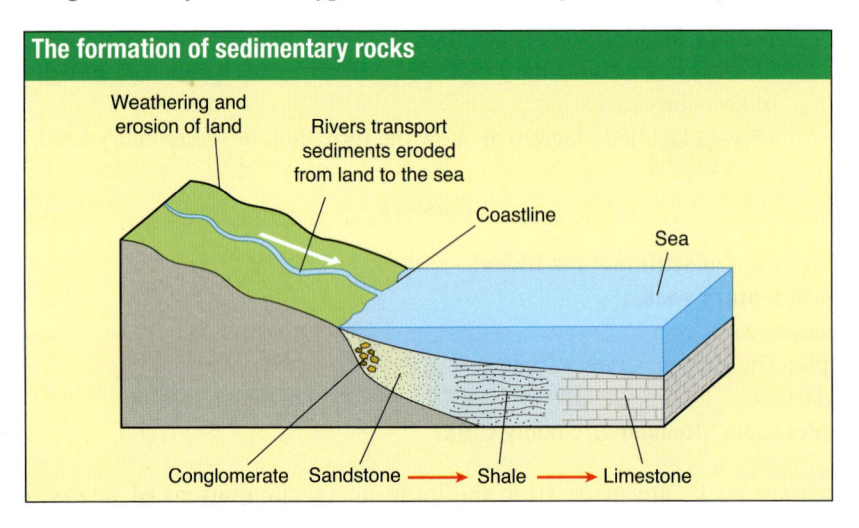

The formation of sedimentary rocks

- Weathering and erosion of land
- Rivers transport sediments eroded from land to the sea
- Coastline
- Sea
- Conglomerate Sandstone ⟶ Shale ⟶ Limestone

Q

Sedimentary and metamorphic rock: 2012 Question 1B
Describe the formation of one sedimentary rock and briefly explain how this rock may be converted into a metamorphic rock. **[30 marks]**

Marking scheme:
Name one sedimentary rock: 2 marks
Name one metamorphic rock: 2 marks
Describe formation of sedimentary rock: 11 x SRPs (11 x 2 marks = 22)
Explain formation of the metamorphic rock: 2 x SRPs (2 x 2 marks = 4)

> **What You Need To Do:**
> - Choose which sedimentary rock you will describe.
> - Name its metamorphic version.
> - Describe how the sedimentary rock is formed.
> - Explain how it is converted to a metamorphic rock.

Answer

A In this answer I will describe the formation of sandstone and explain how it is converted to quartzite, its metamorphic version.

Sandstone is an inorganic sedimentary rock. Inorganic sedimentary rocks form when weathered and eroded particles of igneous, metamorphic or other sedimentary rocks are deposited under water in rivers, lakes and seas.

The loose sediments turn into rock by the process of lithification. During this process, the great weight of the layers of sediment compact the grains of rock together. Under pressure, silica leaks from the grains and sticks them together to form solid rock.

The layers of sediment visible in sandstone are called strata. The junction between each layer is called a bedding plane.

Irish sandstone formed 400 to 350 million years ago when Ireland lay 30° south of the equator. At this time and latitude, Ireland experienced very dry desert conditions. Huge rivers flowed across this dry landscape carrying the sediments that eventually formed the old red sandstone that today is found in the Cork and Kerry mountains.

Sandstone is porous. This means it has spaces between the grains that hold water, oil and gas. For this reason sandstone is an important reservoir for groundwater (an aquifer).

Sandstone is also permeable. This means that liquid/gas can pass through the pores and flow through the rock. This enables people to drill into sandstone and pump water, oil or gas from the rock.

Old Red Sandstone is red/brown in colour because the grains of rock contain small amounts of iron that were weathered by oxidation into iron oxide.

Sandstone is converted to quartzite during thermal metamorphism caused by tectonic plate movement. During thermal metamorphism, great heat (over 200° Celsius) from magma in the mantle bakes the sandstone and causes the grains to melt slightly and lose its sandy texture. When the rock cools down the grains re-crystallize. Metamorphism gives the rock a different texture and colour and makes it much harder. Metamorphism also removes the pores from sandstone so quartzite is not porous.

Quartzite is white and extremely resistant to weathering. Quartzite is found in Mount Errigal, Co. Donegal.

Metamorphic Rocks

Q

Formation of metamorphic rocks: 2013 Question 1B
Explain the formation of metamorphic rocks with reference to examples from Ireland. **[30 marks]**

Marking scheme:
Name two metamorphic rocks: 2 marks + 2 marks
Name two associated Irish locations: 2 marks + 2 marks
Examination: 11 x SRPs (11 x 2 marks = 22)

What You Need To Do:
- Name two metamorphic rocks and give their locations.
- State what metamorphism is.
- Discuss the formation of metamorphic rocks making sure to mention the types of metamorphism and the effects of metamorphism.

A

Answer

The formation of metamorphic rock
Two metamorphic rocks:
(a) Marble (formerly limestone)
Example: Connemara, County Galway
(b) Quartzite (formerly sandstone)
Example: Mount Errigal, County Donegal

Metamorphism is the changing of rock by the action of great heat and/or pressure. Metamorphism of rock occurs at temperatures higher than 200°C and pressures higher than 300 megapascals (3,000 times normal atmospheric pressure). Rocks experience these high temperatures and pressures as they become buried deep in the earth. Burial of rock occurs as a result of tectonic processes such as tectonic plate collision and subduction.

There are three types of metamorphism.

(1) Thermal metamorphism occurs when rocks are affected by the great heat supplied by magma moving deep inside the earth's crust or where it erupts as lava to the surface. Quartzite (Irish example: Sugar Loaf Mountain, County Wicklow) is an example. In this case sandstone is baked by the heat from the magma below and changes into quartzite.

(2) Dynamic metamorphism occurs where rocks are changed by great pressure due to plate movements and along fault lines. Slate is an example found in Valentia, County Kerry. In this case shale is changed into slate by pressure.

(3) Regional metamorphism occurs where rocks are changed by both heat and pressure. This type of metamorphism usually occurs over large areas and is due to the gradual movement of the earth's plates. Gneiss is an example.

Metamorphism has several important effects on rocks. It causes foliation (banding) and changes their hardness and colour. Foliation means the mineral grains or crystals are flattened and rearranged into thin bands due to the great pressure upon them, e.g. gneiss.

During metamorphism rock grains and crystals are heated and their outer surface may melt very slightly. When the rock grains cool, they are stuck together and the metamorphic rock is now much harder than the original.

Metamorphic rocks are often a different colour to the original. The colour change happens as the minerals in the parent rock are metamorphosed. Marble has many colours because any mineral impurities present in the limestone affect the colour of the marble that forms. The purest calcite marble is white. Marble containing hematite (iron oxide) has a reddish colour. Connemara marble, which contains the mineral serpentine, is green.

Igneous Rocks

Rocks: 2014 Question 1B
Explain the formation of igneous rocks with reference to Irish examples.
[30 marks]

Marking scheme:
Name two Irish igneous rocks: 2 marks + 2 marks
Give an explanation of formation: 13 x SRPs (13 x 2 marks = 26)

What You Need To Do:
- Name two igneous rocks and give their locations in Ireland.
- Discuss the formation of igneous rocks, making sure to mention two types, e.g. extrusive/volcanic and intrusive/plutonic.
- Draw a labelled diagram.

Answer

The formation of igneous rocks
Two igneous rocks:
(a) Granite **Example:** The Wicklow Mountains, County Wicklow
(b) Basalt   **Example:** The Giant's Causeway, County Antrim

Igneous rocks are formed from magma which cools and solidifies either below ground or on the earth's surface.
Igneous rocks can be divided into two groups depending on the depth at which they formed.

(a) Extrusive or volcanic igneous rock (basalt) Basalt forms when magma from the mantle reaches the earth's surface at volcanic cones, hotspots and mid-ocean ridges. The magma which erupts as lava on the earth's surface cools rapidly due to contact with water or air to form basalt rock.

Basalt is dark black or brown in colour. It is a hard rock and very resistant to weathering and erosion. Volcanic igneous rocks have microscopic crystals because the lava cools so rapidly. In Ireland, basalt formed about 60 million years ago when highly fluid basic magma containing less than 55% silica erupted to the surface through large cracks or fissures in the crust. The lava cooled into hexagonal (six-sided) columns which can be seen at the Giant's Causeway, County Antrim. Today basalt is forming in Iceland at the mid-Atlantic ridge and in Italy at the Mount Etna volcano.

Acidic lava contains more than 55% silica and does not flow across the surface very easily. Basalt domes often form in this case, e.g. Mount St Helens, America.

(b) Intrusive or plutonic igneous rock (granite) Granite forms when magma from the mantle cools slowly deep underground. This happens at destructive plate boundaries where an oceanic plate sinks beneath a continental plate, e.g. the Nazca plate meets the South American plate. As the oceanic plate sinks into the mantle, it melts and is recycled in a process called subduction. The magma then rises into the continental plate above it but does not reach the surface. The magma cools slowly over millions of years at a depth of several kilometres below the surface. Granite rock is formed. Because the magma cools so slowly, large crystals of feldspar, mica and quartz grow. Granite has a pale grey, white, pink or green colour. In Ireland granite was formed 400 million years ago during the Caledonian mountain building. Magma was injected into the crust as it was folded during plate collision. It slowly cooled to form a granite batholith. We see granite rock on the earth's surface today because the overlying rocks have been eroded away.

Sometimes the magma pushes closer to the surface and cools faster, forming smaller-grained intermediate/hypabyssal igneous rock such as dolerite. This rock is often found in dykes, sills and laccoliths. In Ireland dolerite is found in Fair Head, County Antrim.

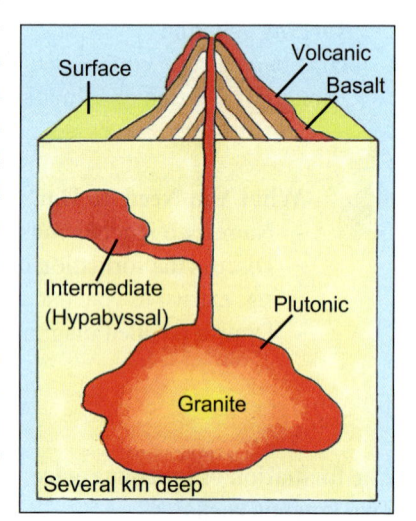

Chapter 4

Rock Types and Landscapes

Q

Different rock types: 2014 Question 2C
Examine how different rock types produce distinctive landscapes, with reference to examples that you have studied. **[30 marks]**

Marking scheme:
Rock 1 and associated landscape: 2 marks + 2 marks
Rock 2 and associated landscape: 2 marks + 2 marks
Examination: 11 x SRPs (11 x 2 marks = 22)

What You Need To Do:
- Name two rock types you have studied.
- Name the landscape formed by each rock type.
- Give an Irish example of each.
- Describe how each landscape was formed making sure to discuss how each rock type was formed.

Answer

A

Limestone

The rock type discussed in this answer is limestone, an organically formed sedimentary rock. This means it is made from the remains of dead sea creatures. Limestone forms a distinctive limestone pavement typical of karst (bare limestone rock) landscapes, e.g. the Burren in County Clare.

The formation of limestone

Irish limestone formed in warm, shallow seas about 350 to 300 million years ago when Ireland lay close to the equator. Over thousands of years the bodies of dead marine creatures such as shellfish and corals fell to the seafloor and built up on the seabed. Sand particles and mud from rivers were also added to the seafloor.

Over time the weight of the sediments compressed the grains together. Water was pushed out of the pore spaces between the grains of sediment and gradually the grains were cemented together with calcium carbonate (calcite) from the shells and corals. Solid limestone rock was formed. The remains of shells are seen as fossils in the rock. The process by which the loose grains of sediment are turned into rock is called lithification. Because limestone is sedimentary rock, it contains horizontal layers or strata which are separated by flat surfaces called bedding planes. Vertical cracks or joints are also present. They formed when earth movements folded and split the rock as Ireland moved northwards during plate movements.

Limestone is a permeable, pervious rock. This means that water passes through the joints and bedding planes but is not passed through the body of the rock itself.

Limestone landscapes

Bare limestone rock forms a distinctive karst landscape of limestone pavement, e.g. the Burren in County Clare.

Limestone pavement forms because limestone is chemically weathered by the process of carbonation.

Carbonation occurs when rainwater absorbs carbon dioxide from the air and forms weak carbonic acid with a pH of 5·6. This naturally acidic rainwater falls on the limestone and a chemical reaction takes place between the acidic rainwater and the alkaline limestone. Limestone is converted into soluble calcium bicarbonate which is washed away in solution by the rainwater.

Because limestone contains many vertical joints and horizontal bedding planes, rainwater passes through these cracks and carbonation easily erodes them. They are widened and deepened to form a unique surface landform: limestone pavement. The joints are deepened to form grikes that separate large flat areas called clints. Other surface landforms associated with karst landscapes are swallow holes and dolines. Underground, carbonation leads to the formation of caves which contain stalactites, stalagmites and pillars. In Ireland there are many show caves where these features can be seen, e.g. Ailwee Cave in the Burren or Crag Cave, County Kerry.

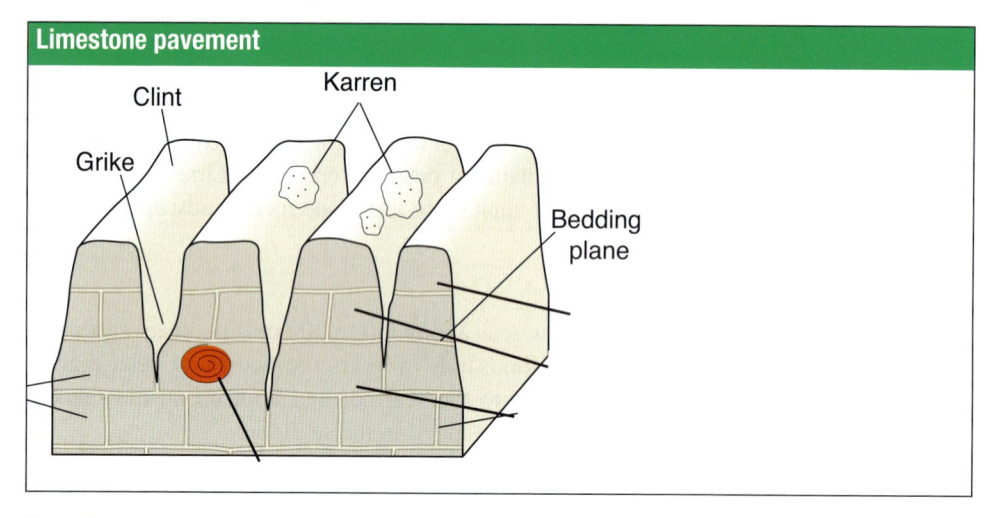

Limestone pavement

- Clint
- Karren
- Grike
- Bedding plane

Basalt

The rock type discussed in this answer is basalt, a volcanic igneous rock. Basalt forms a distinctive plateau landscape, e.g. the Giant's Causeway of County Antrim.

The formation of basalt rock

Basalt is formed when molten rock from the mantle flows onto the earth's surface, rapidly cools and solidifies into basalt rock. Basalt is dark brown or black in colour. The lava cools so quickly that crystals of mica, quartz and feldspar contained in the lava do not have time to grow very big and are not visible to the eye. Basalt can form during volcanic eruptions. Volcanoes release massive amounts of magma which flows out of the vent and travels downhill. As it moves it may cool quickly to form basalt rock. This occurs in active volcanoes such as Mount Etna in Italy. At other times magma may reach the surface at mid-ocean ridges where the crust is being pulled apart by mantle currents. Basalt forms new sea floor as it reaches the surface. On land where mid-ocean ridges occur such as in Iceland, long cracks or fissures form and basic magma can flow out and spread over the landscape either side of the fissure.

The formation of basalt landscapes

A landscape formed by basalt rock is a basalt rock plateau, e.g. Giant's Causeway, County Antrim. A basalt plateau is a flat-topped upland area made of basalt rock. These plateaux form during huge fissure eruptions of basic lava that can occur when the earth's crust is split apart by plate movement at constructive plate boundaries or at hotspots.

Over time the basic lava from many thousands of fissure eruptions build up either side of the fissure into a high basalt plateau. The basalt in the plateau can form distinctive landscapes because of the way it cools during the formation of the plateau. During the cooling of a thick lava flow, distinctive polygonal basalt columns can form. These basalt columns form because as the lava cools it contracts slightly and polygonal-shaped columns form. The columns may be from 3- to 12-sided but in the Giant's Causeway, County Antrim, most have 6 sides (hexagonal). In Ireland a distinctive basalt plateau landscape formed 90 to 60 million years ago when plate movement led to large fissure eruptions in the Antrim area.

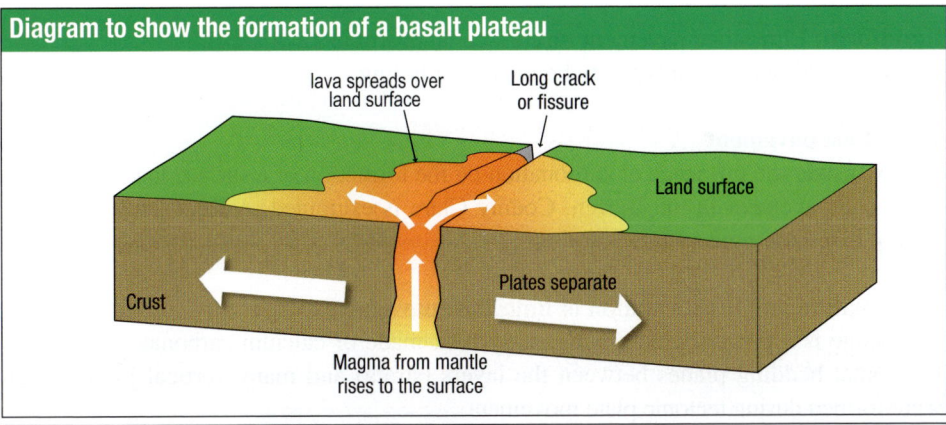

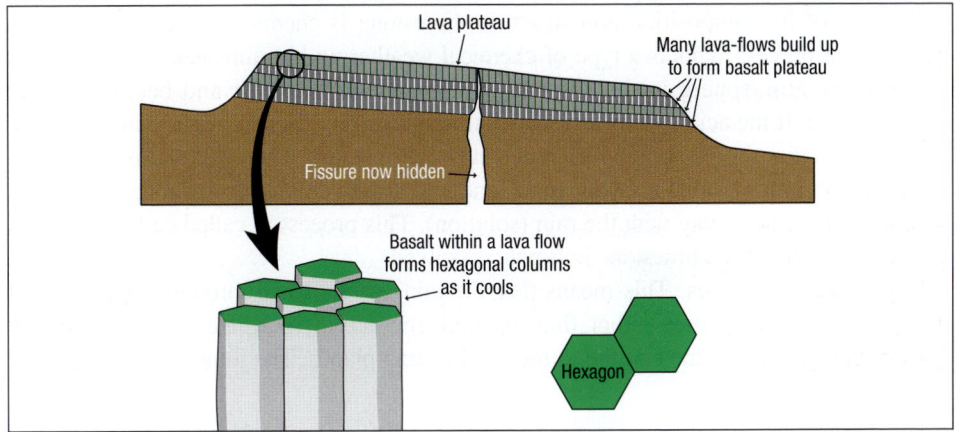

Diagram to show the formation of a basalt plateau

- lava spreads over land surface
- Long crack or fissure
- Land surface
- Crust
- Plates separate
- Magma from mantle rises to the surface

- Lava plateau
- Many lava-flows build up to form basalt plateau
- Fissure now hidden
- Basalt within a lava flow forms hexagonal columns as it cools
- Hexagon

Chapter 5
Weathering

Surface Limestone Landforms

Q

Limestone pavement: 2012 Question 3B
With the aid of a diagram(s), explain how chemical weathering has shaped the limestone pavement in a karst region. **[30 marks]**
Marking scheme:
Name process: 2 marks
Diagram(s): 4 marks
Explanation: 12 x SRPs (12 x 2 marks = 24)

What You Need To Do:
- Name and explain the process of carbonation.
- Discuss the formation of the feature referring to carbonation.
- Draw a labelled diagram of the feature.
- Give Irish example.

Answer

A

Landform: Limestone pavement - a surface landform in karst areas.
Process: Carbonation - a type of chemical weathering.

Limestone pavement
In this answer the influence of carbonation on the formation of a surface landform called limestone pavement in the Burren, County Clare is examined. A karst landscape is an area of bare limestone rock.

Carbonation and the formation of limestone pavement
Limestone is a grey, organic, sedimentary rock made of calcium carbonate. It contains horizontal bedding planes between the layers (strata) and many vertical joints which were formed during tectonic plate movement.

Because of its composition and structure, limestone is chemically weathered by the carbonation process. This is a type of chemical weathering by rainwater. As rain passes through the atmosphere it absorbs carbon dioxide from the air and becomes weak carbonic acid. If the acidic rainwater passes through soil it picks up humic acids from the rotting vegetation in the soil and becomes even more acidic. The acidic rainwater reacts with the calcium carbonate in the limestone and forms calcium bicarbonate which is soluble and washes away with the rain (solution). This process is called carbonation. As a result of carbonation, limestone is slowly dissolved.

Limestone is pervious. This means that the rain passes down through the joints and along the bedding planes rather than through the actual rock itself. Weathering by carbonation is concentrated on the joints and bedding planes. The joints are widened and deepened and become long, deep grooves in the rock surface called grikes. The rock between the grikes is divided into large sections called clints. The combination of clints and grikes looks a bit like paving slabs and so this feature – bare limestone surface with clints and grikes – is called limestone pavement. It is well developed in the Burren of County Clare near Black Head.

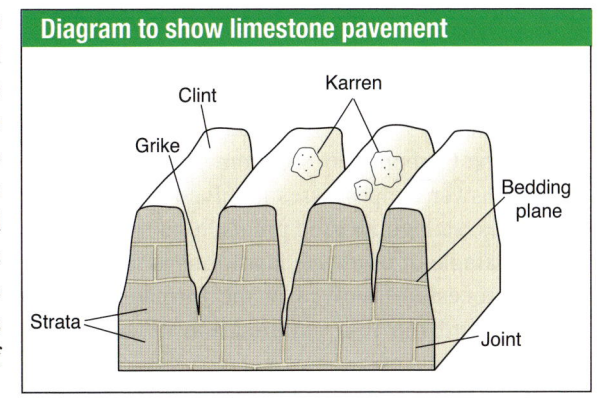

Diagram to show limestone pavement

(Labels: Clint, Karren, Grike, Bedding plane, Strata, Joint)

In this area the limestone pavement formed underneath the soil which covered the land before the Ice Age. However, glaciation and human activities removed the soil and the limestone pavement is now exposed.

Over the years, soil has been washed into the grikes by the rain and plants can grow in them.

The clints are further dissolved by carbonation as rainwater collects on the surface and then flows into the grikes. Evidence of this is the development of 'Karren'. Karren is a collection of small pits and gutter-like channels found on the top of clints.

Underground Limestone Landforms

Karst Landscape: 2010 Question 3C
With reference to the Irish landscape, examine the processes which have influenced the development of any **one** underground landform in a karst region.
[30 marks]

Marking scheme:
Name process: 2 marks
Identify underground landform: 2 marks
Irish example: 2 marks
Discussion: 12 x SRPs, including 2 SRPs for a well-labelled diagram
(12 x 2 marks = 24)

What You Need To Do:
- Name the underground landform.
- Give an Irish example of this landform.
- Name and explain the process that forms the landform.
- Explain how the landform is made.
- Draw a labelled diagram of the landform.

A | Answer
The formation of dripstone

Landform: Stalactites, stalagmites and pillars (dripstone) – an underground landform in karst areas.

Processes: Carbonation, solution.

In this answer the processes involved in the formation of the underground landform of stalactites, stalagmites and pillars, together known as dripstone, will be explained.

An example of dripstone landforms is found in Crag Cave, County Kerry.

The processes involved in the formation of dripstone landforms are carbonation, solution and the re-crystallisation of calcite during evaporation of rainwater in underground caves.

Carbonation occurs when rainwater absorbs carbon dioxide from the air and becomes weak carbonic acid. When the rain falls on limestone rock, a slow chemical reaction occurs. The acidic rainwater reacts with the alkaline limestone rock causing it to dissolve. The rain reacts with the calcium carbonate in the limestone forming calcium bicarbonate. This new substance is very soluble and is washed away, dissolved, in the rainwater. The removal of dissolved limestone by rainwater is called solution. As rainwater flows through the joints and bedding planes of limestone, it carries the dissolved limestone (calcium bicarbonate) in solution deep underground.

When the rainwater eventually reaches the roof of a cave it forms droplets of water which drip constantly from the roof to the floor. Every water droplet evaporates slightly, reversing the carbonation process and leaving a tiny ring of calcite attached to the roof. The calcite ring gradually builds up to form a straw-like tube that hangs from the ceiling. If a tiny rock fragment blocks the tube, water flows over the outside of the tube and the calcite is deposited on the outside of the straw to form a carrot-shaped formation called a stalactite. In some cases water evaporates slowly from long cracks or fissures in the cave roof. In this case calcite is deposited along the path of the crack and hangs down as a curtain-shaped formation.

At the same time the water droplets splash onto the floor beneath the stalactite and evaporate on the ground, leaving an irregularly-shaped mound of calcite known as a stalagmite. Over many thousands of years the stalactite and stalagmite slowly grow towards each other. When they eventually join together, a pillar/column is formed.

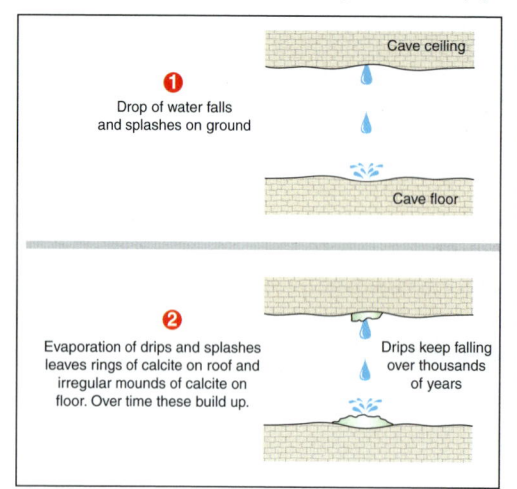

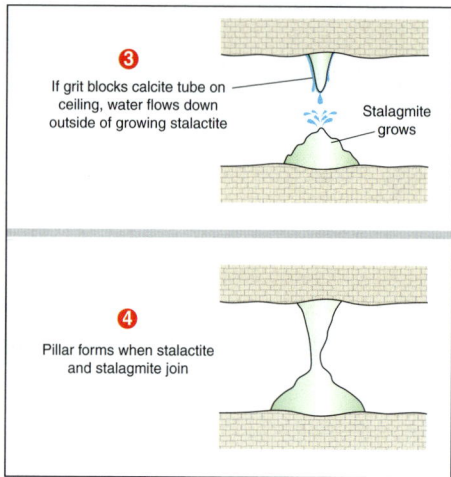

① Drop of water falls and splashes on ground

Cave ceiling

Cave floor

② Evaporation of drips and splashes leaves rings of calcite on roof and irregular mounds of calcite on floor. Over time these build up.

③ If grit blocks calcite tube on ceiling, water flows down outside of growing stalactite

Stalagmite grows

Drips keep falling over thousands of years

④ Pillar forms when stalactite and stalagmite join

Types of weathering

Q

> **Physical weathering: 2013 Question 3B**
> Explain the process(es) of physical weathering OR the process(es) of chemical weathering. **[30 marks]**
>
> **Marking scheme:**
> Name process: 2 marks
> Explanation: 14 x SRPs (14 x 2 marks = 28)

> **What You Need To Do:**
> - State what weathering is.
> - Name a process of chemical weathering OR Name a process of mechanical weathering.
> - Discuss how chemical weathering occurs OR mechanical weathering occurs.
> - Draw a labelled diagram where relevant.

Answer

A

Answer 1. Mechanical Weathering:
In this answer I will explain the processes of freeze – thaw action and exfoliation/onion weathering.

Weathering processes break down rocks into smaller pieces. Weathering processes may be mechanical/physical or chemical.

Mechanical weathering is the breakdown of rock into smaller pieces and no new substances are formed. This can happen by the action of frost (freeze – thaw action) and temperature changes (exfoliation/onion weathering). In Ireland, mechanical weathering such as freeze-thaw action occurs in areas where the temperature varies above and below freezing point (0°C). This happens on high mountain tops or on lowlands during very cold weather.

During freeze-thaw action, water gathers in tiny rock cracks during wet weather. If the temperature drops below freezing point, water in the cracks freezes and expands by about 10% and this expansion enlarges the rock crack.

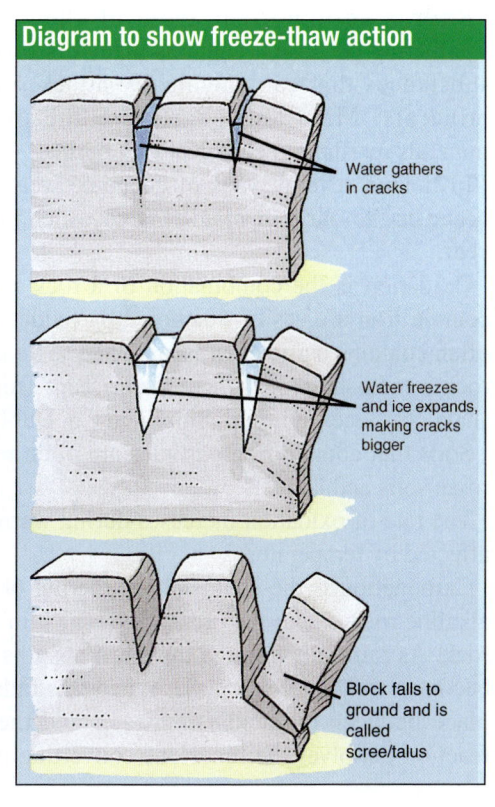

Diagram to show freeze-thaw action
- Water gathers in cracks
- Water freezes and ice expands, making cracks bigger
- Block falls to ground and is called scree/talus

When the ice melts the pressure on the rock is released. Over time repeated cycles of freezing and thawing weakens the rock and eventually pieces of rock fall away and gather at the foot of the hillsides as scree. Scree-covered slopes are found in the Wicklow Mountains and the Cooley Mountains in Louth.

Onion weathering causes the rock surface to peel away in layers. It occurs in desert areas such as Arizona, USA. The desert climate has a very large range in temperature (about 40°C) between day and night (diurnal range). Extreme heat during the day causes the top few centimeters of the rock to expand. At night, the rock cools and contracts (shrinks). This process is repeated each day and the rock surface is weakened and begins to peel away. The peeled layers fall to the ground as scree. The rate of onion weathering increases if the rock is composed of many different minerals, e.g. granite, as the minerals expand and contract by different amounts. This weakens the rock even more. Small amounts of water will also speed up the process.

OR

Answer 2. Chemical Weathering
In this answer I will discuss the processes of oxidation and carbonation.

Chemical weathering is the breakdown of rock during a chemical reaction. The rock dissolves and changes into a completely new substance.

Rain is an important agent of chemical weathering because it contains many dissolved substances that can chemically attack rock minerals. Mica and quartz are the only minerals resistant to chemical weathering.

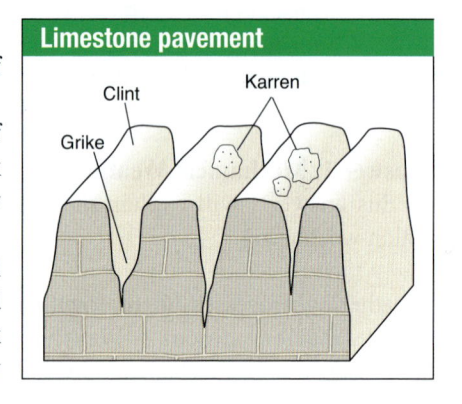

In Ireland several types of chemical weathering such as oxidation and carbonation occur due to our temperate climate which provides water and warmth throughout the year.

Oxidation is the combination of a rock mineral with oxygen (rusting). Rocks that contain iron are easily weathered by oxidation and often appear red or orange. Shale often contains particles of iron. When shale is oxidized to form iron oxide, it gives the rock a reddish colour where water seeps from the rock. Oxidation can be seen in the shale cliff faces at Lough Shinny in Co. Dublin.

Soils that contain iron particles are often red due to the oxidation process, e.g. terra rossa soils and latosols.

The rate of oxidation increases during warm weather as many chemical reactions are affected by temperature.

Carbonation is the chemical weathering of limestone by rainwater. Limestone is an alkaline rock due to the presence of calcium carbonate from sea shell fragments in the rock. As rain falls through the air, it absorbs carbon dioxide from the atmosphere and becomes weak carbonic acid. When this falls on limestone, a chemical reaction takes place between the acidic rainwater and the alkaline limestone rock. The chemical reaction dissolves the limestone converting it to calcium bicarbonate which is washed away in solution by the rainwater. Carbonation occurs on limestone rock throughout Ireland but its effects are best seen in the Burren in Co. Clare. The vertical joints in limestone are weathered by carbonation into deep grooves called grikes while the surface slabs between the grikes are called clints. The flat surface of the clints are further dissolved by carbonation into small sharp-edged pits and tiny channels that together are called karren.

Chapter 6
Human Interaction with the Rock Cycle

NOTE

In this topic students have a choice. They can answer a question on:
A. Mining **OR** B. Quarrying **OR** C. Oil/gas exploration **OR**
D. Geothermal energy

Answers to all four choices are supplied in this chapter.
You need to study one of the choices **A** or **B** or **C** or **D**.
Sometimes the interactions are listed in the question.
However, this is not always the case.

Q

Human Interaction: 2015 Question 3C
Examine how humans interact with the rock cycle with reference to one of the following: • Mining • Extraction of building materials • Oil/gas exploration • Geothermal energy production   [30 marks]

Marking scheme:
Examination: 15 x SRPs (15 x 2 marks = 30)

What You Need To Do:
- State which topic you will examine.
- Discuss briefly how the topic you have chosen (minerals, quarry materials, oil/gas, geothermal energy) is formed as part of the rock cycle.
- Discuss how your chosen topic is used economically.
- In your discussion name a benefit and or disadvantage associated with interaction.

A

Answer
A. Mining

Mining enables humans to benefit from many useful materials produced by the rock cycle.
   Humans interact with the rock cycle by mining rocks for useful minerals such as

gold and diamonds and for fuels such as coal, oil and gas. These substances are economically important. They provide energy, food additives, metals and raw materials for the chemical industry. Mines, mining companies and their products are sold internationally and this trade alone is worth more than €150 billion worldwide annually.

Metals are often found within igneous and sedimentary rocks. The metals are deposited when hot, metal-rich fluids produced by volcanic activity pass through joints in rocks and cool, allowing the metals to collect in the cracks as veins of metal. The lead and zinc deposits in limestone rock at Tara Mines in Navan were formed in this way.

Sometimes metals are eroded from igneous or sedimentary rocks and are re-deposited in sands and gravels by river action. This occurred with gold in the Avoca River, County Wicklow.

In order to extract metals and fuels formed as part of the rock cycle, humans have to find them, dig them up and process them. These primary activities are important to the economies of countries such as Ireland and South Africa. In Ireland the mining industry is an important economic activity. Mining employs nearly 6,000 people and generates over €1 billion per annum for the Irish economy.

A good example of the economic benefits of human interaction with the rock cycle is the mining operation at Tara Lead and Zinc Mine in Navan, County Meath. This is the largest lead and zinc mine in Europe, employing 680 people and generating €100 million per annum for the local economy through wages and spin-off industries. It produces over 2.7 million tonnes of zinc and lead concentrate per year. Lead and zinc are very useful metals. Sixty per cent of the lead mined is used in batteries. Other uses include weapons and X-ray gowns. Zinc is used to galvanise other metals to protect them from rusting. It is also used in cosmetics and paint. These uses have many economic applications in business, health, transportation and computing.

In order to extract the ore (metal-bearing rock) from the ground the stope and pillar method is used. Large areas underground are blasted (the stopes) and pillars of rock are left standing between the stopes to support the tunnels. Underground remote-controlled equipment crushes the rock and lifts it to the surface. On the surface it is again crushed to a powder and mixed with water and chemicals to release the metal from the powdered ore. This mix is then filtered. When it is dried it becomes what is known as the concentrate. The concentrate is sent by rail to Dublin Port and shipped to Europe for smelting.

Waste water from the mine is pumped to a settling pond and solid waste is collected here. The waste rock is mixed with cement and used to fill the stopes when they are finished supplying ore. All these mine-related activities provide a variety of jobs for the economy.

A

OR
Answer
B. Quarrying

Quarrying is the removal of stone from large open pits dug into the earth's surface. It is an important economic activity across the world. Quarries provide materials for the construction industry as well as rock salt, marble for sculpture and stone for paving and kitchen work-tops. Quarries are used to extract many types of rock from the ground. Such is the variety of rocks that can be quarried that every part of the rock cycle is involved.

Igneous rocks such as basalt and granite, sedimentary rocks such as rock salt and limestone and metamorphic rock such as marble are all removed from quarries. Weathered and eroded rock particles such as sands and gravels are also an important resource extracted by quarrying.

Quarry operators use several methods to remove rock from the ground depending on the rock type involved or its proposed use once sold. The plug-and-feather method involves drilling holes into the rock and then using steel wedges to lever large slabs of rock from the ground. This is used to supply large decorative slabs for flooring or wall covering, e.g. Liscannor flagstone. This method works best in sedimentary rocks where the wedges can be pushed into the bedding planes between the layers of rock.

Explosives are used to remove large volumes of rock that do not need to be in large pieces, e.g. to supply the cement industry with limestone or to supply farmers with powdered lime.

Another method called channelling is used to cut large slices of rock that can then be cut to particular shapes, e.g. marble blocks for sculptures.

Quarrying has an important economic impact. Sand and gravel quarries are found in most counties and provide jobs in construction, distribution and in the quarries themselves. Over 1,000 people are involved in the quarrying industry in Ireland. The value of quarrying and mining products produced in Ireland is over €758 million. Two major quarry companies in Ireland are Roadstone and Readymix.

In some areas local road infrastructure may be improved along access routes to the quarry. This can encourage other industries to locate in the area. Limestone quarries provide an important raw material – lime – for the agricultural industry. Lime is used to promote grass growth and leads to higher milk yields and income for farmers.

A

OR
Answer
C. Oil/gas exploration

Humans interact with the rock cycle through the activities of oil and gas exploration. The oil and gas industry is economically important to countries such as Norway and Saudi Arabia. In 2010 the global value of this industry was over €186 billion.

Oil and gas are formed when organic material buried in sedimentary rocks is subjected to heat and pressure. The organic material is converted to oil and gas and these hydrocarbons are held in the pore spaces between the grains of sedimentary rocks such as sandstone.

Oil and gas are less dense than water and slowly rise through the rock until they either get trapped by a layer of impermeable rock such as shale (the cap rock) or they escape to the surface.

Humans interact with this process by searching for and extracting oil and gas from the rock reservoirs underground. Humans also use the hydrocarbons as a source of energy and as a raw material for many useful materials such as plastics.

In Ireland geologists have discovered several gas deposits offshore. These are located in the Kinsale Gas Field off the Cork coast in the Celtic Sea and the Corrib Gas Field in the Atlantic Ocean, 70 kilometres west of Belmullet, County Mayo.

The Kinsale source is nearing the end of its life and the Corrib gas has yet to be brought ashore but is expected to supply approximately 60% of Irish gas requirements.

At present most of our gas is piped from the North Sea, across Scotland, through an undersea inter-connector pipeline to Ireland. There are many jobs associated with the exploration and exploitation of oil/gas resources. Globally 2.5 million people work in the oil industry. Direct employment occurs on the rigs and a large network of people on land supports these workers, e.g. pilots, geologists, medical staff, clothing suppliers, engineers, divers and caterers.

On land, pipeline construction and maintenance workers, pumping station operators, environmental consultants and archaeologists are all involved in the provision of gas pipeline infrastructure to homes and businesses.

The benefits of the existence of oil and gas deposits are very important to national economic security in times of recession. One such benefit is the independence of fuel supply which protects the economy from fuel shortages and from rising world fuel prices.

Oil and gas are the raw material for many important products. The plastics industry is dependent on hydrocarbons as is the chemicals industry. Several clothing fabrics such as nylon are made from oil. The cosmetic industry also uses oil and its products, e.g. petroleum jelly (Vaseline) and shampoo. Petrochemicals are also used as food additives.

OR
Answer
D. Geothermal energy

Geothermal energy production uses heat from hot igneous rocks to heat water and generate steam which can be used to make electricity. Several countries, including Iceland and New Zealand, use geothermal energy.

Geothermal energy uses the rock cycle to provide heat and power. Iceland is located on the Mid Atlantic Ridge. Here, the Eurasian plate is pulled apart from the North American plate. Hot magma from the mantle rises to fill the rift between the plates. The hot igneous rock heats the rainwater that seeps into the ground to a temperature of 200 °C.

This hot water can be captured by drilling 2 kilometres down into the hot rocks above the magma. The hot water can be distributed directly to homes and industries to supply hot water and central heating. It is also used to heat greenhouses for vegetable production. In this way Iceland can produce salad crops cheaply and reduce expensive imports.

At present 26% of electricity in Iceland is generated using geothermal energy. Iceland has five geothermal power plants and geothermal heating provides hot water and heating for over 89% of the country's housing. It is such a cheap source of heat that some footpaths in Iceland's capital (Reykjavik) are heated.

In other power stations water is pumped into wells drilled into the hot rock below. It is then heated and turned into steam which is returned to the surface and used to make electricity. Geothermal energy also reduces the need for fossil fuels and helps reduce harmful greenhouse gas emissions. Iceland also plans to sell its geothermal electricity to Europe through undersea cables measuring 1,170 km in length which will be connected to the UK.

In Iceland geothermal energy is also a tourist attraction. One power plant just south of Reykjavik uses mineral-rich water from the power station to fill up a nearby lake known as the Blue Lagoon. This has become one of Iceland's most famous tourist destinations and has a spa complex beside the lagoon where the water is kept at a cosy 40°C for bathers. Other effects of geothermal energy are geysers and geothermal springs which are tourist attractions in Iceland. The Geysir area is one of Iceland's most famous tourist destinations due to the geothermal activity that occurs there. It has several hot, bubbling mudpools and geysers which attract thousands of tourists to the area each year. In 2014 just under one million tourists visited Iceland.

Chapter 7
Surface Processes – Rivers/Ice/Sea/Mass Movement

NOTE

In this section students have to study **one** topic (rivers, ice, sea or mass movement) in detail. This means students must be able to describe the formation of landforms created by either rivers, ice, sea or mass movement processes.

For all topics students must be able to recognise the landforms/features from maps, photos and diagrams and state which processes were involved in their formation.

This is a very common question on the exam paper and **all** students should be well prepared to do this question. Students should know one landform of erosion and one landform of deposition from their chosen topic. Students could be asked to locate a landform on a map. Students may be asked to discuss one or two landforms in an answer.

A. Fluvial processes (Rivers)

(i) Landform of river erosion: Waterfalls

Q

Landform Development: 2015 Question 1B (i)
Examine the impact of the processes of erosion on the formation of one fluvial, coastal or glacial landform that you have studied. **[30 marks]**

Marking scheme:
Name processes of erosion: 2 marks + 2 marks
Name landform of erosion: 2 marks
Examination: 12 x SRPs (12 x 2 marks = 24)

> **What You Need To Do:**
> - Name the landform.
> - Name an Irish example of that landform.
> - Draw a well-labelled diagram.
> - Explain the formation of the landform focusing on the processes of erosion.
> - You must name and explain at least two processes of erosion.

Answer

A **Waterfalls**

This answer will examine the processes involved in the formation of waterfalls, landforms formed by river erosion. **Irish example:** Torc Waterfall, County Kerry.

The river erosion processes involved in the formation of a waterfall are hydraulic action, abrasion and solution.

Hydraulic action is the force of moving water on the land. Fast-flowing water forces out loose rock and soil from the riverbed and banks. Over time the banks collapse. Soft rocks are eroded faster than harder ones. (Differential erosion)

Abrasion is the wearing away of the riverbed by its load. Stones carried by the river scrape away and smooth the river channel as they move along, deepening and widening the river channel.

Solution occurs when river water dissolves the soft rock over which it flows.

The erosion processes mentioned above combine to form waterfalls in the youthful stage of a river's course. Waterfalls occur where a band of hard rock, e.g granite, lies across a river's bed. Soft rock (e.g. shale) is eroded more quickly. Gradually a small fall forms in the riverbed. The hydraulic force of water and abrasion combine to deepen the fall. A plunge pool forms at the base of the waterfall due to erosion caused by the weight of the water and stones carried by the river over the hard rock. Water also splashes against the back wall of the waterfall and erodes it by the process of solution. Eventually the overhanging piece of hard rock collapses and slowly the waterfall moves or retreats upstream. This is called headward erosion. Sometimes a steep-sided gorge is formed if headward erosion forms very quickly and the sides of the valley have not had time to be widened by mass movement.

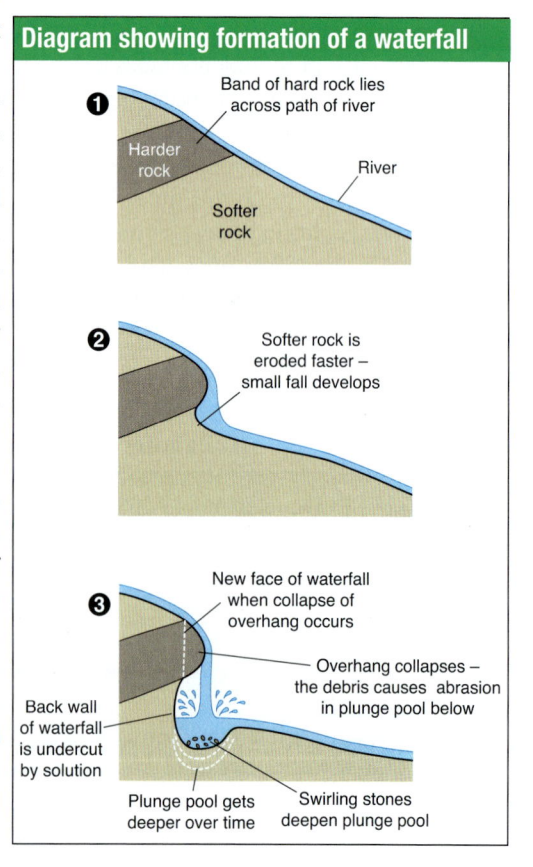

Diagram showing formation of a waterfall

❶ Band of hard rock lies across path of river
- Harder rock
- Softer rock
- River

❷ Softer rock is eroded faster – small fall develops

❸ New face of waterfall when collapse of overhang occurs
- Overhang collapses – the debris causes abrasion in plunge pool below
- Back wall of waterfall is undercut by solution
- Plunge pool gets deeper over time
- Swirling stones deepen plunge pool

(ii) Landform of river deposition: Levees

Q

Landform Development: 2012 Question 2B (i)
Explain with the aid of a labelled diagram(s) the formation of **one** landform of deposition that you have studied. **[30 marks]**

Marking scheme:
Named landform: 2 marks
Labelled diagram: 4 marks
Explanation: 12 x SRPs (12 x 12 marks = 24)

What You Need To Do:
- Name the landform.
- Draw a labelled diagram.
- Give an example.
- Explain the formation of the landform focusing on the processes of deposition.

Answer

A **Levees**

In this answer the processes involved in the formation of river levees will be examined. Levees are landforms formed by the processes of river deposition during flooding.
Irish example: The banks of the River Moy in County Mayo.

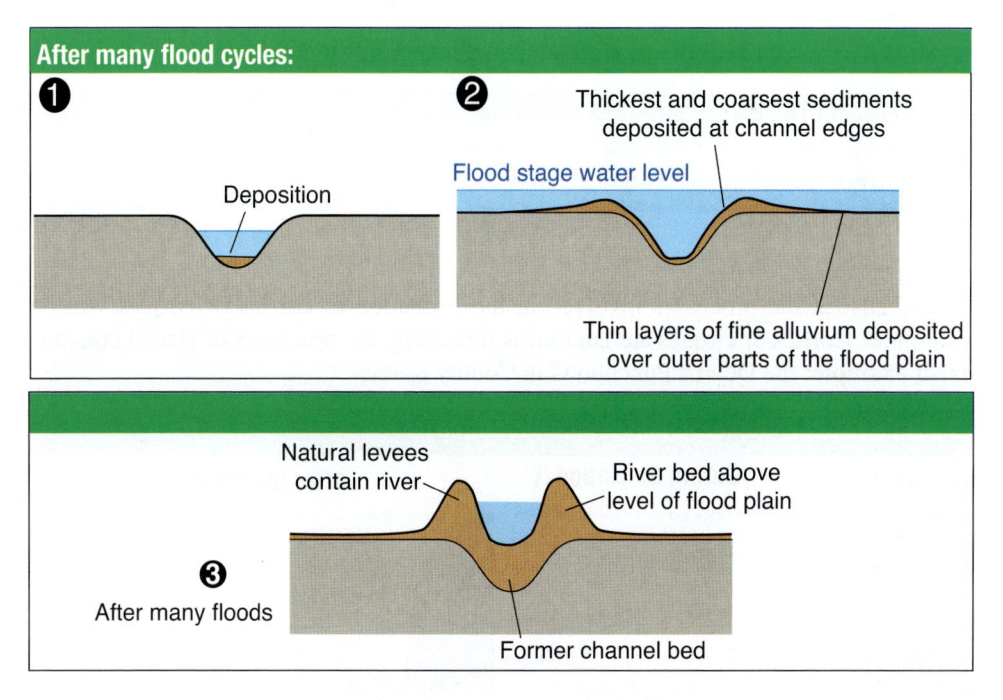

After many flood cycles:

❶ Deposition

❷ Thickest and coarsest sediments deposited at channel edges
Flood stage water level
Thin layers of fine alluvium deposited over outer parts of the flood plain

❸ After many floods
Natural levees contain river
River bed above level of flood plain
Former channel bed

The formation of levees

A levee is a wide ridge of sediment on the banks of a river. They are landforms of deposition often found in the lower stage of sediment-laden rivers.

River deposition occurs when the river loses energy and cannot carry its load. This can happen for a variety of reasons, e.g. the river may slow down when it floods onto its flood plain and suddenly becomes shallower. Levees form because of flooding. During normal flow the river is confined in its channel and deposition will occur on the riverbed. However, during flood events the river overflows its channel and pours over the flood plain.

Once the river has overflowed its channel, it will slow down due to the sudden decrease in depth and the fact that it has escaped its channel and now has a wider area to flow over. The loss of energy causes deposition. The heaviest stones are deposited first and closest to the banks while the finer alluvium is carried further away across the flood plain.

Over repeated flood events the deposits of heavy sediment build up on the banks and form ridges called levees. Levees are a river's natural defence against flooding. They keep the river within its channel as every time the river floods it will have to rise higher to escape over the levees. Eventually, deposition on the riverbed combined with natural levee-building leads to a situation where the bed of the river channel is above the level of the flood plain and the levees are the only thing preventing it flowing over the flood plain.

When humans reinforce levees or build artificial ones, it can interfere with the river's natural flood processes and trigger more extreme floods further downstream as has been seen along the Rivers Rhine and Mississippi.

B. Glacial processes

(i) Landform of glacial erosion – Corries/Cirques

Q

Landform Development: 2015 Question 1B (i)
Examine the impact of the processes of erosion on the formation of **one** fluvial coastal or glacial landform that you have studied. **[30 marks]**

Answer

A

Corrie/cirque
In this answer the processes involved in the formation of corries or cirques will be examined. Corries or cirques are landforms formed by the processes of glacial erosion.
Irish example: the Devil's Punchbowl in County Kerry.

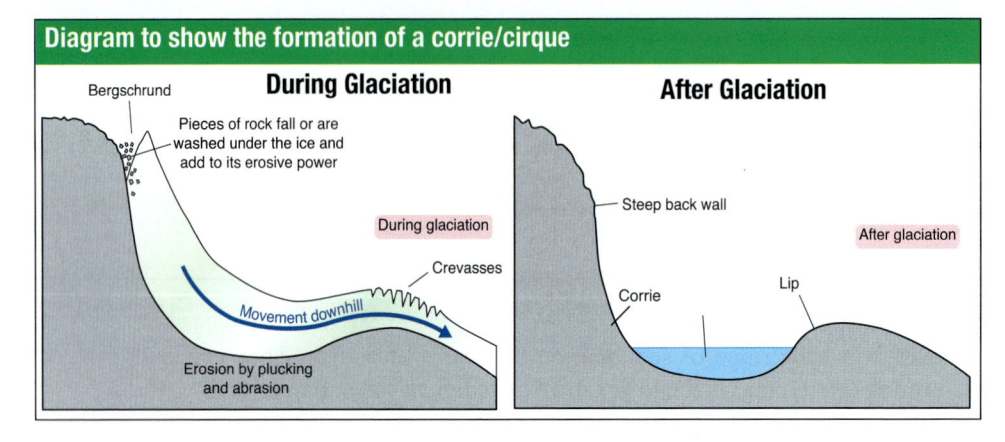

Diagram to show the formation of a corrie/cirque

During Glaciation
- Bergschrund
- Pieces of rock fall or are washed under the ice and add to its erosive power
- During glaciation
- Crevasses
- Movement downhill
- Erosion by plucking and abrasion

After Glaciation
- Steep back wall
- Corrie
- Lip
- After glaciation

The formation of a corrie/cirque
A corrie is a horseshoe-shaped hollow in mountainous areas. Several processes form a cirque: freeze-thaw action, plucking, abrasion and nivation.

Freeze-thaw action is a mechanical weathering process. Water collects in small cracks in rocks. It expands as it freezes and the pressure caused by the expansion weakens the rock. If the rock is repeatedly stressed it may crumble away when the water melts.

Plucking occurs when meltwater formed at the base and sides of the ice of a glacier seeps into rock cracks. When the meltwater refreezes it sticks to the rock. As the glacier moves downhill the ice plucks rock fragments away from the ground.

Abrasion occurs when rock fragments that are stuck to the ice are used to wear the rock surface away by scratching or abrading it. This is a similar process to how sandpaper is used to smooth rough surfaces.

Corries form mainly on north-facing slopes where snow lies on the ground all year. Freeze-thaw action provides loose rock fragments that fall onto the snow and during the brief summer melt, some rock fragments are washed under the snow. Over time the snow builds up and its weight compresses the bottom layers of snow into Firn ice and eventually blue glacier ice. All the time freeze-thaw action adds rock fragments to the ice and these are used to abrade the mountain when the ice eventually moves.

When the weight of the ice is great enough the ice moves downhill with a motion called rotational slip. This curved sliding motion combined with plucking and abrasion forms a hollow in the mountainside. The process of making a deep hollow or corrie by rotational slip, plucking and abrasion is called nivation. Eventually the ice is able to flow out of the hollow (corrie) and down the mountainside.

As the ice moves, some of it is pulled away from the back of the corrie to create a huge crevasse called a Bergschrund. When the ice melted after the Ice Age, corries were often filled with a lake. Corrie lakes are called tarns.

(ii) Landform of glacial deposition - Drumlins

Q **Landform Development: 2012 Question 2B (i)**
Explain with the aid of a labelled diagram(s) the formation of **one** landform of deposition that you have studied. **[30 marks]**

Answer

A **Drumlins**
In this answer the processes involved in the formation of drumlins will be examined. Drumlins are landforms of glacial deposition.
Irish example: the drumlin belt of Sligo–Monaghan.

Diagram to show the formation of drumlins

Ice movement →

STOSS SIDE — LEE SIDE
Boulder clay
30–100 m
1 km

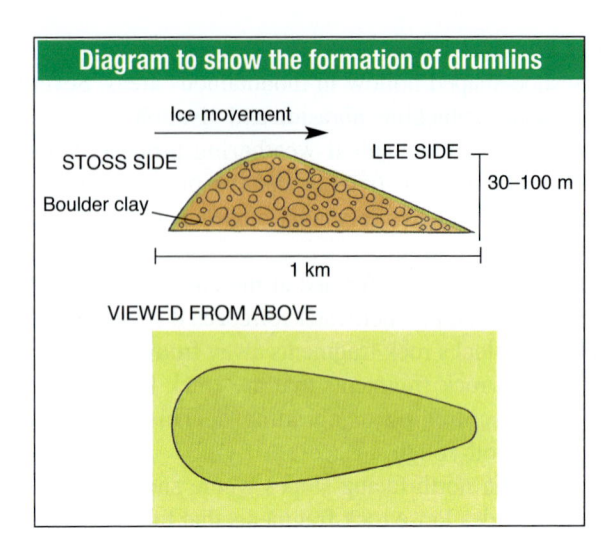

VIEWED FROM ABOVE

Processes involved in the formation of a drumlin

Drumlins are low oval-shaped hills composed of unsorted boulder clay. Boulder clay consists of sand, gravel and clay mixed up with larger stones or boulders. Drumlins vary in height from 25 to 100 metres and may be up to 1 kilometre long and 0.5 kilometres wide.

Drumlins are usually deposited parallel to the movement of the ice that formed them. As a result of this they have a steeper side (called the stoss side) which faces the ice movement and a gentler slope (called the lee side) which faces away from the direction of movement. This means that the highest point of any drumlin is always on the stoss side with the lowest point at the end of the lee side. Drumlins were deposited beneath the ice when an ice sheet laden with boulder clay melted.

There are several theories proposed to explain the formation of drumlins. One accepted theory is that an ice sheet became overloaded with sediment, and deposition occurred when the ice lost the ability to carry its load. The loss of energy was due to melting and/or a reduction in its speed of movement. However, the ice still had enough energy to move forward and mould the boulder clay deposits into their characteristic shape.

Another explanation suggests that the boulder clay was deposited beneath the ice and that large amounts of meltwater shaped the boulder clay deposits in the same way that sand ripples are formed on a beach. This explanation is used to explain why drumlins occur in large numbers (drumlin swarms) in some areas but are not found in others. Landscapes with many drumlins, such as County Monaghan, are sometimes called a 'basket of eggs' landscape.

Some drumlins are known to have formed around a large rock boulder. It is thought that the boulder acted as an obstruction to the moving ice and triggered deposition due to the extra friction generated between the ice and the boulder.

C. Marine processes

(i) Landform of marine erosion - Sea cliffs

Q

Landform Development: 2015 Question 1B (i)
Examine the impact of the processes of erosion on the formation of **one** fluvial, coastal or glacial landform that you have studied. **[30 marks]**

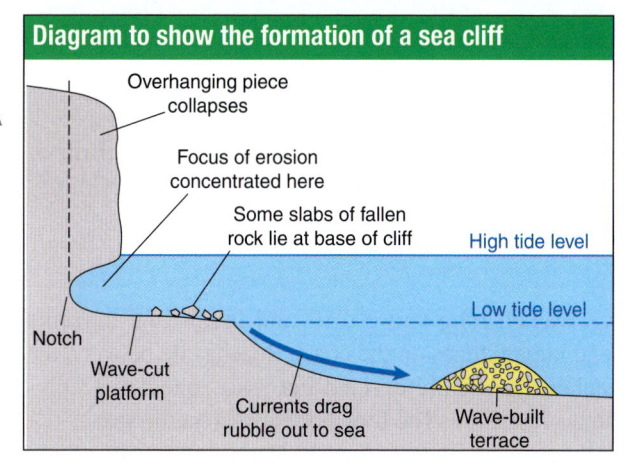

A

Diagram to show the formation of a sea cliff

Answer

Sea cliffs
In this answer the processes involved in the formation of sea cliffs, landforms of marine erosion, will be examined. **Irish example:** the Cliffs of Moher, County Clare.

The formation of sea cliffs
Several marine erosion processes combine to form sea cliffs. The two most powerful are hydraulic action and air compression. Hydraulic action is the force of water hitting against the land every time a wave breaks over it. A wave contains hundreds of tonnes of water and in storm conditions destructive waves hit the land several times a minute. The constant battering by the sea weakens the rock and loosens it.

Over time cracks appear in the rock and every time a wave breaks against it air is suddenly compressed into the crack (air compression). When the wave falls away from the rock the air in the crack suddenly escapes with explosive force. This constant compression and release of air in rock cracks is a very powerful method of marine erosion, especially in storm conditions when waves are larger and hit the land more often.

The above methods of marine erosion are involved in cliff formation. But abrasion (when sea sediment is used to wear the land away) and chemical action (dissolving the rock) also play a role.

The constant wave attack on the land is concentrated in a zone between the high and low tide mark. Gradually this area is eaten away and an overhang or notch is formed. As the notch is enlarged the overlying rock is unsupported and eventually collapses and a steep cliff face is formed. The continual cycle of notch formation and cliff collapse causes the cliff face to move or 'retreat' inland. The exposed base of the cliff forms a flat area in front of the cliff which is visible at low tide. This area is called the wave-cut platform.

The cliff debris falls to the bottom of the cliff and is itself broken up by the forces of erosion and then used in abrasion to wear the cliff face away. Some of the debris is dragged out to sea by hydraulic action and local tidal currents. This debris collects in a ridge underwater and is called a wave-built terrace.

(ii) Landform of marine deposition – Beach

Q **Landform Development: 2012 Question 2B (i)**
Explain with the aid of a labelled diagram(s) the formation of **one** landform of deposition that you have studied. **[30 marks]**

Answer

A **Beach**
In this answer the processes involved in the formation of a beach, a landform of marine deposition, will be examined. **Irish example:** Tramore Beach, County Waterford.

The formation of a beach
Beaches form when constructive waves, long-shore drift and local tidal currents combine to deposit sand, shingle and larger stones on the coast. Beaches lie between the high tide and low tide mark. Beaches are usually divided into two zones: a steeply-sloping upper shore and a much flatter foreshore. The foreshore is nearest the sea.

Several conditions must exist before beach material can be deposited on the shore: There must be a sheltered area to trap sediment, long-shore drift must bring material to the sheltered area and then constructive waves must occur to keep depositing material on the beach. Long-shore drift is the movement of beach material along the coast by the swash and backwash of waves.

Bays usually provide all these conditions and are ideal places for beaches to form. Many of Ireland's beaches are found in bays, e.g. Lahinch, County Clare.

Constructive waves build beaches in the following way: the swash of a constructive wave is more powerful than the backwash. The swash is able to drag sediment and larger stones up the shore but the backwash is unable to pull them away again. As the swash moves up the shore it slows down, seawater then percolates (seeps) into the ground depositing its load of sand and stones. The heavier stones and shingle are left higher up the beach but finer sand is dragged back down the shore and left there. As a result of this sorting of material, beaches usually have an area of stony material at the top of the beach while sandier material is found closer to the sea. In storm conditions powerful waves carry or throw much larger stones to the top of the beach and deposit them as a storm beach.

Wave action and local currents shape the beach deposits into a variety of forms such as cusps, berms, ridges and runnels. Cusps are crescent-shaped hollows formed in shingle beaches by constructive wave action. Berms are long steps or terraces formed in the storm beach by powerful constructive waves that push shingle stones towards the backshore when they surge up the shore. Ridges are long, low, sandy mounds that are built parallel to the beach in the foreshore. They are separated from each other by deeper channels called runnels. Ridges and runnels are formed by constructive waves and local long-shore drift currents.

Diagram to show the formation of a beach

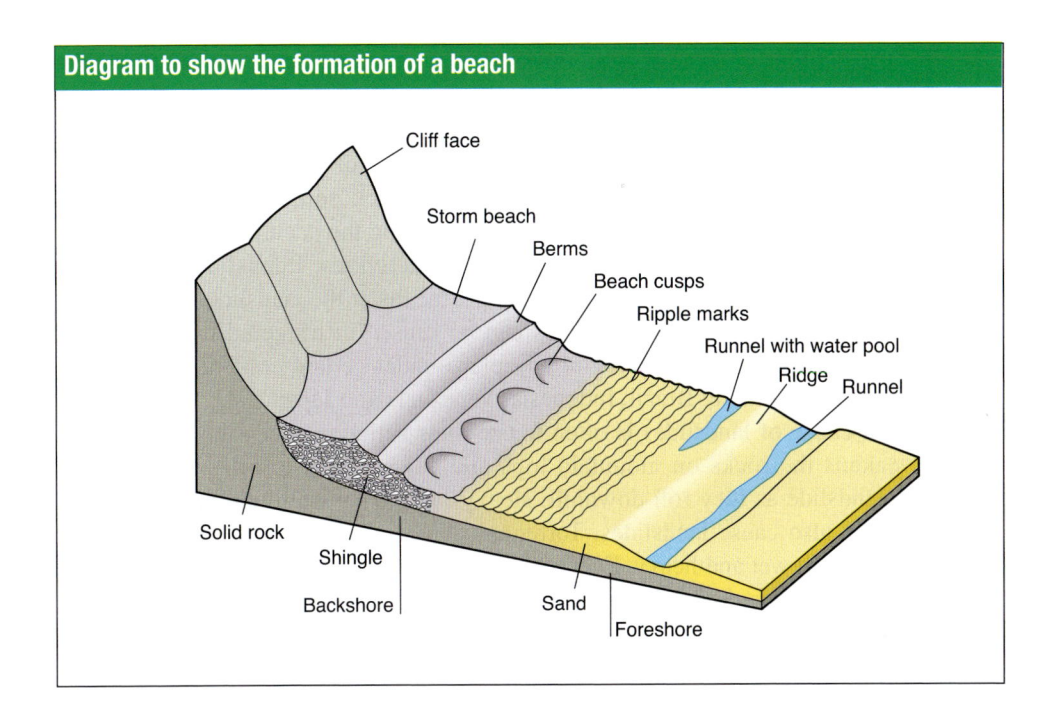

Labels: Cliff face, Storm beach, Berms, Beach cusps, Ripple marks, Runnel with water pool, Ridge, Runnel, Solid rock, Shingle, Backshore, Sand, Foreshore

D. Mass Movement Processes

Q

Landform Development: 2015 Question 1B(ii)
Describe and explain the factors governing the operation of **one** mass movement process that you have studied. **[30 marks]**

Marking scheme:
Identify factors: 2 marks + 2 marks
Name mass movement process: 2 marks
Description/explanation: 12 x SRPs (12 x 2 marks = 26)

What You Need To Do:
- Name a mass movement process.
- Draw a labelled diagram to show how it happens.
- Discuss why it happens focusing on factors such as gradient, rainfall, vegetation and human activities.
- Give examples.
- Discuss effects and possible solutions if relevant.

Answer

A Mass Movement Process / Landslides

Mass movement is the movement of material downhill due to the influence of gravity. In this answer I will describe and explain the occurrence of landslides, a fast type of mass movement process. Landslides occur when loose rock, soil or sediment known as regolith suddenly moves downhill. The factors governing the occurrence of landslides include gradient, rainfall, earthquakes and human activities. Landslides happen on steep slopes of 45° or more. The steeper the slope, the faster the landslide will be.

Like many mass movements, landslides can be caused or triggered by natural and human events. Landslides can occur in any place under certain conditions described below; they are common in Brazil, Indonesia, Venezuela and Japan.

A **natural cause** of landslides is often freeze-thaw action on steep mountain slopes which weakens the rocks on mountain tops and causes them to fall as scree. This triggers a landslide as they roll downhill. Heavy rainfall/snowfall and earthquakes or volcanoes can also cause landslides. Torrential rainfall during storms and hurricanes makes the regolith wet and heavy. Eventually it becomes so saturated and slippery that the land surface slides downhill under its own weight. This type of landslide is very common in mountainous tropical countries such as Venezuela. Countries such as Haiti which lie in the path of hurricanes regularly experience landslides because the ground becomes saturated by heavy rainfall during hurricanes.

Earthquakes also cause landslides. As the land is shaken, loose rock and soil falls downhill. In China in 2008 a major earthquake caused thousands of landslides. A major river was blocked with landslide debris and this led to the formation of a 'quake lake' which threatened to burst through the landslide debris and affect 1.3 million people. The landslide blockage was eventually cleared by blasting the rock debris away and slowly draining the lake.

Human activity can also cause landslides. The most common human cause of landslides is deforestation of mountainous land and road building on steep ground.

Plant roots anchor the soil which prevents mass movement. Branches provide natural protection for soil from rain and wind. When deforestation happens the bare soil is exposed to the wind and rain and easily slides downhill on steep slopes. In places like Brazil and Madagascar large-scale deforestation for timber has led to an increase in the amount of landslides occurring.

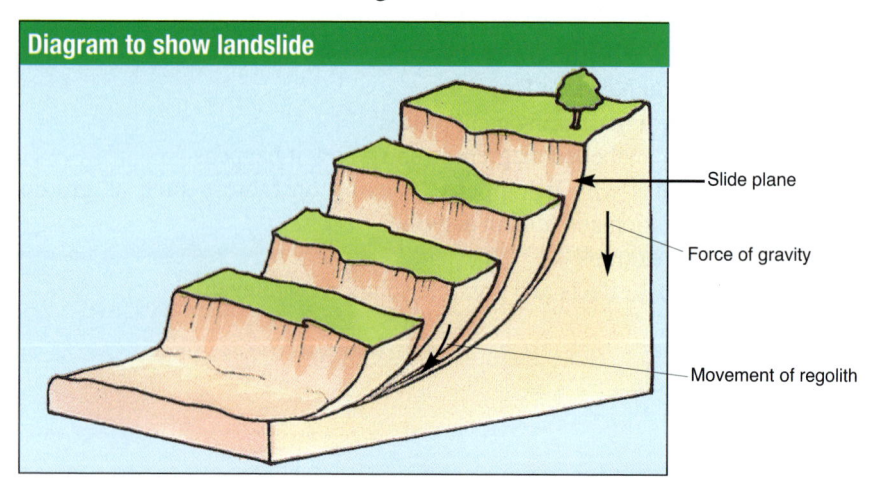

Diagram to show landslide

- Slide plane
- Force of gravity
- Movement of regolith

Landslides are a major problem in Japan, a densely populated mountainous country with frequent earthquakes. The construction of roads and railway tracks across steep ground in Japan has weakened the slopes and can trigger landslides which destroy large sections of routeways and damage settlement. The road/rail routes also weaken slopes during an earthquake.

The Japanese have invested in landslide prediction, mapping and prevention technologies. These include strain meters and laser measuring of land to map where the land surface is slowly beginning to move. People are warned and evacuated if a landslide seems likely. Engineers also strengthen slopes below routeways by building supporting walls as well as draining water from hillsides. This reduces the weight of the regolith and therefore also its ability to slide.

Mass movement process 2
Soil creep

Soil creep is a slow mass movement process, usually 1 cm/year. It is the slow but continuous movement of soil downhill under the force of gravity. The factors that govern the operation of soil creep are weather and gradient. Soil creep occurs due to the combination of freeze-thaw action on soil grains and the alternate wetting and drying out of soil caused by the weather.

During rainy weather, clay particles in soil grains absorb moisture and expand slightly (hydration). As they expand, they push up and away from each other. During dry spells, the clay grains dry out and shrink (dehydrate). As they dry out, they move closer to each other and roll slowly downhill. During frosty weather, ice forms between the soil grains and as the ice expands, it pushes them apart. When the soil thaws out, the grains move closer together and roll slowly downhill.

Repeated wetting and drying combined with frost causes a slow continuous movement of soil grains downhill. Soil creep happens on grassy slopes across Ireland.

Evidence that soil creep is occurring include: small steps or terracettes in grassy slopes, tilted fence posts, soil gathering on the uphill side of stone walls, bulging or burst stone walls, cracks in hillside road surfaces and curved tree trunks on slopes.

The rate of soil creep depends on the gradient of the slope. Steeper slopes cause faster creep. Plant roots, while anchoring soil grains together, add to the weight of the soil and contribute to soil creep during wet conditions.

Building engineers guard against soil creep by sinking metal rods into the ground close to foundations to prevent soil creep affecting buildings on slopes.

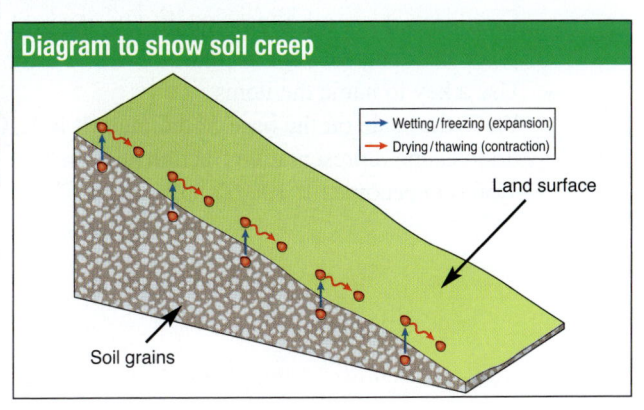

Diagram to show soil creep

→ Wetting/freezing (expansion)
→ Drying/thawing (contraction)

Land surface

Soil grains

Chapter 8
Map Skills

Q

Ordnance Survey extract: 2011 Question 1A
Examine the 1: 50,000 Ordnance Survey map and legend that accompanies this paper.
Draw a sketch map to **half-scale** of the area shown.
On it **mark** and **name** each of the following:
- The complete course of the Garfinny River
- A section of coast with coastal cliffs
- A beach
- An area of land over 600 metres east of easting 50   [20 marks]

Marking scheme:
4 features @ 4 marks each (shown = 2 marks, named = 2 marks)
Proportion: 4 marks (graded 4 – 2 – 0)
Note: proportion involves showing correct scale and coastline.

What You Need to Do:
- Ask the exam attendant for graph paper if you do not have any. Graph paper may be worth 2 marks!
- Put the title of the sketch at the top of the page.
- Count the grid squares across the top of the map. This is the length in centimetres of the top and bottom edges of your frame.
- Count the grid squares up the side of the map. This is the length in centimetres of the left and right edges of your frame.
- Using a ruler, draw the frame to the size you have just calculated.
- With a pencil lightly divide your frame and map area into nine equal sections.
- Mark in the coastline.
- Draw the outline of the items required. Make sure they are in the correct location and not too big or small. Use the grid lines you have drawn to help place the items on your sketch.
- Use a key to name the items.
- Place the scale on the base of the map. It is 1:100,000. Drawing to half scale doubles the representative fraction so 2 cm to 1 km becomes 1 cm to 1 km or 1:50,000 becomes 1: 100,000 or 1 cm = 1 km.

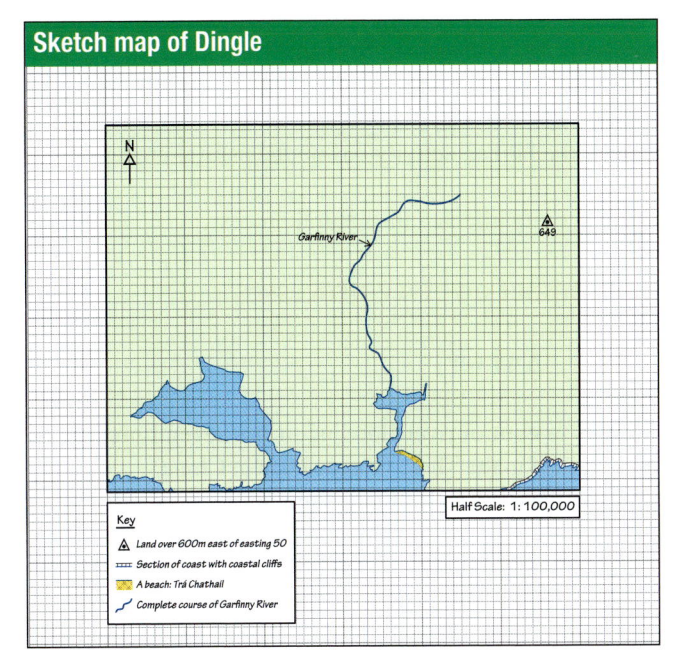

A

Sketch map of Dingle

Key
- Land over 600m east of easting 50
- Section of coast with coastal cliffs
- A beach: Trá Chathail
- Complete course of Garfinny River

Half Scale: 1 : 100,000

Chapter 9

Human Interaction with Surface Processes

NOTE

In this section students have a choice of answering on human interaction with:
A. Rivers **OR**
B. Seas **OR**
C. Mass movement processes.

Q

Human Influence on Natural Processes: 2012 Question 2C
Examine with reference to an example or examples you have studied how human activities impacted on either river, coastal or mass movement processes. **[30 marks]**

Marking scheme:
Identify human activity: 2 marks
Identify impact: 2 marks
Name example: 2 marks
Discussion: 12 x SRPs (12 x 2 marks = 24)

Note: This is a common question and students should be well prepared on this topic. The questions asked may reflect natural events occuring during the year. In late 2013/early 2014, coastal erosion and river flooding were major issues during winter storms and the questions asked in 2014 reflected this, (e.g. 2014 Q1C).

> **What You Need To Do:**
> - State the human activity that has affected the natural process you have chosen.
> - Name at least one impact the human activity has on the natural process.
> - Give an example.
> - Discuss how the human activity affected the natural process.

A. Human impact on river processes

A

Answer

Human impact on river processes

When people build dams and levees to control river flooding, it has several impacts on the operation of natural river processes, e.g. the Three Gorges Dam in China.

Building dams affects river transport processes. Building dams across a river to control flooding interferes with the ability of the river to carry its load of sediment from source to sea. Huge reservoirs are created behind the dams and the river's load is trapped in the reservoir.

At the Three Gorges Dam in China a dam 185 metres high and 1.6 kilometres wide was built across the River Yangtze. A reservoir over 560 kilometres long was created behind this dam. This dam is used to generate power for major cities such as Shanghai and to prevent devastating floods which in the past have killed hundreds of thousands of people.

However, damming the river has prevented the transport of fertile alluvium downstream. The floods have also been stopped. This has saved lives but farmland downstream from the dam is becoming infertile as it is starved of the life-giving alluvium which would have been deposited by the floods. Farmers now have to use expensive artificial fertilisers on their land.

Building levees prevents natural flood processes from occurring, e.g. along the River Rhine in Germany. Levees are raised river banks deposited in the lower stage of a river's course. These are natural river landforms but humans also build levees and raise existing levees to stop a river flooding onto its flood plain. Flood plains are flat, fertile areas. Over the centuries many have become densely populated areas. Large cities have been built on them, e.g. Duisburg - the largest inland port in the world was built on the flood plain of the River Rhine. Preventing rivers overflowing onto their flood plains by interfering with the natural flood process has stopped damage to economically important developments such as factories and transport infrastructure.

Because the levees are so high, the river cannot flood naturally; so it deposits its load on the riverbed. Over time this raises the riverbed above the level of the flood plain and so the levees are the only thing containing the river. This creates a need for higher, stronger levees which are expensive to build and maintain. Floodwater which would normally escape onto the flood plain is now trapped in the river and is funnelled downstream until it can overflow where it then creates extreme damage. Levees also cause the river to flow faster as it is constrained in narrower channels. The Rhine now flows 30% faster than before the levees were built.

OR
B. Human impact on coastal processes

> **Human Influence on Natural Processes: 2012 Question 2C**
> Examine with reference to an example or examples you have studied how human activities impacted on either river, coastal or mass movement processes. **[30 marks]**

Answer

Human impact on coastal processes
Coastal processes are marine erosion, transport and deposition. Humans can have an impact on all of these processes.

1. Human impact on marine erosion processes
People can impact on marine erosion processes by protecting the coast from the effects of abrasion, hydraulic action and air compression – the most damaging coastal processes. Coastal protection methods can be hard or soft. Hard methods such as sea walls and rock armour work to resist the power of the sea and prevent erosion from damaging the coastline and the buildings on it. Hard methods have been used in Lahinch, County Clare where large two-tonne stones have been piled in front of a large curved sea wall to protect the coast there. Soft methods use the power of the sea to build up the coastline. Soft methods usually encourage deposition as a beach protects the coast and prevents further erosion. Soft methods include sand dune protection. Fences and beach mats placed in front of the dunes to trap windblown sand also encourage deposition. Soft methods such as beach mats have been used at Bull Island in Dublin.

2. Human impact on marine transport processes
Long-shore drift uses the swash and backwash of sea waves to transport large volumes of sediment along the coast. People can affect this natural coastal process by building beach groynes to trap the sand as it is moved along the shore. Groynes are wooden or concrete walls placed at right angles to the shore. They allow the build-up of beach material in an area and prevent the sea from removing beaches. Groynes are used at Rosslare Strand, County Wexford. However if they are not correctly spaced they can lead to further erosion along the coast because they prevent sediment from moving along the coast.

3. Human impact on marine deposition processes
People can affect coastal depositional processes by diverting sea currents so that deposition occurs in an area that does not affect shipping. This has happened in Dublin Bay where the North and South Bull Walls were built to keep the port clear of sand. The walls have changed the natural deposition process so that the port channel is kept clear by the tides while the sand that used to be deposited there is now carried away from the port entrance and deposited at the Bull Island instead. The sea walls are also an obstacle to marine transportation in Dublin Bay and have led to the deposition of sand against the North Wall. Over time a large sand spit of 5 km in length called Bull Island has formed.

OR
C. Human interaction with mass movement processes

> **Human Influence on Natural Processes: 2012 Question 2C**
> Examine with reference to an example or examples you have studied how human activities impacted on either river, coastal or mass movement processes. **[30 marks]**

Answer

Mass movement

Mass movement is the movement of loose soil and rock (known as regolith) downhill. Fast mass movements include landslides, rock falls, bog bursts and avalanches. The natural factors that control whether mass movement will occur are vegetation cover, the steepness of a slope and water content of the soil. However, human activity can interfere with these factors and cause mass movement to occur.

Deforestation: Vegetation is important in anchoring the soil to the ground. Plant roots hold soil grains together and prevent them being blown or washed away. Leaves and branches protect soil from the force of wind and rain, preventing erosion and slowing mass movement. Human activities such as deforestation and overgrazing remove the protective cover of vegetation. On mountain slopes deforestation can increase the occurrence of landslides in times of wet weather. This has been seen in Brazil, Venezuela and Indonesia where large areas of forest have been cleared. In these countries when hurricanes and tropical storms bring torrential rain, devastating landslides occur on the deforested slopes. Many thousands of people have lost their lives and roads and rail lines have been destroyed.

Overgrazing removes the protection of vegetation. In Ireland the hills of County Mayo have been overgrazed due to the overstocking of sheep on the uplands. In the 1980s and 1990s more than two million sheep grazed the uplands. The sheep cleared the protective covering of heather and moss from the blanket bogs and this led to the erosion of boglands across Mayo. Bog bursts occur more easily when the plants are removed and rain washes the peat away into rivers and streams.

Construction on hillsides can also increase the occurrence of mass movement. Japan is a mountainous country and many roads are built along the sides of mountains. The road cuttings remove support for the slope and this can lead to landslides triggered by heavy rain or by the great weight of the hillsides bearing down on the road cutting. Also in Japan earthquakes often trigger landslides on slopes affected by road construction.

Irrigation: Making the soil wetter can also trigger mass movement. Water increases the weight of the regolith and provides lubrication, allowing it to slip more easily. Irrigation of crops on sloping hillsides is a problem in many areas of California and Southern Italy as the rate of soil creep is increased.

The occurrence of mass movement can be reduced or prevented in a number of ways. Methods include improving drainage. This reduces both the weight of the regolith and its ability to slide. Another method is to reduce the angle of the slope by terracing or levelling. This reduces the influence of gravity on an unstable hill. Re-planting slopes with trees and shrubs will anchor the soil and protect the surface from erosion by wind and rain. Placing artificial hard covers of wire or flexible concrete on disintegrating cliff faces will prevent rockfalls which can trigger larger slides.

Chapter 10

Isostatic Processes

> **NOTE:** Isostatic processes include topics such as river rejuvenation, changes in base level and the landforms that result.

Q

Isostatic Processes: 2013 Question 1C
Explain how rivers adjust to a change in base level with reference to example(s) that you have studied. **[30 marks]**

Marking scheme:
Identify adjustment: 2 marks
Name Irish example: 2 marks
Explanation: 13 x SRPs (13 x 2 marks = 26)

What You Need To Do:
- Explain the term **isostatic changes**.
- Name and explain two river landforms made by isostatic processes.
- Give examples.
- Draw a labelled diagram.

> **NOTE:** This topic was also examined in 2015 (Question 2C).
> **'Explain how isostacy has impacted on the Irish landscape.'**
> The answer below applies to both the 2013 and 2015 questions.

A

Answer

Landforms: Knickpoints and river terraces
Example: Both found on River Barrow near Saint Mullins, County Kilkenny

Isostatic processes involve changes in sea level due to the uplift or sinking of the earth's lithosphere. This is caused by the removal or addition of huge ice sheets on the land during the Ice Ages.

The great weight of ice pressing down on the lithosphere during an Ice Age causes it to sink slightly under the weight. This can cause a local rise in sea level affecting only the area of land that is sinking under the weight. Once the ice has melted, the weight of great ice sheets on the land is removed. The lithosphere slowly returns to its original level and the land is uplifted out of the sea. The uplift of land is called isostacy.

The effect of isostatic processes on the Irish landscape is to change the base level (sea level) of any rivers flowing over the land. If the land is uplifted then a river's base level is lowered and it has renewed ability to erode. This is termed rejuvenation.

The formation of knickpoints

Knickpoints are rapids and small waterfalls found in the mature or lower stage of a river's course. They represent the place where the river once entered the sea. Due to isostatic uplift the sea level was lowered and the river had to travel over a longer course to reach the sea. The river was rejuvenated or made young again as it was given renewed ability to cut down into the land (vertical erosion) in order to reach the sea. The rejuvenated river cuts a new profile for itself and the place where the new profile meets the old profile is seen as a knickpoint. They are visible on many Irish rivers in the south and east regions at a height of about 150 metres above sea level, showing that the sea level was once this much higher around Ireland.

The formation of river terraces

When a river is rejuvenated it begins to cut down into its existing floodplain and makes a deeper, narrower channel for itself. The rejuvenated river makes a new flood plain for itself at a lower level.

The original valley floor is left high above the new flood plain and is seen as steps in the land on either side of the rejuvenated river channel. These steps are called river terraces and are often seen in pairs on either side of the river. Sometimes a river can be rejuvenated more than once and so another set of terraces are formed resulting in a river valley with stepped sides. River terraces are found on the River Barrow in County Kilkenny.

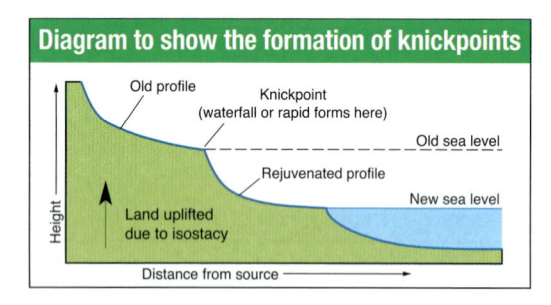

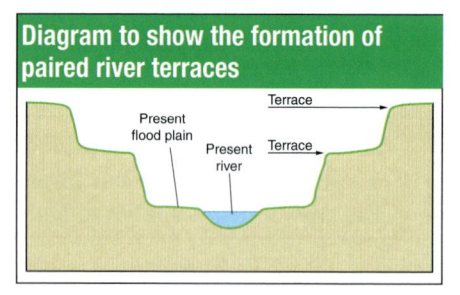

SECTION 2

Core - Regional Geography

→ This topic is examined in Questions 4, 5, and 6 on the Leaving Certificate exam paper. Each question is divided into three parts: A, B and C. The marks allocated are usually 20 marks, 30 marks and 30 marks. Timing should be: 5 to 7 minutes on Part A and 12 to 15 minutes each on Parts B and C.

→ In the regional questions you may be asked to draw a graph of data supplied in a table or picture. See the note on page 7 on how to get full marks in graph drawing. You may be asked to read a graph or find information from a diagram or picture. Do not spend more than 5 minutes drawing a graph. Practice drawing graphs and make sure to bring a calculator, ruler, eraser and pencil into the exam.

→ If drawing a sketch map of a country, make sure to draw the outline accurately. Show the outline of any regions. Position items such as cities, rivers and mountains properly and do not make them too big. Sketching maps and aerial photos can take more time than you may think. Practice these skills in advance of the exam. Always use a key and be neat.

NOTE

The detail required in any answer is determined by:
• the context and the manner in which the question is asked
• the number of marks assigned to the question.
Requirements and mark allocations may vary from year to year.

Contents

11.	Types of Regions	74
	(A) Physical/Geomorphological Regions	74
	(B) Cultural Regions: The Gaeltacht, Brazil, India, South-West USA, Belgium	77
	(C) Urban Regions: Dublin, Paris, São Paulo, Los Angeles, Mumbai	81
	(D) Socio-economic Regions: Core Regions, Peripheral Regions and Regions of Industrial Decline	86
12.	Irish regions: The Border Midlands West and the Greater Dublin Area	89
13.	EU regions: The Paris Basin and the Mezzogiorno; Human processes in European regions	102
14.	The Influence of the EU	113
15.	Non-EU Regions: Brazil, India, South-West USA	116
16.	The Dynamics of Regions: Human Processes in Ireland, the EU and Non-EU regions	128

Chapter 11
Types of Regions

(A) Physical/Geomorphological Regions

Q

Concept of a Region: 2011 Question 5C
A region is an area on the earth's surface which can be defined by one or more criteria. Explain this statement with reference to example(s) that you have studied. **[30 marks]**

Marking scheme:
Name criterion: 2 marks
Name example: 2 marks
Discussion: 13 x SRPs (13 x 2 marks = 26)

What You Need To Do:
- Name the type of region you will discuss – physical, cultural, socio-economic or urban.
- Give an example.
- Discuss the characteristics of that region in 13 SRPs.

Answer 1: The Burren, County Clare – a geomorphic region

A The Burren region of County Clare, Ireland, is defined by one major criterion – its limestone rock forms a unique karst landscape.

A karst landscape is one of bare limestone rock. In the Burren, the area of karst covers about 250 square kilometres. Landforms such as limestone pavements, cave systems, dry valleys, dolines and swallow holes are unique to this area.

The Burren also contains alternating layers of limestone and shale which form terraces or steps. In the terraces, thick beds of limestone are separated by thinner beds of shale. The terraces are easily seen around Black Head in the north-west of the Burren region.

The limestone and shale found in the Burren formed during the carboniferous period about 340 million years ago.

Limestone is composed of the calcium-rich skeletons of marine organisms that lived in the warm, shallow sea covering the region at that time. These were eventually compressed into limestone rock. The shale rock formed later when mud, carried by rivers flowing from the land, was deposited and turned to rock. About 300 million years ago, plate movements uplifted the limestone and shale to form the Burren upland area.

Limestone weathers easily by carbonation – a type of chemical weathering by rainwater. Rain absorbs carbon dioxide from the air to become weak carbonic acid. When rain falls on the alkaline limestone rock, a chemical reaction occurs and dissolves the limestone. Carbonation of limestone in the Burren has formed a unique surface called limestone pavement. Carbonation widened the rock joints into deep grikes which are separated by flat areas called clints. Smaller hollows are weathered onto the surface of the clints by rainwater and are called karren. The limestone pavement is a major attraction for tourists who visit it to walk across the barren beauty of the area.

The limestone rock has also influenced human economic activities in the Burren. Because of its unique karst landscape, the area is defined by tourism based on the rock type, caves and scenic landscape. The region is promoted as an eco-tourism destination. Alpine flowers such as the Spring Gentian and rare butterflies, e.g. the Burren Blue Butterfly, are not found anywhere else in Ireland. Doolin cave and the Ailwee caves are major attractions for tourists. The Ailwee caves received over 92,000 tourists in 2010 while several hundred thousand visitors arrive each year to walk the Burren hills and tour the villages such as Ballyvaughan. This tourism activity is a direct result of the rock type in the Burren. Tourism based on the landscape has also led to the widespread availability of B&B accommodation and tourist shops across the region.

OR

Answer 2: The North European Plain

In this answer the key characteristics of the North European Plain, a geomorphological region in Europe, will be discussed.

The North European Plain is located in the northern half of the European continent. It stretches northwards from the Paris Basin to include Southern Scandinavia and stretches eastwards as far as Russia. Its key characteristic is that it is a lowland region. It was formed during the last Ice Age when glaciers and ice sheets deposited sands and gravels as they melted and retreated north. The resulting topography is one of lowlands with gently rolling hills of sand and gravels.

The climate of the North European plain has cold winters and warm summers. The west has a maritime climate. Summers are warm (15°C), winters mild (5°C) with rain throughout the year (800 mm). Moving further east, the climate becomes more continental as the influence of the sea decreases. Rain is concentrated in the summer months. Summers are hot (21°C) and winters are cold (2°C).

Another characteristic of the North European Plain is its fertile limon soil. This was deposited after the ice melted. Winds blew fine-grained soil from the glacial deposits further north and left them in some areas of the Plain where they formed the very fertile, stoneless soil called limon/löess. Today, the limon soil is the basis of the commercial grain-growing regions of the North European Plain such as the Paris Basin.

The North European Plain has another key characteristic. It is crossed by several large rivers such as the River Seine, River Elbe and River Rhine. These have been used as important natural east/west and north/south route-ways for commerce and trade across the Plain.

Q

Characteristics of a Region: 2007 Question 5A
A region is an area that has one or more characteristics that distinguish it from other areas. Describe the key characteristics of a climatic region **OR** a geomorphological region of your choice.

[20 marks]

Marking scheme:
Name region: 4 marks
Description/Explanation: 8 x SRPs (8 x 2 marks = 16)

What You Need To Do:
- Name your chosen type of region.
- Write 8 points of information about the region, e.g. location, characteristics, reasons for these characteristics.

A

Climatic Regions
Answer: Cool Temperate Oceanic Climatic Region

In this answer the key characteristics of the cool temperate oceanic (maritime) region of North West Europe will be discussed.

This type of climate is found between latitude 40°-50° North/South of the equator on the western edges of continents. Because of its latitude a key characteristic of this climatic region is its moderate climate. It has a temperature range of approximately 9°C. Summer temperatures are 15°C on average and winter temperatures average 6°C. Rainfall occurs throughout the year with most rainfall in winter. On average 1,500 millimetres of precipitation is recorded but variations in relief may increase this in mountainous areas (e.g. relief rain in the west of Ireland). Rainfall amounts may be lower than average in some areas due to the rain shadow effect (e.g. the eastern coast of Ireland).

A key characteristic of the cool temperate oceanic climate is that it is influenced by the sea. The warm North Atlantic Drift ocean current flows along the west coast of Europe keeping winter temperatures warmer than they should be for this latitude. Summer temperatures are cooler than normal. This is due to the fact that the sea is warmer than the land during the winter which helps increase winter land temperatures. The sea is cooler than the land in summer which helps lower summer land temperatures.

A key characteristic of the cool temperate oceanic climatic region is that it is also influenced by warm, prevailing south-westerly winds. This wind brings warmth and moisture to Europe having taken up heat and water vapour from the Atlantic Ocean.

Another key characteristic of this climatic region is the presence of frontal depressions that pass across the region. These bring very changeable weather to Western Europe. The depressions develop where the tropical air mass meets the polar air mass close to latitude 60° North. They move eastwards across the region bringing a variety of weather conditions to the area. In summer the region is under the influence of the Azores high pressure belt so that anti-cyclonic (high pressure) conditions are more common bringing warm temperatures, clear skies and generally dry weather.

(B) Cultural Regions: The Gaeltacht, Brazil, India, South-West USA, Belgium

Q

Culture: 2010 Question 4B
Describe and explain the importance of culture in defining any regions studied by you. [30 marks]

Marking scheme:
Name region: 2 marks
Identify aspect of culture: 2 marks
Examination: 13 x SRPs (13 x 2 marks = 26)

What You Need to Do:
- Name the region you will discuss.
- Name the aspect of its culture that makes the region unique, e.g. ethnic origin of people, language.
- Discuss the aspect in 13 SRPs.

A

Answer 1: Cultural regions in Ireland – the Gaeltacht

Culture describes how people live their lives. Culture includes ethnic origin, language, religion, foods, music, literature and festivals. In this answer the importance of language culture in defining the Gaeltacht region in Ireland will be discussed.

The Gaeltacht is a group of Irish-speaking communities found in the western and south-western areas of Ireland. In the Gaeltacht, Irish is spoken in daily life and at home. Donegal is the largest Gaeltacht region while Dingle (An Daingean), County Kerry is the largest Gaeltacht town. Approximately 60% (54,000) of people living in the Gaeltacht regions speak Irish in their daily lives and in the home.

A Gaeltacht region is defined mainly by its language but other cultural activities are associated with the Irish language including *sean nós* singing, set dancing, *céilís* and storytelling.

The Irish language defines the economic and social development of the Gaeltacht. The Department of Arts, Heritage, Gaeltacht and the Islands promotes the cultural, social and economic wealth of the Gaeltacht region. In 2011 it provided €6 million in government funding to develop the Gaeltacht economy, to stop depopulation and to preserve the Irish language, culture and traditions. This money is spent by Údarás na Gaeltachta which created just over 700 full-time jobs in 2010. Other agencies also support the development of the Gaeltacht. These are the GAA, TG4 television station, *Cúla4* (an Irish language children's TV station), Raidió na Gaeltachta and Foras na Gaeilge.

Unlike in other areas of Ireland, the Irish language is a recognised source of income for people living in the Gaeltacht. The government provides financial support to Gaeltacht families through a series of grants. These include a grant paid to families with school-aged children in the Gaeltacht who can satisfy the Department that Irish is their usual spoken language and a grant paid to qualified families in the Gaeltacht to accommodate learners of Irish while they attend recognised Irish Colleges. Grants are available for organisations working to maintain the Irish language in the Gaeltacht. Grants are also paid for cultural events in which the Irish language has a central role or that will benefit the Irish language and the cultural and social life of Gaeltacht areas.

One of the most important cultural issues defining the Gaeltacht is the survival of the Irish language in everyday life. The number of Irish speakers is decreasing and this is a threat to the survival of Gaeltacht regions. There are several reasons for this; the harsh remote physical landscape has limited economic development leading to out-migration of younger people who are the future of the language. Also, in-migration of non-Irish speakers and the influence of English-speaking media such as satellite TV and the internet have reduced the use of Irish and the number of Irish speakers in the Gaeltacht.

Answer 2: Cultural regions in Brazil

A In this answer the importance of culture in defining regions in Brazil will be discussed. Culture describes how people live their lives. Describing the culture of a region can include descriptions of ethnic origin, language, religion, foods and festivals. In Brazil it is possible to define three regions based on ethnic differences within the population. They are: **(1)** the mainly black African area of north-east Brazil; **(2)** the native Amerindian region of the Amazon rainforest area; and **(3)** south-east Brazil where the majority of people are descended from white Europeans. These regions are culturally different because of European colonisation in the fourteenth century and the resulting trade in slaves from Africa.

The Portuguese colonists were white Europeans in origin and these people tended to settle close to the south-east coast of Brazil in the port cities of Rio de Janeiro and São Paulo. After independence in 1882, further migration from Europe was encouraged by the government to provide workers for the newly industrialising cities of São Paulo and Rio de Janeiro. Today this area has more people of European descent than other parts of Brazil.

The white colonists operated huge sugar plantations in the north-east of Brazil. These plantations needed large numbers of workers. Slave labour was used to work the plantations and Brazil's Atlantic slave trade began. Salvador, a port city in Bahia State, became the most prosperous and important slave trade centre in Brazil. Because the number of black Africans outnumbered the white Europeans in this region, African customs and culture were established and remain strong in north-east Brazil. Today in Bahia the African candomblé religion is the strongest in the region and the population of the city of Salvador is 80% black.

Before the arrival of the Portuguese colonists, Brazil was populated by an estimated 6 million native Amerindian people, e.g. the Yanomami. These native people live in tribal groups with their own languages, customs and beliefs. They live in the rainforest of northern Brazil. They are well adapted to tropical forest conditions, settling in one place for a few years and then moving to a new location when the soil or other local resources are exhausted. However, colonisation and the exploitation of the forests for timber, metals and hydroelectric power has reduced the numbers of native Amerindians to less than 600,000.

Answer 3: Cultural regions in India

In this answer the importance of culture in defining regions in India will be discussed. Culture describes how people live their lives. Describing the culture of a region can include descriptions of ethnic origin, language, religion, foods and festivals. India is a large country with over one billion people. Its culture has been influenced by religion, British colonialism and the spread of ancient European migrants.

In India, there is cultural diversity throughout the country. However it is possible to recognise several regions which have different cultures based on their language and religion.

There are over 1,600 languages spoken in India. Most of them are descended from languages spoken by ancient European migrants. Language can be used to divide India into two main regions. In the far north of the country in the mountainous regions of the Himalayas, people speak languages that are related to Chinese and Tibetan. Southern India has a different language culture. In the south people speak Dravidian languages. This language group has over 200 million speakers and is unrelated to other languages used in India. Hindi, the official language of India, is spoken throughout the country. English is also spoken and is the language of business and commerce in the country.

Religion is also used to define regions of India. India has two main religions: Hinduism and Islam. The majority of people are Hindus and this religion occurs throughout the country. However, a minority of the population is Muslim and they tend to live in the north of the country along the plains of the Indus and Ganges rivers. This distribution is due to the presence of ancient Muslim trading routes in this area. People living in this area converted to Islam and encouraged more Muslims to settle here.

Religion has played a very important part in defining regions of the Indian landmass. In 1947 after India became independent from Britain, two states – Pakistan and India – were created. Pakistan is an Islamic state and India is Hindu. The division caused one of the largest migrations in the world when over 12 million people moved between the newly-created states to be with people of their own religion. Muslims moved to Pakistan and Hindus moved to India.

Answer 4: Cultural regions in the South-West USA

In this answer the importance of culture in defining regions in the South-West USA will be discussed. Culture describes how people live their lives. Describing the culture of a region can include descriptions of ethnic origin, language, religion, foods and festivals.

The South-West USA has three defined regions based upon the origin of people living there. The states of Arizona and New Mexico hold nearly half of America's Native American Indians. The American Indians were the first inhabitants of the South-West USA. Today people belonging to five major tribes are found there. Of these, the Navajo tribe is the largest in the USA, with 200,000 people living in Arizona, Utah and New Mexico. Originally most Native American Indians were either nomadic hunter gatherers or settled farmers. Today they are found mainly on reservations of land and are responsible for their own local government and laws. Much of the economic wealth in the reservations is generated from gambling casinos.

Another culturally distinct region includes the states of California, Arizona, New Mexico and Texas. They have been strongly influenced by Spanish-speaking Mexican culture because they all share a border with Mexico and millions of people have moved to the USA from there. These states have a very strong Spanish influence. Spanish-speaking people who have migrated to the USA from Mexico are called Hispanics. Pull factors such as jobs and better living standards have attracted hundreds of thousands of Hispanics to the South-West USA. In fact so many now live there that the border states are called 'Mexamerica'. Texas and Southern California have Spanish-speaking TV, radio and newspapers and some schools teach through Spanish.

A third cultural region can be defined in California where there is a large Asian community of Chinese, Japanese and Korean people. Many Chinese migrated to California during the nineteenth-century Gold Rush. They worked on the construction of the railroad and the Los Angeles aqueduct. In the past, discrimination against Chinese and other Asians in California was severe and many lived in poor ghettos where they could escape from it and live in their own communities. As a result, today, in San Francisco, the Chinatown area has more than 30,000 Chinese people. It was once a ghetto but is now a successful economic and social centre.

A Answer 5: Cultural regions in Belgium

In this answer the importance of language as a factor in defining the culture of Belgium will be discussed. Regions where people share a specific language, religion and way of life are called 'cultural regions'.

Belgium has three separate cultural regions based mainly on language. Northern Belgium is known as Flanders and in this cultural region the people speak Flemish, which is similar to Dutch. The majority (60%) of Belgium's 10 million people live in Flanders.

Southern Belgium is called Wallonia and is French speaking, while in the south east, close to the border with Germany, people speak German. All regions share the Catholic religion but traditionally Flanders has been a religiously conservative region with a less developed economy based on farming. Wallonia is regarded as more liberal and wealthy, with an economy once based on coal deposits in the Sambre-Meuse Valley and on the steel industry.

Belgium is unique in Europe in that it is socially, economically and culturally divided according to the language regions that occur. An officially recognised 'language line' separates Flanders from Wallonia. This line acts as a cultural border between the regions. It has also had an important political influence on the country. Each language region has a separate government and education system. Elected politicians represent their region in the national parliament in Brussels. Even media celebrities, TV stations and newspapers are different in Flanders and Wallonia. Schools offer different courses in each region. Libraries must keep a copy of every book in both French and Flemish.

The language divide is so strong that villages that are close to each other but which lie on different sides of the language border have little contact with each other. Road signs in each region are also monolingual.

The only bilingual region occurs around the city of Brussels, situated in Flanders. Brussels is the centre of the Flemish parliament but is mainly French speaking because it is the headquarters of the EU parliament.

The cultural and political divisions based on language affect the country's national government. In 2010 it took several months to form a government because the Flemish and Walloons could not agree on power-sharing negotiations. Flemish-speaking separatists want more political powers for their region with surveys showing that 43% of Flemings want a separate and independent Flanders.

Some French and Walloon newspaper commentators suggest that Wallonia should become a province of France.

(C) Urban Regions: Dublin, Paris, São Paulo, Los Angeles, Mumbai

> **NOTE:** Students need to know three cities: for example, Dublin (an Irish city), Paris (a European city) and a non-European city. It should be clear from the question which region they want you to discuss but they will not identify cities by name. The questions below show how the topic can be examined.

Urban Development: 2013 Question 6B
With reference to an urban area in a Continental/Sub-Continental region (not in Europe) that you have studied, explain why this urban area developed at its present location. [30 marks]

Factors Influencing Urban Growth: 2012 Question 5C
Examine how any two of the factors listed below have influenced the development of one urban area in a European region (not in Ireland) that you have studied: • Transport • Location • Primary Economic Activity. [30 marks]

Urban Growth: 2011 Question 4B
Discuss the factors which influenced the development of one urban area in a European region (not Ireland) that you have studied. [30 marks]

Urban Regions: 2010 Question 5B
Examine the development of one urban area in any Irish region studied by you. [30 marks]

Urban Regions: 2008 Question 4C
Describe and explain the growth of one major urban area in a Continental/Sub-Continental Region that you have studied. [30 marks]

Marking scheme:
Name region: 2 marks
Name urban area: 2 marks
Examination: 13 x SRPs (13 x 2 marks = 26)

What You Need To Do:
- Name your city and what country it is in.
- Describe and explain the factors affecting the growth of the city.
- Make sure you state two dates to show the growth of the city over time.
- Outline the problems and solutions associated with urban development.

81

Answer 1: The development/growth of Dublin City

A The boundaries of the Dublin city region have expanded since the 1950s up to the present day. An important factor influencing the growth of Dublin has been rural-to-urban migration. This has caused urban sprawl whereby the city spreads into the surrounding countryside. Growth of the Dublin city region has increased so much that its zone of influence now covers much of the eastern region of Ireland rather than just Dublin city and county.

Dublin is the capital city and centre of government and offers thousands of civil service job opportunities. This combined with the wide variety of educational and health-care services (TCD, UCD, Mater Hospital) has made Dublin an attractive place in which to live and work.

Dublin is a very attractive location for industry. Its communications, such as road, rail, port and air links, have encouraged a wide variety of industries to locate there, e.g. food processing, light engineering and financial services.

As a result of the above attractions the population of the Dublin region has grown rapidly over time. In 1971 it had over 35.7% of the Irish population. Today, the city and its suburbs contain over one million people and it will contain 46% of the national population by 2020. Much of this population growth is due to rural-to-urban migration from the west of Ireland.

In the 1970s, to accommodate the rising population, three new towns were built on the edge of the city: Tallaght, Blanchardstown and Lucan/Clondalkin. These encouraged the spread of the city to the west and south west. In 2007 another new town called Adamstown was built to the west of the city. It is expected to house 70,000 people.

During the 1990s such was the demand for housing that residential development spread out beyond these new towns to include Maynooth and Leixlip in County Kildare.

Increased wealth before economic recession began in 2007, higher rates of car ownership and more expensive house prices in the city led to traffic congestion. People who could not afford houses close to the city bought homes in the surrounding counties such as Meath and Kildare and commute to work each day.

Many commuters now live in towns such as Mullingar and Carlow, 90 kilometres away from the city. This has expanded the zone of influence of the Dublin city region into the surrounding counties.

So, while in the past the Dublin city region had its boundaries close to Howth, the Phoenix Park and Dun Laoghaire, today its boundaries are closer to Swords, Celbridge and Bray.

In order to control the growth of Dublin the Local Government Act was established in 1993. Under this act three new county councils were created to manage the provision of services to the city region. Creating three more county councils (Dun Laoghaire/Rathdown, Fingal and South Dublin) enabled a more efficient provision of waste, water, sewerage and other public services to the expanding city region.

Answer 2: The development/growth of Paris, France

A In this answer the growth of the city of Paris in France will be discussed.

Paris is the largest city in Europe with a population of over 10 million people. Paris has grown into an important city for several reasons:

In medieval times defence was an important factor. Paris developed on an island, the Ile-de-France, in the River Seine. The Ile-de-France location provided a defensive settlement and bridging point. The city grew as people moved here for safety and communications. Other natural factors such as soils also influenced its growth, e.g. Paris lies at the centre of a fertile, limon-covered lowland: the Paris Basin. This region is the most important cereal-growing region in France and many industries developed to process the grain and other products grown there such as vines and dairy products. This made the city a centre of employment.

Paris is the centre of government (a human factor) and provides thousands of civil service jobs that attract people to the city region leading to more growth.

These advantages attracted people from rural areas to the city and Paris has a migrant population of over 1·4 million people. Paris is expected to have a population of 14 million by 2050. Many migrants live in the city suburbs. The construction of these suburbs has led to the urban sprawl of the city into the countryside.

Paris has social and economic problems because of its growth. These problems include traffic congestion, social deprivation in poor suburbs, urban sprawl and inner city decline. In order to combat these negative social factors and control the growth of Paris, planners developed the Schéma Directeur. The aims of this scheme are to control the growth of the city, improve housing in poor suburbs, provide more recreational space and provide employment in towns outside of Paris.

Five new towns have been built around the city. One of these, St. Quentin-en-Yvelines, is located 30 kilometres south west of Paris. It now houses 150,000 people and provides over 40,000 jobs. This new town is an important alternative location for industry and services. The Schéma Directeur has been successful in slowing the growth of Paris and improving living standards in the city region. However, the Parisian riots of 2005 and 2007 highlighted the problems of high unemployment rates among the young migrant population and the lack of opportunity in the poorest suburbs.

Answer 3: The development/growth of São Paulo, Brazil

A In this answer the growth of São Paulo in Brazil will be described and explained.

São Paulo is a mega-city with a population of over 27 million people. It is the largest and most important economic centre in Brazil. It has grown rapidly since it was established in the sixteenth century by Portuguese missionaries. What began as a village is now a sprawling city covering more than 23,000 square kilometres.

Two factors have influenced the growth of São Paulo:

The first factor is rural-to-urban migration (a human factor). Millions of poor people from north-east Brazil have moved to São Paulo to find work and use the services there. Push factors from the countryside include extreme poverty due to the lack of work on newly mechanised farms as well as drought and lack of health and education services in rural areas. The main pull factor attracting migrants is the availability of work in the port, industries and services in the city.

The second human factor is in-migration of European and Asian migrants. These migrants arrived because of state-sponsored advertising schemes which attracted migrants to work in the coffee trade after the abolition of slavery in the nineteenth century. Many more European and Asian investors were attracted to São Paulo because of the business opportunities there. Investment in industry also occurred which required more workers who then moved to the city. Today 65% of urban growth in São Paulo is due to in-migration.

São Paulo continues to grow because of its services. It is the most important financial and educational centre in Brazil. It is also the preferred location for many multinational companies attracted by the large market, e.g. Intel. This has led to the presence of many skilled workers who are very wealthy.

However, the growth of São Paulo has also caused several problems. Combating these problems is an important element in the future growth of the city.

Because of the shortage of housing, the growth of favelas (urban slums) is a major problem in the city. São Paulo has over 1,600 favelas. Millions of people build their own shelters and the favelas lack sewerage, water and electricity services. Favelas are often built on steep hillsides on the edge of the city where land is cheap and nearby industries provide work. Favela redevelopment is underway in some areas which provide water, power and better housing.

Another major problem is traffic congestion and air pollution. Although the government has invested in a modern metro and public transport, there are over 5 million cars in the city. More than 1,000 cars are added to the city each day. To avoid delay most wealthy business people use helicopters to move around and São Paulo has the highest number of helicopter pads of any city in the world.

Other problems facing the city include crime and lack of hospital beds and school places.

Answer 4: The growth of Mumbai, India

A In this answer the growth of Mumbai in western India will be described and explained. Mumbai is an island mega-city with a population of 23 million. It is the second largest city in the world after Tokyo, Japan.

The land that is now Mumbai was originally made up of seven islands joined together by reclaimed land. In the seventeenth century trade was an important factor leading to the city's growth. Mumbai was controlled by the East India Trading Company who built sea defences and developed the area as a major trading port.

Many merchants moved to Mumbai and the city also grew because it was politically stable and allowed religious freedom. As a result, its strength as a trading centre grew even more. By the late seventeenth century Mumbai had a population of 60,000.

In the nineteenth century religious conflict between Hindus and Muslims in other parts of India forced many people to flee to Mumbai for security, leading to further increases in population and associated economic growth.

Later in the nineteenth century the cotton-spinning and weaving industry was established and supplied the British Empire with textiles. When the Suez Canal in Egypt was built, Mumbai was closer to Europe and became even more important as a trading centre between Asia and Europe. It was a stop-off point between these two continents.

Today Mumbai is the financial capital of India. It is also the centre of the world-famous Bollywood film-making industry. The port of Mumbai is the largest in India and handles 25% of India's international trade.

However, its rapid growth has caused many problems typical of mega-cities in the developing world, e.g. air pollution and slum settlements.

Nearly 10 million people in Mumbai live in slum settlements. The largest slum in Asia called Dharavi is in Mumbai. As Mumbai grew and industrialised, Dharavi became the first stop for landless workers and poor migrants who arrived to seek their fortune in India's commercial capital.

Dharavi was once a swamp on the edge of the city but it now occupies prime development land right at its centre. Managing the slum is important to the future growth of the city. State officials have plans to demolish Dharavi and move residents to apartments elsewhere. An €800 million development of business parks, hotels, restaurants and a university is planned for the site. Before this happens, however, new suburbs are being built to ease congestion and provide space for new industrial parks elsewhere in Mumbai.

Answer 5: The growth of Los Angeles, South-West USA

A In this answer the growth of Los Angeles in the South-West USA will be described and explained.

Los Angeles (LA) has a population of nearly 14 million people and is the second largest city in the US today after New York. Its container port is the largest in the US and generates over $39 billion in wages and taxes for the state of California.

The Gold Rush was an important factor in the early growth of the city. LA became a city in the 1800s and grew rapidly during the Gold Rush when tens of thousands of people arrived to the area looking for gold. For example, in 1870 there were 5,000 people in LA; 30 years later it had a population of over 100,000.

People arrived in LA not just to find gold but to work in the growing port, railroad construction and oil industries. Oil was discovered in the late 1800s and by the early twentieth century LA was producing one quarter of the world's oil.

Another important factor affecting the growth of LA was water supply. The growing urban population needed water and because the climate was so dry, local supplies could not cope with the demand. A massive aqueduct, over 400 kilometres long, was built to bring water to LA from the north east. The availability of water led to increased urbanisation and the city area increased to cover more than 1,000 square kilometres of land.

Transport is another factor affecting the growth of LA. The growth of the city into the surrounding area was further encouraged by the construction of the railway. This allowed passengers and cargo to move easily into the city and encouraged the growth of suburbs farther out of town.

In 1932 LA hosted the Olympic Games and this led to the development of recreational facilities and new roads in the city.

In the 1940s the local tram system was closed down and LA became a car-dependent city. Buses replaced trams and this, combined with the increase in car production, led to the terrible air pollution that is still associated with LA today.

As a result of World War II, LA became a major industrial centre producing aircraft and ammunition. It also produced cars, furniture and clothing. By the 1990s these industries declined and they relocated to low wage areas such as Mexico.

Because of its location close to the Mexican border and on the Pacific coast of the

USA, LA has many people of Mexican, Asian and African origin. Today the largest ethnic group is Mexican. The Asian population is mostly Chinese who first came to LA during the Gold Rush years and then stayed as workers on the aqueduct and railroad.

(D) Socio–economic Regions: Core Regions, Peripheral Regions and Regions of Industrial Decline

Q

Economic activity: 2014 Question 6B
Economic activity in core regions differ from those in peripheral regions. Examine this statement with reference to examples that you have studied.
[30 marks]

Marking scheme:
Name core region: 2 marks
Name peripheral region: 2 marks
Examination: 13 x SRPs (13 x 2 marks = 26)

What You Need To Do:
- Name and locate the core and peripheral regions.
- Explain the terms core region and peripheral region.
- Discuss the development of economic activity in each region.

A

Answer: Economic activity of the Paris Basin of France and Mezzogiorno Region of Italy

In this answer differences in economic activity between the Paris Basin and the Mezzogiorno Region of Italy will be discussed.

Paris Basin
Economic core regions are wealthy, accessible regions of Europe. They possess a variety of natural resources such as fertile land and coal. Because of these advantages they are attractive locations for people and industry. Core regions usually have excellent communications infrastructure and high population densities. Core regions are also centres of government administration and services. Industry and agriculture are successful in core regions and incomes are generally 10% higher than the EU average. As a result of their many natural and economic attractions, core regions are also centres of in-migration.

The Paris Basin developed as a core region due to a number of physical and human factors. The Paris Basin is a flat, low-lying area covered by a variety of fertile soils such as limon, alluvium and clays. The climate is cool temperate oceanic (maritime) in the west, changing to more continental conditions in the east of the region. The soil and climate support the development of commercial intensive cereal production. Both rainfall and temperature are suitable for cereal growing and the Paris Basin is known as 'the bread basket of Europe'. Other agricultural activities include dairying (cheese production in Brie) and viticulture (champagne production).

Because of the presence of a profitable farming industry, the region also has a well-developed food processing industry based on cheese, cereals and wine. Such is the level of industrial development in the region that the Paris Basin now has more industry than any other region in France.

The Paris Basin is an attractive location for industry because it has an excellent communications infrastructure. It is accessible by road, rail, canal and river. Several large rivers such as the River Seine and River Marne drain the Paris Basin and these have provided natural route-ways for industries in the region. Major ports exist at Paris and Rouen that allow for the import and export of raw materials and finished goods. The Channel tunnel and the high-speed train system (the TGV) connect Paris to other major European cities such as London and Brussels. These human factors have encouraged the development of commercial and service industries in the region.

Paris is an educational centre for France and this has led to the high population densities in the Paris Basin region. Paris contains more than 20% of the French workforce and many workers are educated in the universities and colleges in Paris (e.g. the Sorbonne).

Like all economic core regions the Paris Basin is a centre of in-migration. Paris has a population of over 10 million people and more than 1.4 million of these are immigrants.

Mezzogiorno Region

Peripheral regions are generally remote, inaccessible, poor regions of Europe. They possess few natural resources and their soils are infertile. They may rely on primary activities such as fishing and forestry as a source of employment. However, peripheral regions are often very scenic, coastal regions and therefore they also depend on tourism for economic development. They are remote with a poor transport infrastructure and low population density. Services are not well developed. They are not favourable locations for industry because of these problems. Peripheral regions are areas of out-migration and incomes are generally 10% lower than the EU average.

The Mezzogiorno is economically underdeveloped due to a number of physical and human factors. A physical factor is the Apennine Mountains. The mountainous relief has prevented the development of an efficient transport network. Roads are narrow and winding and unable to carry large trucks. Because it is remote from the rich core region of Northern Italy, transport costs and travel times are high. These physical problems have discouraged economic development as industry avoids locating in the Mezzogiorno. A human factor is the poor uneducated population. This has slowed economic development in the Mezzogiorno. Industries find it hard to find skilled labour and the local market may not be able to afford their products. Another human factor that has discouraged economic development is the land ownership system. In the past large estates called latifundia were owned by absentee landlords who rented the land in small farms called minifundia to tenant farmers. Over 70% of minifundia were smaller than 3 hectares. The tenant farmers had no incentive to work their land efficiently and produced low-value products such as sheep, goats and cheap table wine for the local market.

In order to overcome the problems preventing economic development, an investment programme called the Cassa Per Il Mezzogiorno Scheme was set up in 1950 to improve agriculture, transport, industry and tourism. The latifundia were split up and the land given to tenant farmers. Education programmes to help farmers use their land more efficiently were provided. A massive motorway called the Autostrada del Sole was completed in 1964 to reduce travel times while ports at Taranto and Siracusa were built and state-owned steel industries located there. The Metapontino region has benefitted most from the Cassa Scheme. Farms there now produce high-value cash crops of flowers, fruit and salad crops. However, much of the Mezzogiorno is still underdeveloped compared to Northern Italy.

Q

Industrial decline: 2015 Question 4B
Examine the causes and impacts of industrial decline with reference to any region(s) that you have studied. **[30 marks]**
Marking scheme (provisional)
Identify cause of decline: 2 marks
Identify impact of decline: 2 marks
Examination: 13 x SRPs (13 x 2 marks = 26)

What You Need To Do:
- Name a region of industrial decline.
- Describe the reason for its original industrial growth.
- Name and explain two reasons for the decline.
- Name and describe two impacts of the decline.
- Describe how the decline is being reversed or managed.

Answer: Industrial Decline in Belgium

A Belgium is a developed economy. In the late 1880s the Sambre-Meuse river valley in Wallonia, Southern Belgium was the industrial core region of the country. The success of its industrialisation was due to large deposits of coal and iron ore that were exposed by the river as it cut its valley into the land. The industrial growth of Wallonia was based on coal mining and the traditional heavy industries of iron and steel, engineering and chemicals. At peak production, more than 120 mines employed over 120,000 people and produced 30 million tonnes of coal per year. However from the 1960s the mines in the region declined and mining stopped completely in 1992. The decline of the mining industry caused a decline in the iron and steel industries that depended on them for coal, their raw material.

Physical and human factors led to industrial decline in Belgium.

A physical factor leading to decline was the size and depth of the coal reserves. Over time the most accessible coal seams were used up and the remaining coal seams were too small, deep and fractured to be worth extracting.

Several human factors also contributed to the speed of the industrial decline. At EU level, the European Coal and Steel Community had a policy offering financial support to the most efficient mines across Europe. The Belgian mines did not qualify for this and could not compete with mines in Germany and Britain. In the mid 1980s, the Belgian government decided that the mining industry should be closed and the government presented a plan that would close all the mines by 1994. The government provided a €2.5 billion redundancy package to the miners to encourage them to leave mining. The combination of EU and government policy led to the end of mining in Wallonia.

Competition with more efficient coal mines and the availability of cheap coal imported from the USA and Poland also caused the mines to decline.

The impact of the closure of the mining industry in Wallonia was felt throughout the region. Many industries associated with mining, such as steel, chemicals and engineering closed. This led to unemployment levels as high as 20% and higher levels of poverty in Wallonia compared to Northern Belgium. People left the region to seek work in the richer areas of northern Belgium, e.g. Antwerp. Wallonia's GDP is less than 75% of the EU average so it now qualifies for EU Structural Funds and is classed as a Convergence region.

To overcome the social and economic problems, the European Structural Funds programme for 2007-2013 has allocated a budget of €15 billion to support the economic development of the region.

Chapter 12
Irish Regions: The Border Midlands West and the Greater Dublin Area

Sketch Maps

> **NOTE:** For questions on Irish regions, you will be expected to draw an outline map of Ireland and show a selection of regions on it. This sketch map should take 5 to 7 minutes to draw and is usually worth 20 marks at Higher Level. Always name the items required in a Key. The secret to doing well in questions that require sketch maps is to PRACTISE! Refer to sketching tips on page 63.

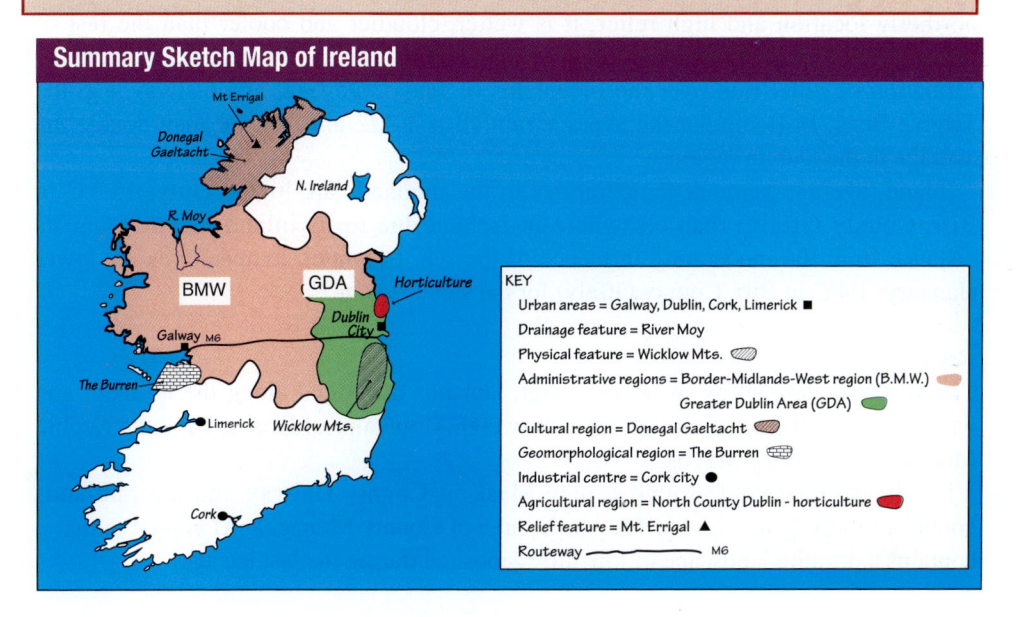

Summary Sketch Map of Ireland

KEY
- Urban areas = Galway, Dublin, Cork, Limerick ■
- Drainage feature = River Moy
- Physical feature = Wicklow Mts.
- Administrative regions = Border-Midlands-West region (B.M.W.)
- Greater Dublin Area (GDA)
- Cultural region = Donegal Gaeltacht
- Geomorphological region = The Burren
- Industrial centre = Cork city ●
- Agricultural region = North County Dublin - horticulture
- Relief feature = Mt. Errigal ▲
- Routeway ———— M6

Factors Affecting Regions in Ireland

Q

Irish Regions: 2010 Question 6B
Regions can be defined by many factors including:
- Economic
- Human
- Physical

Explain how any **one** of the above factors has defined an Irish Region studied by you. [30 marks]

Marking scheme:
Name region: 2 marks
Examination: 14 x SRPs (14 x 2 marks = 28)

What You Need To Do:
- Name your region.
- Name the physical **or** human **or** economic factors that affect the region you have named.
- Discuss the factors in 14 SRPs

A

Answer

Physical factors defining the BMW

The Border Midland West (BMW) region can be clearly defined by its physical factors such as climate, relief and soils.

Climate

The BMW region has a cool temperate oceanic climate. However, because of its more northerly location and high relief, it is wetter, cloudier and cooler than the rest of Ireland. It is wetter and cloudier mainly along the mountainous coastal areas due to the formation of relief rain over the mountains of Mayo, Donegal and Galway, e.g. the Twelve Bens. In Belmullet the average rainfall is 1,422 mm – more than double the average in the Dublin region.

Inland, average summer temperatures in the midlands are higher (July: 15·3°C in Birr, County Offaly) than elsewhere in Ireland due to its inland location and its distance from the moderating influence of the sea. In winter, temperatures are lower (January: 1·4°C in Birr, County Offaly) for the same reason.

Relief

The BMW is defined by its varied relief. Uplands are found along the northern and western coasts of the region, e.g. the Derryveigh Mountains of Donegal and the Nephin Mountains in County Mayo.

Lowlands are found around Lough Mask in County Galway and the midlands counties of Offaly and Laois. The border area of County Monaghan is unique in that it contains a drumlin landscape of low hills deposited during the last ice age.

The coastline of the BMW region is made of dramatic headlands and sheltered bays such as Malin Head and Clew Bay. Rising sea levels after the last ice age have influenced the coast. The sea flooded the drumlin landscape of Clew Bay creating its many islands. Killala Bay in County Mayo is a ria and Killary Harbour is a sheltered fiord – important for aquaculture and marine tourism.

Soils

Soils in the BMW region are varied and generally of poor quality. It has infertile peat soils on the uplands of Donegal and poorly drained gley soils in parts of Monaghan and Cavan. The Midland region has areas of raised bog as well as fertile brown earth soils.

As a result of glacial deposition, the Border region is unique with drumlins of boulder clay soil which is fertile and produces good grassland in County Monaghan for cattle fattening. In Connemara, glacial erosion has removed the soil cover completely, leaving a unique landscape of lakes and shallow peat soils. In East Galway, the limestone parent rock has led to the formation of shallow lime-rich soils which produce profitable grassland for cattle rearing.

Primary Activities in Ireland

NOTE

You may be asked to **examine** factors affecting one or more primary activities or to **describe and explain** the development of one or more primary activities in an Irish region. In this context, **examine** and **describe and explain** mean the same thing. The only difference will be in the number of factors you have to discuss and whether you talk about **one** or **two** primary activities, so read the questions carefully. If it doesn't state how many factors to discuss, focus on two.

Physical Factors: climate, relief and soils
Human Factors: transport infrastructure, population, market, labour force, government incentives

Q

Agriculture in Ireland: 2011 Question 4B
Contrast the development of agriculture in **two** Irish regions that you have studied. **[30 marks]**

Marking scheme:
Clearly state contrasts: 2 marks + 2 marks
Discussion: 13 x SRPs (13 x 2 marks = 26)

What You Need To Do:
- Name two Irish regions.
- State two differences in agriculture between the two regions.
- Explain the differences.

A   **Answer**

Differences in the development of agriculture between the Greater Dublin Area (GDA) and the Border Midlands West (BMW)

Agriculture in the GDA is a successful mix of grazing of livestock, cattle fattening, tillage crops and horticulture. In contrast, agriculture in the BMW is based on pastoral hill farming, especially rearing of sheep on the uplands and cattle on lower ground.

Physical factors of climate, relief and soils account for these differences.

Climate

While both regions have a cool temperate climate, it is drier in the GDA due to its location in the rain shadow of the western mountains. The GDA receives only about 800 mm per year of rain; the BMW receives about 1,800 mm per year. This means farmers in the GDA can make a better living from crop farming than those in the BMW. The mild maritime climate also allows a long growing season for grass (9 months), making specialist beef fattening the most common agricultural activity in the GDA. There are over 3,800 beef cattle farms in the region. Beef cattle are mainly produced on the rich grasslands of County Meath. In contrast, farmers in the BMW tend to rear young cattle and sell them on to farmers in the GDA for fattening. This is because cattle do not fatten as well in the cooler, wetter climatic conditions in the BMW. The impact of climate on the development of cattle farming is shown by annual income figures from cattle farming. In the BMW it is about €140 million compared to around €664 million in the GDA.

Relief

Relief also accounts for the differences in agriculture between the two regions. Because of the low-lying relief in the GDA, farms there are large intensive commercial farms with an above national average farm size of 42.3 hectares. These farms grow crops such as barley, wheat and maize. Because of the large farm sizes, yields are higher than in the BMW. In contrast, the mountainous relief in the BMW has led to smaller, fragmented farms. The average farm size in the BMW is just 26.7 hectares. The mountains (e.g. the Twelve Bens) also cause relief rain to fall and because of the wetter climate few cereals can be grown in the BMW.

Farmers in the BMW are more reliant on sheep farming, (sheep are well suited to the upland areas) earning €91 million per year from sheep compared to €25 million from sheep in the GDA.

Soils

Soils also account for the differences in the development of agriculture between the two regions. There is a variety of fertile, well-drained loam, boulder clay and sandy soils in the GDA region. This allows profitable cereal growing in the boulder clays of Meath, greenhouse horticulture in the sandy soils around Rush and Lusk in North County Dublin and cattle fattening across the GDA.

In contrast much of the BMW region has infertile peat, gley and podzol soils which are an obstacle to the development of profitable agriculture.

In the border region, boulder clay soil is used for pasture and cattle rearing. Poultry and mushroom production are also found in border counties (e.g. Monaghan) as they are not dependent on soil quality. As a result of the poor soils and high relief much of the land in the BMW is classified by the EU as disadvantaged for farming and is used for sheep and forestry.

Human factors
Human factors such as transport also account for the differences in agriculture between the two regions. The availability of large urban markets and better transport facilities mean farms in the GDA are more profitable due to lower transport costs. Farmers benefit from the large nearby urban markets of Dublin, Arklow and Navan. Good transport links such as the M1 and M7 keep costs low and the shorter distances between farm and market ensure fragile perishable fruit and vegetables arrive from the greenhouses to the markets in perfect condition. In the BMW the population is smaller and more dispersed. Galway, Sligo and Dundalk are the main market centres. Transport costs are higher due to greater distances to market and travel times are slower due to the high land and winding roads. This situation combined with the harsher physical factors explain the lack of horticulture in the BMW region.

The physical and human factors mean that farm incomes are lower in the BMW region than in the GDA and many farmers only work part time on their farms. In order to make a living, 50% of farmers in the midlands west region have an 'off-farm' job.

Q

Primary Activities: 2007 Question 6C
Examine **two** factors that have influenced the development of primary activities in any **Irish region** you have studied. [30 marks]

NOTE
Pay attention to the use of **activities** in this question.
You must refer to **more** than one.

Marking scheme:
Name region: 2 marks
Identify two primary activities: 2 marks + 2 marks
Name two factors: 2 marks + 2 marks
Examination: 10 x SRPs (10 x 2 marks = 20)

What You Need To Do:
- State the region you have chosen.
- State two primary activities in the region.
- State two factors that influence these two primary activities, e.g. two physical factors, two human factors or one of each.
- Discuss how the factors you have named affect primary activities.

A

Answer 1: Factors influencing fishing and farming in the BMW region

In this answer the way in which physical factors such as relief, soils and ocean currents have influenced the development of fishing and farming in the Border Midlands and West (BMW) region of Ireland will be discussed.

93

Relief and ocean currents influence the development of the fishing industry in the BMW region

The west coast of the BMW region (Mayo, Galway, Donegal and Sligo) has several physical factors that have allowed the development of a successful sea fishing and aquaculture industry. The most important are the coastline and the presence of the North Atlantic Drift. The coast is indented with lots of sheltered bays providing safe harbours for fishing vessels (Killybegs, County Donegal) and sheltered calm water for fish farms (Killary Harbour, County Galway). Aquaculture needs sheltered water to prevent damage to fish cages and oyster beds. Sheltered harbours in Mulroy Bay, County Donegal and Drumcliff Harbour, County Sligo are the main centres of the scallop and clam production industry.

The west coast is affected by the warm North Atlantic Drift ocean current which keeps the shores ice-free and brings a variety of fish species (herring, mackerel) to Irish waters.

The relief of the seabed is also important. The sea off the west coast is shallow (less than 100 metres) due to the presence of the continental shelf. This allows plankton to grow, providing a source of food for fish. It also makes trawling easier than in deeper water further offshore.

These natural advantages have encouraged people to turn to fishing as a source of income. Donegal is the most important fishing county and holds the largest fishing port in Ireland, Killybegs. This port is the centre of the Irish open ocean (pelagic) fleet and over 1,000 people work in this sector at the port.

Climate, relief and soils influence the development of farming in the BMW region

Physical factors such as climate, relief and soils have hindered the development of agriculture in the BMW region. Because much of the BMW region is upland, it receives relief rain and so has a wetter, cooler maritime climate than the rest of the country. This has led to the development of infertile peat and gley soils in many areas of Mayo, Galway and Donegal. These factors (soil and climate) have generally prevented the development of large-scale commercial cereal farming in the region. Farms are smaller – they have an average size of 26·7 hectares. Much of the BMW is classified as 'disadvantaged for farming' by the EU in recognition of these problems.

Pastoral farming of sheep and cattle is the main agricultural activity in the region. Sheep are well suited to upland areas and are reared on the uplands of Mayo and Donegal, e.g. the Bluestack Mountains, while cattle rearing occurs on the more fertile lowlands of County Galway and County Monaghan.

Mushroom and poultry production is more common in the BMW region than elsewhere in Ireland because these activities do not depend on fertile land. Cereal production requires a drier climate and more fertile soil. As a result it is limited to the drier areas and fertile, boulder-clay-covered regions of the eastern border region such as Louth.

Answer 2: Factors influencing primary activities in the GDA

In this answer the way in which physical and human factors have influenced the development of agriculture and forestry in the Greater Dublin Area (GDA) will be discussed.

Physical factors: climate, relief and soils

There is a variety of intensive commercial agriculture in the GDA. Arable farms growing wheat are large and profitable. This is due to the generally low-lying relief of the area which has enabled farmers to create large regular fields suitable for mechanised farming. The climate of the region is cool temperate oceanic but it is warmer and drier than the west of Ireland. Frost is rare due to the influence of the Irish Sea which is an advantage for crop growing.

There is a variety of fertile soils in the GDA. In North County Dublin at Rush and Lusk, light sandy soils are used for market gardening. The soil heats up quickly in spring and is easily worked. Salad vegetables are grown in greenhouses while cabbage, onions and potatoes are grown in large fields. In Kildare the sands and boulder clay deposited by glaciers at the end of the last Ice Age are well drained and support good quality grassland. Cattle are fattened for the beef industry here. Kildare is also the centre of the bloodstock industry and produces racehorses for export. In County Meath fertile boulder clay and brown earth soils are used for arable farming.

Relief has influenced the development of the forestry industry in the GDA. The region generally lacks forests except for County Wicklow. The Wicklow Mountains rise to over 1,000 metres. The steep slopes and high altitude are a disadvantage for arable farming. However, the mild maritime climate encourages tree growth and so farmers have turned to forestry to make best use of their land. Trees mature earlier and can be harvested sooner than in the west of Ireland. Pastoral sheep farming is also carried out on upland farms.

Human factors: market and transport

The GDA has over one million people. Dublin city is the largest market in the country. Combined with the availability of lowland, fertile soils and a drier climate, this large market has encouraged the development of commercial farming in the GDA. Farmers in the GDA can sell their produce directly to consumers at the many 'Farmers Markets' that occur throughout the region. They also have quick access to the wealthy urban population who shop in the many supermarkets and discount stores and who demand fresh produce. The GDA contains food-processing industries such as bread manufacturing, brewing and vegetable canning. These industries buy farm produce in large quantities. For example, Largo Foods in Ashbourne, County Meath sources 90% of its food ingredients from within 20 km of the plant.

Transport infrastructure is well developed in the GDA, e.g. the M50, Port Tunnel. As a result transport times from farm to market are short. This allows easy delivery of fresh produce such as vegtables. Farmers therefore have lower costs than farmers in the west of Ireland. Farm incomes in the GDA are generally 40% higher than the national average.

Secondary Activities in Ireland

NOTE

You may be asked to **examine** factors affecting one or more secondary activities or to **describe and explain** the development of one or more secondary activities in an Irish region. In this context, **examine** and **describe and explain** mean the same thing. The only difference will be in the number of factors you have to discuss and whether you talk about one or two secondary activities so read the questions carefully. If it doesn't state how many factors to discuss, focus on two.

Physical Factors: climate, relief and soils
Human Factors: transport infrastructure, population, market, labour force, government incentives

Q

Secondary Activities: 2013 Question 4B
Examine the factors that influence the development of secondary economic activity in an Irish region that you have studied. **[30 marks]**

Marking scheme:
Name example of secondary economic activity: 2 marks
Name influencing factors: 2 marks + 2 marks
Examination: 12 x SRPs (12 x 2 marks = 24)
Note: Examiner will not accept European or Continental/Sub-Continental regions.

What You Need To Do:
- Name the Irish region you are discussing.
- Name two manufacturing activities.
- Discuss why these activities developed.
- Hint: market, transport links, educated workforce

A
Answer 1: Manufacturing industry in the BMW Region

In this answer the development of manufacturing industry in the Border Midlands West (BMW) region of Ireland will be discussed.

Physical e.g. relief and human factors e.g. low population density have combined to limit the development of industry in the BMW region. The region does not have a wide variety of industry because it is a generally unattractive location for industry. It is a peripheral economic region with a low population density (32 per km^2) and contains few urban centres. It has a poorly developed transport network. There are no major port facilities, unlike in Dublin. The main industries are: food processing, timber processing and textiles. The knowledge-based IT and medical technology industries are concentrated in Galway.

The road and rail network has been underdeveloped because of the relief. The region is generally mountainous and has many large lakes such as Lough Ree. Roads are often narrow and winding. This has prevented the development of industries dependent on fast, efficient road transport to deliver goods and raw materials. The BMW is a peripheral region: Donegal, for example, is over 200 kilometres from Dublin. This adds to transport costs (fuel) for industries that locate in the BMW region and discourages industrial development. Rail links are poorly developed north of Sligo.

Another factor influencing industry in the BMW region is the low population density (32 per km^2). The population is dispersed across the region. There are few large towns – Galway and Sligo are the largest centres. This means that industries that require large numbers of workers may have difficulty finding enough people in an area and the workers may have to commute long distances to their jobs. Train and bus services in the BMW region are underdeveloped. As a result many workers commute by car.

Finding skilled workers in the BMW region is a problem for industry in the area. Galway city has the only university in the region and so many knowledge-based IT and medical technology industries locate close to Galway, e.g. Merit Medical. In Galway, industry has access to an airport and road/rail links to Dublin as well as an educated workforce.

The government has recognised the importance of encouraging industrial development in the BMW region. As part of the National Development Plan (NDP), transport links to the region are being upgraded which will reduce transport costs and travel times. The Dublin/Galway rail service has been improved and motorways are under construction between Galway and Limerick. The Galway-Dublin motorway (M6) has reduced journey times and fuel costs for companies.

Answer 2: Manufacturing industry in the GDA

A

In this answer factors influencing the development of secondary activities in the Greater Dublin Area (GDA) of Ireland will be discussed. Two manufacturing activities associated with the GDA are the computer industry and the food processing industry.

The GDA has many human factors that have encouraged industrial development.

First, the GDA contains Dublin city, Ireland's capital, which is the most economically important urban area in Ireland. It has a young population (45% under 25 years) who provide a labour force for manufacturers. The population of the GDA is also wealthy as wages are 10% above the EU average and this provides a market for manufactured goods.

Second, the GDA has a well developed transport system (rail, motorway) which connects it to all parts of Ireland. Ireland's main seaport and international airport are both in Dublin and these provide a gateway to Europe for manufacturers who need to import and export raw materials and finished products. For example, the silicon disks that are used by Intel in Leixlip are flown into Dublin for processing here.

Because of the well developed transport network, manufacturing is dispersed across the GDA, e.g. computer chip manufacturing at Leixlip, newspaper production at City West and Wavin pipe production in Balbriggan.

The construction of the M50 motorway around the city has encouraged inner city manufacturers to relocate to suburban locations and so the GDA contains many industrial estates, e.g. Sandyford Industrial Estate.

Third, the GDA is a nationally important education centre. It has several universities and colleges of technology (TCD, DIT) and these provide an educated workforce for knowledge-based industries such as computer manufacturing and software development, both of which require highly skilled graduate employees.

Fourth, the GDA is also a financial services centre (IFSC in the Docklands) and this has encouraged manufacturers to locate in the region because of the provision of financial management services and business development advice services.

Physical factors such as fertile soils and a frost-free maritime climate have encouraged farming and led to the development of food processing. The GDA contains large areas of fertile farmland with brown earth and loam soils such as in North County Dublin. Farms in this area provide vegetables for the food-processing industry (tinned peas/beans, e.g. Batchelors Foods). Grain is produced in the southern and western areas of the GDA, e.g. in North Kildare and East Meath. This grain is used in the food processing industry and brewing industry (Jacob's Biscuits and Guinness).

Before economic recession the construction of roads, office blocks, apartments and houses also provided high levels of employment in the region. Since economic recession, employment in this sector has been severely reduced.

Tertiary Activities/Services in Ireland

> **NOTE**
>
> You may be asked to **examine** factors affecting one or more tertiary activities or to **describe and explain** the development of one or more tertiary activities in an Irish region. In this context, **examine** and **describe and explain** mean the same thing. The only difference will be in the number of factors you have to discuss and whether you talk about one or two tertiary activities so read the questions carefully. If it doesn't state how many factors to discuss, focus on two.
>
> **Physical Factors:** climate, relief and soils
> **Human Factors:** transport infrastructure, population, market, labour force, government incentives

Tertiary Activities: 2012 Question 6B
Discuss the factors that influence the development of one tertiary economic activity in an Irish region that you have studied. **[30 marks]**

Marking scheme:
Factors: 2 marks + 2 marks
Name tertiary activity: 2 marks
Discussion: 12 x SRPs (12 x 2 marks = 24)

What You Need to Do:
- Name your chosen Irish region.
- Name one or more tertiary economic activities.
- Name two factors affecting tertiary activity.
- Discuss their development in 12 SRPs.
- Focus on transport and tourism.

> **NOTE**
>
> This topic was also examined in 2015 (Question 4C).
> 'Account for the development of transport or tourism in an Irish region that you have studied.' [30 marks]
> The answers below apply to both the 2012 and 2015 questions.

A

Answer 1: Factors influencing Transport in the Border Midlands West region

In this answer, the physical and human factors influence the development of transport services in the Border Midlands West (BMW) region of Ireland is discussed.

Transport services are generally underdeveloped in the BMW region. There are several reasons for this. Physical factors such as the landscape/relief have affected the development of the road and rail network. The BMW region is very mountainous, e.g. the 12 Bens Co. Galway and has many lakes, e.g. Lough Erne.

Because of these natural barriers, roads are often narrow and winding; this adds to fuel and driver fees and increases wear and tear on vehicles. The steep ground has prevented the development of an efficient rail network. There is no direct rail link between Sligo to Dundalk for example. Rail goods between these towns are transported via Dublin, which is expensive.

There are few national primary roads with the best roads connecting Galway, Dundalk, and Sligo to Dublin, e.g. M1, M4.

The main shipping ports are located at Galway and Sligo but these are shallow and cannot take large container ships, neither do they have international passenger services. Small airports are located at Galway, Knock and Donegal.

Human factors such as the low population density (32/km2) have also affected transport services. The low population means that profits for service providers of air, road and rail transport are limited due to the lack of demand. Public transport is expensive to supply in an area with few people. Services are infrequent and most people in the area rely on private cars to get around. Only 4% of the population use public transport to get to work compared to 11% nationally.

Government policy is a factor affecting transport in the BMW region. The government programme Transport 21 aims to improve transport connections in the BMW. Under this scheme €11.4bn will be spent on transport facilities between 2010 and 2016. The government is funding the Atlantic Corridor, a motorway and dual carriageway connecting Waterford to Donegal. This should reduce transport costs and encourage economic development along the route way. The Western Rail corridor is being upgraded as part of Transport 21.

OR

A

Answer 2. Factors influencing Tourism in the Border Midlands West Region

In this answer, the physical and human factors influence the development of tourism services in the Border Midlands West (BMW) region of Ireland is discussed.

Relief is an important physical factor in the development of tourism services in the BMW region. The mountains, lakes and valleys are scenic, attracting thousands of tourists interested in walking and golf e.g. Glencar Co. Sligo. The region has several marked walking routes such as the Bangor Trail in County Mayo. The annual climb of Croagh Patrick attracts over 20,000 walkers each year. The coastline has many beaches and golf links. Bundoran, County Donegal is popular for surfing holidays. However, the tourism industry is seasonal and many facilities shut down over winter.

A human factor preventing the full development of tourism services is the lack of access to the region. Tour operators offer fly-drive packages to airports at Knock and Galway to try and overcome the problem of access. Most tourists arrive into Ireland at Dublin airport on the east coast and may be discouraged by the long distances to the BMW region's main tourist areas. It is expensive to hire a car in Ireland and bus services are not attractive for tourists with young children. The removal of the Shannon Stop over for trans-Atlantic flights has also reduced the number of visitors arriving in the BMW region. Only about 830,000 of the 6.5 million tourists who arrive into Ireland each year visit the BMW region.

Another human factor affecting tourism in the BMW is investment by Fáilte Ireland the government's tourism development agency. Under a three-year plan, Fáilte Ireland is investing €2m in the North West of Ireland developing walking routes, attractions and tourist information centres. This encourages more visitors to travel to the BMW region.

Culture is human factor attracting tourists to the BMW region. Donegal is Ireland's largest Gaeltacht. This attracts tourists interested in language, music and dance to the region.

OR

A **Answer 3: Factors influencing Transport in the Greater Dublin Area**
In this answer, the development of transport in the Greater Dublin Area of Ireland (GDA) is discussed.

Several human factors have led to the development of transport services in the GDA.

The rapid population growth and urban sprawl of the suburban areas of Dublin city such as Tallaght and Swords has led to a high dependence on cars for commuting to work. This dependence on cars combined with the fact that 90% of all commercial transport is by road has resulted in the GDA experiencing high levels of traffic congestion. The failure of public transport to provide full services to the surrounding commuter towns such as Naas and Navan has made traffic congestion worse.

A physical factor affecting transport services in the GDA is the location of Dublin Port close to the centre of Dublin city. Dublin Port handles over one million trucks each year and this has led to increased congestion in the port access routes such as the M1 and N11.

To overcome the problems of traffic congestion in the Dublin region, the government is funding a scheme called Transport 21. This project includes the Dublin Port Tunnel, the M50 motorway upgrade and the construction of seven new Luas lines in the city. DART lines have been extended and quality bus corridors provided. These improvements have reduced congestion, travel times and costs.

The reduction of the speed limit in Dublin city centre has reduced accidents and air pollution in the area.

The upgrade of the M50 at Newlands Cross will remove the last traffic light controlled junction on the motorway. This will reduce journey times and fuel consumption for motorists using this vital transport artery in the GDA.

Dublin airport is a major access point for people travelling to Dublin. The Dublin Airport Authority has upgraded the airport and Terminal 2 carries over 15 million passengers per year.

OR

Answer 3: Factors influencing Tourism in the Greater Dublin Area

In this answer, the development of tourism services in the Greater Dublin Area (GDA) of Ireland is discussed.

Tourism is a major service in the Dublin area, it earns over €1 billion for the Dublin region and just over €4bn for the country.

A human factor encouraging the development of tourism is Fáilte Ireland, the Irish tourism development agency. It promotes Dublin as a city break destination. Dublin city has many attractions such as museums, art galleries, music venues (the O2) and shops (Dundrum SC).

In 2013 approximately 6.7 million tourists visited Ireland with the majority of these arriving through Dublin. Tourism services are well developed with many 4- and 5-star hotels in the city e.g. The Westbury, as well as budget hotels e.g. Jury's Inns.

Dublin tourism is an 'all year' business and caters for people wishing to experience a city break as well as visiting nearby countryside attractions such as golf in the K-Club or horse racing in the Curragh, County Kildare.

Economic recession from 2008 - 2013 lowered hotel and restaurant prices making the Greater Dublin Area a more affordable location to visit.

Fáilte Ireland promoted The Gathering in 2013 to encourage more visitors to Ireland. This was successful, leading to a 13% increase in visitors from the USA.

The transport network is another human factor affecting tourism in the GDA. Dublin airport has traditionally been the main point of entry into Ireland and since the removal of the Shannon stop-over for aircraft, tourist numbers have risen even more. There are bus tours and rail tours throughout the GDA and river taxis on the Liffey.

Relief is a physical factor encouraging tourism in the GDA. The Wicklow Mountains were glaciated and contain attractive glacial valleys and lakes. Glendalough in County Wicklow is a major attraction. The coastline has scenic headlands and sandy beaches, e.g. Brittas Bay and Howth Head. These features are close to the urban area of Dublin and attract many thousands of local and foreign visitors.

Chapter 13

EU Regions: The Paris Basin and the Mezzogiorno; Human Processes in European Regions

Q

Non-Irish Regions: 2010 Question 6A
In your answer book, draw an outline map of a European Region [not in Ireland] that you have studied.

On it show and name the following:
(i) Any two physical features in the region.
(ii) Any two urban centres in the region. [20 marks]

Marking scheme:
Map outline: 4 marks [graded]
Show and name physical features: 2 x (2 marks [graded] + 2 marks)
Show and name urban centres: 2 x (2 marks [graded] + 2 marks)

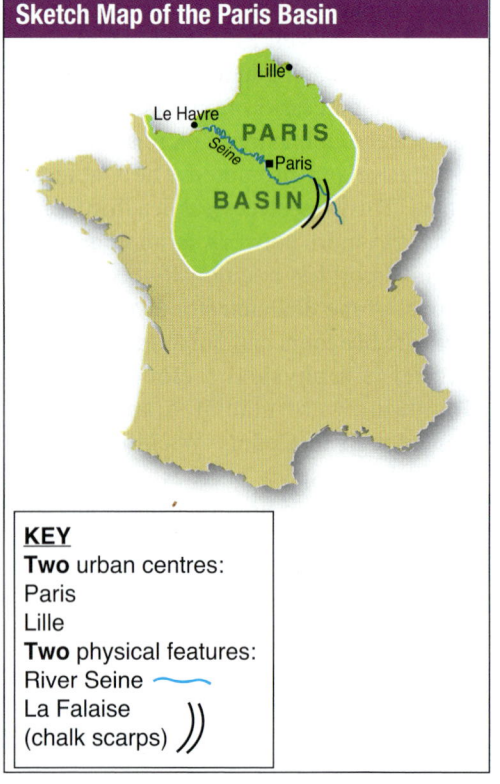

A

Sketch Map of the Mezzogiorno

Labels: ITALY, Northern limit of Mezzogiorno, Apennine Mts., Naples, R. Agri, SARDINIA, Palermo, Mt. Etna, SICILY

KEY
- Urban centres: Naples, Palermo
- Physical feature = active volcano, Mt Etna
- Physical feature = Apennine mountain range
- Drainage feature = R. Agri

Sketch Map of the Paris Basin

Labels: Lille, Le Havre, PARIS BASIN, Seine, Paris

KEY
Two urban centres:
Paris
Lille
Two physical features:
River Seine
La Falaise (chalk scarps)

102

Primary Activities in EU regions –
The Mezzogiorno and the Paris Basin

> **NOTE**
>
> The phrases **examine the development of** and **describe and explain** in this context mean the same thing. When answering any of the questions on primary activities, you should focus on the main factors influencing primary activities. If it doesn't state how many factors to discuss, focus on two.
>
> **Physical Factors:** climate, relief, and soils
> **Human Factors:** transport infrastructure, labour force, market, population, government policy

Q

Economic Activities: 2012 Question 4B
Account for the development of agriculture in a European region (not in Ireland) that you have studied, with reference to any two of the factors listed below:
• Relief • Climate • Markets   [30 marks]

Marking scheme:
Discussion Factor 1: 8 x SRPs = 8 x 2 marks = 16
Discussion Factor 2: 7 x SRPs = 7 x 2 marks = 14

What You Need To Do:
- Name your chosen EU region.
- Write 8 SRPs on the first factor you choose.
- Write 7 SRPs on the second factor you choose.
- Make sure to give examples and names of places in each region.

A

Answer 1: Agriculture in the Mezzogiorno, Italy

The Mezzogiorno is a poor, peripheral less developed region in Europe. It has physical and human factors that have affected agriculture. In this answer, I will discuss how the factors of relief and climate have affected the development of agriculture in the Mezzogiorno region of Italy.

Relief

The mountainous relief in the Mezzogiorno has delayed (hindered) the development of agriculture. The Apennines are Alpine fold mountains (50 million years old) and are steeply sloping. They run north to south along the entire length of the Italian peninsula. Over 85% of the region is mountainous, and nearly half of it is useless for agriculture. The Apennines contain limestone plateaux and granite hills. The steeply-sloping granite relief has thin, infertile, acidic soil that is easily eroded by mass movement during winter rain and summer thunderstorms. The high mountains are used for sheep and goat grazing and the lower slopes produce grapes and olives.

Because of the slow movement of the African Plate northwards into the Eurasian plate, the Apennines are tectonically active and earthquakes occur. These cause landslides and contribute to soil erosion, reducing available farmland.

In other areas active volcanoes, e.g. Mount Etna and Mount Vesuvius have produced fertile soils that have encouraged farming, e.g. olives.

Lowland is found along the coast and in the few river valleys that occur, e.g. the flood plain of the Volturno river. Here high-value wheat and olives are produced on fertile alluvial soils. Since the 1950s low-lying marshes have been reclaimed under the *Cassa Per Il Mezzogiorno* scheme. This land now produces vegetables, salad crops and wheat, e.g. Metapontino.

Intensive farming occurs on the narrow coastal lowlands close to Naples. Here irrigation and fertilisers produce high yields of salad crops and citrus fruits in commercial market gardens.

Climate

The Mezzogiorno has a Mediterranean climate that has a major influence on all farming in the region. This is a two-season climate with hot dry summers and warm wet winters.

Summer temperatures reach 29°C and there is drought between June and September due to the influence of the Azores High Pressure system.

Winters are warm, (11°C), frost is rare. Atlantic depressions travel across the region in winter bringing rain. The Apennines have relief rainfall (900 mm) on their west coast with a drier rain shadow (500 mm) in the east. In summer, convectional rain causes violent downpours that cause soil erosion.

The Mediterranean climate promotes farming in the Mezzogiorno. It is perfect for growing olives and the region is a major producer of Olive oil. Olive trees are drought resistant have adapted perfectly to this climatic zone. The Mezzogiorno produces 80% of Italy's olive oil with Puglia being the main olive growing region. Globally Italy produces just over 21% of the world's olive oil.

The Mediterranean climate provides warmth and sunshine for the early ripening of vegetables for the domestic and European market. It produces salad and citrus crops early in the year and these are sold to countries further north such as Ireland and Denmark.

Several crops harvests are possible using irrigation from the few rivers in the Mediterranean region, e.g River Agri. In winter, crops are produced in market gardens close to urban areas such as Bari and Brindisi.

Answer 2: Agriculture in the Paris Basin, France

A The Paris Basin is a wealthy, core/developed socio-economic region in Europe. In this answer I will discuss how the factors of climate and market have affected the development of agriculture in the Paris Basin.

Climate

The climate of the Paris Basin contributes to the success of farming in the region. The climate changes from west to east across the region.

In the west, there is a cool temperate oceanic (maritime) climate, similar to that in Ireland. The influence of the sea causes cool summers (16°C) and mild winters (5°C).

Average rainfall is 800 mm and falls throughout the year. This climate is perfect for grass growing. The western areas of the Paris Basin e.g. Brie (famous for its pasture and dairy products) have wetter soils and produce dairy cattle. Orchards grow apples used in cider production in the north-west near Normandy.

The influence of the sea cannot reach the eastern regions of the Paris Basin and the climate becomes continental. This type of climate is hot in summer (19°C) and cooler in winter (2°C) with frequent frost. The continental climate is drier – 700 mm of convectional rain falls in summer.

The continental climate has influenced agriculture in the Paris Basin. The hot sunny summers are perfect for wheat growing and viticulture. The Ile-de-France region is called the Bread Basket of Europe; it is one of the world's major grain-producing regions. The region's fertile limon/loëss soils and large flat expanses of land mean farms are large (400 hectares), capital intensive and highly mechanised. The combination of climates, soils and relief has led to the development of different agricultural regions known as *pays* in the Basin. These all produce a great variety of agricultural products, e.g. grapes, cereals and cattle. Champagne grapes are produced in the Champagne *pays*; this region is the most northerly wine-producing region in Europe due to its climate and soils. Summer rain and sunshine help to ripen wheat crops; dairy cattle produce milk and cheese in the wet clay soils of the Brie area. Barley and maize cereal crops as well as sugar beet grow in the wetter western areas of Picardy and Artois.

Markets

Market is an important factor affecting agriculture in the Paris Basin. Local domestic and international markets create demand for the produce of the region. The local consumer market is large: the City of Paris contains over 10 million people and there are 22 million people in the entire Paris Basin region. This population needs fresh food. Therefore land is intensively farmed to get maximum yields from the soils.

The large urban population of Paris has led to the development of wheat and dairying in the Ile-de-France and Brie regions. Brie is close to the city and provides fresh milk and cheese (e.g. Brie cheese) to the population. Market gardening on the outskirts of Paris provides fresh vegetables.

European countries are the main international market for French cereal production. The Paris Basin produces 24% of Europe's cereal harvest. The Paris Basin is located in the centre of Europe. It has well developed transport links to nearby countries such as Germany, Belgium and Italy. Farmers in the Paris Basin export their products to neighbouring countries using road, rail and canal links. Brussels is just 3 hours away and Barcelona is 12 hours by road so farmers have easy access to national and international markets with low transport costs.

The Paris Basin is a global centre for grain production; it is fifth in the world for wheat production. After the EU, the former French colonies in Africa, such as Tunisia, are its main market. France exports grain by ship from Le Havre and Marseille. Export of wheat is worth €3.4 billion. Other agricultural produce such as cheese, wine and cereals is exported along the River Seine through the inland port of Rouen to the North Sea, via the port of Le Havre. Air transport is also important for the export of the world famous champagnes to a wider international market.

Secondary Activities / Manufacturing in EU regions – The Mezzogiorno and Paris Basin

> **NOTE**
> The phrases **examine the development of** and **describe and explain** in this context mean the same thing. When answering any of the questions on secondary activities, you should focus on the main factors influencing secondary activities. If it doesn't state how many factors to discuss, focus on two.
> **Physical Factors:** climate, relief, and soils
> **Human Factors:** transport infrastructure, labour force, market, population, government policy

Q: European Regions: 2015 Question 5B
Account for the development of manufacturing in a European region (not in Ireland) that you have studied. **[30 marks]**

Marking scheme:
Examination: 15 x SRPs (15 x 2 marks = 30)

What You Need To Do:
- Name your chosen region.
- Name the two factors you are going to discuss.
- Discuss each factor in 6/7 SRPs.

A: Answer 1: Manufacturing in the Mezzogiorno

In this answer I will account for the development of secondary/ manufacturing activities in the Mezzogiorno region of Italy. Two factors have affected industrial development: government policy and relief.

Government policy
Government policy is a human factor affecting manufacturing in the Mezzogiorno region of Southern Italy. The Mezzogiorno region is a peripheral less developed region of Europe. Its mountainous relief and remote location have hindered industrial development in the area. In order to encourage industrial development, it became government policy to set up the Cassa Per Il Mezzogiorno (Cassa), a fund for the South. It began in the 1950s and over the next 25 years over €2·3 billion was invested in industry under the Vanoni Plan, a part of the Cassa scheme dealing with industry. The Cassa developed industry in the Mezzogiorno by creating four industrial growth centres that were the focus of investment in industry.

The Bari-Brindisi-Taranto industrial triangle was developed for heavy industries such as steel, petrochemicals and engineering. The Naples and Latina region was developed for chemicals, oil refining, shipbuilding and car manufacturing. In Sicily, oil refining and the petro-chemicals industry were further developed by the construction of a massive oil terminal. These heavy industries were state-owned and provided thousands of jobs across the region. Other incentives to help industry included giving tax relief, grants and subsidies. A new law was passed requiring 40% of new state investment to locate in the Mezzogiorno.

Relief
Relief is a physical factor affecting manufacturing in the Mezzogiorno. The mountainous relief and remote location of the region have hindered industrial development there. The Apennine Mountains stretch from the toe of Italy in Calabria northwards over 1,200 kilometres to Northern Italy. They form a barrier to communications across the Italian Peninsula and to the wealthy core area of Northern Italy. In winter they are snow covered and dangerous for heavy traffic. The steep slopes have hindered rail transport. The Mezzogiorno is an earthquake zone and these cause landslides on steep ground which can block roads.

A massive road-building project called the Autostrada del Sole was completed in 1964. It was built to overcome the problems of relief and reduce the time needed to travel between the new manufacturing centres in the Mezzogiorno and the wealthy markets in the core regions of Northern Italy and Central Europe.

Over 1,000 kilometres of motorway was constructed. Bridges were built over deep valleys and tunnels were blasted through mountainous land in the Apennines. This important road link between the north and south of Italy reduced transport costs and helped encourage industry to locate in the Mezzogiorno. In particular it helped the development of the food processing industry which depends on getting fresh food to the factories in a short time.

The coastline contains many sheltered harbours. These were developed to aid the shipping industry. Deep water ports were constructed at Taranto and Siracusa. These attracted the steel- and oil-refining industries to the region and encouraged further economic development. Today EU Structural Funds continue to upgrade transport services. Of those Structural Funds, 85% are being spent in the Mezzogiorno region.

Answer 2: Manufacturing in the Paris Basin

A In this answer I will account for the factors that have influenced the development of manufacturing activity in the Paris Basin region of France. Two factors have affected development: relief/drainage and population. As a result of these physical and human factors, Paris has more manufacturing industry than any other region in France. It is an economic core region.

Relief/Drainage
Paris is attractive to industry because of physical factors such as its low-lying landscape (relief) and the presence of large rivers (drainage). These have made it one of the most accessible cities in Europe. The low-lying relief enabled the construction of rail and road networks across the region and so it has an excellent transport infrastructure and low transport costs which benefit industry. The River Seine runs

through Paris for over 13 kilometres and the city has an inland port with access to the Atlantic Ocean through the port of Le Havre. Raw materials and finished goods can be imported/exported through the port of Paris, encouraging industrial development. Rail construction is easier on flat low-lying land. The French high-speed rail network (TGV) has its centre in Paris so business people can reach the rest of France and Europe easily. This has attracted many companies to the region, e.g. Lancôme.

Because the region is a low-lying highly productive farming region there are plenty of raw materials such as wine, milk and wheat for the food processing industry. Industries providing equipment and fertilisers have developed across the region.

Population

A human factor encouraging industry is the large wealthy population. The Paris Basin region has over 22 million people. They provide an educated labour force and market for manufactured goods. The Paris Basin is such an attractive location for industry that the region now contains 25% (6·5 million) of the French workforce. Of this 6·5 million, 44% work in manufacturing.

There is a wide variety of industry found in Paris because of the large, educated, wealthy population in the region. Heavy industry such as steel and oil refining are located close to the river on the Canal St. Denis. Lighter industries are located in the newer suburbs such as Marne-La-Vallée. Here industrial estates have been built to encourage industry away from the city centre. Car manufacturers such as Renault and Citroën are also located in the suburbs. Paris is world famous for its fashion. The fashion industry relies on a wealthy population with disposable income to spend on fashion items. Many industrial units are found in the city centre which manufacture luxury clothing (Chanel) and jewellery (Cartier). The Paris Basin is also a centre of cosmetic manufacturing. Research and development of cosmetics is spread across the south and west of the region. The industry employs over 47,000 people.

Tertiary Activities / Services in EU Regions – The Mezzogiorno and the Paris Basin

> **NOTE**
>
> The phrases **examine the development of** and **describe and explain** in this context mean the same thing. When answering any of the questions on tertiary activities, you should focus on the main factors influencing tertiary activities. If it doesn't state how many factors to discuss, focus on two.
> **Physical Factors:** climate, relief, and soils
> **Human Factors:** transport infrastructure, labour force, market, population, government policy

This topic has been examined in two ways.
➤ You may be asked to discuss **ONE** tertiary activity in detail.
➤ You may be asked to discuss **TWO** tertiary activities.

Q

Economic Activities: 2010 Question 4B
Examine the factors that influence the development of one tertiary economic activity in a European region (not in Ireland) that you have studied.

[30 marks]

> **NOTE:** The sample answers below discuss the development of **TWO** tertiary economic activities (tourism AND transport) to provide students with a choice of topics. However the question only requires **ONE** tertiary economic activity to be discussed.

Marking scheme:
Name one tertiary economic activity: 2 marks
Identify two factors: 2 marks + 2 marks
Name the region: 2 marks
Examination: 11 x SRPs (11 x 2 marks = 22)

What You Need To Do:
- Name your chosen tertiary activity.
- Name two factors that affect it.
- Discuss these factors.

A

Italy
Answer 1: Factors affecting the development of tourism in the Mezzogiorno

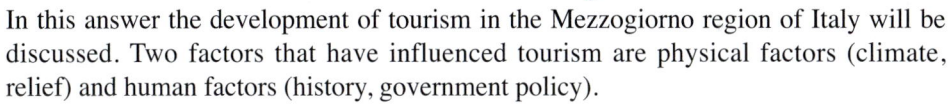

In this answer the development of tourism in the Mezzogiorno region of Italy will be discussed. Two factors that have influenced tourism are physical factors (climate, relief) and human factors (history, government policy).

Tourism
The Mezzogiorno region has many natural and cultural attractions for tourists. However the peripheral location and poor transport services have prevented the development of tourism which is still limited to the coastal regions.

The region has a Mediterranean climate with hot (29°C) and dry summers. Temperatures rarely fall below 11°C. The hot, dry climate is a major attraction for tourists who like to visit the beach for sunshine holidays. In winter the Apennine Mountains are snow covered and suitable for skiing. Tourism could be a year-round activity in some regions near the ski areas.

The relief of the region has provided a variety of mountain scenery and beautiful beaches, e.g. the Bay of Naples and the Amalfi Coast, which attract those looking for sun holidays and walking tours.

The volcanic activity of Mount Etna on Sicily and the volcanic springs are very popular tourist attractions.

History is a human factor affecting the development of tourism in the Mezzogiorno. Ancient Roman culture is widespread and the most well known attraction is the ruined town of Pompeii outside Naples. Thousands of people tour these ancient ruins each year.

Government policy has been very important in developing the tourist industry in the Mezzogiorno. The main policy was the Cassa Scheme which began in the 1950s. Fifteen per cent of the Cassa budget was spent on encouraging tourism in the region. Grants were given to build hotels and tourist accommodation. Roads were improved and training schemes were provided for hotel workers.

A new airport was built at Calabria so that tourists could arrive to the region directly. Tourist ferry boats to Sicily and Sardinia were provided.

However a factor preventing development of tourism is access to the inland areas away from the coast. Facilities are lacking and road and rail access across the mountains is not well developed. The region is also far from the main population centres of Northern Europe. Many people choose the south of France or Spain because they have better developed facilities to cater for mass tourism and are closer.

Answer 2: Factors affecting transport services in the Mezzogiorno region of Italy

In this answer I will discuss the development of transport services in the Mezzogiorno region of Italy. The two factors affecting transport in the Mezzogiorno region are relief and government policy.

Relief

Relief is a physical factor and has an important influence on the development of transport in the Mezzogiorno. Relief has delayed the development of transport services. It has also added to the expense of building roads in such steeply-sloping ground.

The land is very mountainous due to the presence of the Apennine Mountains. They stretch along the length of the Italian peninsula and also into the 'toe' of Italy in Calabria.

The only lowlands are found along a narrow coastal strip of land between the mountains and the sea. This means there is little flat land available for road and rail development.

The mountains are steep and cut by deep valleys. They are snow covered in winter. Roads are steep, narrow and winding. Many bridges have had to be built across the valleys. Tunnels are also required through the steepest hills. This has added to the cost of providing transport services in the Mezzogiorno region.

The Apennine Mountains are also a barrier to road and rail communication from west to east across the peninsula. The mountainous relief has led to long journey times to the wealthy north of Italy and roads are too narrow and winding to carry large modern 40-tonne container lorries. Train services are often disrupted by snow in winter and landslides which can occur on the steep ground after storms.

Government policy

Government policy is a human factor which has influenced the development of transport services in the Mezzogiorno.

In order to overcome the problems for transport caused by the relief, the government set up an investment programme called the Vanoni Plan. This plan was part of the Cassa Per Il Mezzogiorno Scheme. Over €2.5 billion was spent on transport infrastructure to encourage more industrial development and tourism in the region. A major motorway project, the Autostrada del Sole, was constructed in 1964 connecting Milan to Naples. It is the longest Italian autostrada (754 km) and is now the most important routeway of the Italian road network. The project straightened and widened roads so that they could carry large trucks. Bridges were built over deep valleys and tunnels were blasted through mountainous land in the Apennines. This important road link between the north and south of Italy reduced transport costs and helped encourage industry to locate in the Mezzogiorno. It reduced the peripheral location of the Mezzogiorno region.

The government also invested in shipping ports. Deep-water ports were built at the towns of Taranto and Brindisi. These became the location for steel manufacturing. Steel products are now exported across the world from those ports. In Sicily a deep water port for huge oil tankers was built at Siracusa and is now the largest oil importing centre in Italy and has oil-refining industries.

France
Answer 3: The development of tourism in the Paris Basin

In this answer the factors affecting the development of tourism in the Paris Basin region of France will be discussed. France is the world's number one tourist destination. It receives over 75 million visitors per year. Tourism is worth over €35 billion to the French economy. Within France the Paris Basin is a major destination. Tourism in the Paris Basin is focused on the city of Paris. Over nine million tourists visit the city each year. The most popular visitor attraction in the entire country is the Louvre art gallery located in Paris.

The relief and climate are physical factors that have encouraged tourism. The Paris Basin has a low-lying landscape but in the Champagne area there are large limestone ridges called scarps, e.g. the Falaise. The more continental climate on south-facing slopes of these scarps is suitable for wine production. Reims is the centre of wine production and has a well developed wine tourism industry. Human factors such as many historic buildings and excellent transport services have also encouraged the development of tourism in the Paris Basin.

Medieval towns such as Caen attract people who are interested in history. The Normandy beaches on the west coast of the Paris Basin region are visited by thousands of tourists who wish to remember lost relatives from World War II or to trace the development of the war in France.

The wide variety of historic and modern attractions and the excellent transport infrastructure make Paris an easy destination for those tourists who want a city break. Tourists are well supported by an excellent city transport system (the Metro) and a network of tourist information offices across the region.

Another reason for the development of tourism in the Paris Basin is the wide variety of tourist attractions that appeal to a range of tourist types, from young to old. Younger tourists are attracted to facilities such as Disneyland Paris located to the east of the city at Marne-La-Vallée. More mature visitors spend time in art galleries and museums such as the Louvre and Musée D'Orsay as well as visiting the famous cabaret shows at the Moulin Rouge.

Shopping is a major reason for tourists to visit Paris. The Champs-Elysée and Boulevard Haussmann are world-famous shopping streets.

Answer 4: The development of transport and communications in the Paris Basin

The Paris Basin has an excellent transport and communications infrastructure. Today, 22 million people live in the Paris Basin. Physical and human factors encouraged the development of transportation services in the Paris Basin. Relief is a physical factor. It was not difficult to develop the road and rail transport network because the region is part of the North European Plain, an area of low-lying flat land. Transport of agricultural products, such as wheat, to urban food processing plants is required. A human factor is the location of government. Paris is the capital city and economic engine of France. Paris quickly became the centre of the transport network in France. The road and rail systems radiate out from Paris like the spokes of a wheel. One disadvantage of this is that the rail transport network is so centralised, it is difficult to travel across France without having to go through Paris.

In the past the development of railways in the region was slower than in other countries. This was due to historic factors, such as (a) the Napoleonic wars which destroyed many railway lines and (b) opposition from canal and shipping operators who did not want competition. In modern times the French government has invested in the development of the high-speed rail network (TGV). This is focused on Paris and links the city to Marseilles (the second largest city in France) in the south, to Lille in the north and to the UK via the Channel Tunnel. It has been important in connecting industrial zones in the south and west to Paris. The railways in France have always been under government control.

The Paris Basin has several large rivers (the Seine, Marne and Oise) flowing roughly westwards across it. These have encouraged the development of both inland port towns such as Lille and canals across the region, e.g. the Canal St. Denis. Canals link the rivers to each other and carry industrial and tourist traffic. During the Industrial Revolution they were major industrial routeways connecting the Paris region to the rest of the country and to Germany and Belgium.

Paris is an internationally important trading centre and has developed as an inland port. Although it is 130 kilometres from the sea, it provides access to the English channel at Le Havre. International airports are located at Charles de Gaulle and Beauvais.

Chapter 14

The Influence of the EU

Q

> **European Union: 2011 Question 5B**
> Examine the economic impact of enlargement of the European Union on Ireland.
> **[30 marks]**
>
> **Marking scheme:**
> Identify economic impact: 2 marks
> Examination: 14 x SRPs (14 x 2 marks = 28)

> **What You Need To Do:**
> - Name one impact of EU expansion on the Irish economy.
> - Discuss this impact in 14 SRPs.

> **NOTE:** This topic was also examined in **2014 Question 4B**

A

Answer

Impact of EU expansion on Ireland's economy

Since the EU was established, it has expanded from 6 member states in 1957 to 27 today. Several EU treaties have been enacted during the expansion process to allow people from EU countries travel to other countries within the EU and find work without the need for visas, e.g. the Maastricht Treaty in 1993. The movement of labour that has occurred as a result of these treaties has impacted on the Irish economy.

Labour force: The expansion of the EU to 27 member states provided a new source of labour for the Irish economy. Between 1995 and 2008 (before the current economic recession), a rapidly growing Irish economy required over 420,000 new workers to fill the many jobs available. During this time there were not enough Irish workers to fill these employment vacancies. However, with the expansion of the EU in 2004 and 2007 and the agreed EU treaties among members, a new source of labour was made available to the Irish jobs market.

Many workers from the newer EU states, e.g. Poland and Latvia, moved to Ireland to find work. By 2009 over 349,000 foreign national workers were employed here. These new workers have had a positive impact on the Irish economy as their taxes contribute to important health and education services and help fund the Irish National Development Plan. EU workers also provided skills and knowledge that were in short supply in Ireland at the time such as in construction and healthcare.

New market: Non-Irish EU workers support the Irish economy when they rent property, buy houses and purchase goods and services in Ireland. The migration of many thousands of EU citizens to Ireland provides a wider domestic market for clothes, food and recreational facilities. Along with this, many new businesses opened to cater for this new market, e.g. Polish shops (Polski Sklep), Baltic food markets, bars and restaurants. In this way, foreign national and Irish workers continued to maintain the growth of the

Irish economy.

The expansion of the EU also created a wider market for Irish manufacturers. The EU now has a population of over 500 million people. The value of Irish exports increased and much of these exports go to this bigger duty-free EU market. The EU is Ireland's main market for its food and drink exports which were worth €7.3bn in 2013 (42% of exports). The EU is a source of Irish imports in 2013, the UK supplied 35% of Irish imports.

However, since the onset of recession in 2007, Irish economic growth declined. Many Irish and foreign workers lost their jobs. Some Irish workers are now taking advantage of the same EU rules/policies, allowing people to move to other EU countries to find employment. Irish workers are taking up employment in countries such as the UK and Poland.

Eurozone problems: The expansion of the EU can also have a negative impact on our economy. The current economic problems experienced by other EU states, such as Greece and Portugal, also affect Ireland. This is because as Ireland is part of the eurozone, any economic problems that affect the value of the Euro also affect the Irish economy. Also the manufacture of goods in the new EU states is cheaper than the cost of production in Ireland. This therefore caused greater competition for Irish manufacturers when selling to EU and international markets. An example of this is the outsourcing of production from Ireland to cheaper EU locations such as Poland. This occurred in 2009 when Dell outsourced its entire Irish manufacturing base from Limerick to the town of Lodz in Poland.

Q

European Union Expansion: 2009 Question 5B
Describe and explain two impacts on Ireland of the enlargement of the European Union. [30 marks]

Marking scheme:
Identify impacts: 2 marks + 2 marks
Examination: 13 x SRPs (7/6 SRPs x 2 marks for each impact = 26)

What You Need To Do:
- Name two impacts of EU enlargement.
- Discuss each impact in 7/6 SRPs.

A

Answer: Impact of EU expansion on Ireland

The expansion of the EU to 27 members in 2007 has had two impacts on Ireland.
1. An impact on Ireland's economy.
2. An impact on Ireland's culture.

1. Impact of EU expansion on Ireland's economy

The expansion of the EU to 27 member states in 2007 provided a new source of labour for the Irish economy. Between 1995 and 2008, i.e. before the economic recession began, the Irish economy required over 420,000 new workers. Without EU expansion there would not have been enough Irish people available to fill these jobs and maintain Irish economic growth. However, since 2008 Irish economic growth has declined and some Irish workers are now taking advantage of an EU rule which allows most EU citizens to move to other EU countries to find employment.

The EU has expanded from 6 member states in 1957 to 27 in 2007. Several EU treaties have been enacted during the expansion process to allow people from EU countries travel to other countries within the EU and find work, e.g. the Maastricht Treaty in 1993.

Many workers from the newer EU states moved to Ireland to find work, e.g. Poland and Latvia. By 2009, more than 349,000 foreign national workers were employed here. These new workers have had a positive impact on the Irish economy as their taxes have contributed to important health and education services and helped fund the Irish National Development Plan. EU workers also provided skills that were in short supply in Ireland during the economic boom years (1995-2007) such as construction and healthcare.

Non-Irish EU workers also support the Irish economy when they buy houses, goods and services in Ireland. The migration of many thousands of EU citizens to Ireland provides a market for clothes, food and recreational facilities. As a result new businesses open to cater for this new market, e.g. Polish shops (Polski Sklep), Baltic food markets, bars and restaurants.

The expansion of the EU can have a more negative impact on our economy. The economic problems experienced by other EU states such as Greece and Portugal also affect Ireland as we are part of the eurozone where the common currency is the Euro. Any economic problems that affect the value of the Euro also affect the Irish economy.

2. Impact of EU expansion on Irish culture

Ireland has become a multicultural society as a result of EU expansion. The Maastricht Treaty and the introduction of the Euro enable EU citizens to arrive and work in Ireland and use a common currency.

The composition of the Irish population has become more varied. The census shows that just over 555,000 people from other EU countries now live in Ireland, e.g. Poles (115,000) and Lithuanians (35,000). The migration of Eastern Europeans to Ireland is having an impact on our culture as Irish people adapt to become familiar with EU citizens working in primary, manufacturing and service industries. Irish people hear different languages in their daily lives and now work and socialise with people from other cultures. Eastern European shops, bars and restaurants have opened in many parts of Ireland and this encourages an increase in cultural mixing between Irish people and those of other nationalities. Several Irish daily newspapers now publish Polish editions to cater for this new market. The food culture of Ireland is changing as restaurants and shops serve foods, e.g. Baltic and Polish meat dishes, from other EU nations. Irish people may also meet and marry migrants to Ireland. In this way multicultural families become more common and children are raised in bi-lingual households. Schools have to cope with students from other countries and integrate the newcomers into school society. Many schools offer English language classes to help new students settle in and have 'multicultural days' to introduce different cultures to the school.

Irish people can travel to Europe and pay for goods and services in Euro. This enables a direct comparison of services and products between Ireland and EU countries. Irish people can now view how the economy and culture of different EU countries operate.

a direct comparison of services and products between Ireland and EU countries. Irish people can now easily see how the economy and culture of different EU countries operate.

Chapter 15

Non-EU Regions: Brazil, India, South-West USA

> **NOTE**
>
> You will study one non-EU/continental/sub-continental region. Most students study one of the following regions: Brazil, India or the South-West USA. This chapter focuses on sketch maps, economic activities, urban growth and population distribution in Brazil, India and South-West USA. Answers to questions on urban growth and cultural regions are found in Chapter 11. You may be asked to draw a sketch map of your chosen non-EU/continental/sub-continental region. You are required to show and name a selection (usually 4 or 5) of features. These questions are usually worth 20 marks at Higher Level and should not take you more than 5 to 7 minutes to do.
>
> There are three sketch maps (Brazil, India, and the South-West USA) – one map below and two more maps on page 117. These maps show all types of regions, e.g. physical, urban, relief. Note that students would not be required to draw all the items shown.

Summary sketch map of Brazil

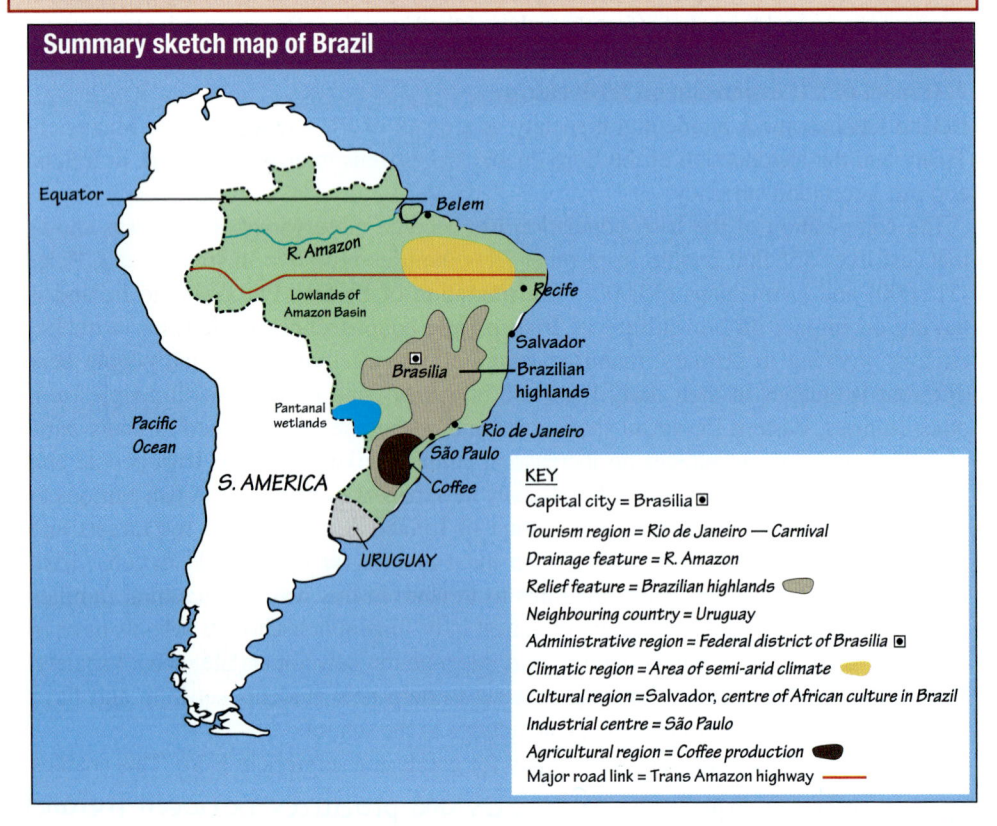

KEY
Capital city = Brasilia ◉
Tourism region = Rio de Janeiro — Carnival
Drainage feature = R. Amazon
Relief feature = Brazilian highlands
Neighbouring country = Uruguay
Administrative region = Federal district of Brasilia ◉
Climatic region = Area of semi-arid climate
Cultural region = Salvador, centre of African culture in Brazil
Industrial centre = São Paulo
Agricultural region = Coffee production
Major road link = Trans Amazon highway

Summary sketch map of India

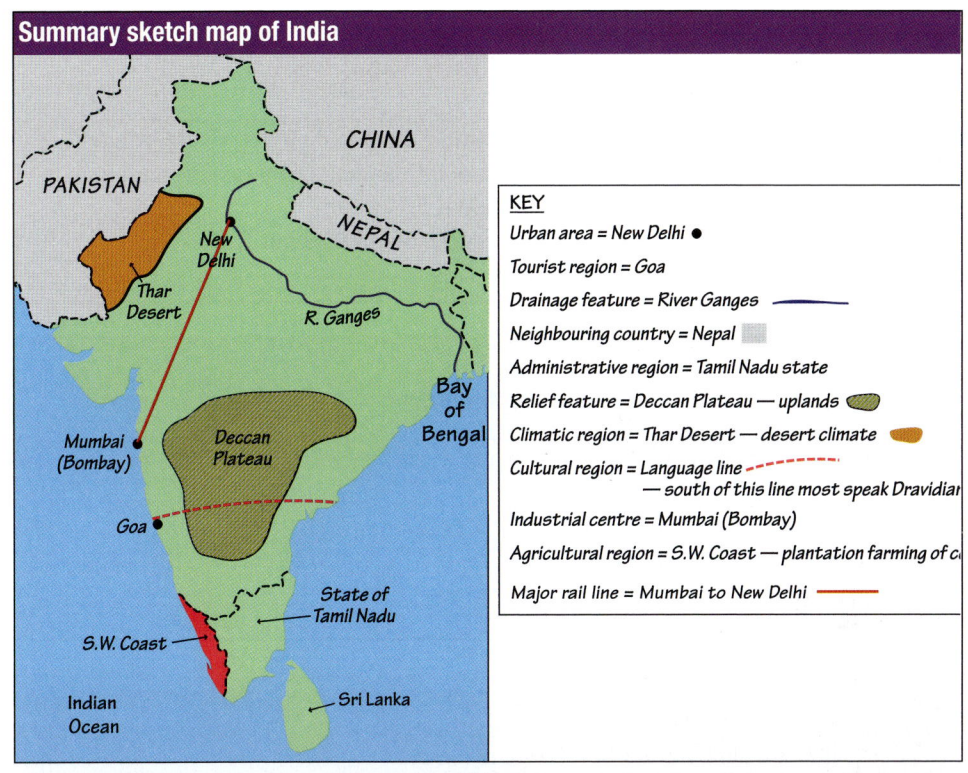

KEY
- Urban area = New Delhi ●
- Tourist region = Goa
- Drainage feature = River Ganges
- Neighbouring country = Nepal
- Administrative region = Tamil Nadu state
- Relief feature = Deccan Plateau — uplands
- Climatic region = Thar Desert — desert climate
- Cultural region = Language line — — — south of this line most speak Dravidian
- Industrial centre = Mumbai (Bombay)
- Agricultural region = S.W. Coast — plantation farming of c...
- Major rail line = Mumbai to New Delhi

Labels on map: PAKISTAN, CHINA, NEPAL, New Delhi, Thar Desert, R. Ganges, Bay of Bengal, Mumbai (Bombay), Deccan Plateau, Goa, State of Tamil Nadu, S.W. Coast, Sri Lanka, Indian Ocean

Summary sketch map of South-West USA

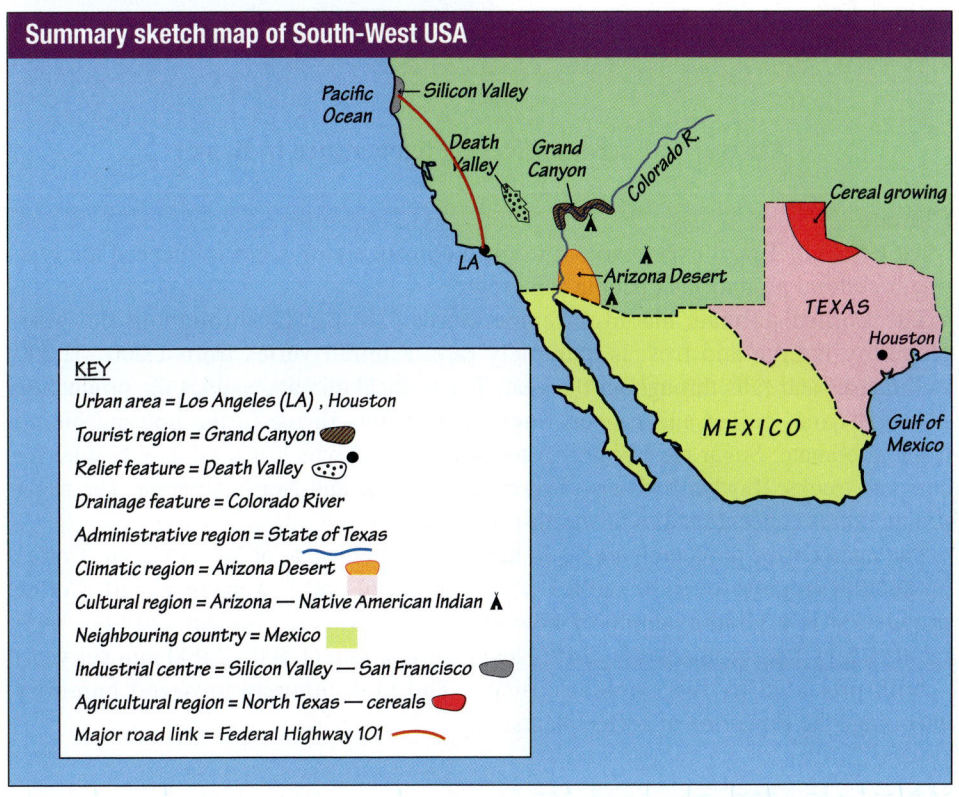

KEY
- Urban area = Los Angeles (LA), Houston
- Tourist region = Grand Canyon
- Relief feature = Death Valley
- Drainage feature = Colorado River
- Administrative region = State of Texas
- Climatic region = Arizona Desert
- Cultural region = Arizona — Native American Indian
- Neighbouring country = Mexico
- Industrial centre = Silicon Valley — San Francisco
- Agricultural region = North Texas — cereals
- Major road link = Federal Highway 101

Labels on map: Pacific Ocean, Silicon Valley, Death Valley, Grand Canyon, Colorado R., Cereal growing, LA, Arizona Desert, TEXAS, Houston, MEXICO, Gulf of Mexico

117

Primary Activities in a non-EU region: Brazil, India, South-West USA

NOTE: When answering any of the questions on primary activities, students should focus on **two** of the main factors influencing primary activities:
Physical Factors: climate, relief, drainage and soils
Human Factors: transport infrastructure, market, labour force, government incentives

Q

Agriculture: 2015 Question 6B
Examine the factors that influence the development of **one** primary economic activity in a continental / sub-continental region (not Europe) that you have studied. **[30 marks]**

Marking scheme:
Identify factors: 2 marks + 2 marks
Examination: 13 x SRPs (13 x 2 marks = 26)

What You Need To Do:
- State the non-European region.
- Name two factors affecting the development of agriculture.
- Discuss the influence **each** factor has on agriculture in 6 SRPs per factor.

A

Answer 1: Factors affecting agriculture in Brazil

Climate
Most (90%) of Brazil experiences a tropical climate and this has influenced the type of agricultural produce that people can grow.

The tropical climate has high temperatures (28°-32° C) throughout the year. Humidity is high and frost is extremely rare. Rainfall varies from 1,000 - 2,000 millimetres and falls throughout the year. The tropical climate enables the production of sugar cane, coffee and timber. Sugar cane plants thrive in the hot and humid tropical climate. Sugar cane is grown to make ethanol which is used as a biofuel for cars and trucks. Raw sugar is also exported to Europe and North America. The sugar production is concentrated in the north-east coast.

The main coffee producing area is in the south-eastern state of Minas Gerais. Coffee production employs over 10 million people in Brazil and is a major export. Coffee production is a good example of how climate has affected human activities as it requires high temperatures (15 - 24°C) and plenty of rain (1,500 - 2,000 mm per year) – both provided by the tropical climate. The high temperatures and humidity encourage the flowering of coffee plants.

Soils
The soil in south-eastern Brazil is called 'Terra Rossa'. It is deep, red coloured, fertile and rich in humus. Terra Rossa soils have developed from limestone parent rock. In Brazil this soil is used for coffee production. Coffee plants require deep, well-drained soils and high altitude (to reduce pests). These conditions are found in south-east Brazil mainly in the state of Minas Gerais. As a result of the combination of climate, soil and relief conditions, Brazil is the world's most important coffee producer.

Soils in the west central area of Brazil are generally infertile. At first Brazilian farmers were able to increase crop production in this area by applying expensive fertilisers and lime to the soil. However they now use a system of 'no-plough' farming. This means that the ground is left permanently covered by vegetation and crops. Sixty per cent of cultivated land in Brazil is now farmed in this way. No-plough farming increases soil fertility and reduces soil erosion. Yields of maize and wheat have increased.

A   Answer 2: Factors affecting agriculture in India

In this answer the way in which climate and soils have influenced agriculture in India will be discussed.

Influence of climate
India has a tropical climate with high temperatures (20°- 32°C) throughout the year and this has influenced the type of crops that people grow. The tropical climate allows the production of crops such as rice and sugar cane which require high temperatures. The amount of rain that falls in India is controlled by the monsoon. The monsoon is a reversal of wind patterns over the continent which creates a wet season (June – September) and dry season (October – June). The monsoon rains control which crops people can grow and when they can be planted or harvested. If the monsoon rains are late or bring low rainfall, then irrigation, planting and crop yields are affected. During the wet season thirsty crops such as rice are grown in the eastern half of the country, along the Ganges Valley and the Eastern and Western Ghats. In these areas rainfall can total over 2,500 millimetres. In the dry season millet is grown throughout India.

In drier regions of north-west India wheat, maize and chickpeas are grown.

The tropical climate is suited to tea production and Assam state in the north east is a major supplier to the global tea trade. In the extreme north-western region of India is the Thar Desert. The desert climate is unsuited to many crops but cotton and millet are grown where irrigation is used.

Influence of soils
Soils have influenced the pattern of primary production in India. In the south-west state of Kerala deep, fertile red soils are found which allow the production of coffee. As a result Kerala is the main coffee-producing state in India. Rice requires fertile, wet, alluvial, clay rich soils. These soils are found along the Ganges Valley and are renewed each year when the Ganges overflows onto its flood plain. In the far north of India the high relief of the Himalaya Mountains has caused the formation of thin, infertile mountain soils and as a result the main primary activities are subsistence

farming and goat herding.

Well-drained, well-aerated, red-coloured soils are essential for the successful growth of tea. Because these soils occur in the states of Assam and Himachal Pradesh in northern India, tea is the main crop produced in these regions.

The sandy desert soils of the Thar region are suitable for agriculture when they are irrigated.

Answer 3: Factors affecting agriculture in the South-West USA

A

In this answer the way in which climate and soils have influenced agriculture in the South-West USA will be discussed.

Climate

The South-West USA is a dry region with a desert or semi-desert climate. Annual rainfall is below 250 millimetres per year and temperatures are high (average = 25°C). The Central Valley region of California has a Mediterranean climate with hot dry summers and warm winters (average = 10°C). These climatic conditions have influenced primary economic activities such as farming in the region. Crops that do well in high temperatures can be grown, such as citrus fruits, avocados and vines. However due to the lack of rain, irrigation is widely used. Most of the South-West USA is used for pastoral farming. Cattle ranching is carried out on huge ranches in the states of Nevada, Arizona and Utah. Because rainfall in these states is unreliable, the vegetation is sparse and large areas of land are needed for the cattle. Climatic conditions have therefore led to the use of extensive farming methods in the region and to the existence of a monoculture based on cattle production. Texas has higher rainfall due to the influence of wet sea breezes from the Gulf of Mexico and this has allowed the production of crops such as cotton, soya and wheat.

Drainage

There are several major rivers in the South-West USA that influence farming in the region. In the Central Valley of California the Sacramento and San Joaquin Rivers are used to supply irrigation water and water for homes and industry. The Colorado River flowing through Utah and Arizona is also used for hydroelectric power and irrigation of farmland. The Rio Grande forms the border between Mexico and Texas. These rivers are important to the economy of the region because agricultural production is dependent on them. The economy of California depends on the Sacramento and San Joaquin Rivers for its irrigation systems, which are the largest in the world. Intensive production of fruit, vegetable and vines would be impossible without the river water. California is the largest agricultural producer in the US due to the plentiful supply of irrigation water from these rivers. For example it is the largest producer of tomatoes in the US and its orange production is second only to the 'Orange County', Florida. The availability of water has enabled farmers to specialise in the production of one crop. Such monoculture is common in vine-producing areas such as the Napa Valley.

Secondary Activities in a non-EU region:
Brazil, India, South-West USA

> **NOTE**
> When answering any of the questions on secondary activities students should focus on **two** of the main factors influencing secondary activities:
> **Physical Factors**: climate, relief and soils
> **Human Factors**: transport infrastructure, market, labour force, raw materials and government policies

Q

Secondary Activities: 2014 Question 5C
Discuss the factors that influence the development of secondary economic activity in a continental/sub continental region (not in Europe) that you have studied.
[30 marks]

Marking scheme:
Name factors: 2 marks + 2 marks = 4
Examination: 13 x SRPs (13 x 2 marks = 26)

What You Need To Do:
- Name your chosen non-EU region.
- Name two factors affecting manufacturing.
- Discuss how these factors influence manufacturing.
- Hint: market, raw materials, transport links, labour force, government policies

A

Answer 1: Secondary activities in Brazil

In this answer the development of secondary economic activities in Brazil, such as steel production and car manufacturing, will be discussed.

Several factors have influenced the development of the manufacturing industry in Brazil. It has a large market with a population of over 185 million people, it has many natural resources and it has been government policy to encourage industrial development.

Manufacturing is concentrated in the south-eastern states, especially São Paulo and Belo Horizonte. This is because these states have many natural resources such as iron ore and limestone that are raw materials for the steel factories. Offshore, there are reserves of oil and gas, which have encouraged the location of the petrochemical industry in Rio de Janeiro.

All of the cities in the region have large populations that provide a workforce for industry. There is also great wealth in the region, which provides a market for manufactured products. For example, São Paulo has the highest rate of helicopter ownership in the world as wealthy business people use them instead of road transport to avoid traffic congestion.

Brazil is a newly industrialised country because of government programmes to develop manufacturing. After World War II, the government started an import substitution scheme. The aim was to produce goods in Brazil rather than import them from the US or Europe. This programme led to the development of cars that used ethanol produced from locally-grown sugar cane instead of imported oil. Car manufacturing is now a major industry in Brazil. Several factors account for this. The market is undeveloped. There is only 1 car for every 6.5 people. The market is getting wealthier due to economic growth which is increasing demand for cars. The government has removed taxes on new cars to encourage car manufacturing.

The government's decision to remove taxes on new cars has successfully increased sales. In 2010 car sales increased by almost 10% and by 2011 Brazil had become the fourth largest car-maker in the world after China, the USA and Japan.

The import substitution scheme developed the textile industry in Brazil. Today Brazil produces 3% of the world's textiles, employing 2 million people. The textile industry is worth 5% of Brazilian GDP.

Answer 2: Secondary activities in India

In this answer the development of secondary economic activities in India, such as software, pharmaceuticals, electronics and steel production, will be discussed.

Two factors have affected industrial development: Government influence and the availability of raw materials. Before India became independent from Britain in 1947 industrial development was generally underdeveloped and limited to textile production and food processing. Just 2% of the labour force was employed in manufacturing. Industry was located in Kolkata, Mumbai and Chennai. After independence the government aimed to spread industry into rural areas across the country by investing in labour-intensive local craft industries and food processing. These used locally-produced raw materials. It also developed fertiliser production and the manufacture of agricultural machinery. However, today the main manufacturing centres are still Kolkata, Mumbai and Chennai.

India has many advantages for industry, such as resources and labour. The main advantage is its well-educated but low-cost labour force. The Indian government has invested in education and now has more third-level graduates than Canada and the USA combined. About 40% of the graduates have engineering and science degrees. This has attracted multinational companies in the high-tech software sector to India. Here they can employ skilled graduates at less than a third of the cost of their American or European workers. Bangalore is the centre of the Indian software industry and is known as India's Silicon Valley with companies such as IBM located there.

Availability of raw materials has also influenced industrial development in India. Resources such as coal and iron ore are located close to Kolkata and this city is the centre of iron and steel manufacturing in India. Transport is another factor that has influenced the development of industry. Beyond the cities, road and rail is poorly developed so industries locate in the cities to use the superior transport networks there. The main port is Mumbai and the pharmaceutical industry, whose products are exported, is located here to lower transport costs.

Answer 3: Secondary activities in the South-West USA

In this answer the development of secondary activities in the South-West USA, such as software, manufacturing and petrochemical production, is discussed.

The region has many advantages for industrial development. Availability of raw materials is a major influence in Texas where the huge oil and gas reserves are used to make fertilisers and petrochemicals. These industries are concentrated in Galveston and Houston.

Elsewhere in California's Silicon Valley a well-educated labour force and the availability of globally important research centres such as Stanford University have attracted knowledge-based high-tech industries. Apple computers, Hewlett-Packard, Intel and IBM all began production in Silicon Valley.

Another important factor influencing the development of industry in the region is a well developed transport system. Ports such as San Francisco provide access to the large markets of Pacific Rim nations such as China. Many industries export to these countries so locating in San Francisco reduces transport costs.

Government influence has also encouraged the development of the Aerospace industry in Texas. The American government located many of its Air Force bases in Texas and New Mexico. These bases require aircraft, satellite navigation and military equipment, all of which are manufactured nearby. The government also chose Houston as its centre for NASA so this city has become a centre for space flight industries making the space shuttle and space research equipment.

Many other industries have located close to the Mexican border so that they can operate low-cost 'maquilladoras' or 'twin factories'. Unskilled, low-paid work such as product assembly is carried out in the Mexican plant. Across the border in the US plants, highly-skilled work such as research, development and marketing is carried out.

Tertiary Activities in a non-EU region: Brazil, India, South-West USA

> **NOTE**
>
> When answering any of the questions on tertiary activities you should focus on **two** of the main factors influencing these activities:
> **Physical factors:** climate, relief, and soils
> **Human factors:** transport infrastructure, tourism, market, population

> **Tertiary Economic Activity: 2009 Question 5C**
> Account for the development of **one** tertiary economic activity in any **one** Continental / Sub-Continental Region that you have studied. [30 marks]
>
> **Marking scheme:**
> Name region: 2 marks
> Name tertiary activity: 2 marks
> Examination: 13 x SRPs (13 x 2 marks = 26)

> **What You Need To Do:**
> - Name your non-EU region.
> - Name one tertiary/service activity.
> - Discuss two factors affecting its development in 6/7 SRPs.

NOTE: Two sample answers are provided for each region.

Brazil

Answer 1: The development of tourism services in Brazil

In this answer the development of tourism in Brazil will be discussed.
Tourism is an underdeveloped but growing industry in Brazil. In 2011 around 6.5 million tourists visited Brazil which is a very low figure compared to France or Spain who receive roughly 75 million and 47 million tourists per year, respectively. Tourism income – from both international and domestic tourism – is worth 3·3% (€55·5 billion) of Brazilian GDP each year. More than eight million people are employed in tourism and 2·8 million of these are directly employed in the sector.

Physical and human factors affect the development of tourism in Brazil. Physical attractions include the Amazon rainforest and the Pantanal wetlands. Brazil has a warm tropical climate and beach holidays are popular along the Bahia Coastline.

Human attractions include the Brazilian culture in cities such as Rio de Janeiro and Salvador. Each year millions of people visit Rio de Janeiro for the annual four-day carnival. The largest tourism development is Costa do Suipe which can cater for more than 10,000 tourists. This purpose-built resort is designed to attract European tourists.

Domestic tourism is important in Brazil. It accounts for 11% of tourism-related spending in Brazil. Most domestic tourists are from São Paulo, a city with hundreds of thousands of wealthy people.

International tourism to Brazil is hindered by the long distances required to get there (a physical factor), a reputation for crime and a lack of tourism infrastructure such as hotels, well-trained staff and guides (human factors). The government is trying to overcome these issues. The Brazilian government has launched Plan Watercolour 2020. This international campaign aims to double the number of foreign visitors in the next ten years. The plan promotes five tourism sectors: (1) sun and beach holidays, (2) ecotourism, (3) sports, (4) culture and business and (5) event holidays. Events such as the 2014 World Cup and the 2016 Olympic Games hosted by Rio de Janeiro will also result in a large increase in international visitors. Tourism workers are now well trained and airport facilities and accommodation are improving.

OR

Answer 2: The development of transport services in Brazil

In this answer the development of transport services in Brazil will be discussed.
Transport services in Brazil are underdeveloped for several reasons. It is extremely expensive to build and maintain road and rail facilities in Brazil. This is due to physical

factors such as the large size of the country and barriers such as forests and wetlands which make the provision of a transport network costly and difficult. The population density is low outside of cities. Large urban areas are far apart, thus requiring thousands of kilometres of road and rail lines. The government has not invested in road or rail infrastructure until recently and just 10% of Brazil's road network is paved.

Over the last ten years human factors such as government policy have led to improvements in infrastructure. The government now aims to invest one per cent of GDP in transport infrastructure.

The best roads connect the main tourist and industrial cities in the south-east, such as São Paulo. The main toll roads managed by private operators are also in good condition, e.g. the main São Paulo-Rio de Janeiro motorway. However, most internal roads are old and do not have tarmac surfaces. To improve transport connections to neighbouring countries, the Trans Amazon Highway is being built across the Amazon to Colombia and Peru. This project is the largest in Brazil and will open up isolated regions to development.

In the cities public transport is well developed and São Paulo has one of the most modern tram and bus systems in the world. Public transport in São Paulo is very important as it is one of the most congested cities in South America. It has over six million cars and is the focus of several major national routeways which bring commuter and business traffic to the city. To cope with the demand for transport, São Paulo already has 17,000 buses and 3 rapid transport systems.

In order to cope with the volume of passenger traffic caused by the 2016 Olympic Games, airports in São Paulo and Rio de Janeiro are being modernised.

Rail transport is poorly developed and underused outside of the cities. Transport costs are high because of the long distances. Efficient rail routes are limited to a few well developed tourist routes. Only the lines operated by iron ore exporters are used to their full capacity. However, the rail network has grown by 20% since it was privatised and upgraded in the late 1990s.

Ports have poor loading facilities and ships visiting Brazil carry their own cranes to unload their goods. Some ports are being modernised, e.g. Santos near São Paulo has increased its capacity and now handles 25% of Brazil's port trade.

India

Answer 1: The development of tourism in India

A In this answer the development of tourism activities in India will be discussed.

Tourism is the largest service industry in India and accounts for roughly 10% of employment. Tourism is worth about 6.0% of Indian GDP per year.

Each year about 5.2 million international tourists travel to India. The USA and the UK are the two largest groups of foreign visitors to India.

Physical and human factors have influenced tourism development in India. Because of its size, the landscape is extremely varied with high mountains, river valleys, beaches, rainforest and rare wildlife such as the Bengal tiger found only in India. The Himalaya Mountains attract thousands of climbers and trekkers to northern India each year. India has many human attractions. Most people tour the 'Golden Triangle' of the cities of Delhi, Agra and Jaipur in northern India. These three cities are very well connected with regular train services and luxury tourist coaches.

Indian culture is a major attraction for many people who travel to experience Indian meditation and yoga holidays in Goa in the south-west of the country. Kerala, in south India, is known for its beaches, elephants and temple festivals. It is marketed as a honeymoon destination.

The tourist industry has to overcome several problems: factors such as poverty have hindered the development of internal tourism in India. Many people are poor and do not have money to spend on holidays. Also, India is a long-haul destination for many American and European visitors so flights are long and expensive. Foreign tourists are often upset by the obvious poverty and overcrowded cities. Terrorist bombings, such as the bombing of a well-known tourist hotel in Mumbai in 2008, also discourage tourists.

Government policy and improvements in transport are helping the development of tourism. The Indian Tourism Development Plan is upgrading tourist facilities and marketing India abroad. Government policy aims to increase international tourist numbers to 8 million by 2015. Improved air transport facilities in Mumbai and Bangalore and new luxury hotels are having an impact. Over the last ten years internal tourism has increased as wealthy IT workers from Bangalore and Chennai travel to the south-west coast for 'monsoon holidays'.

OR

Answer 2: The development of transport services in India

A In this answer the development of transport services in India will be discussed.

The transportation system in India is enormous. The human factors slowing its development are the old and failing infrastructure, lack of investment and a rapidly growing population. A physical factor is the huge size of the Indian continent. The cost of providing transport services across such a large area means it is extremely difficult to give transport services equally to every region. It has been estimated that India will need to invest €1.2 trillion in its transport services to support the growth of the Indian economy. Already the demand for transport infrastructure and services is rising by around 10% each year. Transport facilities are unable to meet the growing demand.

Public transport is the main method of transport for most of the population. Levels of car ownership are very low due to poverty; many people still travel by ox and cart. There are about 13 million cars in India yet the population is over one billion. Only around 10% of Indian households own a motorcycle so buses make up over 90% of public transport in Indian cities.

The economic backbone of the country is the network of 'National Highways' connecting all the major cities and state capitals. These roads are congested so travel times are longer than they need to be.

To improve road services, the government is funding the construction of a nationwide system of motorways. The main routeways will be the 'Golden Quadrilateral' connecting Delhi, Mumbai, Chennai and Kolkata. Two other major corridors running north/south and east/west will link the other cities in India. In rural areas the government began the Prime Minister's Rural Road Program. Its aim is to build all-weather roads to connect settlements with a population of 500 people or more.

India's rail network is the longest in the world and is an important method of transport. It carries over 18 million passengers per day. However the rail system is outdated with steam engines from colonial times still in use. Rail links between India and neighbouring countries are not well-developed. Only two train lines connect to Pakistan. Just two trains per week run to Bangladesh. In cities, modern suburban railway and metro services are extremely limited and are available only in four cities – Mumbai, Kolkata, Chennai and Delhi.

Sea ports are the main centres of international trade. In India about 95% of the foreign trade (by tonnage) takes place through the ports. Mumbai Port is the largest and handles 70% of sea trade in India.

South-West USA

Answer 1: The development of tourism in the South-West USA

In this answer the development of tourism activities in the South-West USA will be discussed.

Climate and relief are two physical factors that have made the region a world-famous tourist destination. The Mediterranean and desert climates in California and Arizona cause hot, dry sunny weather which attracts people from wetter parts of the world.

The relief, a second physical factor, contains many stunning landforms such as the Grand Canyon. This famous landscape receives over five million visitors a year. Yosemite National Park is another major natural attraction. Its landscape is based on glacial valleys carved through granite rock. It attracts those interested in climbing and other outdoor activities.

For those not interested in the landscape, there are many urban attractions such as the casinos of Las Vegas. The gambling industry is a human factor which encourages the development of tourism in the region. The casinos in Las Vegas are the second most visited tourist attraction in the entire USA. Over 36 million tourists travel to Las Vegas each year. This is worth over €6.2 billion to the state of Nevada each year.

The location of the film industry and many celebrity homes in Los Angeles has also led to the development of tourism in the South-West USA. The film industry tours of Hollywood in Los Angeles are very popular with tourists. Los Angeles has many other film-related attractions with 15 million people visiting Disneyland alone each year. Many tourists also visit the region to experience the 'Wild West' cowboy lifestyle in areas such as Phoenix.

The development of tourism in the South-West USA is helped by the fact that due to the climate, landscape and urban centres, it is a year-round destination. Winter sports are available in the Rocky Mountain resorts such as Aspen. The Californian coastline has mild winters. Urban areas can be visited throughout the year.

OR

Answer 2: The development of transport services in South-West USA

In this answer the development of transport services in the South-West USA will be discussed.

Road transport services are very well developed in this region. There is one car for every 1.8 people in the USA. Los Angeles County and Texas have the most cars.

Human factors have encouraged the development of the road transport network in the South-West USA. Migration of workers, rapid urbanisation, urban sprawl and economic development all combined to create a demand for road and rail networks across the region.

The South-West USA has experienced rapid urban growth and urban sprawl of its cities, especially Los Angeles. To cope with the increased population, a dense network of motorways has been built. Commuting long distances is common. Instead of investing in public transport, roads were developed and today people still prefer to use cars rather than use public transport. Cars and fuel are cheap which has also encouraged car ownership. Los Angeles has over 8 million cars, creating both crippling traffic congestion and the worst air pollution of any American city. A survey found that each person in California spends 2.6 days a year in traffic jams.

Because of the severe smog pollution and rising fuel prices, there is now a demand for better rail and bus services. Several new schemes are in operation to reduce car use. These include toll roads to discourage car use, lanes for cars carrying four people to reduce congestion, car pooling schemes and investment in public transport.

California is leading the introduction of electric cars with a law that demands that 10% of new cars are pollution free.

Government funding is vital for public transport development. In 2011 the government passed its Public Transportation Plan. Each year California spends over €1.6 billion on its transportation services and 20% of this is for public transport. The state of California has introduced several laws to help fund the development of public transportation to such a rapidly growing population. The most important is the Transportation Development Act. Under this law, sales of diesel and petrol are taxed at a rate of 5% and the money is used to fund transport projects. The public is in favour of more investment as each dollar invested generates six dollars in local income.

Chapter 16

The Dynamics of Regions: Human Processes in Ireland, the EU and Non-EU regions

Q

Distribution of populations:

2014 Question 4C: Account for the growth and distribution of population in a continental/sub-continental region (not in Ireland) that you have studied.

2013 Question 5C: Account for the distribution of population in a European region (not in Ireland) that you have studied.

2012 Question 4C: Account for the distribution of population throughout an Irish region that you have studied.

2011 Question 6B: Describe and explain the distribution of population in a continental/sub-continental region (not in Europe) that you have studied.

[30 marks]

Marking scheme for 2011, 2012, 2013 and 2014
Discussion: 15 x SRPs (15 x 2 marks = 30)
Discussion without link to a named or clearly inferred region = 0 marks
If you do not name the region or refer to specific places in your region you may lose nearly half the marks.

> **What You Need To Do:**
> - Name your chosen region.
> - Describe the population distribution/density in that region.
> - Explain the factors affecting the population distribution/density in that region.

Answer 1: Population distribution in the Border Midlands West Region of Ireland

Population distribution in the Border Midlands West (BMW) region is uneven. Rural areas (e.g. Co. Leitrim) have few people while urban centres (e.g. Galway) have higher population densities. Most people live in small urban centres along the main coastal and inland route ways (e.g. Dungloe, Co. Donegal). Physical and human factors affect the distribution of population in the region.

Physical factors affecting population distribution in BMW region

The high relief and infertile soils have prevented people from living in many areas of the BMW, e.g. Connemara and Mayo. Therefore, these areas have lower than average population densities, e.g. 20 per km^2 Leitrim, the Irish average is 60/km^2. In Connemara, mountain ranges such as the 12 Bens are too steep and rocky to build on. People avoid living there as these areas lack road and rail access and the land is not suitable for profitable farming. In Mayo, the wet cool temperate climate over the last 10,000 years has formed large areas of peatland that is too wet and soft for settlement.

People prefer to live on lowland areas of the BMW region. In Achill and Donegal, the narrow coastal plain between the sea and mountains supports a higher population density. Here the flat land enables farming, settlement and road construction; in Donegal, people are distributed in small urban centres along the coastal route way, e.g. Dungloe.

The many bays and headlands along the coast of the BMW are scenic and provide shelter; therefore, small towns have developed whose economic activity is based on fishing and tourism, e.g. Westport in Co. Mayo and Killybegs in Co Donegal.

Soils have affected the population distribution in the BMW region. The area with the most fertile soil is east Galway where shallow brown soils support small scale beef and dairy farming; the population density is higher in this area. In Cavan and Monaghan, Drumlins left behind by glacial deposition contain poorly drained boulder clay soil. This has prevented profitable farming and these areas have low population densities.

Human factors affecting population distribution in the BMW region

The availability of services and transport has affected population distribution in the BMW region. The main centres of population in the BMW region are Galway, Sligo and Castlebar. Galway is the largest centre with a population of nearly 73,000. Galway has many services such as hospitals, schools and shops. It has the region's only university (UCG) and is a route focus for road and rail transport. It is connected to Dublin by the M6/M4 motorway and has a regional airport. The range of services and excellent transport facilities has attracted knowledge based IT and healthcare industries, e.g. Merit Medical.

The population distribution is affected by rural to urban migration; due to its services, Galway is a centre of in-migration from other areas in the BMW. Across the region, 43% of rural dwellers work in urban areas. This means people commute and need transport services. However, public transport is underdeveloped due to the low population density. Rural depopulation is a challenge for the BMW region as young people leave for college and workers migrate to live in the towns.

The National Development Plan (NDP) is a government policy that helps reduce rural depopulation by funding local community schemes such as Irish language schools. This brings employment and income to rural areas and helps keep local services in place. Under the National Spatial Strategy (NSS), towns such as Galway, Sligo and Letterkenny are 'Gateway Towns'. Gateway towns promote economic development in the BMW region. They receive extra funding to generate employment in industry, healthcare, education, community and transport services. This helps people live and work in their local area rather than migrate to Dublin or leave Ireland. Development of smaller 'Hub Towns' such as Castlebar and Ballina, aims to prevent rural depopulation by providing employment and services in more rural areas.

Answer 2: Population distribution in the Mezzogiorno region of Italy

The Mezzogiorno contains about 21 million people, with 65% living in rural areas. The average population density is 40/km². The distribution of population in the Mezzogiorno region of Italy is uneven. Physical and human factors affect the population distribution in the Mezzogiorno region of Italy.

Physical factors affecting population distribution in the Mezzogiorno region of Italy

Soils and relief (landscape) affect where people can live. The Campania region around Naples and Mt. Vesuvius has the highest population density (400/km²) due to the low lying land covered with fertile volcanic and alluvial soils. The lowest population density is in Basilicata (<99/km²), a remote upland region with poor soils.

In the past, the narrow coastal plains were uncomfortable humid, mosquito infested marshlands, even though they had fertile alluvial soils. People avoided these lowland areas, preferring to live in small hilltop villages that were also easy to defend. Therefore, today, the rural population is distributed across a network of small to medium sized villages in upland areas.

The Apennine Mountains stretch north to south through the Mezzogiorno. These Alpine fold mountains contain limestone and have few rivers. The Apennines have low population density because the land is very steep, 45% is mountainous (over 400m) and soil erosion is a problem. The mountains prevent profitable farming and are a barrier to communications; in Abruzzo, snow covers the high mountain passes in winter.

Human factors affecting population distribution in the Mezzogiorno

The Mezzogiorno is a poor peripheral economic region. The Mezzogiorno attracts just 1% of Italy's Foreign Direct Investment; organised crime bleeds healthy firms of money they might otherwise spend on investment so there is a lack of well paid industrial work. With unemployment at 25% out migration is a problem, as educated people leave to find work in the north of Italy. Over 4 million people left the region between 1950 and 1970, mostly from rural areas this lowering the population density.

From 1950, a government policy called The Cassa Per Il Mezzogiorno Scheme funded agricultural and industrial development. This affected the distribution of population. Drainage of marshes, irrigation and reclamation of coastal lowlands made these areas suitable for farming and settlement. People were encouraged to relocate from their upland villages to farms on the coastal plains. This lowered the population density in the uplands and increased densities on the lowlands.

The Cassa Scheme developed heavy industry at growth poles in Bari, Brindisi and Taranto as well as Naples and Palermo. This attracted people to live in these coastal port towns. The towns provided jobs in heavy industry such as oil refining and steel. Population density increased in the towns e.g. Palermo in Sicily.

Investment in tourism under the Cassa Scheme attracted people to work in scenic coastal areas such as Sorrento. Airports and rail services were improved providing employment in these sectors.

Escape from conflict is a push factor that makes the Mezzogiorno attractive to illegal migrants from Africa, Albania and Syria. During the 1990's thousands of Albanian refugees fled conflict in the former Yugoslavia, to Apulia in eastern Italy. This led to a rapid rise in population density there. Since then, migrants have continued to arrive almost daily, causing an increase in the population density in the Apulia region.

Today, the population density in Sicily is rising rapidly due to the arrival of African migrants and Syrian refugees. They travel by boat from Lybia and arrive in Sicily daily straining housing and medical services. In April 2014, over 4,000 migrants arrived in Sicily over 2 days and 15,000 were rescued from sinking boats.

Answer 3: Population distribution in Brazil

A In this answer I will describe and explain the population distribution in Brazil. Brazil has a population of more than 193 million people. This population is unevenly distributed across the country.

Over 70% of Brazilians live close to the south-eastern and north-eastern Atlantic coast. In these areas the population density is over 160 people per km^2.

In the centre of Brazil, the capital city of Brasilia is a man-made urban centre of just over 2.3 million people.

The centre-west and the northern regions have very few people with a population density of under 10 people per km^2. These two areas cover just over 64% of the land area of Brazil but have only (15%) of the population.

The population distribution in Brazil is also changing from rural to urban. Over 88% of the population will be urban by 2015.

Physical and human factors have caused the population distribution described.

A human factor was the early colonisation of Brazil by the Portuguese who first settled on the coast. Their settlements became Rio de Janeiro, Salvador and Recife. The level of economic development is another human factor. The south-east of Brazil is an economic core region. Per capita GDP in the south-east is 300% greater than that of the north-east. The business and industrial capital of the country is São Paulo which is located in the south-east. Unlike the centre-west and northern regions, there are many resources and opportunities for skilled and unskilled workers. Rural to urban migration has also led to the high population density in the south-east. Poverty and drought in the northern regions are push factors that have also led to a high population in the south-east.

Government policy is another human factor that has affected population distribution in Brazil. Brasilia was built between 1957 and 1960. This planned capital city was intended to be a gateway to the resources such as land, timber and metals in the Brazilian interior. Many migrant labourers were attracted to work there and stayed on after the city was built. The government was relocated to Brasilia and thousands of civil servants and business people now live there. The city also has food processing, finance, IT and banking activities.

Climate is a physical factor that has affected population distribution. Because much of the interior of Brazil is tropical and equatorial, the natural vegetation is rainforest. This is not attractive for settlement. The hot (32°C) and humid (88% humidity) conditions are uncomfortable; insects and diseases are common. In other areas of the north-east, the climate is hot and dry and has thorny scrub vegetation, making it a difficult region in which to live. This is another factor causing the low population density there. The cooler tropical climate along coastal areas of the south-east and north-east are much more comfortable areas in which to live.

Answer 4: Population Distribution in India

A In this answer I will describe and explain the distribution of population in India.

India has a population of over one billion but the population distribution is very uneven. This is due to physical factors such as the climate and relief. It is also due to human factors such as availability of jobs and services.

The population density is highest along river valleys, in narrow coastal plains and in cities and their hinterlands. The population density is lowest in the Himalaya Mountains in the north and in the Thar Desert area of the north-west.

The most densely populated zone is along the Indus and Ganges river valleys. Here the population density is above 250 people per km^2. This region has constant water supplies, fertile alluvial soils and flat land. Millions of people live in this zone and survive by intensive subsistence farming of rice.

Another area of high population density is along the narrow coastal plains of the eastern and western Ghats. These regions have intensive subsistence rice farming as well as more commercial farming of tea, coconuts and cotton. Because there are so many large plantations, population density is lower in the Ghats than in the river valleys.

The major cities of Kolkata, Mumbai and Chennai have very high population densities. In Kolkata the population density is over 2,050 people per km^2. This high density is due to rural to urban migration and high birth rates. Poor people move to the cities for work, education and better healthcare services. Chennai is the centre of the high tech IT industry and attracts international migrants and local software developers to work there.

Mumbai is India's largest port and has many port-related jobs that attract migrants to the city.

The high relief and steep ground in the Himalaya Mountains cause low population density in northern India. This region is snow covered and lacks soil. Road access is poor and these factors prevent settlement in the area.

In the north-west, the dry desert climate of the Thar Desert causes a low population density below 100 people per km^2. Lack of water prevents agriculture and the population is dispersed among small communities where water is available.

Answer 5: Population distribution in the South-West USA

A

In this answer the distribution of population in the South-West USA will be discussed.

The population of the South-West USA has grown by approximately 1,500% over the last 90 years but the population is not evenly distributed across the region.

The population of the South-West USA is concentrated in urban areas and along the eastern and southern coastlines. The cities with the highest densities are San Francisco, Los Angeles, San Diego and Houston. These cities have over 400 people per km^2. The coastline between Los Angeles and San Diego is also densely populated. Much of the interior of the South-West USA is lightly populated with under 50 people per km^2. South-Eastern Texas has a slightly higher population density (100 people per km^2).

Physical and human factors have contributed to this distribution. Gold and oil are physical factors. In the past, the availability of gold attracted hundreds of thousands of people to the region to work in the gold-mining industry. Many of these people stayed even when the gold ran out. The hot Mediterranean climate in the south-west coastal region is a physical factor that attracts older people from northern states who retire to the region. Large retirement settlements have affected the growth of towns such as Sant Cruz in California. Tourism and recreational businesses have become important in the warm climate.

Many people move to the south west for better quality of life, more open space, less congestion and increased recreational opportunities along the coast and inland in the national park areas such as the Grand Canyon.

Government policies are a human factor that has affected the population distribution in the region. The Mining Act of 1879 encouraged the mining industry during the Gold Rush. The Homestead Acts made inexpensive land available for farmers. Public works such as irrigation, power generation, road building and water projects have encouraged urban growth. For example, the construction of Hoover Dam in the 1930s enabled the development of the Las Vegas area attracting thousands of people to work and live in the region. Before and during the Second World War, the expansion of military bases and ship and aircraft building industries brought many workers to the South-West USA.

Many local and state governments offer incentives such as low taxes, cheap utilities and inexpensive land to businesses that relocate from other states. All these draw people to the area for work. The presence of the high tech industry in Silicon Valley in California attracts educated migrants from the north-east of the country.

Q

2015 Question 5C

| Population dynamics | Language | Religion |
| Urban development | Rural development | |

Examine the influence of any **two** of the human processes in the table above, on the development of a **continental / sub-continental** region (not in Europe) that you have studied. **[30 marks]**

Process 1: influence = 2 marks
Examination: 7 x SRPs (7 x 2 marks = 14)
Process 2: influence = 2 marks
Examination: 6 x SRPs (6 x 2 marks = 12)

What You Need To Do:
- The information required for this answer can be found in answers already provided in this book. You can combine the material provided to build your answer to this question.
- Population dynamics can be taken to mean population distribution. See Answers 3 (page 131), 4 (page 132) and 5 (page 133) in this chapter for information on population distribution for your chosen region.
- Urban development for your chosen region is discussed in Answers 3 (page 83), 4 (page 84) and 5 (page 85) in Section (C) Chapter 11.
- Language and Religion can be discussed under the heading of Culture. See Answers 2 (page 78), 3 (page 79) and 4 (page 79) in Section (B) of Chapter 11 for information on culture/language/religion in your chosen region.

SECTION 3
Electives

→ Students must choose either Patterns and Processes in Economic Activities
<u>OR</u> → Patterns and Processes in the Human Environment.
→ You must do **ONE** question from your chosen elective.
→ Each question has three parts.
→ Choose the question for which you can do **ALL** three parts.

NOTE

The detail required in any answer is determined by:
• the context and the manner in which the question is asked
• the number of marks assigned to the question.
Requirements and mark allocations may vary from year to year.

Contents

Elective 4: Patterns and Process in Economic Activities
17. Industrial Location 136
18. Developed Economies 137
19. Colonialism, Globalisation and MNCs 141
20. Local and Global Interests 146
21. Ordnance Survey Map Interpretation and Photo Skills 149
22. Ireland and the EU 154
23. The Economic and Environmental Impact of Economic Activities 157
24. Sustainable Development 160

Elective 5: Patterns and Processes in the Human Environment
25. Population/OS Map Interpretation/Overpopulation 162
26. Migration 170
27. Settlement: OS Map and Aerial Photo Interpretation Skills 176
28. Urban Land Use and Functions 181
29. Central Place Theory 188
30. Urban Problems and Planning Strategies 193

Elective 4: Patterns and Processes in Economic Activities

Chapter 17
Industrial Location

> **Q**
>
> **Secondary Economic Activity: 2007 Question 7B**
> Transport, Labour, Capital, Environment, Energy, Markets
> Examine the influence of any **two** of the factors listed above on the location of one secondary economic activity that you have studied. **[30 marks]**
>
> **Marking scheme:**
> Name two influences: 2 marks + 2 marks
> Name an economic activity: 2 marks
> Examination: 12 x SRPs (12 x 2 marks = 24)

> **What You Need To Do:**
> - Name your secondary industry.
> - Choose two factors from the list in the question.
> - For **each** factor state one way in which it has affected the location of your named industry in 6 SRPs.

Answer

A

Two factors affecting the location of Johnson & Johnson (Vistakon) in Ireland
In this answer I will discuss the influence of markets and transport on the location of Vistakon, a contact lens manufacturer in Ireland owned by Johnson & Johnson.

Influence of transport
Vistakon is part of the American multinational company Johnson & Johnson and is the largest producer of disposable contact lenses in the world. It makes Acuvue lenses. Its Limerick plant is the only Johnson & Johnson lens manufacturing plant outside of the USA.

Transport facilities and accessibility influenced the decision of Vistakon to locate in Ireland. Ireland is a cost effective location for the manufacturing plant when considering the cost of transporting raw materials.

One of the main ingredients in the contact lens is a gel called Etafilcon A. This is manufactured in the USA and transported to Ireland by ship. Ireland's location on the western edge of Europe provided the nearest European location for Vistakon. This means that shipping is less expensive to Ireland than to elsewhere in the EU. Ireland's motorway network allows rapid transport of raw materials and finished products. The ingredients are transported by ship to Cork and Dublin where it is then carried by container lorry on the motorway routes to Limerick. Ireland's improved motorway network is an advantage. The motorway network of the M7 and M20 makes transport cheaper and faster within Ireland.

Influence of market

The location of the market for disposable contact lenses influenced the decision of Vistakon to locate in Ireland. Ireland offers the most cost effective manufacturing location between the markets and the source of the main raw material.

Although the lenses are sold worldwide, Japan is the main market. Ireland is closer to Japan than the Johnson & Johnson manufacturing plants which are on the east coast of the USA. So it makes economic sense to locate in Ireland to serve that market. Europe's population of 500 million is another reason to locate in Ireland as it provides access to this large market. Ireland's EU membership also reduces costs for Johnson & Johnson as there are no customs and excise duties payable on products sold within the EU.

The finished lenses are exported to the market in Japan from Heathrow airport in London. Heathrow is the nearest airport that offers daily flights to Japan. Heathrow also serves the large European market (500 million people) as well as the North American and South American markets. Motorway and ferry transport connections between Limerick and Heathrow are efficient. Lenses are transported to Rosslare by motorway via Cork. They are then shipped daily to the UK where the lenses are carried by road to the airport and flown to Japan, Europe and the North American markets.

Chapter 18
Developed Economies

> **NOTE**
>
> For the Leaving Certificate exam, you need to be able to describe changes in a developed economy over time under the headings:
>
> - Mass tourism and/or financial services
> - Financial services
> - Industrial decline
> - Footloose industries
>
> You will be asked to discuss the developed economy under one or two of these headings, e.g. 2012 Q8C and 2014 Q7C.
>
> Sample answers are provided below for each of these headings.
>
> Do not be confused if industrial decline is mentioned in a question on 'economic growth'. Decline can be considered as 'negative growth'!

Developed Economy: 2010 Question 8B

Explain the growth of any **one** developed economy you have studied under one or more of the following headings:

- Financial services
- Tourism
- Industrial decline   [30 marks]

Marking scheme:
Name developed economy: 2 marks
Examination: 14 x SRPs (14 x 2 marks = 28)

137

> **What You Need To Do:**
> - Name the developed economy you have studied.
> - Choose your heading and discuss the changes in the economy under that heading in 14 SRPs.

A

Answer 1: Financial Services in Ireland

Ireland is a developed economy. Financial services consist of businesses such as insurance, banking, investment fund management and aircraft leasing. The Irish financial services sector has grown considerably since the 1980s when it was first promoted by the government. Today there are over 500 financial service companies in Ireland.

Ireland is a preferred location for financial service companies for several reasons:
- A low corporate tax rate at 12.5% is a major attraction. In Japan it is 41%.
- Ireland has a unique workforce – 36% of the population is under 25 years of age.
- Ireland also has an experienced and skilled workforce.
  (The combination of youth and experience is very attractive to financial companies.)
- Ireland also has an excellent telecommunications and airline network. Furthermore the government has invested in transport and telecommunications infrastructure.
- Our membership of the EU also gives companies access to a market of 501 million people. Europe is midway between the American and Asian economies so European companies benefit from the time difference between both continents. European companies can do business easily with both regions.

The International Irish Financial Services Centre (IFSC) was established in 1987 to attract investment into Ireland from global financial services organisations. The main centre of the financial services industry in Ireland is located in the Dublin Docklands but financial service companies are located in 20 counties throughout Ireland.

Financial services are very important to Ireland's economy. Financial services employ around 32,000 people and contribute 7.4% of Irish GDP. Financial services account for 10% of multinational employment in Ireland. The selling of financial services from companies based in the IFSC contributes €2.1 billion in tax annually, including 36% of the total corporation tax take.

Ireland is a leading centre for aircraft leasing. Nine of the world's top 10 leasing companies currently operate in Ireland. It is a global market worth €104 billion with Irish-based companies owning or managing 19% of the roughly 18,000 commercial craft flying today.

During the current economic recession the financial services industry is losing jobs but doing better than might be expected. The IFSC provides insurance services across Europe and this sector is growing strongly with companies such as Zurich and Aviva deciding to establish European centres in Dublin.

Answer 2: Tourism in Spain

A

Spain is a developed economy. Mass tourism involves large numbers of tourists. Spain has the largest mass tourist industry in Western Europe. With over 60 million visitors in 2011, Spain is the second most visited country in the world after France.

Up until the 1960s many resorts in Southern Spain were quiet, traditional fishing villages but tourism in Spain has developed rapidly since then. This growth has occurred for several reasons.

Government influence was an important factor in the growth of the tourism industry in Spain. Mass tourism to Spain began when the Spanish government devalued the Spanish currency (the peseta) in the 1960s. This made Spain an inexpensive destination for tourists who were attracted to its low cost of living.

In the 1960s the Spanish Ministry of Tourism provided cheap loans and grants to build hotels, apartments, villas and camping sites in the coastal areas of Spain. This was done to encourage the development of what was then a backward and peripheral economic region. The ministry also planned and built a chain of national tourist hotels across the country. As the Mediterranean resorts have become overcrowded, the ministry has been actively promoting travel to the interior of the country, e.g. Seville. It has promoted the culture, history and festivals of the interior regions.

Social and cultural factors also led to the growth of tourism in Spain. Improved working conditions across Europe mean that workers have paid holiday time. Standard annual paid leave is now 5 weeks in many jobs. This has encouraged more people to take holidays and Spain is a popular destination due to physical factors such as the hot, dry and sunny summers in the Mediterranean climate.

The availability of cheap flights, car hire and rail links have encouraged millions to travel to Spain. The Spanish government has invested in new airports and high-speed rail services in southern coastal resorts such as Malaga in order to attract visitors to the region. The growth of tourism in Spain has led to many problems. Water is in short supply in many hotels and resorts in high season. Sometimes irrigation water for farmland goes to the tourist resorts instead. Investment in reservoirs has occurred but is very expensive. Overcrowded beaches and crime discourage some tourists from visiting more than once. Land prices have increased in scenic coastal areas due to the demand for holiday homes and locals cannot afford to live in the place where they were born.

Answer 3: Industrial Decline in Belgium

A Belgium is a developed economy. In the late 1880s the Sambre-Meuse river valley in Wallonia, Southern Belgium was the industrial core region of the country. The success of its industrialisation was due to large deposits of coal and iron ore that were exposed by the river as it cut its valley into the land. The industrial growth of Wallonia was based on coal mining and the traditional heavy industries of iron and steel, engineering and chemicals. At peak production, more than 120 mines employed over 120,000 people and produced 30 million tonnes of coal per year. However from the 1960s the mines in the region declined and mining stopped completely in 1992. The decline of the mining industry caused a decline in the iron and steel industries that depended on them for coal, their raw material.

Physical and human factors led to industrial decline in Belgium.

A physical factor leading to decline was the size and depth of the coal reserves. Over time the most accessible coal seams were used up and the remaining coal seams were too small, deep and fractured to be worth extracting.

Several human factors also contributed to the speed of the industrial decline. At EU level, the European Coal and Steel Community had a policy offering financial support to the most efficient mines across Europe. The Belgian mines did not qualify for this and could not compete with mines in Germany and Britain. In the mid 1980s, the Belgian government decided that the mining industry should be closed and the government presented a plan that would close all the mines by 1994. The government provided a €2.5 billion redundancy package to the miners to encourage them to leave mining. The combination of EU and government policy led to the end of mining in Wallonia.

Competition with more efficient coal mines and the availability of cheap coal imported from the USA and Poland also caused the mines to decline.

The impact of the closure of the mining industry in Wallonia was felt throughout the region. Many industries associated with mining, such as steel, chemicals and engineering closed. This led to unemployment levels as high as 20% and higher levels of poverty in Wallonia compared to Northern Belgium. People left the region to seek work in the richer areas of northern Belgium, e.g. Antwerp. Wallonia's GDP is less than 75% of the EU average so it now qualifies for EU Structural Funds and is classed as a Convergence region.

To overcome the social and economic problems, the European Structural Funds programme for 2007-2013 has allocated a budget of €15 billion to support the economic development of the region.

Answer 4: Footloose Industry in Ireland

A In this answer, I will discuss the development of footloose industry in Ireland, a developed economy.

Footloose industries are those that do not have to locate close to their raw materials. However, they may locate close to transport routes and a labour force. Many Pharmaceutical industries are footloose. The pharmaceutical (pharma) industry makes chemicals for medicines, healthcare products and medical equipment.

Since the 1970's Ireland has become a major location for the pharma industry. Nine of the top ten pharmaceutical companies in the world have plants in Ireland, e.g. Johnson & Johnson. The pharmaceutical industry is economically important to Ireland because it employs over 47,000 people and accounts for about 50% of Ireland's exports.

Pharmaceutical manufacturing is concentrated in Cork due to several human and physical factors. Government policy and Labour force are two human factors encouraging the location of the pharma industry in Cork. Since the 1950's it has been government policy to encourage foreign direct investment by pharmaceutical companies in Ireland. In the 1970's the Industrial Development Authority (IDA) purchased land banks in the Cork Harbour area at Little Island and in Ringaskiddy. The IDA also provided water, wastewater and power infrastructure to these sites. Then, using its contacts in North America, the IDA attracted several multinational pharmaceutical companies to the Cork Harbour area with a combination of grants and tax incentives.

The pharma industry requires a skilled labour force. During the 1960's and 1970's a government report called the Buchanan Report called for the development of industry across Ireland to counterbalance the growth of Dublin. The report identified Cork as a growth centre for industry because of its labour force and availability of suitable sites. Cork has a young educated workforce, 37% of its population is under 25. Cork has a university and Institute of Technology and several other third level colleges. University College Cork has developed specialist pharmaceutical degree courses and is an important supplier of qualified graduates to the pharmaceutical industry in the area. The availability of skilled labour is a major factor encouraging the location of the footloose pharma industry in the Cork region.

Another human factor encouraging the location of the footloose pharma industry in Cork is the transport network. Cork is connected to the rest of Ireland and Dublin by an efficient motorway (M8, M7) and rail network (hourly intercity trains to Dublin). This allows cheaper distribution of finished goods and raw materials. It also has an international airport used for the distribution of light, high value products.

Several physical factors have encouraged the location of the pharma industry in Cork. Cork Harbour is a natural sheltered deepwater port. The availability of a deep water port attracts multinational companies to Cork Harbour. The Port of Cork offers weekly transatlantic container shipping and handles all six shipping modes i.e. Lift-on Lift-off, Roll-on Roll-off, Liquid Bulk, Dry Bulk, Break Bulk and Cruise shipping.

Water supplies are another physical factor that encouraged the development of footloose industries in the Cork Region. Pharmaceutical plants use large amounts of water in their production; they also generate waste water that needs safe disposal. Effluent discharge systems were built at Ringaskiddy and Cork County Council built the largest freshwater supply system in the country to provide the required volumes of fresh water to the industrial sites.

Pharmaceutical production is often automated and therefore, energy intensive. The development of the Kinsale Gas Field was an important attraction for the pharmaceutical industry. In the 1980's a gas fired power station was built at Aghada near the harbour. This provides cheap electricity to the manufacturing plants in Cork Harbour. Natural Gas is also a raw material in some pharmaceutical processes.

Chapter 19

Globalisation, Colonialism and MNCs

Adjusting to the Global Economy After Colonisation

Q

Developing Economies: 2015 Question 7C
Examine the impacts of colonialism on an economy in the developing world that you have studied. **[30 marks]**

Marking scheme:
Impact identified: 2 marks
Name developing economy: 2 marks
Examination: 13 x SRPs (13 x 2 marks = 26)

> **What You Need To Do:**
> - Name the developing economy.
> - State the impacts of colonialism.
> - Discuss these impacts in 12 SRPs (making sure to say which are positive and which are negative).

Answer

A Brazil was a Portuguese colony for over 400 years and this has had a positive and negative impacts on the economy and society of Brazil.

Colonialism affected the pattern of trade between Brazil and the rest of the world.

Brazil was used as a source of cheap, unprocessed raw materials such as Brazilian wood, sugar and coffee.

While it was a colony a negative impact was that most Brazilian exports went to Portugal, other European countries and the USA. These exports were unprocessed timber, coffee and sugar. Brazilian industry could not develop fully as all processing of raw materials occurred in the colonial power — Portugal — and in other countries. Brazil's development was prevented as it sold the raw material cheaply to Portugal but in turn bought back the more expensive, finished product from Portugal. Even after Brazil gained independence in 1822, colonialism continued to negatively affect its economy for the next 100 years. Most exports still went to Portugal, Europe and the USA. Also the variety of products exported was very limited. By 1950 70% of Brazil's exports were just one product – unprocessed coffee. This meant that the Brazilian economy was hugely affected by changing world trade prices for coffee. As a result its income would rise or fall dramatically each year, making economic progress difficult.

To prevent this situation continuing post independence, Brazil introduced the Import Substitution Industrialisation Programme (ISI). This began in 1950 and was designed to replace imported manufactured goods with home-produced goods instead.

This scheme changed the Brazilian economy from being dependent on exports of a few raw materials, e.g. coffee, to being an exporter of a wide variety of high-value manufactured goods such as aircraft. Today, coffee makes up just 2% of Brazilian exports and Brazil is a world leader in the manufacture of steel, chemicals and engineering products. However the ISI scheme that financed the growth of Brazilian industry has led to huge international debts. *Car manufacturing – Belo Horizonte, São Paulo*

After colonialism Brazil was free to enter trade agreements with other nations. The *Rio* formation of a common market (MERCOSUR) amongst South American nations allowed Brazil trade freely with neighbouring countries such as Paraguay and Argentina. Exports to Argentina were worth €12.2 billion in 2010. National and foreign direct investment (FDI) allowed the country to prosper and pay back its debts.

Colonialism also affected society in Brazil. As a result of Portuguese colonialism and the importation of slaves to work on the sugar and coffee plantations, Brazilian society became divided into a rich, powerful, land-owning group of colonists and a poor, landless group of workers.

Inequality between these two sectors of Brazilian society led to social tension and positive political and economic changes in the country after independence. The first of these was the abolition of slavery in 1888. This was followed by political unrest leading to dictatorship rule that finally ended in 1985.

A positive impact of colonialism on Brazil has been the influence of Portuguese rule on social and political life in Brazil. Racial tension associated with slavery in North America is lacking in Brazil, people of all skin-colours mix well with each other. Also Brazil gained independence from Portugal without a major political conflict and slavery abolished without a civil war, unlike in the USA.

Colonialism also led to the development of the road/rail network across Brazil.

Q

Impact of Globalisation: 2013 Question 9B
Examine the impact of globalisation on a developing economy that you have studied.   **[30 marks]**

Marking scheme:
Name developing country: 2 marks
Identify impact: 2 marks
Examination: 13 x SRPs (13 x 2 marks = 26)

What You Need To Do:
- Name your developing country.
- Name two effects of globalisation (you may discuss positive and negative effects).
- Discuss these effects in 12 SRPs.

A

Answer

A developing country that I have studied is Brazil.

Globalisation can be seen as the increased economic interdependence between countries. The interdependence may be on trade, borrowing/loans, aid, migration and investment. Most developing countries want to benefit from globalisation. They can do this by increasing foreign trade, receiving more direct foreign investment (FDI) by MNCs as well as getting more foreign aid and loans.

Globalisation has affected the Brazilian economy in several ways.

In order for Brazil to benefit from globalisation, it had to undergo important political and economic changes.

A major political change included tackling corruption at government level. Up to the 1990s business in Brazil was difficult due to high levels of corruption in banking and government. Foreign companies and investors were discouraged by this. Many did not want to be associated with corrupt politicians and so would not invest in Brazil. In order to benefit from the global economy and attract foreign investment, Brazil had to have an honest and open legal and banking system. Laws to reduce corruption were introduced. The legal system was reformed. These changes have been successful and encouraged more external investment in Brazil. Over the last ten years FDI into Brazil has averaged 5.5 % of its GDP.

Important economic changes were also made in order to increase trade. For a country to participate in a globalised economy it must open its industries, agriculture and services to competition from other countries. Brazil did this by becoming a member of Mercosur, the southern common market, and by negotiating with the World Trade Organisation to reduce or remove trade barriers.

143

The removal of barriers to trade and investment had a major influence on the Brazilian economy. During the 1950s-1980s industries and agriculture in Brazil was heavily protected by trade barriers and tariffs. The Import Substitution Industrialisation (ISI) scheme also protected Brazilian industries from international competition. While this protection did allow economic growth, it limited the amount of growth that could occur. The impact of globalisation has led Brazil to open its economy to global competition and avail of International Monetary Fund (IMF) loans to allow further growth in the economy. The government also introduced a major privatisation programme and sold many state-owned industries such as telecoms, power, steel and cars to investors. This encouraged more FDI into the country by multinational companies such as Ford Motors. These economic changes were successful and Brazil is now one of the most powerful developing countries and could become part of the G8 group of rich economies.

Globalisation of the Brazilian economy had other important impacts by giving the population better access to consumer goods such as food, modern cars, personal computers and household appliances.

However, having a globalised economy also means that Brazil is at the mercy of international stock markets. In the 1990s foreign investors rushed to leave Brazil when its close South American trading partner, Argentina, suffered a financial crisis. At the time Brazil's economy was strong but was soon threatened by decisions made by investors in other countries. This is typical of the impact of globalisation, where the fate of countries does not seem to depend on the health of their economies, but on the passing waves of good and bad expectations that wash over the stock markets in New York, Tokyo, Frankfurt, Shanghai or London.

Multinational Companies

NOTE: Multinational companies is a popular topic. Examiners usually look for a discussion of the factors influencing where an MNC will locate. Students should be prepared to answer on a variety of factors as the questions listed below show. Be careful to answer the question and not just write everything you know about your chosen MNC as your answer must be relevant.

Q

2015 Q8B: Examine the mobility of modern economic activities with reference to one multinational company that you have studied.

2014 Q8B: With reference to one multinational company that you have studied, describe and explain any two of the following:
– Sourcing of raw materials and components
– Location of processing units
– Location of markets   **[30 marks]** (Answered on page 145)

2013 Q9C: Examine the factors that influence the global distribution of one Multinational Company that you have studied.   **[30 marks]**

2012 Q9B: Examine how corporate strategies influence the opening and the closing of branch plants of **one** multinational company that you have studied.
[30 marks]

Multinational Companies: 2011 Question 8B
Describe and explain the operation of **one** multinational company (MNC) that you have studied. **[30 marks]**

Marking scheme (2014 Question 8B):
Name a multinational (MNC) company: 2 marks
Examination: 14 x SRPs (14 x 2 marks = 28)
Note: Be sure to treat each heading equally, providing 7 SRPs per heading.

What You Need To Do:
- Name an MNC.
- Describe your chosen heading and its relevance to an MNC under each of your chosen headings.
- Discuss why the MNC operates in different locations.

Answer

A multinational company that I have studied is Johnson & Johnson. It is an American pharmaceutical company with research, development, and manufacturing operations in 53 countries including Ireland. Johnson & Johnson and its subsidiary companies make chemicals for medicines such as pain killers and cough mixtures as well as a variety of other products, e.g. skin care items and contact lenses. It employs about 1900 people in Ireland.

MNCs locate in many different countries in order to lower their production costs and maximise their profits. Where an MNC locates is affected by the sourcing of its raw materials/components and the location of its market.

Sourcing of raw materials/components
Sourcing of raw materials and components is an important factor affecting the location of and MNC. They will locate where power supplies and other raw materials are cheaply available. Johnson & Johnson manufactures contact lenses in Limerick and replacement joints (knee/hip) in Cork. The manufacturing process is highly automated and requires a dust free atmosphere; air conditioning, cooling and machine operation is energy intensive (requiring large amounts of power). Johnson & Johnson is the second largest energy user in Munster. Power supplies and carbon dioxide emissions are major costs therefore the company has invested €30million building two wind turbines at its Cork facility. These will lower energy costs by 30%. At its contact lens plant in Limerick (Vistakon) geothermal energy is used to run the powerful air conditioning systems that change the air 20 times per hour in the "Clean Rooms" where the lenses are made. This reduces carbon dioxide emissions by 512 tonnes per year.

A major raw material for contact lenses is Silcone gel. This is cheap to transport in large volumes by ship and is manufactured in specialist factories in the US. Transatlantic container ships arrive weekly in Cork Harbour and the gel is transported by truck to Limerick.

Water is another important raw material for the pharmaceutical industry. The industry requires large volumes of water both as an ingredient and to dilute waste products for disposal. In Limerick, the plant uses two wells on site to supply its needs and control the quality and volume of water used to make the contact lenses. In Cork, the County Council built the largest freshwater supply system in the country to attract industry to the Cork Harbour area. It also built effluent disposal systems to remove waste safely.

Location of Markets

Multinational companies increase their profits by locating close to their markets to reduce transport costs. Johnson and Johnson located in Ireland to gain access to its three major markets – Europe, the US and Japan. Ireland is a member of the EU, so by locating in Ireland, Johnson & Johnson sells its products free of import tariffs to the large (503million) EU market. Products are transported by road, ship, and air to the UK and mainland Europe (via Rotterdam). Although Johnson & Johnson is an American MNC, corporation tax in the US is 40%, compared to Ireland's rate of just 12.5%. It is cheaper for Johnson & Johnson to locate in Ireland and transport its products back to the US by air and ship from Cork. Japan is another major market for Johnson & Johnson. However, Japanese corporation tax is 35% so Johnson and Johnson increases its profits by locating in Ireland rather than in its market - Japan. Ireland is more than 3000km closer to Japan than the east coast of America is, so transport costs are lower from Ireland to Japan.

A variety of transport methods to the markets is used; road from Limerick/Cork to Rosslare, ship from Ireland to the UK and then air transport from the UK to Japan. Currently there are no direct flights from Ireland to Japan, so daily flights from Heathrow are used.

Taking raw materials, market location, corporation tax, and transport costs into account, Ireland is the cheapest manufacturing location for Johnson & Johnson.

Chapter 20
Local and Global Interests

> **NOTE:** In 2014, students were required to refer to **two** examples on this topic.

> **Conflicts of Interest: 2012 Question 9C**
> Examine how conflict can arise between economic interests and environmental interests, with reference to example(s) that you have studied.
> [30 marks]
>
> **Marking scheme:**
> Conflict identified: 2 marks
> Reference to example: 2 marks
> Examination: 13 x 2 SRPs (13 x 2 marks = 26)

> **What You Need to Do:**
> - Name the type of conflict, e.g. between economic and environmental issues.
> - Name the resource over which conflict is occurring, e.g. natural gas.
> - Discuss the example in 13 SRPs.
> - Mention the local and global aspects of the conflict.
> - Mention the environmental and economic aspects of the conflict.

A

Answer 1: Conflict over Fracking

Fracking

Fracking is one of the most modern methods of gas exploitation. Fracking is used to extract gas from shale, a sedimentary rock. Shale is a porous rock containing large amounts of natural gas known as 'shale gas'.

Although shale is extremely porous, it is not very permeable, meaning the gas does not flow through the rock. In fracking, a well is drilled, large volumes of water are mixed with sand, and chemicals are injected underground at high pressure to break up or fracture the rock. This frees the trapped gas, allowing it to flow to the surface where it is captured.

Shale is found under large areas of the Eastern USA and in Europe. In Ireland shale is found in Counties Sligo, Leitrim, Fermanagh and Clare.

There is much controversy over this method of gas extraction but it has many advantages. Because of this, conflict occurs between environmentalists, local lobbyists and governments over fracking.

Local people and environmentalists are concerned that the environment and peoples' health may be put at risk by fracking. Local communities and environmentalists argue that it contaminates water supplies with toxic chemicals. Fracking uses a mixture of water, sand, lubricants and poisons to keep bacteria and other micro-organisms from clogging the pipes. It uses hydrochloric acid to dissolve the excess cement in the pipes. If these fluids stayed far underground, they might not damage the human environment. The problem is that they find their way back to the surface through accidents at well heads, well blowouts, backflow of fluids to the surface and leaks throughout the system. Underground water supplies may be polluted putting human and animal health at risk.

Fracking can cause underground instability. In the USA, UK and Canada fracking has caused small earthquakes. The problem is that underground water released by fracking unlocks previously stable faults, creating a slippage that triggers a 'shalequake'. It also releases gas into the air and people are worried this will affect their health.

Huge amounts of precious water are used in this method of gas extraction. Some sites require 13 million litres per well. In addition noise, air and light pollution all occur at fracking sites.

However, as yet there is no scientific evidence to support some of these claims so governments are in favour of fracking and see advantages to its use.

From a government's point of view, it provides cheap fuel for countries with large shale deposits thus replacing expensive imported gas. In Ireland, we import 90% of our gas and fracking would replace some of this. In the USA, more than one third of gas used comes from fracking wells and shale gas is now cheaper than coal.

It provides 'energy independence' in Europe. Europe imports gas from Russia at high cost. Due to recent conflicts in the Ukraine which threatened energy supplies, energy security is a major concern. Furthermore, fracking provides jobs in areas that have few other resources. Using natural gas instead of coal or oil helps countries reduce their greenhouse gas emissions and slows down global warming.

Fracking is causing an 'energy boom'. In the USA 100 new wells are drilled every day and 2.1 million jobs have been created. This extraction method has helped the US reduce its carbon emissions to their lowest level in 20 years. Gas prices in the US are one third of what Irish and UK customers pay.

Some countries such as France have banned fracking but others are in favour of it. In the UK, Prime Minister David Cameron has pledged support for fracking and given companies licences to drill for gas. He knows it will create thousands of jobs and has offered incentives to communities to allow fracking in their areas. People opposed to the idea see this as a form of bribery.

Cameron believes that pollution from fracking can be reduced by having strong and enforced regulations to protect the environment. In the US the installation of proper gas collection equipment reduces leaks of methane gas by 99%.

In Ireland, Counties Sligo, Leitrim, Fermanagh and Clare are under exploration as suitable fracking sites. It is estimated that shale gas reserves are three times the size of the offshore Corrib gas field. In 2013 the Irish government instructed the Environmental Protection Agency (EPA) to carry out a two-year programme to assess the potential for and impact of fracking. No fracking is allowed during this assessment.

Fracking is a controversial issue but has the potential to provide cheap energy for many years. It will continue to cause debate and conflict.

A Answer 2: Conflict over the Corrib Gas Terminal, County Mayo

In Belmullet, County Mayo there is conflict between local and global economic interests. Local people have environmental concerns about the proposed site of a gas-processing terminal and pipeline bringing gas ashore from the Corrib Gas Field. These environmental concerns are in conflict with the economic interests of the Irish government and multinational oil companies.

The Corrib Gas Field lies 70 kilometres offshore from Belmullet, County Mayo. The Shell Consortium received a licence to exploit the gas, bring it ashore and sell it to the Irish government. This is part of their global oil and gas exploration activities. The Corrib Gas Field is economically important to Ireland as it will provide gas for about 20 years and will supply 60% of Ireland's gas demand. This will reduce Irish imports of other fuels and make the country less dependent on international gas prices and suppliers. This should have a positive impact on Ireland's balance of payments by reducing our bill for imported gas. It will also provide a secure supply of gas.

Development of the Corrib Gas Terminal and extraction of the gas has provided jobs for the local economy. Construction of the terminal provided 500 jobs and subsequently 50 permanent jobs. This has made an important economic contribution to a less developed peripheral region of Ireland where there are few industries.

The gas is piped from the gas field to the mainland. A high-pressure pipeline was constructed on land to carry the gas to a gas-processing terminal where it is made suitable for domestic and industrial use. The gas is then piped into the national gas grid and sold to Irish homes and industries. Local people were concerned that the pipeline bringing gas ashore to the terminal was located too close to houses (70 metres) and posed a risk to people living nearby.

In fact, local people did not want the gas-processing terminal located on land at all. They based their objections on safety issues and pointed out that an offshore processing plant would not need a high-pressure pipeline on land. Their fears were linked to Shell's pipelines in Nigeria, Africa where leaks and fires, with loss of life, have occurred on more than one occasion.

During construction of the terminal large amounts of peat were removed and placed on a nearby blanket bog. People were worried that this would be unstable and cause landslides similar to those that occurred at Derrybrien, County Galway and nearby Pollathomas.

After several years' delay, discussion and protest regarding the overland pipeline, the Environmental Protection Agency granted permission in 2011 for construction of an onshore pipeline in a tunnel under Sruwaddacon estuary. The area is still being monitored by the Garda and by human rights organisations to ensure that the development proceeds without further conflict. The gas supply started in 2015.

Chapter 21
Ordnance Survey Map Interpretation and Photo Skills

OS Map Interpretation Skills

> **NOTE**
>
> You will need a book of past exam papers containing OS maps and photos referred to in the book.
> When giving reasons for the location of any activity you must consider:
> - Transport links
> - Labour force
> - Market
> - Services
> - Availability of suitable space and site
>
> The answers below are chosen to provide a range of OS map interpretation skills.
> The points can be applied to any town or industrial estate/factory using evidence relevant to the map provided.
> Students should be prepared to discuss factors affecting a variety of activities, e.g. industrial estates, processing plants and MNCs.

Q

Ordnance Survey: 2009 Question 7B
Examine the Ordnance Survey extract that accompanies this paper. Using map evidence to support your answer, state and explain **three** reasons why the industrial estate is located at grid reference T 285 955. **[30 marks]**

Marking scheme:
3 reasons @ 10 marks each (broken down as follows):
Identify reason: 2 marks
Provide map reference: 2 marks
Examination: 3 x SRPs (3 x 2 marks = 6)

A

Answer

1. A suitable site with space to expand is available.
At that location the industrial estate would probably have been built on a greenfield site which would have been cheaper to develop and easier to provide water, power and sewerage. The site is on the outskirts of Rathnew and there are only two or three houses nearby (T 286 957) so disturbance to local residents would be minimal. The land is low-lying as it is under 20 m in altitude. This would also make construction and access easier when building the industrial estate. The area around the estate is probably farmland and this land may already be zoned for industrial use because it is close to Rathnew so there is land available should the industrial estate need to expand.

2. The site is accessible via several methods of transport.
The site of the industrial estate is on a regional road, the R750. This road is within 1 km of a junction with a national road, the N11, which is a major north-south route in the area. Any raw materials and finished products made in the industrial estate could be easily transported by road from this location which would lower the cost of the products. The closeness to the N11 means that trucks have access to the national road network within minutes. There is a railway line and station in Wicklow just 2.5 km away. It may be possible to transport bulkier raw materials/products by rail from this location. If not, the rail and road network allows workers to reach the industrial estate from the nearby settlements of Rathnew, Wicklow and elsewhere.

3. The site is serviced.
From the map we can see that the location has all the services that an industrial estate requires. To the west of the estate an electrical power transmission line runs across the land (T 283 958). The factories in the industrial estate may require power at higher levels than for homes and an electrical sub-station could be connected to the power line.

Because the industrial estate is close to the town of Rathnew, it is most likely connected to the water supply. Waste and sewage disposal would also be supplied to the estate from the local urban network. Because the industrial estate is close to the R750 and the town of Rathnew, it would be cheaper to provide these services and not require expensive pipeline extensions.

OS Map

Q

Ordnance Survey Map: 2008 Question 7B
Study the Ordnance Survey 1:50,000 extract that accompanies this paper. Using map evidence to support your answer, explain three reasons why Galway has developed as a growing economic centre. **[30 marks]**

Marking scheme:
3 reasons @10 marks each (broken down as follows):
Identify reason: 2 marks
Provide map reference: 2 marks
Examination: 3 x SRPs (3 x 2 marks = 6)

What You Need To Do:
- Focus on the reasons for the growth of a town, e.g. route centre, bridging point, labour, market, services.
- Name three reasons for the development of Galway.
- Give a six-figure grid reference to show where on the map your named reason appears.
- Discuss each reason giving three detailed points.

Answer

A In this answer three reasons why Galway has developed as a growing economic centre will be discussed.

1. Galway is a route focus.
Galway has developed because it has a variety of transport services and is very accessible. It is connected to its hinterland by national roads (e.g. N6) and several regional roads (e.g. R338). It also has a train station (M 302 253) and there is an airport to the north-east of the city. Economic development depends on transport to deliver goods and services to the local, national and international markets. The great range of transport services in Galway is an attraction to industry and for those providing services. Industry can locate in the Carrowkeel industrial estate north of Oranmore, which is a suburb of Galway. This estate is beside the N6/N18 junction, making it very accessible by road. It is also close to housing areas for workers and markets in Galway city.

2. Galway is a services centre.
The economic development of a town grows if it has a variety of services to attract people to live and work in the town.

Galway is a well-developed services centre. There are many schools in the area and third-level education is available at University College Galway (M 294 259). This attracts a large number of students to the area who all buy food and clothing and use the recreational facilities in the town, encouraging more economic development.

There is a hospital at M289 256 that provides health services. Hospitals are supported by many other businesses such as laundry, catering and cleaning suppliers and this encourages economic development. The city is also a tourism centre as indicated by the presence of two information offices, boating activities and a caravan site. Tourist centres always have many people passing through who buy food and accommodation. This money goes directly into the local area encouraging economic development.

3. Galway has a labour force and market.
There are many housing estates visible in the town, e.g. at Wellpark and Rahoon M 274 259. This shows that Galway has a large population and these people act as a market for businesses in the area. The population also provides a skilled and unskilled labour force for local industries. The labour force is likely to be well educated because of the university in the city and this may attract high-tech industries to the area. The presence of such a labour force and a strong market encourages trade and economic development.

Aerial Photo Interpretation Skills

Q

Multinational Companies: 2010 Question 7B
Examine the aerial photograph and the Ordnance Survey map accompanying this paper.
Using evidence from the Ordnance Survey map and the aerial photograph, explain **three** reasons why Carrick-on-Suir would be a suitable location for a multinational company.

Marking scheme:
3 reasons @ 10 marks each (broken down as follows):
Identify reason: 2 marks
Provide map / photograph evidence: 2 marks
Examination: 3 x SRPs (3 x 2 marks = 6)

Answer

A

1. There are suitable sites available.
Carrick-on-Suir would be a suitable location for a multinational company (MNC) because it has space and land available for a factory building. On the OS map there is a suitable site at S 442 238.

This site is flat, low-lying (under 30 m) farmland and it is less than 4 km from the town on the N24 national primary road. Multinational branch plants require large areas of flat land for their factory and car parking for workers. The site would also need space for product distribution trucks to enter and leave the factory. It has no large housing developments nearby so disturbance of residents would not be a problem during construction or plant operation. The site is on the eastern side of Carrick-on-Suir and therefore closer to Waterford, which is a major port. The site is beside the

N24 and would have water, sewerage and power supplies installed along or under the road.

On the photograph the only suitable site seems to be the fields in the right background. But although space is available, it seems too close to suburban housing and the town centre and may have planning permission problems.

2. The town is accessible.

Carrick-on-Suir is a suitable location for an MNC because it is accessible by several methods of transport. The town has national primary road and rail services. Although the River Suir flows through the town, this river is probably not used for shipping transport as there is no evidence of a port. There is also evidence of river deposition downstream of the town at S 415 216. Here there are small islands and the river is braiding. These islands are visible in the right foreground of the photo and are an obstacle to shipping. They show the river is not used for commercial shipping.

The town has a railway line and railway station which would provide access for the labour force and a possible means of transporting finished goods and raw materials. The station is on the edge of the town at S 407 220 and is seen in the right foreground of the photo.

The N24 provides road access to Waterford and Cork which are both major ports and may also have companies that would use the products of the MNC as components in their factories. The N24 would also provide access to workers and would probably be the main method of transporting finished goods and raw materials.

3. There is a labour force and services.

From the photograph we can see that Carrick-on-Suir is a town that probably has a large enough population to provide a labour force for an MNC in the area. It also has a variety of services such as a shopping centre in the left background, education and recreation in the centre background (school and playing pitches) and housing for workers in the right foreground. These would attract MNC workers to the area from other areas of Ireland and from abroad. They could also be used by local workers. On the OS map we can see that the whole region is very scenic with forested hills such as Carrigadoon Hill to the north (S 403 290) and the valley of the River Suir. The South Leinster Way walking route runs through the town. These suggest that the area is attractive to those interested in outdoor activities and quality of life would be an attraction for the employees of an MNC.

Chapter 22

Ireland and the EU

Q

This is a common topic and students should be prepared to discuss several EU policies within an answer, e.g. 2015 Q9C, 2014 Q8C, 2013 Q7C, 2012 Q7C.

European Union: 2011 Question 9C
Examine the impact of any **one** European Union policy on the Irish economy.
[30 marks]

Marking scheme:
Name policy: 2 marks
Impact on Irish economy: 2 marks + 2 marks
Examination: 13 x SRPs (13 x 2 marks = 26)

NOTE

You have several policies to chose from. The four main policies you may have studied are:
- Common Agricultural Policy
- Common Fisheries Policy
- Regional Development Funds
- Social Funding

An answer is provided for the first three policies.

What You Need to Do:
- Name the policy you will discuss.
- State the impact of the policy on Ireland's economy.
- Discuss the impact in 13 SRPs.

Answer 1

A In this answer the impact of the **Common Agricultural Policy** (CAP) on Ireland's economy will be discussed.

The CAP is the EU system for supporting and managing agricultural production in Europe. The CAP combines a direct subsidy payment to farmers for their crops and cultivated land with guaranteed minimum prices for farm produce. It also includes import tariffs and quotas on certain goods from outside the EU.

The money distributed to Irish farmers through the CAP has had an impact on the economy by supporting jobs, raising farm incomes, reducing rural poverty and improving food standards. CAP payments support directly and indirectly over 250,000 jobs in the farming and food sectors in Ireland. The farming and food sectors provide 9% of Irish GDP and are worth over €17 billion to the economy.

CAP payments raise farm incomes and living standards in rural Ireland. Between 2009 and 2013 Ireland will receive €1·9 billion from the EU in direct CAP payments. This money will be used to make direct payments to farmers and support CAP schemes in Ireland. It then passes through the Irish economy due to the multiplier effect.

Several CAP schemes have been introduced to increase farm income. The Rural Environment Protection Scheme (REPS) has been introduced to encourage farmers to increase the variety of work they do with their farmland. Many farmers now have agri-tourism operations linked to their farms, e.g. having 'open farms' for school tours or operating 'farmhouse B&B' accommodation during the summer months. Also many farmers in areas of poorer land such as County Leitrim have been encouraged to turn their land over to forestry. Other schemes such as the introduction of milk quotas have enabled farmers to get a regular income. Milk quotas work by giving each farmer a set amount of milk that can be produced and a guaranteed income for that milk. Quotas were removed in 2015 to enable farmers to expand production for export. The CAP also includes retirement schemes for older farmers to enable them to have an income after they retire. This has reduced rural poverty in areas of Ireland such as Leitrim that have poor land, elderly farmers and unprofitable farms. The CAP has also impacted on the Irish economy by improving Irish food production standards and therefore the reputation and sales of Irish food worldwide. The agri-food sector includes 600 food and drinks firms selling to over 140 countries and generating €24 billion for the Irish economy. Irish farmers who are supported by CAP supply such companies, e.g. Largo Foods in County Meath which produces Tayto crisps.

Answer 2

A The **Common Fisheries Policy (CFP)** is the EU's system for managing fish stocks and aquaculture. The CFP also funds the development of port infrastructure.

The money received by the Irish fishing industry is used to develop infrastructure and aquaculture. Between 2007 and 2013, the EU will provide €42.5m to support the Irish fishing industry through the European Fisheries Fund (EFF).

This money will improve port facilities, e.g. new ice houses and harbour walls, safety training. It will also be used to develop new markets for Irish fish products across the world. This includes such things as marketing Irish shellfish in Japan. The economic impact of CFP support for the seafood industry is important because 11,600 people are directly employed in the industry. This industry generates over €800 million for the Irish economy.

Under the CFP, the size of the Irish fishing fleet will be reduced to remove old, inefficient boats from the fleet and to help conserve fish stocks. The Irish fleet contains about 1,400 vessels and this is being reduced under the new 2006–2013 CFP negotiations. Although decommissioning of the fleet will lead to a loss of jobs, the CFP pays compensation to fishermen who stop fishing so that the economic impact of extra social welfare costs is reduced.

The CFP controls the amount of fish that Irish fishermen can catch. The Total Allowable Catch (TAC) is decided for each species by the EU. Fishing boats are allotted a portion or quota of the TAC. Inspectors check fishing vessels and catch records to make sure that the fishing vessels do not exceed their quota. This helps to keep fishing at a sustainable level. The TAC/quota system has resulted in a reduction in the number of days that a fishing boat can spend at sea. Currently fishermen can operate for 55 days each year. The value of the fish quota is important to the economy of Ireland. In 2011 the quota was worth €220 million. However Ireland's fish quotas are not as big as they could be. There is potential for an increase in quota sizes which would have a positive impact on revenues from fishing.

Obeying the rules and regulations of the CFP has meant that only the largest factory ships, which can stay out at sea for several months, are profitable. The CFP has contributed to the development of port infrastructure to cope with these large boats, e.g. Killybegs, County Donegal. The economic impact of this has been to reduce the number of small ports and centralise the fishing industry at fewer but larger ports.

Fishing is not always profitable and many fishermen have two jobs and fish part-time in order to make a living. To compensate for this, the CFP offers fishermen a retirement pension scheme which raises income for elderly fishermen in coastal areas.

Answer 3

A **Regional development funds** from the EU are given to all member states as part of its regional policy to tackle the economic and social imbalances between and within EU member states. The regional development funds are divided into Structural and Cohesion funds. Structural funds are given to all countries; Cohesion funds are additional funds given to the poorest member states.

Structural funds are used for the development of infrastructure, telecommunications, education and training and to support research and development in each country. These funds have had a major impact on the Irish economy. Since it joined the EU, Ireland has received €17 billion in Structural and Cohesion Funds.

EU member states are grouped into different categories for structural funding. The South and East region of Ireland (which includes the Greater Dublin Area) is in the Regional Competitiveness and Employment region. Funding for this type of region is provided to improve the job opportunities and economic attractiveness of the region. The Border Midland West region is classed as 'phasing in' to this category. Regions that are phasing into the Competitiveness and Employment group need extra money to increase the level of transport and communications infrastructure and for worker training programmes.

Ireland will be given €901 million in Structural funding from 2007 to 2013. The impact of Structural and Cohesion Funds on the economy is widespread.

Structural Funds have transformed the Irish economy, in particular by bringing about the rapid increase of Irish living standards to EU levels during the 1990s.

The Structural Funds have also contributed to the economy by increasing the flow of money into the economy. They have been used to pay for regional development, construction of road, rail, water and power infrastructure and human resource development.

Without regional funding from the EU many of Ireland's major transport networks would not have been built, e.g. the Dublin Port Tunnel, Waterford and Limerick bypasses, the Luas tram network, the motorway network and the broadband network.

Overall the economic impact has been to raise Ireland's GNP by about two percentage points above the level that it would be without them.

An educated workforce is important to the Irish economy. Many educational facilities are funded under the European Social Fund which is part of EU regional development funding. The expansion of facilities in the network of Institutes of Technology across the country and literacy programmes as well as university access schemes, e.g. New Era awards, are all funded under the regional development funding programme.

Chapter 23

The Economic and Environmental Impact of Economic Activities

Q

Environmental Impact: 2011 Question 8C
Pollution does not recognise boundaries and therefore can impact on the environment locally, nationally and internationally.
Examine the above statement with reference to example(s) that you have studied. **[30 marks]**
Marking scheme:
Identify pollution source: 2 marks
State impact outside source: 2 marks
Provide example: 2 marks
Examination: 12 x SRPs (12 x 2 marks = 24)

What You Need To Do:
- Name one type of pollution and where it is produced.
- Name one area far from the source that is affected by that pollution.
- Name an impact of the pollution.
- Discuss how the pollution affects the region named.

A

Answer
The international impact of acid rain

Acid rain is polluted rainfall with a pH of less than 5.6. Acid rain is produced in the heavily industrialised regions of Central Europe. The environmental impact of acid rain produced in Europe is seen most severely in Southern Sweden over 1,200 km from the source of the pollution.

Acid rain damages soils and lakes, kills aquatic life, poisons trees and damages metal pipes and buildings.

Acid rain is caused by the burning of fossil fuels such as oil and coal in power stations, in homes and in vehicles. Burning fossil fuels releases sulfur and nitrogen oxides into the atmosphere which combine with moisture in the air making it acidic. It is estimated that in 2011 about 7 million tonnes of sulfur were produced by the 27 EU states.

The acidic moisture can be blown thousands of kilometres across national borders before it falls to the ground as acid rain. The sulfur dioxide and nitrogen oxides also combine with dust particles in the air and they can fall to the ground as acidic dust.

Sulfur dioxide produced by coal and oil power stations in Central Europe, Ireland and the UK is blown by the prevailing south-westerly winds to Southern Sweden. Nature is able to absorb some of the acid but once the critical load is passed, damage to soils, plants, animals and lakes will occur.

Over 14,000 Swedish lakes and rivers have been severely acidified by this international pollution. Acid water prevents insects reproducing and leaches aluminium from soils which then washes into rivers and lakes where it poisons fish. Birds then die as their food source disappears. Many Swedish lakes are now classified as dead with no aquatic life at all.

Farmland in Sweden can also be acidified by acid rain and acid dust deposition. The soil becomes acidic and this can reduce crop production and affect tree growth in forests. To counteract the acidification, powdered lime is spread on the land. A dosage of 3–5 tonnes of lime per hectare is estimated to protect soil from acidification for 20–30 years with current levels of acid deposition in Southern Sweden.

In order to reduce the impact of air pollution, the Swedish government designed an international treaty called the Convention on Long-Range Trans-Boundary Air Pollution. Countries that sign this treaty undertake to reduce the amount of sulfur and nitrogen they produce and therefore reduce acid rain. Over 28 countries around the world including Ireland have signed this treaty.

Q **Environmental Impact: 2013 Question 8B**
Examine the environmental impact of burning fossil fuels. **[30 marks]**
Marking scheme:
Identify impact: 2 marks
Examination: 14 x SRPs (14 x 2 marks = 28)

What You Need To Do:
- Name an impact of burning fossil fuels.
- Discuss this impact, how it is caused and its effects.
- Solutions to the impact may be mentioned.

Answer

A An environmental impact of burning fossil fuels is global warming.

Global warming is the rise in temperature of the earth's atmosphere. It is caused by adding carbon dioxide (CO_2) to the air when fossil fuels are burnt in power stations and vehicles. Burning fossil fuels adds about 34.5 billion tonnes of CO_2 into the air each year. CO_2 traps heat from the sun inside the atmosphere and causes the global temperature to rise. As the atmosphere warms up, global climate and weather systems change and sea levels rise.

Due to population growth, increased car ownership and increased shipping trade, there is a steady increase in both CO_2 emissions and the amount of fossil fuel being used. At present, 33% of CO_2 emissions come from fossil fuels used in transport. Developing countries like China and India are increasing their CO_2 emissions from coal used in power stations. Chinese power stations burn 4 million tonnes of coal per day.

The environmental impact of global warming is felt across the world. Global temperatures are rising steadily with 9 of the 10 warmest years on record occurring since 2000. Since 1950, the earth's average temperature has risen by 0·6°C causing parts of the Greenland and Antarctic ice sheets to melt. In Greenland, the rate of summer melting has increased by 30%. In the Antarctic Peninsula, temperatures have risen by 2·5°C since 1950 causing the ice sheet to slide more quickly into the ocean. Together these two ice sheets hold 99% of the world's fresh water. If they melt completely, sea levels could rise by nearly 70 m, drowning most major cities in the world and valuable farmland. The ice sheets also influence global weather patterns by controlling the path of storms in the north and south Atlantic.

Global warming has already heated the oceans causing them to expand and rise by about 22 cm. This has impacted on low-lying Indian Ocean islands such as the Maldives, whose water supplies are contaminated by salt water and coastal erosion increases, leaving even less land to live on. The Maldives' government has bought land in Africa, should it need to evacuate its population.

Another effect of global warming is loss of tourism income. In Australia, the coral of the Great Barrier Reef is dying due to rising temperatures. The reef is worth over €1.5 billion to the economy and attracts over 2 million tourists to the region per year but could be gone by 2047.

Global climate patterns are also changing due to the continued use of fossil fuels. In the Sahel region of Africa, rainfall has decreased by about 30% over the past 20 years and drought has increased. Southern Europe is becoming warmer – extreme heatwaves and forest fires are occurring more frequently in Spain and central Europe. Rainfall patterns have also changed. Rain is falling in short, severe storms rather than over a longer time leading to flash flooding in the UK and Ireland. This has led to costly repairs and insurance claims. Winter storms have also become more severe causing damage to coastal communities such as the storm that occurred in December 2013 in Kilrush in Co. Clare.

As climate changes and governments realise the cost of the impacts to their economies, more investment is being made in renewable fuels. Global use of renewable energy is increasing. Renewables accounted for 21% of power generated in 2011. By 2040, 25% of energy could be generated from renewable sources (solar, hydro, wind and biofuel).

International agreements such as the Kyoto Protocol encourage countries to limit their greenhouse gas emissions and develop new technologies to reduce future emissions, e.g. biofuel development.

> **NOTE**
> In 2015 Question 7B, students were asked to discuss the environmental impact of economic activities on a local and global scale. You will find material to answer the local aspect of this question in Chapter 20.

Chapter 24
Sustainable Development

Energy sources

Q

> **Sustainable Development: 2014 Question 7B**
> Discuss the environmental and economic advantages of using renewable energy sources. **[30 marks]**
>
> **Marking scheme:**
> Identify environmental advantage: 2 marks
> Identify economic advantage: 2 marks
> Examination: 13 x SRPs (13 x 2 marks = 26)

> **What You Need To Do:**
> - Name two sources of renewable energy.
> - Discuss one environmental advantage of using renewable energy in 5 or 6 SRPs.
> - Discuss one economic advantage of using renewable energy in 5 or 6 SRPs.

Answer

A

Renewable energy sources (renewables) are resources that are continuously re-supplied by the earth, e.g. the wind, sun, water and geothermal energy. In contrast, fossil fuels such as oil, coal and natural gas form so slowly in comparison to our rate of energy use that they are classified as non-renewable resources that will eventually run out.

Using renewable energy has environmental and economic benefits for people.

Environmental benefits of using renewable energy

Using renewable energy reduces the amount of polluting fossil fuels that are used in power stations. This in turn reduces production of greenhouse gases such as carbon dioxide (CO_2). It is estimated that to keep global warming under 2°C and limit severe environmental change, the world will need to reduce carbon emissions by 80% by 2050. Using renewable energy will enable us to do that.

Using renewable energy instead of fossil fuels also reduces the amount of harmful sulfur dioxide released by coal- and oil-fired power stations. These contribute to acid rain. Therefore, using renewables reduces acid rain in countries such as Sweden and the north-eastern USA.

Using renewable sources instead of fossil fuels also reduces the amount of air pollution caused by harmful dust particles in the air that are produced by burning oil and coal. These tiny particles (PM10s) contribute to about 380,000 deaths in Europe each year. In the USA scientists estimate that increasing the use of renewables and other measures to reduce global carbon dioxide emissions could save 700,000 lives each year that would otherwise be lost due to air pollution.

Another environmental benefit of using renewable sources of energy is that less oil would have to be transported by huge ocean tankers and less oil would need to be extracted from the sea bed. These two activities lead to oil pollution of the oceans. Each year 1.3 million tonnes of oil are leaked into the sea.

Coal-mining activities would also decrease due to less demand for coal. Open-cast coal mining causes huge amounts of dust to blow over the land and can cause breathing problems in people and damages crops. They are also unsightly in rural areas. This impact would be reduced by increasing our use of renewable energy sources.

Economic benefits of using renewable energy

Using renewable energy sources has economic benefits.

It provides direct employment. These jobs are in the various plants that generate renewable energy, e.g. at hydropower stations and at wind farms.

Using renewable energy also creates indirect employment in jobs and economic activity in supplying goods and services to the renewable energy plant – people such as the banker who provides loans to the plant's owners and the workers who supply parts and materials to the turbine assemblers. Jobs are also available at local level for plumbers and electricians involved in installation of solar panels and geothermal energy in homes.

Using renewable energy also provides 'energy security' to the economy of a country. Ireland currently imports 96% of its gas needs. This dependence on an energy resource makes the country more exposed to rising prices and interruptions to the fuel supply. Since most renewables are not bought and sold on the international fuel markets, they are not subject to price changes resulting from increased demand, decreased supply or speculation on the market. Also, because renewable energy supplies are usually produced within the country, the supply is not controlled or interrupted by other countries, e.g. war or political decisions. Russia supplies 25% of Europe's natural gas. In 2009 Russia turned off gas supplies in a dispute with the Ukraine over payment.

A nation's fossil fuel dependence also has serious implications for its national security, e.g. the US sent troops to Kuwait during the first Gulf War in 1991. American troops were sent in partly to guard against a possible cut-off of their oil supply.

Renewable energy development can also contribute to economic growth by providing opportunities for countries to export their renewable technology and their surplus energy. In Ireland the potential for wind energy is so great that by 2020, Ireland could export as much renewable energy as we use. This could be worth €2 billion to the Irish economy.

Elective 5: Patterns and Processes in the Human Environment

Chapter 25

Population/OS Map Interpretation/Overpopulation

> This is a popular topic having been examined in **2012, 2013 and 2014**.

Q

Population Density and Distribution: 2008 Question 10C
Describe and explain, using examples which you have studied, the difference between the terms **population density** and **population distribution**. [30 marks]

Marking scheme:
Define terms: 2 marks + 2 marks
Name two examples: 2 marks + 2 marks
Explanation: 11 x SRPs (11 x 2 marks = 22)

What You Need To Do:
- Explain the terms population density and population distribution.
- Give examples to support your answer.
- Briefly explain why population density and distribution vary across the world.
- Focus on relief, availability of water, climate and resources.

Answer

A **Population density** refers to the average number of people per square kilometre in a country or region. It is calculated by dividing the population of a country or region by its land area. Ireland has a population density of 54 people per km^2. Population density is an average figure and hides the fact that some areas may have very few people while other areas have more. For example, in Brazil the population density is 20 people per km^2 but vast areas of rainforest in the Amazon have very low population densities (6 people per km^2) while city areas such as Brasilia have high population densities (410 people per km^2).

Population distribution describes where and how many people are found in a country (or region). For example in Ireland the majority of the Irish population is distributed along the eastern and southern half of the country.

Population density and distribution are closely related. The places where people prefer to live have higher population densities. Several factors affect population distribution and population density. They include availability of lowland, water, fertile farmland and resources.

People prefer to live in lowland areas that have plenty of water and fertile farmland as this makes food production easier. They like to live where there are many services and transport is easy. The majority of the world's population lives in a zone between

23°S and 60°N. Places like Europe, South East Asia and North East America have more people and higher population densities. People avoid extreme climates and steep mountains where it is difficult to live. Desert or mountainous regions such as the Sahara desert or the Himalayas have few people and low population densities because they are too dry or steep to support large numbers of people.

OS Map Interpretation skills

> **NOTE**
>
> The reasons for low population density on OS maps are usually the same:
> - Steep ground
> - High altitude
> - Lowland on a flood plain at risk of flooding
> - Lowland at coastal areas with soft marshland
> - Bogland areas
> - Lack of road access (usually due to the factors above)
>
> Students have to see which of the above points apply to the OS map they are provided with in the Leaving Certificate exam.

Q

Population Density: 2011 Question 11C
Examine the 1:50,000 Ordnance Survey map and legend accompanying this paper. Explain using evidence from the map, why the area to the east of easting 44 and north of northing 03 has such a low population density. **[30 marks]**

Marking scheme:
Provide OS map evidence: 2 marks
Identify reason: 2 marks
Explanation: 13 x SRPs (13 x 2 marks = 26)

What You Need To Do:
- State one reason for the lack of people in the area.
- Give a map reference to support your reason.
- Say why your chosen reason causes low population density in the area shown.

Answer

A

Reason for low population density on the OS map

There are few people (low population density) in the area east of easting 44 and north of northing 03 because the land is very mountainous. At Q 460 040 the contours are very close together indicating steep ground. Between the point at Q 510 040 and Q 510 030 the altitude drops nearly 300 m over a distance of 1 km. This is a steep gradient of about 1:3. The mountainous area around Slievanea has been glaciated and has many steep slopes around corries and glaciated valleys on the northern slopes of the upland area, e.g. the Coumahare Lakes.

Mountainous ground is nearly impossible to build houses or other buildings on.

Housing design would need to be modified to fit onto such steep slopes and this would make it very expensive. Providing water, power cables and sewerage pipes would also be difficult and expensive. Steep ground is at a higher risk of landslide and digging foundations would increase this risk. People avoid land like this because of these reasons so the area has a low population density.

Most of the mountainous land in the area is above 150 m in altitude and much of it is well above 400 m. The highest point is an unnamed peak (Q 516 064) which is 670 m. High ground is colder because the temperature decreases by about 6·5°C for every 100 m increase in altitude (the lapse rate). Colder conditions are not comfortable for people and it also makes farming more difficult. The area may be snow covered in winter making access to houses and farm animals impossible. High ground is wetter and cloudier due to the formation of relief rain; this would also discourage settlement in the area. There are no houses above 150 m in the area given.

Mountainous land is inaccessible, causing a low population density in the area. There are only small winding, third class roads and 'other roads' leading into the area. The third class roads stop at a height of about 100 m so anyone living above this height would not have road access. There is only one regional road across the upland region. It is the R 560 which is a major route from north-east to south-west. However in the area Q 506 065 there are Vehicle Restrictions which would mean the road is impassable in times of snow or cold icy weather so this road does not provide reliable access across the mountains. People do not like to live in inaccessible areas. Emergency services would have difficulty reaching them. Travelling to Dingle/An Daingean for education, retail and recreational services would be difficult. As a result of the presence of steep, high mountainous land the area given in this OS map extract has a low population density.

Overpopulation: Causes and Effects

NOTE: When a question asks for **causes** and/or **effects** of overpopulation, e.g. 2015 Q10C, you are expected to name and explain **TWO** causes/effects of overpopulation unless told otherwise. Factors affecting population growth include society, culture, income levels and technology.

Q

Overpopulation: 2011 Question 12B
Discuss the causes of overpopulation referring to examples that you have studied. **[30 marks]**

Marking scheme:
Identify two causes: 2 marks + 2 marks
Name examples: 2 marks + 2 marks
Discussion: 11 x SRPs (11 x 2 marks = 22)

What You Need To Do:
- State what is meant by the term overpopulation.
- Name two causes of overpopulation.
- State an example of each cause (two examples).
- Discuss each cause in 5/6 SRPs.

A   **Answer**

Overpopulation occurs when there are not enough basic resources in an area to support the population. Basic resources include food, shelter, clean water, fuel and farmland. Overpopulation has several causes including high birth rates and overuse (depletion) of resources.

Cause 1: High birth rates
Example: Sudan, Africa

Overpopulation has occurred in Sudan because of high birth rates there. The birth rate in Sudan is 33 per 1,000 and its death rate is 10.28 per thousand. This means there is a large natural increase in the population and it is in Stage 2 of the population cycle/demographic transition. In Sudan women have low social status and do not have easy access to education. Due to the lack of education, women have low literacy levels and this, combined with poor health services, has led to high fertility rates of more than 5 children per woman. The Sudanese government has not been able to provide enough housing, education/healthcare services or employment opportunities for its rapidly growing population. The rapid pace of population growth is putting a strain on existing resources such as water, soil, fuels and farmland leading to overpopulation. The farmland is then overgrazed/overcropped by the growing population of farmers leading to food shortages. As a result the Sudanese population is poor and has a low life expectancy of just 53 years.

    These conditions are evidence of overpopulation in this region.

Cause 2: Depletion of resources
Example: The Aral Sea, Central Asia

The Aral Sea in Central Asia was once the fourth largest lake in the world. This sea has been shrinking steadily ever since the 1960s when the then Communist government controlling the area decided to divert water from the rivers feeding it. The diverted water was used for the irrigation of huge cotton plantations. The diversion of water from the Aral Sea has caused overpopulation.

    The water level in the Aral Sea has dropped and once thriving fishing towns are now over 40 km away from the sea. Fishing trawlers are left abandoned on the now exposed sea floor. Unemployment and poverty have risen as people lost their source of food and income. Drinking water supplies have been severely reduced and the water that is left is contaminated with pesticides and agricultural waste from the cotton plantations. The town of Muynak, once located on the edge of the sea, was a tourist seaside town with a thriving harbour and fishing industry that employed approximately 30,000 people. Today it is a desert town with few jobs and it lies over 100 km from the shore.

    The Aral Sea is now less than 10% of its original size and considered to be one of the world's worst environmental disasters. The coastal communities it once supported have become overpopulated as the resource that once provided water, food and employment has been depleted.

Q

> **Overpopulation: Suggested Question**
> Discuss the effects of overpopulation referring to examples that you have studied. **[30 marks]**
>
> **Suggested marking scheme:**
> Name two effects: 2 marks + 2 marks
> Name two examples: 2 marks + 2 marks
> Discussion: 11 x SRPs (11 x 2 marks = 22)

> **What You Need To Do:**
> - State what is meant by the term overpopulation.
> - Name two effects of overpopulation.
> - State two example of each effect.
> - Discuss the effect in 5/6 SRPs each.

A

Answer

Overpopulation occurs when there are not enough basic resources in an area to support the population. Basic resources include food, shelter, clean water, fuel and farmland.

The effects of overpopulation can include lack of food, the development of shanty towns/favelas in cities, poverty, low life expectancy and conflict.

Effect 1: Lack of food
Example: Sudan, Africa

Lack of food is an effect of overpopulation in Sudan. Across the Sahel region of Africa in general, high birth rates and population growth have led to desertification and reduced food supplies.

Two thirds of the Sudanese population lives within 300 km of the capital city and the signs of overpopulation are obvious in this region of Sudan.

The rising population depends on wood fuel for cooking and this has led to deforestation of the region. Because wood is now scarce, cattle dung is burned as fuel. This deprives the soil of valuable nutrients and leads to increased soil erosion. Increasing numbers of people keep cattle and grow crops on the land. Population growth is leading to a rise in cattle numbers and overcultivation of land. The cattle trample the soil and eat the grass cover which makes it less fertile and easily eroded by desert winds. This overgrazing has reduced food supplies. Constant cultivation of land has depleted the soil nutrients, damaged the soil structure and reduced fertility. Over time the damaged soil is easily eroded and food production decreases leading to food shortages and famine. Overpopulation has occurred.

Effect 2: Shanty towns/Favelas in cities
Example: São Paulo, Brazil

Favelas/shanty towns are overcrowded slum settlements where people live in handmade shelters. Favelas lack basic services of power, water and sewerage. Favelas developed and grew because the city councils in São Paulo could not cope with the demand for housing by the rapidly growing urban population. Five per cent of the population in São Paulo lives in 1,600 favelas across the city. Favelas lack the basic services of a clean water supply, electricity, rubbish collection and sewage disposal. Shelters are often made of wood and the high population densities increase the risk of fire. The shanty towns are often built on wasteland or unused land set in a dangerous location. The land may often flood or be steeply sloping and therefore at risk of a landslide. It could be on a piece of land that has been polluted by local factories. The favelas are often centres of the crime and violence associated with drug gangs.

The government of São Paulo is trying to reduce overpopulation in the favelas by improving favela conditions. They have set up self-help schemes. In these schemes favela residents are given materials by the local council to improve their existing shelters. Residents set up community schemes to improve education and medical services. Local authorities are also providing electricity, water and sewerage disposal. This is happening in the Monte Azul favela in São Paulo.

> **Q**
>
> **Population Growth 2014 Q 12C**
> Examine the influence/impact of **one** of the following on population growth
> • Society and Culture
> • Income levels
> • Technology   [30 marks]
>
> **Marking scheme:**
> Name impact: 2 marks
> Examination: 14 x SRPs (14 x 2 marks = 28)

> **What you need to do:**
> – Choose your topic.
> – State the influence/impact that it has on population growth – this may be to increase or decrease it.
> – Explain how the influence operates.
> – Give examples to illustrate your answer.

Three separate answers are provided, one for each topic named in the question.

Answer 1

A

Impact/influence of society and culture on population growth

The status of women is a cultural factor that influences population growth in a country. In countries that do not treat women equally, e.g. Afghanistan, birth rates and population growth are higher than in countries that have gender equality, e.g. Norway.

The position of women in society is influenced by factors such as religion, availability of education and healthcare, which in turn are affected by the level of economic development in a country. In Afghanistan, the tribal leaders are conservative, religious males and women have low social status.

When the Taliban (a religious political group) came to power in Afghanistan in the 1990s, women's rights were greatly reduced. Women/girls were prevented from leaving their home without a male escort; they could not work or go to school.

Qualified female doctors, teachers and other professional women had to stay at home or risk attack. Women were denied access to education and healthcare, were forced to agree to arranged marriages and were expected to live as a wife and mother in their husband's house. The majority of girls and women could not read or write and were very dependent on male relatives. Lack of education and limited freedom of movement led to higher birth rates as women did not know about and could not access family planning services.

Since the 1990s some improvements in the status of women have occurred but the Total Fertility Rate is high: 5.3 children per woman. This has led to population growth.

Norway is a democratic country with strong laws that protect all citizens from discrimination. In Norway, women have high social status. Women are educated, live and work independently from men, choose their own partner, have access to health and educational services and have political and social equality with men. In Norway, the total fertility rate is 1.8 children per woman and population growth rates are low.

In other countries such as India, where females have low social status, the pressure to have male children increases birth rates. In India, male children are more valuable because they are more likely to work and bring home a wage to the family.

As in Afghanistan, most Indian girls do not have access to education. Over 60% of Indian women are illiterate and cannot access family planning services or get well paid work. They marry young and have large families.

Although it is illegal, the dowry system still operates in India. When a girl marries, her family is expected to provide expensive gifts and/or money (i.e. the dowry) to her husband's family. This is a huge economic drain on families. Therefore, if a woman has a female child, she is expected to continue having children until she has a boy, thus leading to population growth.

Government policy is a social factor that influences population growth. In the 1950s the Chinese government encouraged population growth to increase the country's work force, but this growth was not sustainable. In 1974, the government introduced its one-child policy. Population growth before the policy was 1.9% per year. Since the policy was introduced it has dropped to 0.7% per year. The policy has worked but has caused problems. As in India, male children were favoured and many couples terminated pregnancies if they were carrying a female child. Today, there is a gender imbalance in the population where males outnumber women by 60 million. The one-child policy is being relaxed. Couples can now have a second child if they are both from one-child families.

A
Answer 2
Impact/influence of income levels on population growth
Wealthy countries, e.g. Ireland, with a high standard of living tend to have low birth rates and low death rates. Highly developed countries are usually in stage 4 or 5 of the population cycle. Population growth is low or there may even be a natural decrease in the population.

There are several reasons for this. Highly developed economies, such as Ireland, have access to clean water, sanitation and well-equipped hospitals. In many developed countries, the government pays for medical services and provides unemployment benefit. Infant mortality is low (4 per 1,000 live births in Ireland) and couples are sure that their children will survive. There is no need to have large families to provide an income.

In richer countries, the status of women is often high. Women stay in education longer, work in well-paid, professional jobs (e.g. finance, IT) and marry later in life. The average age of marriage in Ireland is 32 years for women and 34 years for men. This lowers birth rates and population growth.

As a country develops, the population becomes healthier, wealthier and more educated. Many jobs are in well-paid industrial/service sectors. People have more money to spend on services. Laws prevent child labour and children may be economically dependent on their parents into their twenties. Childcare is expensive and this discourages large families. In 2013, the cost of rearing a child to the age of 21 in the UK was estimated at just over £220,000. The cost of child rearing reduces birth rates.

In less developed countries (LDCs) such as India, there is no government support for the unemployed, elderly or sick. In an LDC having a large family is an economic advantage as children and grandchildren can help support their relatives financially. LDCs are often in stage 2 or 3 of the population cycle with high population growth rates.

LDCs have low levels of healthcare. Access to a doctor or hospital is difficult and expensive. Clean water and sanitation are often absent leading to high infant mortality rates (in India the infant mortality rate is 43 per 1,000 live births). Couples cannot be certain that their children will survive. Therefore, they have large families to ensure economic security.

In LDCs the status of women is often low and this contributes to population growth. Women are denied education, marry young (the average age of marriage in Bangladesh is 18 years) and may not have access to healthcare services without their husband's permission. These factors contribute to population growth in less developed countries.

Answer 3

Impact/influence of technology on population growth

A Developments in agricultural technology have increased global food supplies. This has led to population growth. The global population is now over 7 billion people. When people have more food, they are generally healthier, their life expectancy rises and they have more children. These factors lead to a growth in population. There are many technological improvements in farming. It is now possible to support 1,000 people for a year on an area the size of a soccer pitch.

Glasshouse production allows farmers to grow crops all year round in artificial climate conditions. In glasshouses, computers carefully control the temperature, water levels and soil conditions, producing high yields from small areas.

Irrigation schemes provide water to dry areas and increase yields of cotton, rice and cereal crops, e.g. the Aswan Dam in Egypt. This raises the standard of living in poor regions and leads to an increase in birth rates as people become healthier and live longer.

Selective breeding of animals increases milk and meat yields from each animal, while crop breeding produces drought- and pest-resistant plants that can grow in poor climate and soil conditions, e.g. rice and wheat.

Development of farm technology lets farmers carefully control their farm activities. Tractors can be fitted with GPS map systems which control seed planting, fertiliser application, slurry spreading and steering. This reduces costs and raises yields.

Development of medical technology generally reduces population growth. This is due to a combination of factors. Vaccination programmes (e.g. vaccines to prevent polio and measles) reduce child mortality. In the long term these lead to a lowering of birth rates as families realise that their children will survive and so they have fewer children. Improvements in family planning technology reduce birth rates. Combined with access to education for women this leads to a decrease in the total fertility rate. This has occurred in India where the number of children per woman (Total Fertility Rate) has dropped from 5.8 in 1960 to 2.4 today.

Other improvements in medical technology include new medicines for diseases and new techniques for treating illnesses such as cancer and diabetes. Eradication programmes for diseases such as smallpox and polio lower infant mortality rates. These improvements increase life expectancy and lead to a decrease in birth rates over time.

Some countries have not used medical technology available to them, causing a rise in death rates. Today, nearly 28% of South Africans live with AIDS and 47% of deaths are due to AIDS. The government has been criticised for not providing AIDS drug-treatment programmes to its population quickly enough, thus leading to a spread of the disease.

Chapter 26
Migration

Q

Migration and Ireland: 2010 Question 10B
Examine **two** major changes in the patterns of Irish migration within the last one hundred years. **[30 marks]**

Marking scheme:
Name two changes: 2 marks + 2 marks
Refer to two time periods: 2 marks + 2 marks
Examination: 11 x SRPs (6/5 SRPs per change)

What You Need To Do:
- Name two changes to the pattern of migration.
- Say when these changes occurred.
- Discuss why each change occurred in 6/5 SRPS.

Note: The answer provided also applies to 2015 Question 11C.

Answer

Change 1: Emigration (out-migration) in the 1950s

During the 1950s Ireland had the highest emigration rates since the Famine of 1845 - 1848. Roughly 408,000 people emigrated in the 1950s. This was due to economic recession in Ireland at the time. Unemployment was a major push factor encouraging people to leave. High rates of emigration continued and the Irish population reached its lowest level of 2.8 million in 1961.

Most of those who emigrated came from the less developed rural parts of the country, such as the western region. The people who left Ireland were mainly agricultural workers, construction workers and domestic service providers (e.g. cooks, cleaners, child minders). The majority of male Irish emigrants moved to the USA or the UK to work in construction while women who emigrated tended to work in services. The UK and USA were experiencing an economic boom and labour shortages at the time and Irish emigrants supplied their demand for labour.

Change 2: Increase in Immigration (in-migration) 1990-2008

After the 1950s the Irish population slowly increased. But a major change in the pattern of migration was the high rate of in-migration into Ireland between 1990 and 2008. At this time the Irish economy underwent rapid economic growth (Celtic Tiger) and had a labour shortage. The resulting demand for skilled and unskilled labour in construction, healthcare and IT led to the in-migration of workers to Ireland, particularly from Eastern European countries such as Poland. Ireland's average annual net migration rate (the difference between the number of people emigrating and immigrating) increased until it was the second highest in the EU15 between 1995 and 1999. At the height of the economic boom in 2000, Ireland's net population inflow was 8.4 people per 1,000. During the late 1990s and early 2000s Ireland also experienced increasing in-migration by asylum seekers from some EU and African nations, particularly Romania and Nigeria, which contributed to migration inflows.

Today the Irish population is 4.47 million. Due to economic recession a pattern of net outflow of people from Ireland has returned.

Impacts of Migration

Impacts of Migration: 2011 Question 10B
Outline the effects of rural to urban migration in a developing region that you have studied. **[30 marks]**

Marking scheme:
Name developing region: 2 marks
Identify effects: 2 marks + 2 marks
Discussion: 12 x SRPs (12 x 2 marks = 24)

What You Need To Do:
- Name the developing region you will discuss.
- Name two effects of rural to urban migration.
- Discuss each effect in 6 SRPs.

A

Answer

In this answer I will discuss the effects of rural-to-urban migration in São Paulo, a developing world city in Brazil.

People sometimes move from the countryside to cities and towns in search of employment, educational opportunities and higher standards of living. This is called rural-to-urban migration.

Two effects of rural-to-urban migration in São Paulo are (a) the growth of favelas and (b) traffic congestion.

(a) Growth of favelas

São Paulo is a mega-city with a population of more than 20 million people. It is growing rapidly due to rural-to-urban migration. This migration results from pull factors such as jobs, health and education services in the city which attract people. Push factors in the countryside such as high unemployment rates and lack of health and education services drive people to the city.

Favelas/shanty towns are overcrowded slum settlements. Favelas have developed and grown because the city councils in São Paulo cannot cope with the demand for housing by the rapidly growing urban population. Five per cent of the population in São Paulo lives in 1,600 favelas across the city. Favelas lack the basic services of a clean water supply, electricity, rubbish collection and sewage disposal. Shelters are often made of wood and the high population densities increase the risk of fire. The shanty towns are often built on wasteland or unused land which can be situated in a dangerous location. The land may often flood or be steeply sloping and therefore at risk of a landslide. It could be on a piece of land that has been polluted by local factories. The favelas are often centres of the crime and violence associated with drug gangs.

The government of São Paulo is trying to improve favela conditions by introducing self-help schemes. In these schemes favela residents are given materials by the local council to improve their existing shelters. Residents set up community schemes to improve education and medical services. Local authorities are also providing electricity, water and sewage disposal.

This is happening in the Monte Azul favela in São Paulo.

(b) Traffic congestion

Rural-to-urban migration increases traffic congestion. With thousands of people arriving into the city each month, traffic congestion is a major problem in São Paulo. Over 1,000 new cars are bought there every day. Congestion levels are so great that the average speed in the city is just 17 km/h.

To combat congestion São Paulo implemented a rota system called Operation Rota where drivers are banned from using their vehicles one day a week based on their license plate numbers. It also bans traffic from certain city centre areas at peak time.

Due to rural-to-urban migration the city has about 6 million cars and 1 million motorcycles so the government aims to cut traffic by 20% by using Operation Rota and by improving public transport. The underground Metro system and an enormous bus system (over 17,000 buses) also reduce congestion.

Traffic congestion has led to serious air pollution in São Paulo. Public health is affected – adults and children experience pneumonia and other lung diseases. To help combat this problem, new rules have been introduced to reduce pollution from motorbikes as well as cars.

Donor and receiver regions: 2014 Question 10C
With reference to a developed region that you have studied explain the impact of rural to urban migration on donor and receiver regions.   [30 marks]

Marking scheme:
Name developed region: 2 marks
Identify impact on donor region: 2 marks
Identify impact on receiver region: 2 marks
Examination: 12 x SRPs (12 x 2 marks = 24)

What You Need To Do:
- Name your chosen developed region.
- Identify a donor and receiver region.
- Discuss the impact of rural-to-urban migration on the donor region.
- Discuss the impact of rural-to-urban migration on the receiver region.

Answer

A In this answer, I will discuss the impact of rural-to-urban migration on donor and receiver regions in Ireland, a developed region. Rural-to-urban migration is the movement of people from rural (countryside) areas to urban areas. In Ireland, rural-to-urban migration is occurring. In 1926, 68% of the Irish population was rural but by 2030 just 30% will live in rural regions.

Impact on donor region: Rural depopulation in the Border Midlands West (BMW) Region
Underdeveloped/peripheral rural areas such as the BMW region have many push factors causing people to leave. These push factors include unemployment and a lack of educational, recreational and health services.

Rural-to-urban migration has caused population decline in the BMW region. Between 1926 and 2011 some counties, such as Mayo, lost 40% of their population because of out-migration. Most of the people who left were young and educated. This has led to an increase in the elderly age dependency ratio as older people were left behind. Over time, this leads to further natural decrease in the population as death rates rise in an area with few young people.

Rural-to-urban migration also changes the sex ratio in the BMW. This is because the BMW is highly dependent on farming, forestry and fishing for its wealth. These sectors traditionally employ more males than females. There are fewer jobs for young educated females so they leave to find work in urban areas. This leaves a sex imbalance and contributes to lower marriage and birth rates in the BMW region, contributing to population decline in the region.

Rural depopulation in the BMW may cause a cycle of economic decline in rural areas. Once young people leave, it is uneconomic to provide services such as schools, post offices and transport. Local shops may lose business and industries avoid the region due to the lack of an educated workforce. In the western region, 30% of post offices were closed between 1992 and 2010. This further reinforces the existing push factors of unemployment and lack of services. Rural sports clubs find it impossible to get enough people to play matches; in the western region over 500 players have left the area since 2009. This leads to a decline in social events and loss of amenities.

Impact on receiver region: Urban Sprawl in the Greater Dublin Area (GDA)

Wealthy, developed, core urban areas such as the Greater Dublin Area (GDA) have many pull factors that attract people. Dublin is the centre of government with thousands of civil service jobs. It is also the financial services centre of Ireland and attracts workers from rural areas and other cities. The range of educational services such as universities, Institutes of Technology and second-level schools attract young people from across Ireland. These pull factors have caused high levels of in-migration. The GDA will hold 2.4 million (42%) of the population by 2026.

Rural-to-urban migration has caused urban sprawl in Dublin. Unlike other European cities (such as Paris), Dublin has not built high-density, high-rise buildings. Instead, it has become a dispersed city, building new homes and industries on greenfield sites on the edge of the city. This is because rural-to-urban migration causes a demand for new housing and increases house prices. It is cheaper and faster to build new homes on greenfield sites on the edge of the city.

The impact of this sprawl is that traditional commuter towns such as Swords, Naas and Navan are under pressure to provide services for a rapidly growing population. Housing, schools, medical services and water supplies have to be supplied while new residents oppose sewage disposal and landfill sites being located close to them. The population of Donabate in north County Dublin grew by 30,000 in 10 years and the need for sewage treatment is an urgent problem.

Loss of valuable farmland is another impact of rural-to-urban migration in the GDA. In order to reduce urban sprawl, new towns were built in Dublin. Adamstown is the newest and already holds nearly 10,000 people. These new towns were built on fertile brown earth soils, reducing the area of farmland available in the region. Wildlife habitats are also under threat as hedgerows and fields are cleared for new housing.

Traffic congestion is associated with urban sprawl. Commuters travel to the city centre for work and shopping leading to traffic jams and air pollution. The M50 motorway, Luas lines and port tunnel were built to try to reduce congestion in Dublin.

Q

Population Movement: 2007 Question 12C

Migration, both internal and international, continues to play an important role in shaping the populations of states and regions.

Examine one impact of population movement on the donor regions and one impact on the receiver regions. **[30 marks]**

Marking scheme:
State impact on donor regions: 2 marks
State impact on receiver regions: 2 marks
Examination: 13 x SRPs (13 x 2 marks = 26)

What You Need To Do:
- Name a donor region.
- Name the impact of migration on the donor region.
- Discuss the impact in 6/7 SRPs.
- Name a receiver region.
- Name an impact of migration on the receiver region.
- Discuss that impact in 6/7 SRPs.

Answer

A

Donor regions are those countries/regions from which migrants leave. In Europe, Poland is a donor region as many Polish people leave their country to find work elsewhere.

An economic impact of migration on donor countries is the loss of skilled workers from the population.

The loss of over 2 million people from Poland since 2004 has had an important impact on the economy and society in Poland. Skilled workers such as teachers, doctors, engineers and nurses have left the country in search of higher paid work in other EU countries, especially Ireland and the UK. This 'brain drain' of skilled workers from Poland means that there are labour shortages in Poland and this prevents the economic development of the country and the provision of essential services. From the late 1990s until 2009, Polish companies could not find skilled workers and therefore could not expand or provide more services. This situation in Poland has since improved due to the onset of economic recession in Ireland and an economic boom in Poland. Many Eastern European people are now returning to the growing Polish labour market. Associated with the loss of skilled workers is the decreased tax revenue to the government because there are fewer workers in the country. However, economic recession and the uncertain global economic situation means unemployment levels may rise in both donor and host countries. Remittances sent home to the donor region are an important source of income for the donor country. Due to economic recession, Ireland has once again become a donor region as more people leave the country to find work abroad.

Impact on receiver region

A receiver region is a country/region that gains migrants. In Europe, Ireland was a receiver region. In 2008 the country gained over 83,000 migrants at the height of its economic boom. Today countries with growing economies such as Brazil and China are receiver regions.

An impact of migration on receiver regions such as Ireland is the economic impact associated with the addition of workers to the labour force.

Extra workers in the economy raise tax revenue for the government. They also provide a new market for goods and services for business. In Ireland many shops and restaurants opened to cater for the Polish community here. There are also Polish- and Russian-language newspapers. These new businesses contribute to the economy through their tax payments and by employing workers. However there are also economic disadvantages experienced by receiver regions as new migrants place an increased demand on services such as health and education. These services are then stretched and waiting times to access health and educational services increase. The government then has to invest more money to improve the services, which may divert money from other projects such as transport. Economic recession in Ireland is discouraging migration here and some migrants and Irish nationals may leave the country as employment opportunities decrease.

Chapter 27

Settlement: OS Map and Aerial Photo Interpretation Skills

Rural Settlement

NOTE: This topic has been examined in **2006, 2007, 2009, 2010, 2013, 2014, 2015**.

Q

Settlement Patterns: 2009 Question 10B
Examine the Ordnance Survey extract that accompanies this paper. Using map evidence to support your answer, identify and explain **three** patterns of rural settlement. **[30 marks]**

Marking scheme:
3 rural settlement patterns @ 10 marks each (broken down as follows):
Identify settlement pattern: 2 marks
Refer to map: 2 marks
Examination: 3 x SRPs (3 x 2 marks = 6)

What You Need To Do:
- Find and name three patterns of rural settlement.
- Give a six-figure grid reference for each.
- Write three points of information about each type of settlement.

Answer

1. Linear Settlement

Linear settlement is visible at T 267 943 along the R752 regional road.

Linear settlement is seen where houses are built in a line along a road or coastline in rural areas. It develops because services such as electricity, water and sewage disposal are installed and supplied more cheaply along roadsides. Roadside locations are also more valuable because they are more accessible. Roads such as the R752 lead into towns and villages so people can reach town services such as schools and shops more easily while still enjoying a country lifestyle.

Many houses are built on sites made available by farmers as they sell off sections of their land. These sites with road frontage are more valuable and are sold more easily because they may be already serviced with lighting, water, sewerage and power by the local council.

2. Dispersed Settlement

Dispersed settlement is visible at T 269 915.

This pattern is seen where there are houses and buildings scattered across the map. It develops in farming areas. In the area on the map west of Wicklow Town the land is hilly and quite steep which can be seen by the closely-spaced contour lines at T 290 930. The land is probably not suitable for large housing developments because of the relief. As a result dispersed settlement shows isolated farmhouses. The farmhouses are located at the end of small mountain roads that may not be suitable for two-lane traffic. These tracks are classed as 'other roads' on the map legend.

3. Clustered Settlement

Clustered rural settlement is visible at O 299 003.

This type of rural settlement has several houses grouped together. They are often found at the end of small roads branching from larger routeways. The clusters may be family groups of houses or a group of farm buildings close to water. At the location given, the cluster is on a raised dry point at 20 m above sea level. The surrounding area is a low-lying coastal region and may have wet, sandy, unstable ground that is unsuitable for housing foundations. The settlement may date back to the time of the Plantations in the sixteenth century as the nearby land is called Castlegrange. In the time of the Plantation the term 'grange' referred to an area of land with farm buildings. In modern times rural clusters may also be small modern housing developments in the countryside. This can be seen at T 337 913 near Long Rock. This is a planned clustered housing area in a scenic coastal location.

Historic Settlement

Historic Settlement: 2010 Question 10C (See also 2015 Question 12C)
Examine the 1:50,000 Ordnance Survey map of Carrick-on-Suir that accompanies this paper.
Using evidence from the map, describe and explain **three** different examples of historic settlement. **[30 marks]**

> **Marking scheme:**
> 3 historic settlements @ 10 marks each (broken down as follows):
> Identify settlement: 2 marks
> Refer to map: 2 marks
> Examination: 3 x SRPs (3 x 2 marks = 6)

> **What You Need To Do:**
> - Find and name three pieces of evidence of historic settlement.
>   **Note:** They must be from different time periods.
> - Give a six-figure grid reference for each.
> - Write three points of information about each type of settlement.

Answer

A

1. New Stone Age Settlement: 3500 BC
A megalithic tomb is visible at S 430 283 on Kilmacoliver Hill.
Megalithic tombs are evidence of New Stone Age settlement in an area. New Stone Age people were hunter-gatherers who may have begun to live more permanently in an area than their predecessors. They built large burial chambers from massive stones (megaliths). These tombs are usually found on high places in the landscape, as on this map. Building tombs on high ground meant that they were visible from a great distance and that may have had some personal importance to the living relatives of the dead.

Their tombs can be also be found on lowland fertile landscapes, close to a regular water supply and at dry points above a river, e.g. at S 416 243. Many tombs are made of huge stones and the sheer size of these tombs shows the skill these people had in moving such huge stones and boulders.

2. Iron Age/Celtic Settlement: 600 BC
A hillfort is visible at S 369 285.
Hillforts are evidence of Iron Age settlement in an area. During the Iron Age people were very concerned with defence and built large circular enclosures with a ditch on the outer side of hill tops. They are defensive settlements made of earth and are usually found on hilltops, where people can keep a lookout over their land. Hillforts are quite large, often enclosing 20 hectares of land. A large number of people would have been required to properly defend them and the ringforts may also have had several houses built within them. People lived in them and kept animals there. There are four smaller ringforts within a kilometre of this hillfort and the people living in them may have used the hillfort for protection or may have been called upon to defend the area when necessary.

3. Early Christian Settlement: 500 – 800 AD
High crosses are visible at S 414 292 (Ahenny High Crosses).
These crosses are large, carved stone crosses. They are evidence of early Christian settlement in an area. High crosses are found throughout Ireland but especially in the

south-east region on old monastic sites. They are highly decorated and show scenes from the Bible. High crosses often acted as status symbols for a monastery or a wealthy person. These crosses were probably used as meeting points for religious ceremonies. Some were used to mark land boundaries.

Urban Development: OS Map and Aerial Photo Interpretation Skills

> **NOTE**
>
> When asked to interpret a map AND photo remember to give evidence from each.
> Towns develop for similar reasons. These reasons are:
> - Route centre
> - Bridging point
> - Services centre
> - Fertile hinterland
> - Sheltered harbour
> - Dry point
>
> Students have to see which of the above points apply to the map and photo they are given in the Leaving Certificate exam.

Q

Aerial Photo and Ordnance Survey Map: 2011 Question 12C
Using the aerial photograph, the 1:50,000 Ordnance Survey map and the legend that accompany this paper, explain **three** reasons for the development of the urban area of Dingle/An Daingean at this site. **[30 marks]**

Marking scheme:
3 reasons @ 10 marks each (broken down as follows):
Identify reason: 2 marks
Refer to map/photo: 2 marks
Examination: 3 x SRPs (3 x 2 marks = 6)
Note: You must have at least **one** piece of evidence from the OS map and **one** piece of evidence from the photo.

What You Need To Do:
- State each reason. At least one should be based on map evidence.
- Give one/two six-figure grid reference(s) for evidence supporting your stated reason.
- Give one/two aerial photo locations for evidence supporting your stated reason.
- Explain in 3 SRPs each how your chosen reasons led to the development of the town at its location.

Answer

A

1. It is a sheltered site and harbour.
On the OS map the site of Dingle is a south-west facing sheltered harbour. It is located on lowland between the coast and 40 m above sea level. It is also situated at the mouth of a gently sloping valley which is facing south-west. This valley is sheltered by high ground such as An Chorr at Q 468 028.

The sheltered conditions and harbour location would have encouraged settlement in the area which has few alternative places for larger settlements. The land to the north is too high and steep. The sheltered inlet to the east at Short Strand (Q 485 003) is too narrow and shallow for fishing boats to enter. The coast to the south and east has sea cliffs. The land around Dingle/An Daingean is not suitable for commercial farming and so fishing would provide an income for people in the area. There is evidence of fishing activity at Dingle/An Daingean in the aerial photo located in the left foreground where piers and large quaysides have been built for fishing trawlers.

2. It is a route centre.
From the map and photograph, the site of Dingle/An Daingean is seen to be a route centre. It is connected to its hinterland by regional roads such as the R559 from the west and north-west and the national secondary road, the N86, from the east. The junction of these roads is visible at the roundabout in the centre of the photo. Towns develop at route centres because they are accessible and businesses are more profitable because of the greater levels of trade. People in the hinterland can easily reach the town for services they need such as schools and shops. Businesses also need road transport to distribute goods and attract customers. Dingle/An Daingean is the most accessible location in the area shown with routes entering it from all directions. It has a Nodality Index of 6. This would have helped the development of the town at this site.

3. It is a services centre.
From the photograph it can be seen that Dingle/An Daingean is a service centre for its hinterland. In the right foreground there are two large playing pitches and a viewing stand. This suggests that the town is an important recreational centre for GAA/soccer and other games.

In the centre background are a church, housing and shops. These suggest that the town provides religious, residential and retail services for people in the town and its hinterland. In the left foreground recreational boats are tied up at the pier suggesting a tourism function for the town. Boating activities are available for tourists in the harbour at Q 442 005.

This variety of services is an important reason for the development of Dingle/An Daingean at this location. Services attract people to live in the town. The harbour and pitches attract visitors to the town and provide a variety of jobs for its population. Towns with a variety of services continue to grow as they create jobs in other industries which support them such as agriculture, restaurants and clothing. Towns with a range of services also attract other businesses that benefit from the large market and labour force, e.g. light industry.

Chapter 28
Urban Land Use and Functions – Aerial Photo Interpretation

Burgess Concentric Zone Model

Q

Development Models: (Sample paper) 2005 Question 11B
Examine briefly **one** theoretical model which attempts to explain the development of land use zones in a developed world city. **[30 marks]**

Proposed marking scheme:
Name model: 2 marks
Name city: 2 marks
Discussion: 13 x SRPs (13 x 2 marks = 26)

What You Need To Do:
- Name the land use model you are discussing.
- Name a city to which the model applies.
- Discuss how the model was developed and what it shows. In your discussion describe any problems that it might have.

A

Answer

The Burgess Concentric Zone Model of urban land use is one theory which attempts to explain land use in a developed world city.

This theory was developed by Ernest Burgess in 1925. He studied residential land use in Chicago, USA and observed that:

1. Land use was organised in concentric zones around the Central Business District (CBD) of the city he studied.
2. Land values are highest in the city centre.
3. Socio-economic status improved as you travel out from the city centre. Poorer people lived in the city centre and richer people lived in the suburbs or urban boundary.

Burgess recognised 5 zones of land use, which were organised in concentric circles around the CBD.

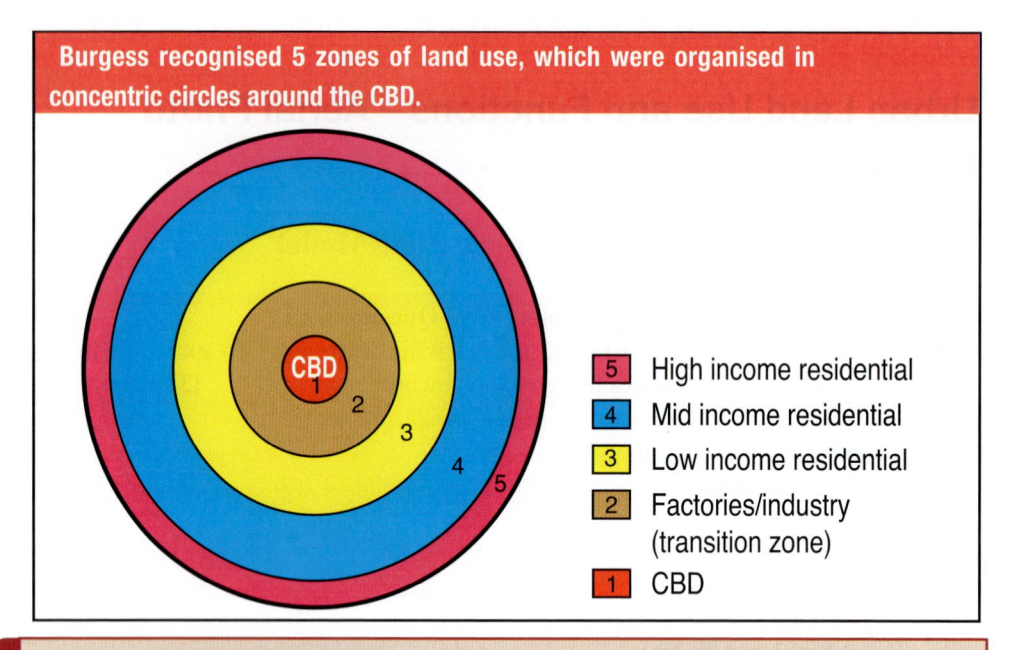

5	High income residential
4	Mid income residential
3	Low income residential
2	Factories/industry (transition zone)
1	CBD

NOTE: You are not required to draw this diagram in the Leaving Certificate exam unless it is asked for in the question.

Burgess recognised 5 zones of land use.

Zone 1 The CBD, containing shops and offices. The CBD generally expands into Zone 2.

Zone 2 The transition zone, an area of changing land use. Here old traditional industrial buildings such as breweries and textile factories were located. The workers in these factories lived in poor quality housing nearby. Today this zone contains a mix of derelict sites and redeveloped buildings.

Zone 3 This zone contained lower income housing.

Zone 4 This zone contained middle income housing, with more space and gardens.

Zone 5 This was the commuter zone containing higher income housing, e.g. large detached housing. Towns and villages within about an hour of the CBD are included here.

In Burgess' time, society was socially and economically segregated. Wealthy people did not live close to or socialise with those who were less well off. Also in his time the poorest housing was found close to the edge of the CBD.

The Burgess Concentric Zone Model of urban land use has several problems that make it difficult to apply to modern developed world cities:

- He assumed that the land a city develops on is flat and featureless. In reality, this is not the case. Many cities are divided by rivers (Dublin), valleys or irregularly-shaped harbours (Cork). These features change the pattern of land use and prevent the development of a concentric pattern.

- Burgess' model was developed before high levels of car ownership and commuting occurred. In his day only the rich could afford transport and live on the outskirts of a city. Today all members of society may live on the edge of an urban area regardless of income levels.
- Burgess did not consider that industry and transport links could impact on the location of residential or other land use.

Hoyt's Sector Model

Q

Dynamics of Settlement: 2012 Question 10C
Describe and explain the land use zones in a city that you have studied.
[30 marks]

Marking scheme:
Name city: 2 marks
Examination: 14 x SRPs (14 x 2 marks = 28)

What You Need To Do:
- Decide which model you are going to discuss.
- Name the city you have studied to which this model applies.
- Discuss the ways in which this model applies to your city in 14 SRPs.
- In your discussion you should mention each land use zone and give a named place for each land use zone in your city. If your chosen city does not exactly match the model, point this out in your answer and say why it is different.

Answer

A

Hoyt Sector Model, Dublin city

A city I have studied is Dublin. Dublin shows several patterns of land use that agree with the Sector Model devised by Hoyt.

Hoyt stated that cities expand outwards from the Central Business District (CBD) along routeways. Spaces in between routeways are later filled in with housing, retail and other developments. In this way a city develops in 'sectors', which is why this is called the Sector Model.

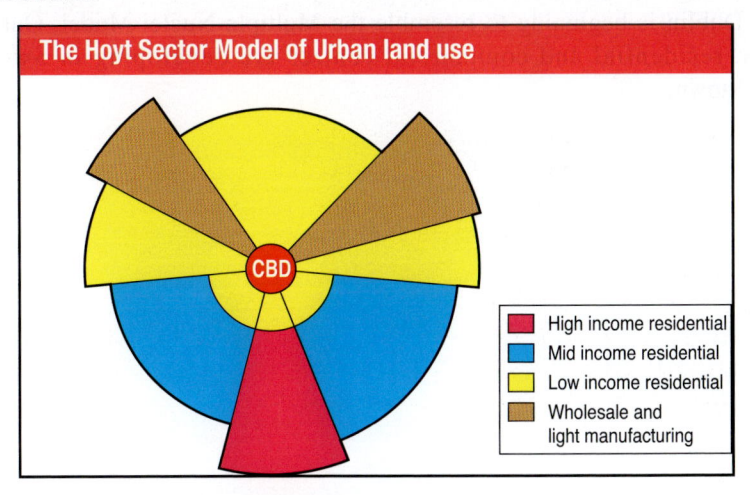

The Hoyt Sector Model of Urban land use

- High income residential
- Mid income residential
- Low income residential
- Wholesale and light manufacturing

> **NOTE:** You are not required to draw this diagram in the Leaving Certificate exam unless it is asked for in the question.

Hoyt stated that certain land uses keep away from each other, e.g. wealthy residents do not live next to factories. Hoyt also said that access to rapid or high quality transport would determine where wealthier people would live and the land values in those areas.

The Sector Model can be used to partially explain the pattern of land use and land values in Dublin.

Dublin has a CBD that stretches north to south from O'Connell Street across the River Liffey to St. Stephen's Green and east to west from Gardiner Street to Smithfield.

Radiating out from the CBD are several major routeways: the River Liffey, the main Dublin to Galway rail line and the main Wexford-Dublin-Belfast rail line. Roads radiate out from the CBD west along the Liffey and north to south along the N1 and N11.

In Dublin different land uses have developed in sectors along and between these routeways according to the Sector Model. For example the area along the N11 is generally a high-income residential region including areas such as Foxrock and Killiney. These high-income areas are separated from lower-income residential zones such as Tallaght by medium/high-income areas such as Rathmines and Ranelagh.

Along the rail lines and River Liffey are light industrial commercial land use areas such as Dublin Port and East Point Business Park. Such land uses developed in these sectors to take advantage of the communications links offered by the river and rail lines which carry workers and goods.

The opening of the M50 motorway led to the development of industrial land use sectors. Dublin has many industrial estates and retail parks located on the edge of the M50, e.g. Sandyford Industrial Estate and Blanchardstown Shopping Centre.

According to Hoyt, land values would be affected by the availability of rapid high quality transport. This is clearly seen in Dublin where the development of the Luas and Dart lines has raised the price of nearby houses by as much as €30,000.

Hoyt's idea that certain land uses repel each other is seen in Dublin with the development of industrial zones well away from high-income residential areas. In Dublin the south east of the city has highest income areas but the south and west is the most industrialised region.

Dublin does not match the Sector Model exactly. For example there is evidence that as it grows Dublin is beginning to resemble the Multiple Nuclei Model. Out-of-town business, residential and commercial centres are developing in Swords and Blanchardstown.

Changing Land Use

> **Urban Land Use: 2014 Question 10B**
> Examine how the function of urban centres can change over time with reference to Irish example(s). **[30 marks]**
> **Suggested marking scheme:**
> Identify two changing functions: 2 marks and 2 marks
> Name Irish example: 2 marks
> Discussion: 12 x SRPs (12 x 2 marks = 24)

> **What You Need to Do:**
> - Name the town you have studied.
> - Discuss how and why TWO of these land use zones change function over time.

Answer

In this answer changes in the Function of land in the Central Business District (CBD) and transition zone of urban areas will be discussed with reference to Dublin City.

The Central Business District (CBD)

The CBD is located in the centre of an urban area. It is the most desirable location for shops and offices. This is due to its accessibility (all routes meet in the city centre) and the high number of customers visiting the area. Rents in the CBD are high because there is a lot of competition for land in the CBD. Consequently buildings are high-rise multi-storey buildings that have more than one function, e.g the ground floor may be a shoe shop that depends on passing trade and having an attractive window display, the second floor might have an accountancy firm and the third level may be an apartment. In Dublin the CBD includes the area stretching from Grafton Street across the River Liffey to O'Connell Street.

The function of land in the CBD changes over the years as the urban area grows. These changes occur so that maximum profit can be gained from rents collected for the buildings there. So we see that in Dublin many old inner city residences that were built in the last century are now redeveloped into modern offices blocks, e.g. Merrion Street.

Buildings that were once well situated in the CBD have now changed their function to better suit the needs of a modern city, e.g. the old Jervis Street hospital was replaced by a shopping centre and new hospitals are located on the outskirts of the city. So we can see that land use in the CBD does change over time in urban areas.

The Transition Zone

Another functional zone found in any city is the transition zone. This zone lies just beyond the CBD and it is close to or part of the old inner city area. The transition zone contains a mix of old terraced housing that may have fallen into disrepair and old factory buildings that may be vacant since the factory operations have been relocated to cheaper sites in the suburbs.

In Dublin the transition zone stretches along the quays between Smithfield and the O2 Arena.

Functional change in the transition zone is very common. It takes two forms: urban renewal and urban redevelopment. Urban renewal schemes keep the land use the same as buildings are upgraded. Old decaying flats are redeveloped into apartments as part of urban renewal programmes, e.g. the Gardiner Street apartments.

Urban redevelopment changes the land use. In Dublin old industrial sites and warehouses have been redeveloped into apartments, business, retail and recreational centres, e.g. The Gasworks, IFSC, the Grand Canal Basin area and Temple Bar.

Aerial Photo Interpretation Skills

NOTE

Remember the urban function memory aid, RICEPOTS:
- Residential/recreation/religious/retail
- Industry
- Commercial
- Education
- Port/public buildings
- Transport/tourism
- Services

Be sure to know the difference between the phrases **land use** and **function**!
Land use means what is built, e.g. a school.
Function means what a building does, e.g. education.

Urban Functions: 2008 Question 10B
Study the aerial photograph of part of Galway that accompanies this paper. Examine any **three** functions of the city, using evidence from the photograph to support your answer. **[30 marks]**
Marking scheme:
3 functions @ 10 marks each (broken down as follows):
Identify function: 2 marks
Refer to photo: 2 marks
Examination: 3 x SRPs (3 x 2 marks = 6)

What You Need To Do
- Identify three urban functions that you can find evidence for in the photo.
- Name the function and state the land use that is in evidence for that function, e.g. for an educational function, the land use would be a school.
- Locate the evidence using the correct referencing system, e.g. left, background, right foreground.
- Describe the function in 3 SRPs.

Answer

A

1. Religious Function

There is a large Roman Catholic church/cathedral in the centre of the photo.

This large church can provide a variety of religious functions for Galway city. In the photo the church car park is full. There may be a confirmation, communion, funeral or wedding taking place inside the church. Large churches in cities are sometimes used for public religious events such as religious prayer weeks.

A large religious building such as this may also have a tourist function attracting visitors to choral events or to view the building.

The church is located at the junction of two major roads. This enables people from outside the urban area to attend services there.

2. Educational Function

There is a large school/college/university in the right background of the photo.

This building probably has an educational function because it has large buildings that are not obviously industrial. There is also an outdoor area containing playing courts and green areas for students. A car park, possibly for staff and students, is also visible on the grounds.

Several large buildings are spread around a single area bordered by two roads and the rivers. This could be a third level college campus. The buildings may hold lecture rooms, a student canteen, libraries and practical laboratories.

Large cities such as Galway can provide educational functions for a large hinterland. Students come from across the western region and further away to study at such a large educational facility as the one shown in this photograph.

3. Retail Function

There is a shopping area in the left foreground of the photo.

This shopping area has off-street parking and seems to be a busy street with people shopping on it. It could be part of the Central Business District in the city which would be quite big in a city such as Galway. Shops provide clothing, food and other services such as sports equipment. Some of the buildings may be restaurants and pubs.

A city like Galway that offers educational, residential, religious and recreational functions as shown on the photo would need a variety of retail outlets to provide the large population with the services and goods that they need to live in the city. The retail outlets would contribute to the growth of the city by paying rates to the city council which are used for urban development such as lighting, roads and water infrastructure.

Chapter 29

Central Place Theory

Central Place Theory

Hamlet	------ Boundary of hamlet trading area
Village	--- Boundary of village trading area
Town	—— Boundary of town trading area
City	▬▬ Boundary of city trading area

Q

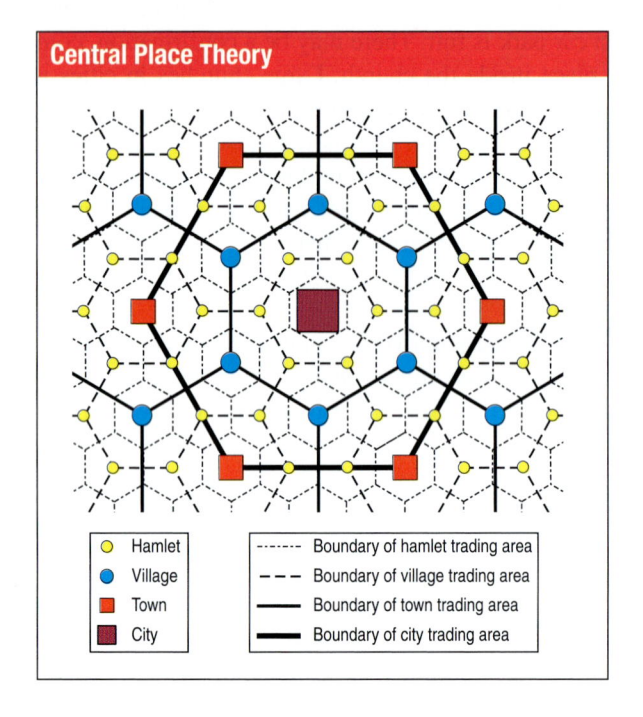

Central Place Theory: 2008 Question 12B
Examine this diagram, which refers to Christaller's Central Place Theory. Explain what you understand by this theory. **[30 marks]**

Marking scheme:
Explain Central Place Theory: 15 x SRPs (15 x 2 marks = 30)

What You Need to Do:
- Explain Central Place Theory.
- Describe the main points of this theory.
- State how it applies to modern settlement patterns.
- Explain any criticisms of this theory.

Answer

A A Central Place is a settlement that provides services and goods for people in the town and the surrounding area (hinterland). Central Place Theory (CPT) was devised by Walter Christaller to explain the way in which settlements (Central Places) are spaced apart according to their size.

His theory stated that settlements are distributed in a pattern according to their size.

This will happen if there is an even distribution of people in a flat and featureless region, all with equal wealth and access to transport services. Central Place Theory has four important ideas to explain why this pattern occurs.

1. Threshold population
This is the number of people required to keep a shop or service in business. Some services have high thresholds, e.g. hospitals. Other services have a low threshold, e.g. a village shop.

2. Range
This is the distance people are prepared to travel in order to use a service or buy a product. The range determines the size of a town's hinterland. For example, Croke Park has a high range as people will travel from all over Ireland to attend matches and concerts there. A local DVD rental store, however, will have a small range as people will not travel far to use this service.

3. Rank order
High-order goods are expensive and bought infrequently, e.g. cars. Low-order goods are inexpensive and bought daily, e.g. newspapers and bread. People travel further to use high-order services. So a settlement that offers many high-order services will have a high range and therefore a large hinterland.

4. Frequency of demand
This is how often a product or service is used or needed. Low-order goods have a high frequency of use while high-order goods are used infrequently.

Combining the four ideas above, Christaller classified settlements in order of size from cities down to hamlets. CPT explains why there are very few large cities and a greater number of towns and many more villages. The largest cities have large hinterlands and offer many high-order goods and services. These require large numbers of people to keep them in business. People are prepared to travel great distances to the city to use the services. If the cities were close together then there would be intense competition (lower profits) between the businesses for customers in the hinterland. So there are usually very few of the largest cities and they are spaced very far apart.

Villages offer many low-order and a few medium-order goods, e.g. hairdressers, with a high frequency of demand. People will not travel far to use these services and so these settlements are usually closer together.

The shape of the hinterlands is hexagonal so that no land is left unserved by its central place.

Several criticisms apply to Christaller's theory. It simplifies the landscape to a flat featureless plain which is unrealistic. It does not take into account the variation in transport services. Some areas have good transport, others do not. Shoppers have preferences about which shop to use and may ignore the distance they have to travel.

> **Hierarchy and Hinterland: 2014 Question 11C**
> Examine the importance of hierarchy and hinterland in Central Place Theory.
> [30 marks]
>
> **Marking scheme:**
> Explanation: 15 x SRPs (15 x 2 marks = 30)

> **What You Need to Do:**
> - Explain the term central place theory.
> - Explain the terms hinterland and hierarchy.
> - Discuss how these concepts fit into Central Place Theory.

Answer

A central place is a settlement that provides services and goods to people in the town and its surrounding area (hinterland). Walter Christaller devised Central Place Theory; he stated that settlements are distributed across the land in a pattern according to their population, function and size of hinterland.

Two concepts are important in Central Place Theory – hinterland and hierarchy.

Hinterland

Hinterland is the area surrounding an urban centre. People living in the hinterland trade with and use the services of the urban centre. In Central Place Theory, Christaller assumed that each settlement would lie in the centre of a hexagonal-shaped hinterland. Hexagons fit together with no unused area between them. Hinterlands of large cities would overlap with those of smaller settlements.

The distance people will travel to use a particular service is called its range. The range of each service provided by a settlement affects the size of its hinterland. People will not travel very far to access low-order services. These are services required every day, e.g. milk, newspapers and fuel. Therefore, small settlements, e.g. Louth Village, providing low-order services have small hinterlands.

Higher-order services include car dealerships, medical centres and universities. These are needed less often and people are prepared to travel further to access them. Large settlements have many high-order services and therefore have a large hinterland.

Services also have a threshold. This is the minimum population needed to make a service profitable. Low-order services such as petrol stations do not need many people to be profitable and can survive in small hinterlands. High-order services such as concert venues, e.g. the 3 Arena in Dublin, need large numbers of people and larger hinterlands.

Hierarchy

In Central Place Theory, Christaller developed an urban hierarchy (ranking) of settlements according to the range, and threshold of services that they provided. Some settlements are more important than others are because they offer a variety of high-order services

The position in the hierarchy of any settlement depends on its population, order of services and the area of its hinterland. In general, the higher up the urban hierarchy a settlement is, the higher the order of services it supplies.

Settlements with large populations, a variety of services and large hinterlands will be near the top of the hierarchy. Major cities such as Dublin, Paris, and New York are at the top of the urban hierarchy in their countries. At the other end of the scale, settlements with small populations, few services and small hinterlands will be placed low down in the hierarchy.

Christaller named the type of settlement in each level of the urban hierarchy. Hamlets are at the bottom of the hierarchy. Hamlets are tiny villages or a small group of rural housing. They might have a small shop supplying low-order services such as basic daily items, e.g. Fanore in Co. Clare.

The next level up in the hierarchy is a village. Villages may have one or two higher-order services, e.g. a primary school, a church and a shop or two, e.g. Ballyvaughan, Co. Clare.

Above villages are towns, e.g. Balbriggan, Co Dublin. Large towns, e.g. Drogheda in Co. Louth, may have retail parks, a range of educational services and a hospital. People will travel to large towns from a wide area to access the services there.

At the top of the hierarchy are cities. These are major regional centres and offer a huge variety of high-order services such as specialist medical care, major recreational events such as sports matches and music concerts, e.g. Croke Park. They will also hold airports and university facilities. The hinterland of large cities may be many hundreds of square kilometres or even the entire country in the case of particular services such as national sports events or neuro-surgery.

These concepts – hinterland, range, threshold and urban hierarchy – help to explain why there are many smaller settlements placed close together and fewer large cities spaced far apart.

Towns as Central Places/Market Centres: OS Map and Photo Interpretation Skills

Q

Central Place: 2010 Question 12C

Examine the Ordnance Survey map and aerial photograph accompanying this paper.

Using evidence from the Ordnance Survey map and aerial photograph, show that Carrick-on-Suir performs the function of a Central Place or market centre for the surrounding hinterland. **[30 marks]**

Marking scheme:
Provide Ordnance Survey Map evidence: 2 marks
Provide aerial photograph evidence: 2 marks
Examination: 13 x SRPs (13 x 2 marks = 26)

> **What You Need To Do:**
> - Outline what Central Place Theory says about the services provided by urban centres referring to high-order and low-order services.
> - Refer to the range of goods.
> - Find and locate evidence of high-order and low-order services in Carrick-on-Suir on the map and photo.
> - Relate these services to Central Place Theory.

Answer

A A central place is a town or urban centre which provides goods and services for people who live in and around it. Carrick-on Suir is the only large settlement shown on the map extract and so is the central place for the area shown.

A town's centrality is the degree to which it serves the surrounding area. This can be measured in terms of the services it offers. From the OS map and aerial photo, Carrick-on-Suir seems to fulfil the functions of a central place.

High-order services are used less frequently and are more expensive. They are found only in larger settlements and have a high range so people are prepared to travel from the hinterland to the town to use them. In central places, businesses and services survive if there is a threshold population large enough to support them. Carrick-on-Suir provides a variety of high-order services for its hinterland.

1. It provides high-order retail and commercial services.
From the photograph we can see that Carrick-on-Suir provides high-order retail services to its hinterland. In the left centre is the main Central Business District. This area seems large and the wide street would accommodate large volumes of traffic. In the left background there seems to be a shopping centre which would offer a variety of retail outlets that are unavailable elsewhere in the hinterland. The non-retail commercial buildings in the CBD would probably hold solicitors, accountancy firms and medical services such as dental surgeries which would be used less frequently by people in the hinterland.

2. The town provides high-order transport services for its hinterland.
From the OS map, we can see that Carrick-on-Suir is a route focus and would be used as a transport centre by people in the hinterland who need to travel long distances.

The town has national primary routes (N24), regional roads (R697) and third class roads leading into it. Most roads reach the town from the southerly and northerly directions. East to west transport across the region is not well developed apart from the N25 and rail line. So anyone wishing to travel across the hinterland would need to travel via Carrick-on-Suir. The only rail station in the region shown is in the town so people would use this high-order transport service to travel to towns and cities further from Carrick-on-Suir and for commuting to work.

3. The town provides educational services for its hinterland.
There are two schools in the town, e.g. S 404 221. There are only three other schools shown in the entire hinterland, e.g. S 365 249 at Ballyneill. The schools in the

hinterland are likely to be primary schools because they are located in small villages and would not have large populations to support them. Carrick-on-Suir seems therefore to be a central place offering higher-order educational services. The schools shown in the town are likely to be second level schools and their students would travel from the hinterland to the town for second level educational qualifications such as the Leaving Certificate. School bus services for students in the hinterland are probably based in Carrick-on-Suir in order to reach them more easily along the regional roads that radiate out from the town.

Chapter 30
Urban Problems and Planning Strategies

Urban Problems in the Developed World

Q

Urban Future: 2008 Question 12C
Examine two of the main problems created by the continued pace of urban growth in a region you have studied. **[30 marks]**

Marking scheme:
Identify two problems: 2 marks + 2 marks
Name urban centre/region: 2 marks
Examination: 12 x SRPs (12 x 2 marks = 24)

What You Need To Do:
- Name two urban problems.
- Name one city where these problems occur.
- Discuss the reasons for the problems.
- Briefly outline a possible solution to the problems.
- Your discussion should be about two problems in one city.

Answer

A

Urban problems in the developed world
In this answer two problems associated with the growth of urban centres in the developed world will be discussed. The two problems I have chosen to discuss are traffic congestion and urban sprawl in Dublin city.

Traffic congestion in Dublin
The Greater Dublin Area now contains over 1.6 million people and the growth of Dublin has led to an increase in traffic congestion. Population growth and an increase in wealth have led to an increase in the number of cars in urban areas such as Dublin. In Ireland there are over 402 cars per 1,000 people. Many of these are second cars for families. Economic growth during the boom years (1995 – 2007) in Ireland has also

led to an increase in the number of Heavy Goods Vehicles (HGVs) on Irish roads delivering goods across the country. These HGVs add to traffic congestion in city areas, especially near port areas such as Dublin Port and Cork Harbour. Commuting is another cause of traffic congestion in growing urban areas. Traffic congestion results in long journey times for commuters, e.g. it can take up to 90 minutes to get from Blanchardstown in the west of Dublin to the city centre at peak times. In Ireland public transport, while being upgraded (e.g. extension of Luas lines, increased number of bus corridors and more frequent intercity train services), still does not provide the service required by many people. There is still a significant number of people who drive their car to work instead.

In Ireland there are several strategies to reduce traffic congestion. In Dublin, traffic restrictions are in place preventing cars from entering certain areas, e.g. the five-axle ban in Dublin city. Also the provision of park-and-ride facilities and quality bus corridors (QBCs) in Dublin allow faster movement of buses and encourage more people to leave their cars outside the city, thus reducing traffic congestion. The Dublin Transportation Office's plan for reducing congestion aims to increase cycling and use of public transport and to reduce car use in the city centre.

Urban sprawl

Urban sprawl is the rapid spread of housing from cities into the surrounding countryside. Increased migration to cities such as Dublin in the developed world is causing urban sprawl. Economic growth combined with an increase in car ownership also contributes to urban sprawl.

The Dublin area has experienced rapid population growth caused by rural to urban migration and immigration which has led to urban sprawl.

Urban sprawl has negative effects on the surrounding countryside. Many small villages on the edges of Dublin have been swamped by residents who commute to work each day from these villages, e.g. Swords, Greystones. These once small villages are now large dormitory towns.

Growth of the villages is due to cheaper housing, the availability of development land on the outskirts of the city and higher land prices closer to the city centre. As a result dormitory towns may have few services for their growing populations. Developing a sense of community is difficult when the majority of people spend long days commuting and have little free time to participate in local events and clubs. Place names and townland names are often lost as builders use names for their developments that are unrelated to the local area. The sense of community in these towns and villages is lost as the population is swamped by many people with no family connection to the local area. Traffic congestion, usually associated with urban areas, then becomes a problem in the rural areas during commuter rush hours. Local schools in the areas surrounding the growing city may become overcrowded as the new residents settle and have families.

As an urban area expands greenfield areas are built upon and used for roads, housing and other developments. This causes problems for farmers and wildlife in the hinterland. It becomes increasingly difficult for farmers to enlarge their farmlands as they are often unable to afford the prices charged for neighbouring land. The price of land which has been rezoned for residential or industrial use is usually much higher than that of agricultural land. Farmers must compete with property developers and often land prices go well beyond their reach.

Urban Problems in the Developing World

Q

Developing World Cities: 2010 Question 11C
'Problems can develop as urban centres expand and grow.'
Discuss this statement with reference to **ONE** developing world city that you have studied. **[30 marks]**

Marking scheme:
Identify a developing world city: 2 marks
Identify two problems: 2 marks + 2 marks
Examination: 12 x SRPs (12 x 2 marks = 24)

What You Need To Do:
- Name your developing world city.
- Name two problems.
- Explain how these problems occur and explain briefly how they are being controlled/solved.

Answer

A

Rural to urban migration in countries such as Brazil is the major economic cause of population growth in developing world cities. By 2015, it is projected that the number of people living in urban areas will exceed the entire globe's population in 1965.

Two socio-economic problems associated with the rapid growth of cities in the developing world are:
1. The growth of favelas/shanty towns.
2. A lack of services and infrastructure.
Both of these problems occur in São Paulo in Brazil.

1. Growth of favelas/shanty towns

São Paulo is a large city of over 22 million people. It has grown so rapidly that the city authorities have not been able to meet the demand for housing in the city. As a result over 5% of the population in São Paulo lives in favelas – shanty towns filled with handmade shelters in which people live. People build their own shelter from any scrap materials they can find. Favelas are built on any spare unused land in the city, but most are found on the edge of the city on waste ground beside factories. Within the favelas there are no services. Sewerage, waste, water and electricity supplies are absent. People live in favelas because they are poor and/or have recently moved to the city from rural areas in search of work or a better life.

São Paulo has 1,600 favela settlements. Favelas have existed for many years and not all residents are recent arrivals. Extended families of children, parents and grandparents live in these shacks.

For the increasing number of middle-income families in the booming São Paulo economy, some improved favelas are becoming desirable locations because of their closeness to industrial areas where many people work.

2. Lack of services

The favelas lack the infrastructure and services to make life bearable. Water is gathered from a communal pump, toilets are filthy communal latrines. There is no organised municipal waste collection service because the 'streets' between the shelters are too narrow for bin lorries to pass through. Rubbish is dumped onto the streets and open drains run down the small alleys between shelters. The lack of electricity supplies means that people must use candles or gas lamps which are fire hazards in the cramped conditions. Because living conditions are so poor in the favelas, social problems are common. In favelas death rates and infant mortality rates are much higher than average. Children die from diseases such as dysentery caused by drinking dirty water and from playing in the unhygienic living conditions.

In São Paulo the city council has self-help schemes to improve conditions for favela residents. This scheme is providing community centres and public sanitation services. It is also replacing poor shelters with brick-built houses and providing school buildings, e.g. Cingapura favela electricity and water supplies. Monte Azul favela in São Paulo is an example. However, projects like this are rare across developed world cities and many millions of people still suffer from the problems of living in rapidly growing cities.

Urban Sprawl

Q

Urban Expansion: 2012 Question 11C
'As cities expand they impact on the surrounding areas.'
Discuss this statement with reference to example(s) you have studied.
[30 marks]

Marking scheme:
Name a city that has expanded: 2 marks
Name two impacts: 2 marks + 2 marks
Discussion: 12 x SRPs (12 x 2 marks = 24)

What You Need To Do:
- Name the city you have studied.
- Name the impact on the surrounding area.
- Discuss the impact in 12 SRPs.

Answer

A

A city I have studied is Dublin.

Urban sprawl is the rapid spread of housing from cities into the surrounding countryside. Increased migration to cities in the developed world is causing urban sprawl. Economic growth combined with an increase in car ownership also contributes to urban sprawl.

In the early twenty-first century the Dublin area experienced rapid population growth caused by rural to urban migration and immigration. This growth has had two important effects on the hinterland.

1. Growth of dormitory towns in the hinterland

Many small villages on the edges of Dublin have been swamped by residents who commute to work each day from these villages, e.g. Swords, Greystones.

This is due to cheaper housing, the availability of development land on the outskirts of the city and higher land prices closer to the city centre. As a result once small villages are now large dormitory towns which may have few services for their growing populations. Developing a sense of community is difficult when the majority of people spend long days commuting and have little free time to participate in local events and clubs. Place names and townland names are often lost as builders use names for their developments that are unrelated to the local area. The sense of community in once small towns and villages is lost as the population is swamped by many people with no family connection to the local area. Traffic congestion, usually associated with urban areas, then becomes a problem in the rural areas during commuter rush hours. Local schools in the areas surrounding the growing city may become overcrowded as the new residents settle and have families.

2. Loss of valuable farmland and wildlife habitat

As an urban area expands, greenfield areas are built upon with roads, housing and other developments. This causes problems for farmers and wildlife in the hinterland. It becomes increasingly difficult for farmers to enlarge their farmlands as they are often unable to afford the prices charged for neighbouring land. The price of land which has been rezoned for residential or industrial use is usually much higher than that of agricultural land. Farmers must compete with property developers and often land prices go well beyond their reach.

As housing estates are built, hedgerows are removed which reduces the number of plant and animal species across the land. Wildlife breeding places such as trees and old buildings that provide nest sites for the Barn Owl or roosting sites for bats are removed. The building of the Kildare bypass has led to a decrease in water levels in Pollardstown fen which is a site of special scientific interest in Ireland as it contains rare vegetation. The light and noise pollution caused by new housing and industry in rural areas also disrupts the night-time hunting abilities of owls and bats.

Q

Urban Planning Strategies: 2015 Question 12B
Examine the impact of urban planning strategies with reference to example(s) that you have studied. **[30 marks]**

Marking scheme:
Give example: 2 marks
Identify impact: 2 marks
Examination: 13 x SRPs (13 x 2 marks = 26)

What You Need To Do:
- Name one planning strategy.
- Name one urban area affected by that strategy.
- Explain how the strategy has affected the urban area.
- You may also discuss another planning strategy and urban area.

Answer

A

In this answer, I will discuss the impact of Ireland's National Development Plan (NDP) and the French *Schéma Directeur*.

The NDP is an Irish government urban planning policy designed to encourage balanced urban and regional development across the whole of Ireland up to 2016 and to reduce the urban sprawl and economic dominance of Dublin city. Under the NDP, larger cities such as Dublin, Waterford, Galway, Limerick and Cork were identified as 'gateway' towns.

Dublin, being Ireland's primate city (twice as big as the next biggest city, Cork) attracts more business than others and is the major economic engine of Ireland. Gateway towns outside Dublin city are seen as engines of growth and development in a region. They attract business and people to a region and help to counterbalance the economic and social attraction of Dublin.

Gateway towns receive increased government investment in transport, healthcare, water, education and housing in order to cope with their planned future growth, e.g. expansion of the University College Galway campus and completion of the M8 motorway.

The NDP was further improved under the National Spatial Strategy (NSS), which will operate until 2020. The NSS identified small to medium-sized towns such as Ennis, Castlebar and Monaghan as 'hub' towns. These receive investment in order to provide services and employment in areas surrounding the gateway towns. The aim is to reduce rural-to-urban migration and control the urban sprawl of Dublin. It also aims to control the rapid growth of the mid-east region by providing services and facilities to people in the rest of Ireland.

These two planning strategies have had an impact on urban areas. Most gateway towns underwent upgrades to their transport infrastructure, e.g. the M1 to Dundalk, the hourly intercity train service to Cork and the Shannon Tunnel in Limerick. Hub towns such as Castlebar received upgrades to their educational facilities, e.g. the GMIT campus.

Cork, Ireland's second largest city, has its own urban development plan: the Cork Area Strategic Plan. One of the aims under this plan is urban renewal/redevelopment of decaying brownfield sites such as the dockland area to provide jobs, services and recreational areas for the city.

Continued government investment in urban planning strategies is linked to economic growth and all were cut back during Ireland's economic recession between 2008 and 2013.

Similar to Dublin, the capital city of France, Paris, has undergone rapid growth and needed a long-term strategy to control its urban sprawl and dominance of the French economy. Its strategy is called the *Schéma Directeur*. Paris city has a population of over 12 million.

The aims of this scheme are to control urban sprawl, promote development in the area surrounding Paris, reduce traffic congestion and improve housing and recreational facilities in the city.

Under this planning strategy, five new towns were built around Paris to provide alternative locations for business, industry and housing. The most successful development is St. Quentin-en–Yvelines which houses 150,000 people and offers over 40,000 jobs.

The *Schéma Directeur* has been successful in slowing the growth of Paris but has still to improve housing for its large migrant population who live in low quality high-rise buildings in the suburbs.

SECTION 4
Options

The Marking Scheme
Higher Level students should always aim to create a logical layout and to make use of headings in their answers. It is well worth taking a couple of minutes to plan your answer before you begin to write.

The Marking Scheme – Overall Coherence
- Your answer to the Option question is in the form of an essay.
- The marking scheme in the Option question is different to the rest of the exam paper as it includes marks for **Overall Coherence (OC)**.
- In awarding Overall Coherence (OC) the examiner will consider how well the candidate deals with the set question and will follow the following marking descriptors:

		Overall Coherence (20 marks)
Excellent	20	Excellent, comprehensive response demonstrating detailed knowledge of subject matter. Excellent ability to relate knowledge to the question.
Very Good	17	Very good response. Very broad knowledge of the subject matter demonstrated. Considerable strength in relating the knowledge to the set question.
Good	14	Good response with worthwhile information. Broad knowledge of the subject matter. Reasonable capacity to relate knowledge appropriately to the set question.
Fair	10	Basic grasp of subject matter with main points covered but limited detail. Some effort to relate knowledge to the set question but only a basic understanding displayed.
Weak	6	Identified some relevant but limited information and has engaged with the set question to some extent
Poor	0	General misunderstanding of the question. Failure to address the question resulting in a largely irrelevant answer

- To successfully answer the Option question, students are expected to write on three or four topics of discussion in their essay. These topics are called aspects. Plan your answer before you write to make sure you have identified which aspects you will discuss and in which order.

If you choose to write on **three** aspects you must:
- Name your aspects (topics of discussion). Since 2014 there are usually 4 marks available for each topic heading.
- Use headings to write 8 SRPs on each aspect. **Note:** you may not get the full OC marks available if you do not give the correct number of SRPs.

If you choose to write on **four** aspects you must:
- Name your aspects (topics of discussion). Since 2014 there are usually 4 marks available for each topic heading.
- Use headings to write 6 SRPs on each aspect. **Note:** you may not get the full OC marks available if you do not give the correct number of SRPs.

> **NOTE:** Three aspects of discussion are usually provided in the answer essays in this section. Each aspect has at least 8 SRPs. If four aspects are given, each aspect has at least 6 SRPs. In this section **aspects of discussion** have an **asterisk (*)** beside them to help you identify them.

Contents

> **NOTE:** The detail required in any answer is determined by:
> - the context and the manner in which the question is asked
> - the number of marks assigned to the question.
>
> Requirements and mark allocations may vary from year to year.

Global Interdependence (Option 6)
- 31. Development 202
- 32. Interdependence: the impact of economic activities 206
- 33. Trade, Aid, Debt and Land Ownership 215
- 34. Sustainable Development, NGOs and Empowerment 227

Geoecology (Option 7)
- 35. Soils 234
- 36. Human Influence on Soils/Soil Erosion 248
- 37. Biomes 252
- 38. Human Influence on Biomes 265

GLOBAL INTERDEPENDENCE (Option 6)

> **NOTE:** Three aspects of discussion are usually provided in the answer essays in this section. Each aspect has at least 8 SRPs. If four aspects are given, each aspect has at least 6 SRPs. In this section **aspects of discussion** have **an asterisk (*)** beside them to help you identify them.

Chapter 31
Development

Views of Development

Q

Development: 2007 Question 15
Examine the idea that attitudes towards development and underdevelopment are subject to change. [80 marks]

Development: 2014 Question 13
Views of development and underdevelopment are subject to change.
Discuss. [80 marks]

What You Need To Do:
- Name three views of development.
- Put them in historic order.
- Describe their main points/problems.
- Describe how they relate to each other, if at all, and how they reflect the ideas of the time during which they were developed.

Answer

A There have been three main views of development/underdevelopment since the late nineteenth century. Each view reflects the attitudes and political thinking of the time in which they were developed. As the world has become more modern, so have the views and attitudes of development that we use today.

1. Nineteenth century attitudes to development*

The earliest model of development is the Environmental Determinism Model. This was developed during the late 1800s/early 1900s.

The main point of the Environmental Determinism Model is that climate and landscapes influence people and can encourage economic development or prevent it.

At the time this model was developed, European geographers considered that the temperate climate and varied landscape of Europe had led to the development of a culture of exploration and science. This, in turn, resulted in Europeans becoming more socially and economically advanced than people from other continents as they discovered resources and inventions that led to developed societies, e.g. coal, steam power and steel making. These Europeans believed that countries with harsh environmental conditions such as deserts or jungles would remain underdeveloped.

This way of thinking also led to the colonisation of other countries by European nations (e.g. India was colonised by Britain) who then exploited new resources such as gold, coffee and timber in those colonies.

However, this model has disadvantages and was criticised during the 1930s because it focused mainly on the development of resources and was used as an excuse for continued colonisation. Countries were seen as sources of raw materials for the colonial powers rather than as independent states. Another criticism is that this model does not account for varying levels of development across the world. For example the Democratic Republic of Congo has many resources yet is undeveloped while Japan is highly developed but has few resources. Today, this model is seen as being too simplistic.

2. Attitudes to development in the early twentieth century*

As the global economy grew after World War II, a second view of development became established during the 1960s. This was the Modernisation Theory of Development proposed by Walt Rostow. He studied changes in the gross national product (GNP) of a country over time. Using GNP as a measure of development, Rostow was able to identify five stages in the economic development of a country as it changed from a poor, rural, agricultural subsistence economy to a highly industrialised urban economy where consumption of resources is high.

Using GNP he stated that the Western world is most developed and other regions would eventually catch up. The development of free trade and global trading systems would help the economies of poorer nations. He observed that many countries have not developed or have fallen behind in their development stages and need help to catch up with the more developed countries. According to Rostow the developed world can encourage the less developed nations to grow.

This view is one of the main problems associated with the Modernisation model. He focused purely on the 'Western' world countries, such as Japan and Europe, with large populations and plenty of resources. Another criticism of this model is that it only considers economic factors such as GNP; it does not take into account human development such as literacy levels or healthcare provision.

3. Attitudes to development in the late twentieth/early twenty-first century*

Today our view of development is not based on one single factor but on several. It is widely believed that development must include consideration of the quality of life that people have and the sustainability of any economic growth that occurs. This combination of growth with sustainable use of resources is the basis of the post modernisation view of development. The main points of this view are:
- Improving quality of life for people is the most important part of development.
- Development should benefit everyone in society.
- Development policies must adapt to changing needs in a country, e.g. in response to natural disasters.

Today our views of development also consider the environment; human rights; cultural, economic and social needs; and who the decision-makers are. One method used to measure development today is the Human Development Index (HDI). This index combines data on life expectancy, literacy and education to rank countries according to their levels of development in these areas. The post modern view of development is that development projects must benefit the people for whom they are intended. Today development is also aimed at empowering women in society as women are responsible for food production and healthcare of their children in many societies. Modern attitudes to development also include plans to protect the environment, e.g. re-forestation of slopes in Nepal. This view is very different to earlier models and shows that our views of development have changed over time.

Problems with Models of Development

Q

Developed world views of development and their limitations: 2011 Question 14
The developed world can often be accused of shortcomings in its view towards developing nations. Examine this statement referring to differing views of development. **[80 marks]**

What You Need To Do:
- This question requires you to examine the different views of development and comment about their limitations in helping developing nations.

A

Answer
Views of development today: Human Development Index*
This statement might have had some truth in the past but today modern views of development are much more helpful to developing nations than older models.

Today, our view of development is based on several factors that give a more complete picture of the needs of developing nations. Today, developed nations and their aid agencies, such as the Irish government's development agency called Irish Aid, realise that development must include consideration of the quality of life that people have and the sustainability of any economic growth that occurs. This combination of growth with sustainable use of resources is the basis of the current view of development. The main points of this view are:
- That improving the quality of life for people is the most important part of development.
- That development should benefit everyone in society.
- That development policies must adapt to changing needs in a country, e.g. in response to natural disasters.

Today, our views of development also consider the environment; human rights; cultural, economic and social needs; and who the decision-makers are. One method used to measure development today is the Human Development Index (HDI). This index combines data on life expectancy, literacy and education to rank countries according to their levels of development in these areas. It has also been expanded to consider total years of schooling available to people. Today, the current view is that development projects must benefit the people for whom they are intended, include women, protect the environment and be achievable. This view is much less authoritarian and enables developing nations to discuss with the aid givers what their needs are rather than have development aid imposed upon them without consultation as has happened in the past. The development of the HDI has helped to overcome shortcomings in the views of the developed world towards developing nations.

The Environmental Determinism view of development and the limitations of this view in helping developing nations*

The earliest model of development was the Environmental Determinism Model. This was developed during the late 1800s/early 1900s.

The main point of the Environmental Determinism Model is that climate and landscapes influence people and can encourage economic development or prevent it.

At the time this model was developed, European geographers considered that the temperate climate and varied landscape of Europe had led to the development of a culture of exploration and science. This, in turn, resulted in Europeans becoming more socially and economically advanced than people from other continents as they discovered resources and inventions that led to developed societies, e.g. coal, steam power and steel making. This way of thinking also led to the colonisation of other countries by European nations (e.g. India was colonised by Britain). These European nations then exploited new resources such as gold, coffee and timber in their colonies.

This model was criticised during the 1930s because it focused mainly on the development of resources and was used as an excuse for continued colonisation. Development of other countries was seen mainly as a source of economic development for the colonial power and it was not for the benefit of the country 'being developed'. Countries were seen as sources of raw materials for the colonial powers rather than as independent states. Another limitation is that this model does not account for varying levels of development across the world. For example the Democratic Republic of Congo has many resources yet is undeveloped while Japan is highly developed but has few resources. In this case political stability, accountable government and democracy are vital to development.

Though it is outdated, this model still has some relevance to developing nations which are at risk from desertification or flooding due to climate change, e.g. Bangladesh. Harsh, inhospitable landscapes and environmental problems do have an impact on the ability of a country to develop. Developed and developing nations still need to consider the impact of environmental change on the needs of people when discussing the type of aid that may be required.

Rostow's Modernisation Theory of Development and the limitations of this view in helping developing nations*

As the global economy grew after World War II, another view of development became established. This was the Modernisation Theory of Development proposed by Walt Rostow. He studied changes in the gross national product (GNP) of a country over time. Using GNP as a measure of development, Rostow was able to identify five stages in the economic development of a country as it changed from a poor, rural, agricultural subsistence economy to a highly industrialised, urban economy where consumption of resources is high. Using GNP, Rostow stated that the Western world is most developed and that other regions would eventually catch up. He observed that many countries have not developed or have fallen behind in their development stages and need help to catch up with the more developed countries. According to Rostow the developed world can encourage the less developed nations to grow.

One of the main shortcomings associated with the Modernisation model is that Rostow focused purely on the 'Western' world countries, such as Japan and France. These countries have large populations, stable government and plenty of resources. This model does not really apply to many developing nations, e.g. Somalia, which lacks any form of government structures and also lacks the educated population to enable it to 'catch up'. Another shortcoming of this model is that it only considers economic factors such as GNP; it does not take into account human development such as literacy levels or healthcare provision. Some oil-rich developing nations such as Nigeria appear to be 'developed' when GNP is considered because of the value of their oil exports. However, this wealth does not reach the majority of the population; in fact basic services such as schooling and healthcare are lacking across much of the country.

Chapter 32
Interdependence: The Impact of Economic Activities

Interdependent global economy/ MNCs

Q

MNCs/Interdependent global economy: 2009 Question 14
We live in an interdependent global economy. Actions or decisions taken in one area have an impact on other areas. Discuss. **[80 marks]**

What You Need To Do:
- Name a multinational company (MNC) you wish to discuss.
- Name the producer and consumer region.
- Discuss the impact of this MNC's location decisions on the producer and consumer region.

A

Answer

Decision-making by MNCs*
In a globalised world, rapid communications and decision making mean that the decisions made by MNCs in one country can quickly cause positive or negative economic changes in another. The positive economic impacts of an MNC locating in a region include jobs, higher tax income and the raising of skills in the local population. Negative impacts can include increased pollution and overdependence on branch plants for employment.

Just 500 multinational companies (MNCs) control over 70% of world trade. The most important issue for an MNC is locating their operations in countries where they can maintain profitability for their shareholders. So they are constantly searching for cheaper production methods and locations. Multinational companies, e.g. Johnson & Johnson, operate in many countries. Usually the headquarters are in a High or Medium

Economically Developed Country (MEDC), e.g. the USA or France, while branch plants are placed in Less Economically Developed Countries (LEDCs), e.g. Morocco, or MEDCs depending on the stage a product is at in its life cycle. This means that if a product is at the stage of being mass produced, the MNC will most likely decide to locate its manufacturing plant in a low labour cost economy such as China. This assumes that the product is labour intensive, e.g. footwear and clothing. For other products such as pharmaceuticals and healthcare products, e.g. contact lenses, the overall 'Delivered Cost' is more important than wage costs and manufacturing plants may decide to locate in higher wage economies such as Ireland. In this case production requires skilled workers, intensive use of technology and high levels of health standard regulation.

Impact of MNC decisions on producer regions*

Most MNCs are very wealthy; some of them are wealthier than actual countries. For example, of the 100 largest economies in the world, 51 are MNCs. This makes MNCs very powerful in trade negotiations with national governments. Individual governments may be willing to negotiate tax laws and environmental protection laws with MNCs in order to influence the company's decision to locate manufacturing plants in their country. When choosing to locate in a region, an MNC will often 'play countries against each other' to try and get the best deal it can in order to minimise its wage bill and other production costs. To compete, countries sometimes offer incentives to MNCs such as tax breaks, pledges of governmental assistance, improved infrastructure or low standards of environmental protection. This, for example, has led to the location of 'maquiladora' manufacturing plants in Mexico. A maquiladora is a foreign-owned manufacturing plant found close to the border of the USA in Mexico. The location of maquiladora plants in Mexico has occurred because Mexican labour is inexpensive and worker protection laws are not as strict as those in the USA. The MNCs' decision to locate in Mexico has had several impacts there. First, it has increased exports from Mexico, thus improving its balance of trade. Maquiladoras account for more than 50% of manufacturing exports between Mexico and the USA. This is helping the Mexican economy. However pollution is a problem as some MNCs are responsible for serious water and air pollution in their area due to low standards of environmental protection. Second, maquiladoras provide jobs in areas that may have few other sources of work. In the state of Chihuahua over 750,000 people are employed in maquiladora plants. The availability of work in MNCs has led to migration from rural to urban areas. This has caused pressure on services. Many thousands of workers live in shanty towns without basic services such as water and power.

Because of their size, MNCs can influence government policy by threatening legal action. This happened in the healthcare industry when 39 major pharmaceutical companies prosecuted the South African government for introducing cheaper HIV/AIDS medicines in an effort to lower the cost of treatment for people. The companies eventually withdraw the case due to international protest.

Some MNCs that have invested large sums of money in pollution control may lobby governments to have higher standards of pollution control. This forces their competitors in the country into a weaker trading position, e.g. the power generation industry.

Impact of MNC decisions on consumer regions*

MNCs choose to locate in consumer regions in order to be close to a wealthy market. They also locate in consumer regions when the product they are making is not at the stage of its life cycle where it is mass produced for global consumption, e.g. Blu-Ray players. When MNCs choose to locate in consumer regions it has several impacts. First, it provides employment in the region. MNCs employ over 500 million people across the world. In Ireland, for example, American MNC Johnson & Johnson employs over 2,000 people across 7 plants. This provides increased tax revenue for the Irish government. It is estimated that in Ireland MNCs contribute over €2.5 billion per year to the Irish economy. Second, there is a spin-off effect of employment on the local economies in the consumer region. Across Ireland in 2011 MNCs employed around 139,000 people. Their wages are spent in local shops and businesses helping to keep these local retailers and service providers in operation and leading to more employment in the area. Employment opportunities in MNCs located outside of Dublin help to develop those regions (e.g. the Border Midlands West Region) and balance economic development more equally across the country. However, if the MNC decides to outsource its employment from consumer regions to lower-cost areas it can have a devastating impact on the consumer region. This happened in Ireland when software MNC Dell moved its operations from Limerick to Poland resulting in 1,900 job losses. This resulted in higher social welfare payments for the Irish government and loss of income for shops and businesses in the Limerick area. In this case the decision to relocate was made at the company's headquarters in Austin, Texas but the impact was felt several thousand kilometres away in the west of Ireland.

Global Warming, Deforestation and Desertification

> **NOTE**
>
> This topic can be examined in several ways. You may be asked to discuss one issue (as in 2012 Question 15 and 2014 Question 15) or you may be asked to discuss more than one.
>
> A selection of single issue answers is provided below. These answers could be shortened and combined if the question asks you to discuss more than one issue.
>
> Depending on the question, when discussing environmental issues your three aspects could be:
> - Causes
> - Impacts
> - Solutions to the problem

Q **Global environmental issues: 2010 Question 15**
Examine the **causes** and the **impact** of **one** global environmental issue studied by you. **[80 marks]**

> **What You Need To Do:**
> - Discuss the causes of your chosen issue, e.g. global warming/deforestation/desertification.
> - Describe the worldwide impact referring to examples.
> - Describe how the issue may be solved or impacts reduced.

Answer 1: Global Warming

A Cause of global warming: burning fossil fuels*

The atmosphere contains gases such as carbon dioxide, methane and water vapour which naturally trap heat from the sun and keep the earth's average temperature (about 16°C) warm enough to support life.

Global warming refers to the rise in the temperature of the earth's atmosphere. This rise is caused by human economic activities, such as burning fossil fuels, farming and deforestation. These human activities release vast amounts of carbon dioxide (CO_2) and methane into the air. These gases trap more heat from the sun within the atmosphere. As the atmosphere warms up, global climate and ocean systems change.

Burning fossil fuels adds about 24.5 billion tonnes of CO_2 into the air each year. The amount of fossil fuels such as coal and oil that humans use is increasing due to population growth, increased car ownership, increased shipping trade and rising demand for electricity. Petroleum is used to fuel our vehicles while coal and natural gas are used to produce electricity for our homes and offices. Burning fossil fuels has caused about three quarters of the increase in CO_2 over the past 20 years. The majority of fossil fuels are used for transport. CO_2 released from transportation contributes to approximately 33% of global CO_2 emissions.

Developing countries such as India and China are also burning more fossil fuels to provide energy for their rapidly growing economies. China has massive reserves of coal which supplies 70% of its energy. Chinese power stations burn 4 million tonnes of coal a day. This situation is not environmentally sustainable.

In order to reduce global use of fossil fuels, an international agreement called the Kyoto Protocol was introduced to reduce CO_2 emissions from fossil fuel use. Countries who have signed it have agreed to reduce their emissions by 5.2% by 2012.

Governments can commit to using more renewable sources of energy such as hydropower and wind power instead of burning fossil fuels in power stations. Investing in nuclear energy can also reduce CO_2 emissions. The Irish government has pledged to reduce its CO_2 emissions and is investing in renewable energy sources.

Individuals can help to reduce their production of greenhouse gases. Insulating homes and switching off appliances and not leaving them in 'sleep mode' are two simple ways to reduce our power consumption and therefore our use of fossil fuels. Across the EU, 10% of electricity is used by machines in 'sleep mode'. Using public transport where available instead of the car is another practical way of reducing harmful CO_2 emissions from transport. One bus can replace 50 cars on the road.

Cause of global warming: agriculture*

Agriculture is another cause of global warming. Two gases are released by agricultural activities: methane emissions are released from decaying plants in water-covered rice fields and CO_2 is released from cattle farming. Cattle production accounts for 9% of CO_2 emissions and the clearing of forest for pasture also increases global warming. Rice fields contribute to 20% of global methane emissions.

Livestock now use 30% of the earth's entire land surface either as pasture or in the form of arable land used to produce feed for livestock. Forests are cleared to create new pastures for cattle production. Forest clearance for cattle is most severe in South America where, for example, some 70% of former forests in the Amazon have been turned over to grazing. Deforestation for pasture reduces the amount of CO_2 that can be absorbed from the air by trees and so contributes to global warming. In Indonesia natural forests are cleared to make way for palm oil plantations which do not absorb as much CO_2 from the air as natural forest.

The manufacture and use of pesticides and fertilisers as well as fuel and oil for tractors, equipment and food transport also release greenhouse gases and increase global warming.

In addition, irrigation of land and intensive agriculture decrease the amount of CO_2 that can be absorbed from the air by soils.

At present, as a result of human activities such as farming and fossil fuel burning, concentrations of CO_2 in the air are just over 394 parts per million (ppm) – an increase of over 50 ppm on levels recorded in the 1970s. In the worst case situation, further increases could cause the global average temperature to rise by as much as 6°C by 2100. Scientists estimate that irreversible change to the global climate and ocean systems is likely to occur if the global climate warms by 2°C.

Buying food that is produced locally reduces CO_2 emissions as there is then less demand for imported food that has travelled by land, air or sea using fossil fuels. Using organically produced food also reduces pesticide use and improves the soil's capacity to absorb carbon dioxide.

Impact of global warming*

The United Nations Intergovernmental Panel on Climate Change says that global warming, if unchecked, will lead to a devastating combination of floods, drought, disease and extreme weather. These effects are already being observed across the planet. Southern Europe is getting warmer and the frequency of heat waves and associated forest fires is increasing. In Africa rainfall in the Sahel region is becoming more unpredictable and has decreased by 30% over the last 20 years. This is leading to increased drought.

The world's oceans are predicted to rise by up to 1 metre by 2100 due to the melting of icecaps in Greenland and Antarctica and the thermal expansion of the oceans. This eustatic (global) rise in sea level will have an impact on many countries across the planet. It is enough to wipe out several small island nations in the Pacific Ocean such as the Maldives and displace tens of millions living in low-lying river deltas in East Asia, e.g. the Ganges Delta in Bangladesh. Even the rise (22 centimetres during the twentieth century) that has already occurred is having an impact on Pacific island nations such as Tuvalu (located between Australia and Hawaii) whose water supplies are contaminated by saltwater and which is being eroded away by the sea.

Tourism and agriculture are also experiencing problems due to global warming. In

Australia the warming ocean is damaging the Great Barrier Reef. The reef attracts over 2 million visitors each year and generates about €1.5 billion per year for the Australian economy.

However the reef could disappear by 2047 due to global warming and the loss of income would severely damage the Australian economy.

Africa, Asia and Southern Europe are also expected to suffer a decrease in agricultural production if global temperatures rise by 2°C. The economies of these regions will suffer as a result of decreased food supplies as there will be millions of people at risk of starvation or economic ruin.

Answer 2: Deforestation

A

Cause of deforestation: economic development*

Deforestation of the world's tropical rainforests is a global problem. Tropical rainforests are found between 23°C north and south of the equator in South America, Africa and South-East Asia. The unsustainable use of these forests for timber and land clearance is widespread. Each day 32,000 hectares of rainforest disappear. There are several reasons for continued deforestation and they are all related to economic development. Industrial logging, conversion of forest land for agriculture (soya farming, cattle ranching) and forest fires – set by people to clear land – are responsible for the bulk of global deforestation today. Rainforests in developing nations such as Brazil are under threat since valuable wood such as teak and mahogany are sold to improve their balance of payments. The developed world has a great demand for hardwood, which it processes into furniture such as garden tables. Deforestation is also caused by mining developments and road building projects. The Trans Amazon highway in Brazil is an example. This highway is being built across Brazil to reach neighbouring countries such as Colombia in order to develop the interior of Brazil, provide trade routes and encourage exploitation of resources. In order to encourage people to move to the region, settlers are granted a 100-hectare plot of land, six-months' salary and easy access to agricultural loans. This is in exchange for settling along the highway and converting the surrounding rainforest into agricultural land. Government-planned urban development has also led to deforestation. In Brazil, the capital city Brasilia was deliberately planned to be in the heart of the Amazon rainforest. The aim was to attract people to the Brazilian interior to exploit its resources and clear the forest for agriculture. It was completed in 1960 and today has a population of about 3.5 million people.

Cause of deforestation: agriculture*

In Indonesia and Malaysia deforestation is driven by the palm oil industry. Palm oil is used in 50% of all consumer goods, from soaps and detergents to breakfast cereals and biofuels. It is grown on massive plantations in tropical nations, mainly Malaysia and Indonesia. In Brazil, deforestation is driven by the soya bean industry. Soya beans are about 18% oil and 38% protein. Because soya beans are high in protein, they are a major ingredient in livestock feed. Most soya beans are processed for their oil and protein for the animal feed industry. A smaller percentage is processed for human consumption and made into products including soya milk and soya flour. Soya bean oil is also used to make biodiesel fuel.

Soya bean farming is associated with new roads and infrastructure projects, which increase the rate of deforestation. Satellite data in Brazil shows more deforestation along the BR-163 road, a highway the government has been paving in an effort to help soya farmers from the state of Mato Grosso transport their crops to export markets. Typically, roads encourage settlement by rural poor who look to the rainforest as free land for subsistence agriculture. In Brazil, famers can claim ownership of land simply by clearing an area of forest and grazing a few cattle on it. This easy way to gain ownership of land has led to many settlers moving into the Amazon forest and burning down a section in order to make pasture land. Commercial beef producers also burn thousands of hectares of forest to make their massive cattle ranches.

Production of soya has increased across the world because it is a cash crop. A cash crop is one that is sold by the government to pay back debts, often to the World Bank. In order for a country such as Brazil to qualify for international development loans the World Bank demands that it must produce more cash crops in order to pay back the loan. This has led to the increase in deforestation in Brazil.

Impact of deforestation*

Deforestation is a significant global problem because tropical rainforests play a vital role in controlling the planet's natural weather and climate systems. If the forests continue to be destroyed, global weather patterns may become more unstable and extreme. The forests regulate local and global weather through their absorption of water and formation of rainfall. For example, the Amazon creates 50-80% of its own rainfall through transpiration (the transfer of water from soil to the atmosphere by plants). Clearing the rainforests changes the reflectivity (albedo) of the earth's surface. This can affect global weather by altering wind and rainfall patterns. A study by NASA in 2005 found that deforestation in the Amazon region of South America influences rainfall from Mexico to Texas and in the Gulf of Mexico.

Rainforests also have an important role in absorbing carbon dioxide from the air and storing it. It is estimated that tropical forests absorb 18% of carbon dioxide added to the air by burning fossil fuels. Deforestation can destroy this 'carbon sink' leading to increased global warming.

Reducing the rate of deforestation is a global problem. Responsible development of rainforests has to occur if countries want to preserve this valuable resource for the future.

Another impact has been international concern about deforestation. Several ways of reducing the rate of deforestation exist and some stop it completely.

Rainforests provide medicines like quinine, which treats malaria, and tamoxifen, which treats cancer. They are also home to 50% of the earth's species. Efforts to restore degraded forest lands along with the establishment of protected areas are vital to securing the rainforests for the future. Responsible farming can also help protect forests. In Brazil new laws aim to prevent soya bean production on newly cleared forest.

Agri-forestry is one way of reducing the impact of deforestation. It involves combining farming and forestry. Agri-forestry protects the forest surrounding the farms. It also reduces soil erosion and improves soil fertility by providing as much vegetation cover for the soil as possible. Agri-forestry also provides an income for native tribal people. Using agri-forestry, farms and forests can exist together in the future. People and wildlife benefit from this system. People can get an income from the forest while the forest biome is damaged as little as possible.

Conservation zones are areas where felling of trees is banned. These areas are used only by native tribes and their way of life is secure from interference from mining, urban settlement, logging, HEP schemes and road building. Brazil has many forest sites that are protected. Some of these sites are so unique they are designated as Biosphere Reserves by the United Nations.

Eco-tourism can fund efforts to protect and rehabilitate degraded forests. In Costa Rica, which was one of the first countries to promote eco-tourism, money from this form of tourism is earned through park entrance fees, employing locals as guides and in the services (hotels, restaurants, drivers, boat drivers, porters, cooks) and handicrafts sectors.

An advantage of conserving forests is that rainforest countries can earn money by allowing scientists to develop products from the plant and animal species in the forests. For example, Costa Rica has entered into an agreement with the American pharmaceutical company, Merck, to look for plants with potential pharmaceutical uses. Under the agreement, a portion of the proceeds from plant/animal products that do prove commercially valuable will go to the Costa Rican government which has guaranteed that some of the royalties will be set aside for conservation projects.

Answer 3: Desertification

Cause of desertification: Population growth*

Desertification is the spread of desert conditions into new areas. Desertified soils are dry, dusty and lack humus. Their fertility is reduced and they are affected by soil erosion.

The Sahel region of Africa is the region most at risk from desertification although Southern Europe, especially Southern Spain, is also at risk. Desertification often occurs as a result of a combination of human factors such as drought, overcropping, overgrazing and deforestation. Overcropping is when the land is constantly cultivated and its fertility is reduced. Overgrazing is when too many animals are grazed on the land and destroy the soil. High population growth in countries such as Sudan, where the natural increase is over 2.5% per year (an extra 6 million people per year), contributes to desertification due to the increased demand for food and fuel. Drought conditions increase the chance of desertification occurring when the soil is already stressed by overcropping and overgrazing.

World Bank debt relief programmes also contribute to desertification. In Sahelian countries such as Chad and Niger, cotton and cashew nuts are grown as cash crops on huge plantations as part of economic reforms (structural adjustment programmes) in return for debt relief. People are removed from their land to make way for the plantations and must make a living on poor land at the edge of the plantations.

This land is overgrazed and overcropped and trees are cut down for fuel and building materials. Because so many trees have been cut down, cattle dung is used for fuel instead. This further deprives the soil of valuable nutrients leading to increased desertification in the region during drought.

Cause of desertification: changing climate patterns due to global warming*

The atmosphere contains gases such as carbon dioxide, methane and water vapour which naturally trap heat from the sun and keep the earth's average temperature (about 16°C) warm enough to support life.

Global warming refers to the rise in the temperature of the earth's atmosphere. This rise is caused by human economic activities such as burning fossil fuels, farming and deforestation. These human activities release vast amounts of carbon dioxide (CO_2) and methane into the air. These gases trap more heat from the sun within the atmosphere. As the atmosphere warms up, global climate and ocean systems change. Global warming is increasing the amount of desertification that is occurring.

In the savanna and tropical regions of the world, global warming is causing crop production to decrease. As the soil becomes drier, fewer plants can survive and cannot protect the soil from being blown away, leading to desertification.

Global warming is expected to reduce annual water run-off from the land by 10–30% in the areas between the tropics and 50° North and South. This will reduce the amount of water available and lead to further desertification in those regions. Agricultural production in many African regions is being severely affected by climate change. In the Sahel rainfall levels have decreased by 30% over the last 20 years. The area suitable for agriculture, the length of growing seasons and the amount harvested are all expected to decrease. In the drier areas of Central and South America, climate change is expected to lead to salinisation of soil and desertification of agricultural land. In Southern Europe, higher temperatures and more frequent drought are reducing water supplies and crop production which are the early signs of desertification.

Impacts of desertification*

Desertification has a number of impacts. Loss of productive farmland and the resulting rural to urban migration of people will occur in many countries of the Sahel affected by desertification, e.g. Mali.

Hunger due to lack of food is another impact. The loss of food production and resulting starvation is a serious threat to populations in desertified regions. Some models show that natural drought cycles combined with human causes of desertification could cause Chad and Niger to lose nearly all their rain dependent agriculture by 2100.

Global warming will also increase the effects of desertification. It is estimated that if global temperatures rise by 1-2·75°C the cereal harvest in Mali by 2030 could be 15-19% lower than at present. This will cause food prices to double. Reduced agricultural production and increased food prices will then cause hunger to affect nearly 70% of the Malian population by 2030.

Another impact of desertification is the decrease in GDP of a country. Decreased agricultural and livestock production threatens to shrink already poor economies of Sahelian nations. The majority of the populations in Sahelian countries work in agriculture and livestock herding and these industries account for 40% of the GDP for those countries. Their economies will then need more aid from richer nations in order to develop.

Apart from hunger, other health risks associated with desertification will affect people. Land destroyed by desertification leads to increased numbers of dust storms, which contributes to air pollution and causes eye infections, respiratory problems and allergies.

Rural to urban migration will increase as people leave the land and move to the cities to escape rural poverty and hunger. This is already putting pressure on services in cities such as Khartoum in Sudan.

Other impacts of desertification are (a) global concern about the loss of vital soil resources and (b) conflicts that arise from the displacement of people as a result of desertification of their land. International aid is now being used to try and reduce desertification. It is possible to reduce the impact of desertification. The main methods involve saving water, improving soil fertility and preventing soil erosion.

Enriching of the soil and restoring soil fertility is often done by plants. Plants that extract nitrogen from the air and fix it into the soil can be grown to increase fertility, e.g. bean plants and barley. Food crop trees such as dates are also used to do this.

Reducing the loss of the rainwater that falls in dry areas is a very important method of reducing desertification. Rainwater is lost when it runs off the land and is not captured for storage or irrigation. Run-off accounts for 20 – 40% of total annual rainfall in the Sahel making this the largest contributor to lack of moisture in the Sahel. Hedgerow systems and stone lines (bunds) are methods used to limit run-off in fields. They work by providing a barrier to run-off and encouraging water to soak into the soil. The greater number of stone lines in a plot allows more water infiltration, thus improving yields. Hedgerow systems also increase water infiltration to the soil and decrease run-off.

Planting trees in and around fields where crops are being grown will also reduce the impact of soil erosion due to desertification. Using trees on farms (agri-forestry) can cause a more humid local climate (microclimate). Trees can also provide an additional source of income for Sahelian farmers.

Sand fences can also be used to control drifting of soil and sand erosion.

The introduction of solar cookers in the Sahel could reduce the need for timber as a fuel. Trees can then be planted which can help slow soil erosion due to desertification in the region.

Chapter 33
Trade, Aid, Debt and Land Owership

Trade

Q

Fair trade, aid and economic inequality: 2010 Question 14
Discuss the idea that Fair Trade not aid is the best way to tackle economic inequality in the world. **[80 marks]**

What You Need To Do:
- Discuss the issue of trade and inequality.
- Discuss the problems associated with aid.
- Discuss the benefits/problems of Fair Trade.
- Respond to the statement in the question. You may agree or disagree with it.

215

A

Answer

Trade and Economic Inequality*

Fair trading relationships between producers and consumers should benefit both sides equally. However across the world producers rarely receive a fair share of the trade that occurs.

Unfair trade rules contribute to economic inequality between developed and developing countries. Developed countries place tariffs on agricultural and manufactured exports from developing countries to (1) make these products more expensive and (2) prevent manufacturers from getting a fair share of the global market. Having a fair share of world trade helps a country earn more money, develop its manufacturing base and expand its economy. If farmers and manufacturers in developing countries were able to trade fairly on the world markets, there would be less need to give international aid.

To reduce economic inequality the World Bank provides debt relief and international aid to poor countries on the condition that they open their markets to foreign companies. This type of 'tied aid' can cripple the local economy. In Ghana, domestic rice production, a vital source of income for the country's farmers, has collapsed since the World Bank and the IMF insisted that Ghana open its agricultural markets as a condition of receiving aid. Cheap American rice now floods the country, while Ghanaian farmers struggle to sell their crops which are now more expensive.

Farmers in developing countries must also compete with farmers in rich countries whose production costs are subsidised by their government. Subsidies are an unfair trade rule that leads to economic inequality. The US spends €20 billion each year in subsidies to its farmers. Subsidies give farmers in rich countries an unfair advantage on the world market because their produce is cheaper than it would be if they did not receive subsidies.

Fair trade is one way in which international aid can be made more effective in reducing economic inequality in trade. If farmers get a fair income for their produce, there is less need for food aid and debt relief. Therefore aid that is given can be directed to more long-term projects such as education and healthcare. Over time fair trade could lead to the reduction in aid required and economic independence for developing countries.

Aid and economic inequality*

One of the main criticisms of international aid is that it is not effective in helping countries develop. For example despite €0.7 trillion in loans since the 1960s, the per capita growth rate of the typical developing country over the past 20 years was zero.

Even though €1.4 billion worth of aid has been given to Zambia, living standards are 40% lower now than when it gained independence in 1964. In 2011, it was ranked as the least 'livable' country in the world on the Human Development Index.

How can so much international aid make so little difference to those in need? First, in many cases aid is diverted by international agencies and never reaches those who need help. In Afghanistan, for example, a €21-million project to deliver roofing timber to people in a war-torn mountain village was not effective as it could have been because 60% of the money was used by foreign agencies to cover their own costs such as administration and transport.

Also, aid money may be stolen by corrupt government officials who bank the money in overseas accounts for their own private use, e.g. President Marcos of the Philippine Islands and Idi Amin of Uganda. According to American and British defence forces, up to half of all foreign aid allocated to help improve living standards of ordinary people in war-torn Afghanistan has been stolen by corrupt government officials and tribal leaders. Fuel, building materials and trucks intended to help rebuild war-torn areas have all been taken. Projects can also be affected by differences in customs between development aid workers and local people. Not respecting local customs may cause severe offence, and thus lead to problems and delay of the projects. However, development aid can be very effective. For example, in Ethiopia the average income is now 40% higher than in 1999. It is now €784 per year.

Even though the amount of international aid given to developing economies is huge (over €87.5 billion in 2010), many times that amount is lost to developing economies through unfair trade systems. It is estimated that for every €1 of aid given to poor countries, over €14 is lost due to unfair trade. This discourages donors from giving more aid and this increases economic inequality in the world. So by increasing the amount of fair trade, the aid that is given can be more effective in reducing inequality.

Benefits and problems of Fair Trade

If trade was organised in a more fair way, the need for development aid would be reduced. One way for doing this is the Fair Trade system.

Goods sold under the Fair Trade system improve levels of human development in the following ways: A fair price is charged for goods, i.e. a price that covers the cost of production and guarantees a living income. This allows communities to improve local services such as water supply and education.

The Fair Trade label ensures that farm workers are protected by labour laws and standards and that a sum of money called a 'premium' has been paid to contribute to community projects.

Farmers have security of income, allowing them to plan for the future. Support is provided to enable farmers in developing countries to gain the knowledge and skills needed to develop their businesses and increase sales.

With sales of over €2.8 billion in 2009, Fair Trade benefited about 6 million poor people in 58 developing countries. Sales are increasing across the world.

Fair Trade is not a perfect solution to economic inequality. It represents only a tiny proportion of world trade. For example, only 1% of global coffee sales carried the label in 2009. The Fair Trade system is not a substitute for 'fair trade', the internationally agreed terms of trade that the poorest countries need to encourage their development.

Also, Fair Trade is largely restricted to agricultural products such as coffee and bananas. It is a subsidy which encourages production rather than efficiency and the poorest farmers still struggle to organise themselves to pay the certification fees to be registered as Fair Trade producers. However, these problems can be overcome if consumers in developed nations demand more Fair Trade produce and the application process is made simpler so more producers will join.

More difficult problems for Fair Trade to deal with are the massive barriers to development that are found across many African nations. These include antiquated port facilities, poor roads, crippling customs bureaucracy and unreliable energy supplies. These factors all combine to raise the costs of doing business. Small-scale farmers and fishermen cannot even hope to export their produce unless these issues are overcome. Infrastructure aid projects are needed in this case to enable trade, fair or otherwise, to occur.

> **Q**
>
> **Global trading systems: 2013 Question 14**
> Examine the impact of global trading systems in relation to both producer and consumer regions with reference to one multinational company that you have studied. **[80 marks]**

> **What You Need To Do:**
> - Discuss the pattern of global trade.
> - Discuss the effects of global trade on producer regions.
> - Discuss the effects of global trade on consumer regions.
> - You must refer to a named MNC in your answer.

A

Answer

The global trading system*

International trade connects many countries both economically and socially. Countries trade with each other because they cannot all produce everything their people want. For example, Ireland buys Brazilian coffee and sells beef to Saudi Arabia. Trade therefore makes countries interdependent. Countries rely on each other to get the things they need. When discussing world trade, the term 'globalisation' refers to the network of trading partnerships and the rapid movement of people, goods and information between producer and consumer regions. More economically developed countries (MEDCs), e.g. Ireland, rely on the less economically developed countries (LEDCs), e.g. Brazil, for foodstuffs, raw materials and cheap labour. In return the LEDCs depend on MEDCs for their market and foreign direct investment.

Global trade is governed by the World Trade Organisation (WTO). This body is responsible for overseeing trade agreements between countries. Decisions about market access and barriers to trade are made by the member countries of the WTO.

Multinational companies (MNCs) have a big influence on global trading patterns. Just 500 MNCs control over 70% of world trade. The most important factor for an MNC is locating their operations in countries where they can maintain profitability for their shareholders. So they are constantly searching for cheaper production methods and locations. MNCs (such as Johnson & Johnson) operate in many countries. Usually the headquarters are in a MEDC while branch plants are placed in LEDCs or MEDCs depending on the stage a product is at in its lifecycle. This means that if a product is at the stage of being mass produced, the MNC will most likely locate its manufacturing plant in a low labour cost economy such as China. In a globalised world, rapid communications mean that the decisions made by MNCs in one country can quickly cause economic changes in another. Johnson & Johnson uses the global trading system in its manufacture of contact lenses. Its headquarters and silicone gel manufacture is located in the US. However, its lens manufacturing plant is located in Limerick in order to lower transport costs to its markets in Japan and the EU.

Impact on producer regions*

Most MNCs are very wealthy; some of them are wealthier than actual countries. For example, of the 100 largest economies in the world, 51 are MNCs. This makes MNCs very powerful in trade negotiations with national governments. When choosing to locate in a region, an MNC will often 'play countries against each other' to try and get the best deal it can to minimise its wage bill and other production costs. To compete, countries sometimes offer incentives to MNCs such as tax breaks, pledges of governmental assistance, improved infrastructure or low standards of environmental protection. This, for example, has led to the location of 'maquiladora' manufacturing plants in Mexico. A maquiladora is a foreign-owned manufacturing plant found close to the border of the US in Mexico. The location of maquiladora plants in Mexico has occurred because Mexican labour is inexpensive and worker protection laws are not as strict as those in the US. The location of maquiladora plants in Mexico has several impacts there. First, it has increased exports from Mexico, improving its balance of trade. Maquiladoras account for more than 50% of manufacturing exports between Mexico and the US. This is helping the Mexican economy. However pollution is a problem as some MNCs are responsible for serious water and air pollution in their area due to low standards of environmental protection. Second, maquiladoras provide jobs in areas that may have few other sources of work. In the state of Chihuahua over 750,000 people are employed in maquiladora plants, e.g. Johnson & Johnson and Electrolux. The availability of work has led to migration from rural to urban areas. This has caused pressure on services. Many thousands of workers live in shanty towns without basic services such as water and power.

Another impact of the global trade system of maquiladoras is the employment of women in low-paid work. The cost of living in maquiladora towns is often higher than elsewhere yet some MNCs do not pay the minimum wage so thousands of women are living in poverty while working long hours.

Impact on consumer regions*

The main consumer regions in the world are Europe, the US and Japan. MNCs choose to locate in consumer regions in order to be close to a wealthy market. They also do this when the product they are making is not at the stage of its life cycle where it is mass produced for global consumption, e.g. Blue Ray DVD players. When MNCs choose to locate in consumer regions it has several impacts. First, it provides employment in the region. In Ireland, for example, American MNC Johnson & Johnson employs over 2,000 people across 7 plants. This provides increased tax revenue for the Irish government. It is estimated that in Ireland MNCs contribute over €2.5 billion per year to the Irish economy. Second, there is a spin-off effect of employment on the local economies in the consumer region. Wages are spent in local shops and businesses keeping them in operation and leading to more employment in the area. Employment opportunities in MNCs located outside of Dublin helps to develop those regions (e.g. the Border Midlands West Region) and balances economic development more equally across the country. However, the MNC may outsource its employment from consumer regions to lower cost areas. This happened in Ireland when software MNC Dell moved its operations from Limerick to Poland resulting in 1,900 job losses.

Aid

> **Q**
>
> **Impact of aid on developing countries: 2011 Question 13**
> Examine the way in which **aid** can have both **positive** and **negative** impacts on developing countries.
> **International aid: 2013 Question 15**
> Discuss the arguments for and against international aid. [80 marks]

> **What You Need To Do:**
> - Discuss two positive impacts of aid referring to examples.
> - Discuss negative impacts of aid referring to examples.
> - Name and describe different types of aid in your discussions.

A

Answer

Positive impact of aid (1): improved health, literacy and infrastructure *

Aid has many positive impacts. International aid is the help given to less developed countries so that they can develop economically and socially. Development aid helps communities to improve their living conditions, education, training and infrastructure in the long term. Emergency aid saves lives and is given in response to natural disasters such as earthquakes and hurricanes. Aid may be in the form of money, equipment or skilled people who can make a difference in the regions in which they work. Aid can be provided by national governments or by voluntary agencies called non-governmental organisations (NGOs) such as Goal and Trócaire. The main donor countries are the US, the UK and Japan. Ireland donated €630 million in development aid in 2010.

Aid has saved lives, increased trade, empowered women and improved literacy levels in Africa, Asia and South America. It has also improved healthcare across many of the poorest nations such as Ethiopia.

The Millennium Development Goals (MDGs) are development targets set by the United Nations (UN). These goals have many positive aims such as eliminating extreme poverty and hunger, providing primary education, promoting equality between men and women, reducing child mortality and improving health. Funding these goals is having an impact in developing countries.

Ireland's MDG programme in Ethiopia is an example of the many positive impacts of aid on developing countries. Ethiopia is the poorest of Irish Aid's programme countries. Over 26% of the population live on less than €1 a day and 80% live on less than €1.50 a day. In 2010 Irish Aid's contribution to Ethiopia totalled €34.7 million.

Irish Aid contributes to the funding of Ethiopia's education sector to expand primary school enrolment to 65%. This includes funding a purchase scheme for school books and supplies.

Irish Aid also contributes to funding the expansion of and access to basic health services. This includes supporting a network of community health workers who provide basic healthcare in villages throughout Ethiopia.

The aid received from Ireland also supports voluntary counselling and testing programmes for HIV/AIDS as well as education and awareness-raising of the disease.

It is also used to improve the local water and sanitation infrastructure. It funds the Water Sector Development Plan which supports community-managed water and sanitation programmes.

Positive impact of aid (2): Government reform in developing countries *

The World Bank warns that one of the biggest threats to development in the twenty-first century is long-term insecurity caused by criminal and political violence in countries receiving aid. Therefore in order for development aid to work and achieve its aims, the government of the receiving nation must be peaceful, well organised and honest. Aid can be given on condition that the government receiving the money introduces regulations to prevent corruption and accounts honestly for the money. Not all governments are corrupt and may just lack the skills required to run an efficient government.

The Irish Aid programme in Tanzania focuses on local government reform and on improving accounting standards in government at local level. Irish Aid is also involved in civic education programmes so that people know what to expect of their government and can use the services it provides.

Irish Aid has also supported the Tanzanian government in increasing its investment in the health sector. Government expenditure on health per person has increased by 500% since 2000.

The department of health has received technical assistance from Ireland and has been able to provide new hospitals, health centres and equipment in areas that five years ago had no health services at all.

A woman in Tanzania is over 500 times more likely to die in childbirth than a woman in Ireland. The high mortality rate has been linked to poor access to medical treatment for basic birth complications. Due to Irish Aid supports for government health service reform, improved government services have been very successful in reducing maternal death rates. Under-five child mortality has fallen from 147 to 67 per 1,000 live births since 2004.

Negative impact of aid: tied aid/ inappropriate aid *

One of the main criticisms of international aid is that it is not effective enough in helping countries develop. For example despite €0.7 trillion in loans since the 1960s, the per capita growth rate of the typical developing country over the past 20 years was zero. One of the reasons for this is tied aid. In this type of aid the giving (or donor) country also benefits economically from the aid. This happens as the receiving country has to buy goods and services from the donor country to get the aid in the first place. Most aid (70%) is in the form of bilateral aid which is given from one country to another, e.g. Ireland has given aid to Zambia and other priority countries in Africa. However, when bilateral aid is tied it has negative impacts on developing economies.

In 2011, 20% of all bilateral aid was tied aid even though developed world countries promised to stop tied aid over ten years ago. Tied aid is often criticised as the aid given must be spent in the donor country or in a group of selected countries. The World Bank itself is involved in tied aid. In Uganda, for example, only 18% of the contract value of World Bank-funded projects went to local firms. In this way tied aid can increase development aid project costs by up to 20 or 30%. In Eritrea, the government calculated that it would be cheaper to build its network of railways with local expertise and resources rather than be forced to spend its aid money on American consultants, architects and engineers under the terms of the aid agreement with the USA.

Another negative impact of tied aid is that aid money is often spent on weapons instead of helping people. Before the UK banned the giving of tied aid, it was criticised for donating €269 million in aid for a hydroelectric dam project in Malaysia. The donation was on condition that the Malaysian government spend €1.1 billion on weapons from the UK.

Other negative side effects of tied aid can include increasing corruption and adverse political effects such as postponements of necessary economic and democratic reforms as aid money is used, for example, to run government services rather than improve infrastructure.

In the past bilateral (government-to-government aid) programmes were often inappropriate because they supported corrupt leaders of countries with valuable resources sought by the developed world. For example, the former dictator of Zaire, Mobuto Sese Seko, was supported by Western countries in order to reduce communist influence in Africa. At the time of his death in 1997 he had accumulated enough money from aid agreements with Western countries to pay off the entire external debt of Zaire.

Q

International Aid Debate: 2008 Question 14
Examine two of the major issues arising from the international aid debate.
[80 marks]

What You Need to Do:
- Briefly outline the types of aid.
- Name two issues associated with the provision of aid (e.g. unfair trade and whether it is effective or not).
- You must cover three or four aspects across the two major issues.

Answer

A

Two of the main issues associated with international aid are: whether it is effective and the impact of unfair trade.

International aid is the help given to less developed countries so that they can develop economically and socially. It can be long-term development aid or emergency aid. Aid may be in the form of money, equipment or skilled people who can make a difference in the regions in which they work.

The effectiveness of international aid*

One of the main criticisms of international aid is that it is not effective in helping countries develop. For example despite €0.7 trillion in loans since the 1960s, the per-capita growth rate of the typical developing country over the past 20 years was zero. Even after €1.4 billion worth of aid was given to Zambia, living standards are 40% lower now than when it gained independence in 1964. How can so much international aid make so little difference to those in need? First, in many cases aid is diverted by international agencies and never reaches those who need help. In Afghanistan, for example, a €21-million project to deliver roofing timber to people in a war-torn mountain village was not effective because 60% of the money was used by foreign agencies to cover their own costs such as administration and transport. Also, aid money may be stolen by corrupt government officials who bank the money in overseas accounts for their own private use. According to American and British defence forces up to half of all foreign aid allocated to help improve living standards of ordinary people in war-torn Afghanistan has been stolen by corrupt government officials and tribal leaders. Fuel, building materials and trucks intended to help rebuild war-torn areas have all been taken.

Inappropriate aid is ineffective*

Aid may not be suitable or appropriate for the people who need it. For example, clothes given in an emergency such as an earthquake may be too warm for the climate. This was a problem for victims of the Asian tsunami of 2004. Large sums of money can be wasted on inappropriate aid projects and these can do long-term harm. In Ghana, the Akosombo Dam was built to provide power and control floods. However the reservoir drowned valuable agricultural land so people ultimately had less food.

However, aid can be very effective when it is delivered directly to those in need and is appropriate for their needs. Voluntary aid is organised by non-governmental organisations (NGOs) such as Goal or Trócaire. People contribute to bilateral and multilateral aid through their government taxes. They can also contribute to non-governmental aid by donating to charity collections, e.g. the annual Trócaire 24-Hour Fast. Emergency aid is given in response to natural disasters such as earthquakes and hurricanes, e.g. the Haiti Earthquake in 2010. Most aid (70%) is in the form of bilateral aid which is given from one country to another, e.g. Ireland gives aid to Zambia and other priority countries in Africa. About 30% of all aid is multilateral aid. This is aid given by many countries to a central fund which is then channelled to those who need it through international agencies such as the UN. In Ghana international aid has been used to supply low-tech solar cookers to villages. Solar cookers do not need wood fuel thus helping to combat desertification in the region. Over the past decade, Uganda has used Western aid to double the number of children in schools, cut the rate of HIV infection among pregnant women by 80% and reduce poverty by about 35%. These are huge social and economic gains due to the effectiveness of international aid.

The effectiveness of bilateral aid can be prevented by political instability in the receiver countries. 1.5 billion people live in countries affected by organised violence. The World Bank states that one of the biggest threats to development in the twenty-first century is long-term insecurity caused by criminal and political violence. It suggests that more aid should be spent on establishing security as well as on health and education.

The impact of unfair trade*
Another major issue surrounding international aid is the impact of unfair trade on developing economies. Even though the amount of international aid given to developing economies is huge (over €87.5 billion in 2010) many times that amount is lost to developing economies through unfair trade systems. It is estimated that for every €1 of aid given to poor countries, over €14 is lost due to unfair trade.

Unfair trade rules mean that poor countries cannot compete in the global market place with rich countries, pushing millions of poor farmers deeper into poverty. At the same time the World Bank makes the giving of debt relief and international aid conditional on poor countries opening their markets to foreign companies. This type of 'tied aid' can cripple the local economy. In Ghana, domestic rice production, a vital source of income for the country's farmers, has collapsed since the World Bank and the IMF insisted that Ghana open its agricultural markets as a condition of receiving aid. Cheap American rice now floods the country, while Ghanaian farmers struggle to sell their crops which are more expensive. Tariffs placed on agricultural and manufactured exports from developing countries make their products more expensive and prevent manufacturers from getting a fair share of the global market. Having a fair share of world trade helps a country earn more money, develop its manufacturing base and expand its economy. If farmers and manufacturers in developing countries were able to trade fairly on the world markets, there would be less need to give international aid.

Farmers in developing countries must also compete with farmers in rich countries whose production costs are subsidised by their government. In 2008 for example the USA spent €10 billion in subsidies to its farmers. Subsidies give farmers in rich countries an unfair advantage on the world market because their produce is cheaper than it would be if they did not receive subsidies.

Fair trade is one way in which international aid can be made more effective. If farmers get a fair income for their produce there is less need for food aid and debt relief and so aid can be directed to more long-term projects such as education and healthcare.

Debt and Land Ownership

Developing Countries: 2012 Question 14
Examine the role that national debt, fair trade and landownership patterns play in the economic development of developing countries. **[80 marks]**

What You Need To Do:
- Explain how national debt, fair trade and landownership affect development.
- Name two examples in your answer.

Answer: Trade patterns, debt and landownership

The cycle of poverty*

The cycle of poverty is a set of social and economic conditions that combine to keep people poor throughout their lives. The social and economic conditions that keep people in the cycle of poverty include unfair global trading patterns, unfair landownership systems and high national debt levels in developing countries such as Ethiopia and Brazil.

People find themselves in the cycle of poverty for many reasons. The most common are a lack of education and unfair trade.

If a family is poor, parents are more likely to send their children out to work to support the family instead of sending them to school. The children then lack the skills and literacy levels needed to get a well-paid job. They grow into adults who cannot get a well-paid job and so the cycle continues.

Poor farmers also find themselves in a cycle of poverty as unfair global trading systems keep down the prices of the food they produce, reducing the farmers' incomes. Their low incomes prevent them from improving their lives. Breaking the cycle of poverty involves the provision of educational services to communities. It also involves the creation of trading systems, such as the Fair Trade scheme, that allow poor farmers to overcome the poverty trap.

Fair trade and development*

The global trade in cocoa for chocolate manufacturing is an example of how trade can affect economic development in poor countries.

Developed countries keep the world market price for cocoa beans low and so the cocoa farmers are left in a cycle of poverty.

Low market prices for cocoa beans lead to a lack of money for cocoa farmers. When a crop is undervalued, farmers have no choice but to take out high-interest loans to pay for food, education and health-care. The farmers are then perhaps hungry and in ill health. They cannot farm to the highest levels and this leads to the production of poor quality cocoa beans.

Cocoa farmers are then left in the following predicament:
- They must secure loans to cover their families' basic needs and medical emergencies.
- High-interest loans are made by unscrupulous money lenders based on anticipated income from the upcoming harvest.
- Farmers try to pay back loans with their harvest, but remain in debt due to high interest rates.
- They are left with no cash flow and often resort to migrating to the cities in the hope of escaping the vicious cycle of poverty.

Fair Trade projects ensure producers get a guaranteed and fair price for their cocoa. This money can then be used to break the cycle of poverty.

Goods sold under the Fair Trade system improve levels of human development in the following ways: A fair price is charged for goods, i.e. a price that covers the cost of production and guarantees a living income. This allows communities to improve local services such as water supply and education.

The Fair Trade label ensures that farm workers are protected by labour laws and standards and that a sum of money called a 'premium' has been paid to contribute to community projects.

Farmers have security of income, allowing them to plan for the future. Support is provided to enable farmers in developing countries to gain the knowledge and skills needed to develop their businesses and increase sales.

With sales of over €2.8 billion in 2009, Fair Trade benefited about 6 million poor people in 58 developing countries. Sales are increasing across the world.

National debt and Economic Development*

Debt relief can free resources for education and thus help economic development. Repaying national debt reduces government spending on education. For example, in Zambia the government spends four times more on debt servicing than on education. Nicaragua spends five times more on paying its debts than on teaching its children.

In Ethiopia, the abolition of school fees and provision of free textbooks could be financed by the transfer of one-quarter of the funds currently allocated to debt repayments.

However, debt repayments are organised by the International Monetary Fund (IMF) and the World Bank. In order to qualify for debt relief, these organisations demand that 'structural adjustments' are made to the economies of poor countries so that they can pay back their debts. Structural Adjustment Policies (SAPs) are imposed to ensure debt repayment. But these SAPs require poor countries to reduce spending on health, education and development, while debt repayment is made the priority. An example of a SAP is the increased export of cash crops such as cotton from countries such as Mali in Africa. Mali, like Zambia and Nicaragua, spends more on debt servicing than on essential services like education and healthcare.

Land ownership and economic development*

In many developing countries such as Brazil, land ownership systems affect development. If a farmer owns his land, he can produce enough food for his family and pay for education and healthcare from crop sales. This enables his children to work in better-paid jobs and raises standards of living in a region. Unfair land ownership systems hinder economic development because when someone works land they do not own the landowner can exploit them and they have no incentive to improve the land or try new farming methods. Tenant farmers lack economic security as they may be evicted from the land they farm. This continues a cycle of poverty and prevents economic development.

In Brazil, land ownership is major issues in rural communities where the majority of farmers do not own the land they farm. In Brazil, a few landowners own vast areas of land - just 2% of landlords own 60% of the land.

When land ownership is unequal, slavery or bonded labour can occur. This is a problem for development of rural areas in Brazil. Under the system of bonded labour, poor workers are tempted to accept verbal contracts of work based on dishonest promises of well-paid work on farms. The workers are taken by lorry to isolated parts Brazil such as the state of Pará. Here they are charged for the cost of transport, rent for their accommodation and food. Their documentation is taken from them and they soon become indebted and have no right to complain or leave the plantations. They are forced to work long hours in poor conditions and are subject to violence. About 25,000 people in Brazil are bonded labourers and this prevents the economic development of the regions they live in.

Chapter 34
Sustainable Development, NGOs and Empowerment

> **Q**
>
> **Sustainable development: 2011 Question 15**
> With reference to examples you have studied, examine how natural resources can be exploited in a sustainable way. **[80 marks]**

> **What You Need To Do:**
> - Explain the phrase 'sustainable use of resources'.
> - Discuss how fish stocks can be used in a sustainable way.
> - Discuss how fossil fuels can be used in a sustainable way.

A

Answer
In this answer the sustainable use of resources will be discussed.

Sustainable use of resources*
If resources are used in a sustainable way, they will be available to future generations. Sustainable exploitation of resources balances the need for economic and social development with conservation and protection of valuable resources such as fossil fuels and food resources such as fish. Nature will constantly resupply most renewable resources such as solar energy and wind energy. Human use of these resources will have little impact on them and they will be available for use by future generations. Yet some renewable resources can be affected by human exploitation. Fish is an example of this kind of resource. If fish stocks are exploited carefully today, they should last into the future. But if fish stocks are used too rapidly, they will be depleted and become unavailable to future generations. Unsustainable exploitation of fish stocks is occurring across the world from coral reefs in Indonesia to the Irish Sea cod fishery. In Canada the Grand Banks Cod fishery in the Atlantic Ocean was seriously overfished leading to the closure of the fishery in 1992 and the loss of 30,000 jobs. The social and economic cost of unsustainable exploitation of resources is high. It can lead to unemployment, migration and poverty, e.g. the unsustainable use of the water feeding the Aral Sea in Central Asia led to the abandonment of coastal towns and the collapse of the fishing and tourism industry in the region.

A. Sustainable exploitation of fish stocks*
Fish are a renewable resource but overfishing is a problem within the EU and several fish species are severely depleted, e.g. Irish Sea cod.

In order to protect these over-exploited fish stocks, two methods are in operation: (1) the Emergency Measures System and (2) Recovery Plans. These methods are designed to enable a more sustainable use of fish resources. They are enforced under the EU Common Fisheries Policy.

1. Emergency Measures
These actions give immediate protection to fish stocks most at risk from collapse. Emergency measures include:
- Closure of fishing grounds.
- Making fishing net mesh sizes bigger to allow younger fish to escape.
- The reduction of fishing time at sea.

2. Recovery Plans
These plans are designed to allow fish stocks to grow while at the same time enabling fishing communities to continue fishing and maintain their livelihood.

Recovery plans use a quota system for fish catches. Each year at a meeting of EU fishery ministers, each fish species is given a Total Allowable Catch or TAC. This is the tonnage of any species that can be caught by all EU fishing boats combined. The TAC is then divided out amongst the EU fishing countries, each of whom gets a share or quota of the TAC. The national quota is then divided out amongst each fishing boat in that country with some boats getting larger quotas than others depending on their capacity. In 2011, Ireland's TAC was worth €220 million.

Boats are closely monitored at sea by fishery protection vessels and on land by inspectors at ports to ensure that they stick to their quota. In this way the amount of fish caught is regulated.

B. Sustainable exploitation of fossil fuels*
In order to exploit fossil fuels in a more sustainable way we have to ensure that:
(i) They last longer.
(ii) Their use does less damage to the environment.

Sustainable use of fossil fuels is not being practiced at the moment. At our present rate of consumption, oil is expected to run out in the next 50 years. The continued burning of fossil fuels also contributes to global warming and the resulting climate change and sea-level rise is already affecting the planet with more frequent extreme weather events and changes to rainfall patterns.

There are many ways in which we can conserve fossil fuels. Switching to alternative sources of energy such as tidal, nuclear, solar and wind power can replace fossil fuel use in electricity generation. Nuclear fuel is already widely used across the world, in particular France where 90% of its electricity is provided by nuclear power.

In Brazil most cars are built to run on ethanol, a biofuel obtained from sugar cane. By using alternative fuel sources we can conserve the fossil fuel reserves we have left for important uses such as the manufacture of essential materials, e.g. carbon fibre.

The EU is committed to replacing fossil fuels with renewable energy sources and aimed to have 22% of its electricity generated by renewable sources by 2010. However by 2011 it had reached just 11%.

In Ireland the development of our wind-power resource is encouraged and the government aims to meet the EU target of receiving 20% of our energy needs from renewable sources by 2020.

Reducing the impact of fossil fuels on the environment is a personal as well as global issue. Most of the environmental impact of the use of fossil fuels comes from power generation and transport. The environmental impact includes acid rain and climate change. We can all make small changes in our daily lives to reduce our power consumption and use less fuel while travelling.

Switching off appliances and not leaving them in 'sleep mode' is one simple way to reduce our power consumption. Across the EU 10% of electricity is used by machines in 'sleep mode'. Using public transport where available instead of the car is another practical way of reducing harmful emissions from transport.

Nationally and globally, countries must agree to limits on the consumption of fossil fuels and on their production of carbon dioxide (CO_2). For example, the Kyoto Protocol is an international agreement to reduce greenhouse gas emissions from fossil fuel use. Countries that have signed it have agreed to reduce their emissions by 5·2% by 2012.

NGOs and Empowerment

Non-Governmental Organisations: 2012 Question 13
Examine the role of Non-Governmental Organisations (NGOs) in empowering people, with reference to examples that you have studied.   [80 marks]

What You Need To Do:
- Describe NGOs referring to what they do and how they operate. Make sure to name 2 or 3 NGOs.
- Discuss 'empowerment' in general and how NGOs work to empower people.
- Describe the problems NGOs encounter in their work to empower people.

Answer

Non-Governmental Organisations (NGOs)*

NGOs are private aid agencies that are independent of governments. They are usually non-profit making and rely on funding from donations from individuals and private voluntary organisations. Goal, Trócaire, Bóthar and Oxfam are examples of NGOs.

NGOs operate in 4 main areas of empowerment. These are education, relief, development and justice. Because these are such large problems, each NGO has a particular focus to its activities and all of them involve empowering people to live in a sustainable way. For example, Goal focuses on saving the lives of people, Concern focuses on education and raising awareness of the need for people in donor countries to give aid. Bóthar provides poverty-stricken families with the means to solve their problems by using livestock in development aid.

Because NGOs are non-political and independent of government agencies, they are welcome in many areas where conflict occurs, e.g. Sudan. They can also openly criticise governments where necessary without being seen as biased. By being non-political, NGOs provide 'people-to-people' aid, reaching people directly without corrupt governments stealing their aid.

NGOs are usually quite small and flexible organisations. This means they can respond quickly to emergencies and send volunteers into famine/disaster areas to organise water, food and sanitation more easily than government agencies, e.g. the Haiti earthquake of 2010.

NGOs empower people by working in small village communities to provide long-term development projects such as wells, sanitation, farming and education facilities. These help people improve their standard of living over time, e.g. solar disinfection of water schemes in Kenya.

Empowerment*

Empowerment gives people/communities choice about how they live their lives. When people are empowered, they can raise their standard of living and increase the level of development in a community. NGOs work to empower people across the world.

Aid provided by NGOs aims to make people independent so that they will not need aid in the future but can support themselves. NGO aid is not tied, unlike much governmental aid, so the benefits of the aid stay in the local communities.

Bóthar is an Irish NGO working in 20 countries across South America, Africa, Asia and Eastern Europe. Bóthar helps poor families to overcome hunger, malnutrition and poverty in a sustainable manner. They provide farm animals to families and communities. The animals – such as goats, chicken and cattle – give struggling families the opportunity to raise their living standards. Bóthar provides veterinary help and breeding advice until the communities can manage themselves. The milk, honey, meat and eggs not only improve a family's diet but the surplus can be sold, thus giving the family possibly their first opportunity to earn an income. This income allows them to feed, clothe and educate their children. The impact that one good quality farm animal has on an impoverished family in the developing world can mean the difference between destitution and security.

Trócaire supports aid projects empowering over 3.4 million people in 20 countries such as Kenya and Ethiopia. In Kenya, Trócaire raises awareness of violence against women and provides medical, legal and educational support for thousands of women and men in the region. It helps to empower women in communities so that they are able to make decisions as to how their community is organised. Trócaire also works to protect and promote human rights in countries such as Honduras and Pakistan.

When people are healthy they are able to work and raise their living standards. In Africa, HIV/AIDS is a major problem accounting for 47% of deaths in South Africa alone. Globally over 15 million children are orphaned by HIV/AIDS. In South Africa 63% of orphans have been orphaned due to HIV/AIDS. NGOs work to raise awareness about how HIV/AIDS is spread and how it can be treated and avoided. Trócaire provides care for those with AIDs and supports orphaned children and families affected by AIDS. Children orphaned by HIV/AIDS are affected by grief, have to drop out of school, suffer poverty and may be stigmatised. NGOs help to empower families affected by AIDS by providing treatment, keeping children in school by providing home care for sick parents and working to educate people about HIV/AIDS.

Problems for NGOs*

The work of NGOs in empowering people is hindered by several factors. Most NGOs are small organisations dependent on voluntary donations. Donor fatigue is a problem. This occurs when donors no longer give to charities or are slow to respond to calls for help. There are a number of causes for donor fatigue, including too much pressure to donate, overstretched personal budgets, frustration with mis-managed charities and seemingly constant disasters, conflicts and famines. Most NGOs are well aware of donor fatigue and do all they can to avoid it by running short, targeted campaigns to raise funds. It is a difficult position for NGOs. They have to advertise what they do but can't put people off donating by producing too many wasteful glossy pamphlets or running expensive advertising campaigns.

Another issue for NGOs is ensuring the safety of their workers in unstable countries such as Sudan. An increase in attacks on aid workers is due to the increasingly violent areas in which they work and the rise in the number of aid workers in conflict zones. In addition, the traditional perception of NGO neutrality may be lost as internal armed forces may see any foreign aid worker as an 'enemy'. In 2012 there were 167 attacks on aid workers across the world. Sudan and Afghanistan were the most dangerous places.

Competition for funding is a major challenge for most NGOs. The best organised can afford to run media campaigns and fundraising events to raise awareness, e.g. the Trócaire Fast or the Concern Debates. Smaller NGOs are less effective because they may not be so well organised and their income is unreliable. A recent controversy involving payment of top-up salaries to consultants out of voluntary donations at the Central Remedial Clinic affected the income of charities across Ireland. Donations dropped by 40% as donors worried about whether their money was really helping those in need.

Global economic recession also affects the income of NGOs. In Ireland, economic recession from 2008-2013 caused thousands of people to lose their job. Personal budgets decreased and individuals had less money to spend on donations to charities. At the height of economic recession, Trócaire reported a 10% decrease in donations.

Q

Economic growth and human development: 2015 Question 14
Empowering people is a way of linking economic growth with human development.
Discuss this statement with reference to aid programmes.   [80 marks]

What You Need To Do:
- Discuss aid and how it works.
- Explain the term 'empowerment' and link it to sustainable development.
- Discuss aid programmes that you have studied and how they encourage human development and economic growth (i.e. how they empower people).

A

Answer

Aid

International aid is the help given to less developed countries so that they can develop economically and socially. It can be long-term development aid or emergency aid. Aid may be in the form of money, equipment or skilled people who can make a difference in the regions in which they work.

Most aid is in the form of bilateral aid, given from one country to another, e.g. Ireland gives aid to Zambia in Africa. About 30% of all aid is multilateral aid. This is aid given by many countries to a central fund, which is then channelled to those who need it through international agencies such as the United Nations (UN). People contribute to bilateral and multilateral aid through their government taxes. Emergency aid is given in response to natural disasters such as earthquakes and hurricanes.

Voluntary aid is organised by non-governmental organisations (NGOs) such as Goal or Trócaire. People contribute to non-governmental aid by donating directly to charity collections, e.g. the annual Trócaire 24-Hour Fast.

All types of aid can empower people. Empowerment gives people/communities choice about how they live their lives. When people are empowered, they can raise their standard of living and increase the level of development in a community.

NGOs operate in four main areas of empowerment. These are: education, relief, development and justice. Because these are such large areas, each NGO has a particular focus to its activities and all of them involve empowering people to live in a sustainable way. For example, Goal focuses on saving the lives of people, Concern focuses on education and raising awareness of the need for people in donor countries to give aid. Bóthar provides poverty-stricken families with the means to solve their problems by using livestock in development aid.

Ireland's official government aid agency is called Irish Aid. Its aim is to reduce poverty and hunger across 80 countries by supporting long-term development.

Aid and sustainable human and economic development*

Sustainable development is human and economic development that meets the needs of the present without compromising the ability of future generations to meet their needs. If aid is to empower people, it has to be sustainable. An example of sustainable aid that empowers people is the United Nations Millennium Development Goal program.

The Millennium Development Goals (MDG) are development targets set by the UN. These goals aim to get rid of extreme poverty and hunger, achieve primary education for all, promote gender equality and empower women, reduce child mortality, improve maternal health, combat HIV/AIDS, malaria and other diseases and ensure environmental sustainability.

Funding these goals is having an impact in developing countries.

Ireland's MDG aid program in Ethiopia is an example of the many positive impacts of aid on developing countries. Ethiopia is the poorest of Irish Aid's programme countries. Over 26% of the population live on less than €1 a day and 80% live on less than €1.50 a day. In 2010 Irish Aid to Ethiopia totalled €34.7 million.

Irish Aid contributes to the funding of Ethiopia's education sector, aiming to expand primary school enrolment to 65%. This includes funding a purchase scheme for schoolbooks and supplies.

Irish Aid also contributes to funding the expansion of and access to basic health services. This includes supporting a network of community health workers who provide basic healthcare in villages throughout Ethiopia.

Irish Aid also supports voluntary counselling and testing programmes for HIV/AIDS as well as education and awareness-raising of the disease.

Irish Aid to Ethiopia funds the Safety Nets Programme, a scheme which provides seven million of the poorest Ethiopians with cash or food in exchange for work, as well as funding the Water Sector Development Plan which supports community-managed water and sanitation programmes.

Sustainable development aid is working in Ethiopia to increase its human and economic development; over the last ten years, Ethiopia's score on the Human Development Index has risen by 32%.

Aid can be most effective when it is delivered directly to those in need and is appropriate for their needs. For example, in Ghana international aid has been used to supply low-tech solar cookers to villages. Solar cookers do not need wood fuel, thus helping to combat desertification in the region. Over the past decade, Uganda has used Western aid to double the number of children in schools, cut the rate of HIV infection among pregnant women by 80% and reduce poverty by about 35%. These are huge social and economic gains due to the effectiveness of international aid.

Empowerment and aid*

Many aid programmes work to empower people across the world. Aid has saved lives, increased trade, empowered women and improved literacy levels. It has also improved healthcare across many poor nations.

Aid provided by Non-Governmental Organisations (NGOs) and governments aims to make people independent so that they will not need aid in the future and can support themselves. NGO aid is not 'tied' (conditional), unlike much governmental aid, so the benefits of the aid stay in the local communities.

Bóthar is an Irish NGO working in 20 countries across South America, Africa, Asia and Eastern Europe. Bóthar helps poor families to overcome hunger, malnutrition and poverty in a sustainable manner. They provide farm animals to families and communities. The animals - such as goats, chicken and cattle - give struggling families the opportunity to raise their living standards. Bóthar provides veterinary help and breeding advice until the communities can manage themselves. The milk, honey, meat and eggs not only improve a family's diet but the surplus is sold, thus giving the family possibly their first opportunity to earn an income. This income allows them to feed, clothe and educate their children.

The impact that one good quality farm animal has on an impoverished family in the Developing World can mean the difference between destitution and security. In this way the aid programme empowers people so that they can contribute to the local and national economy and this leads to economic growth in the area.

Trócaire supports aid projects empowering over 3.4 million people in 20 countries such as Kenya and Ethiopia. In Kenya, Trócaire raises awareness of violence against women and provides medical, legal and educational support for thousands of women and men in the region. It helps to empower women in communities so that they are able to make decisions as to how their community is organised. Trócaire also works to protect and promote human rights in countries such as Honduras, Israel and Pakistan.

When people feel safe and secure they are able to go about their daily business and develop the local and national economy without fear of violence. In conflict zones such as Syria human and economic development is prevented and even more people leave the country.

When people are healthy, they are able to work and raise their living standards. In Africa, HIV/AIDS is a major problem accounting for 47% of deaths in South Africa alone. Globally over 15 million children are orphaned by HIV/AIDS; in South Africa 63% of orphans have been orphaned due to HIV/AIDS. NGOs work to raise awareness about how HIV/AIDS spreads and how it can be treated and avoided. Trócaire provides care for those with AIDs and supports orphaned children and families affected by AIDS. Children orphaned by HIV/AIDS are affected by grief, have to drop out of school, suffer poverty and may be stigmatised. NGOs help to empower families affected by AIDS by providing treatment, keeping children in school by providing home care for sick parents and working to educate people about HIV/AIDS so that gradually the economic development of Aids-affected areas increases.

GEOECOLOGY (Option 7)

> **NOTE**
>
> Three **aspects** are usually provided in the answer essays.
> Each aspect has at least 8 SRPs. If 4 aspects are given, each aspect has at least 6 SRPs. Aspects of discussion have been given an **asterisk** (*) to help you identify them.

Chapter 35
Soils

Soil Composition

Q

Soil Development: 2015 Question 16
Examine the influence of mineral matter, air, water and organic matter on soil development. **[80 marks]**

What You Need To Do:
- The four topics of discussion are given in the question but you will not get 'aspect' marks by just repeating them. Note how they have been made relevant to soil development in each heading.
- Write 6 SRPs on each aspect.

Answer

Mineral matter influences texture, structure, colour and pH of soils*

Mineral matter are the rocky soil grains that make up the 'skeleton' of the soil. Mineral matter is made from particles of bedrock that are produced by mechanical weathering processes such as freeze-thaw action. Mineral matter makes up about 45% of a typical soil.

Mineral matter affects soil development by producing soils of different texture. If the mineral matter originated from shale rock, then the soil will have a large amount of clay particles and a clay texture. If the mineral matter is produced from weathered sandstone, the soil may develop a sandy texture.

Mineral matter also influences the development of soil structures. Crumb-structured soils tend to develop in soils with a mineral matter content that is equal parts sand, silt and clay whereas clay soils tend to develop on soils with a higher proportion of clay particles.

The mineral content forms the largest part of the soil (45%) so if the mineral matter has a particular colour, the soil will also have that colour. For example, sandy soils (>85% sand grains) tend to be pale brown because sand has that colour. Clay soils (clay content >40% clay grains) tend to be dark black or dark grey because shale rock from which the clay develops is also dark black or grey.

Mineral matter influences the water content of soils because the grain size influences the size of the pore spaces between grains and therefore the drainage of water through the soil. Pore size is related to the texture and structure of the soil. Soils with large pore spaces tend to be free-draining drier soils.

If the mineral matter has acidic or alkaline properties then the soil may have similar characteristics, e.g. acid soils tend to develop on soils with a higher proportion of sand grains.

Air influences the colour and amount of living things in soil *

Soil air is located in the pore spaces between the soil grains and makes up about 25% of soil.

Air seeps into soil from the atmosphere. The amount of air in soil depends on the size of the pore spaces between the particles of mineral matter and the weather. Rainy days reduce the amount of air in the soil and large pore spaces can hold more air.

Air affects the development of soil by encouraging the presence of living things. Animals and plants will not survive for long in anaerobic soils (soils lacking oxygen).

Poorly aerated soils are often infertile and lack both structure and organic matter.
Air influences soil colour because it is needed for oxidation. Oxidation is a chemical weathering process whereby iron and other elements combine with oxygen. Oxidation affects soil colour, making soils red/orange in colour. Soils lacking air tend to be a mottled blue/black/grey colour.

Water influences living things, soil colour and the pH of soils*

Water makes up about 25% of a typical soil. Water in soil comes from two sources: from the atmosphere (rain/snow) and from underground (groundwater). Water in soil enables plants to absorb nutrients released from mineral matter. Water reduces soil erosion because water binds soil particles together. Water seeping through soil enables soil horizons (layers) to develop and causes the formation of hard pans.

The amount of water a soil can hold is influenced by the humus content, texture and structure of the soil. Sandy-textured soils are often dry because the water easily drains through the round pores while clay-textured soils are wetter due to the small angular pores. Soils with a high humus content tend to hold more water.

Water in soil can also influence its development by affecting which processes take place in the soil. Leaching (the loss of nutrients down through the soil) doesn't occur in dry soils, gleying (water logging and lack of oxygen) occurs in poorly-drained soils with too much water. Leaching and gleying in turn affect soil colour: leached soils are pale, while waterlogged soils are mottled blue/grey.

If the water in soil has a particular pH, this will affect the pH of the soil as well. In areas affected by acid rain, acid rainwater causes acidity levels in the soil to rise, e.g. central and southern Sweden. Acid soils tend to have fewer bacteria and fungi and therefore lack humus.

Organic matter influences soil colour, texture and water content of soils*

Organic matter includes living things like worms, spiders and plant roots as well as animal droppings and dead things such as autumn leaves. Organic matter also includes humus, a dark black substance made from the bacterial and fungal decay of organic matter.

Organic matter makes up about 5% of a typical soil. The amount of organic matter affects the development of soils in a number of ways. Soils rich in organic matter tend to be dark brown or black in colour because they are rich in humus – derived from the humification process. Soils rich in organic matter develop a crumb structure because the humus helps bind the soil particles together into rounded clumps called peds. Organic matter helps retain moisture in the soil and encourages the presence of micro-organisms, which in turn increases the soil fertility.

Soils rich in organic matter tend to undergo humification. Humification is a soil forming process whereby dead organic matter is converted to humus by bacteria and fungi. Humification increases soil fertility.

The amount of organic matter is affected by the climate and water content of the soil. Soils formed in well watered and highly vegetated temperate climates, such as Ireland's cool, temperate oceanic climate, have more organic matter in them than soils formed in hot, dry, desert climates.

Soil processes

> **NOTE:** Soil-forming processes are: weathering, leaching, humification, laterisation, podzolisation, gleying, salinisation and calcification.

Q

Soil processes: 2011 Question 16
Soil characteristics are affected by their immediate environment and by a combination of processes operating in that environment. Examine any **three** soil processes that affect soil characteristics.

What You Need To Do:
- Consider which soil processes best suit the question. You need to show how processes affect soil texture, colour, pH, structure, water content, humus content and organisms. Not every process affects every characteristic so pick the ones that affect the most characteristics.
- Decide on your three soil processes. These will be your three aspects of discussion.
- Discuss their influence on soil characteristics. You must describe the process AND link it to soil characteristics.

Answer

Soil characteristics include texture, structure, colour, pH, water content and humus content. There are many soil processes that affect these characteristics. In this answer I will discuss three: humification, weathering and laterisation.

A

Humification*

The humification process affects a number of soil characteristics. Humification is the method by which dead organic matter is converted to humus by the action of decomposers such as fungi and bacteria which are microorganisms in the soil. Humus is a black gel-like substance that is washed into the soil by rainfall. It is an important component of soil because it increases soil fertility. The humification process affects soil colour by producing humus. Because humus is dark, soils with a high humus content are usually very dark brown or black in colour.

Humification can also affect soil structure. Humus helps to bind the soil particles together and therefore can influence soil structure by contributing to the formation of a crumb structure.

Humus also increases the water content of soils. Humification contributes to the formation of pore spaces that can hold water.

Humification affects soil pH. Soils with a high humus content are also less likely to be highly acidic or alkaline. Humus helps to keep soil pH within a range that is suitable for microorganisms to grow. Irish brown earth soil is affected by humification. The local environment (relief) affects how much humification occurs. Lowlands have deeper, darker soils due to being warmer and more sheltered. These conditions increase humification.

Weathering*

Weathering is the breakdown of rocks into smaller pieces by chemical or mechanical methods. It is an important soil-forming process. Weathering provides the mineral component for any soil. The mineral part of any soil influences its characteristics.

Chemical weathering of rock affects soil pH, e.g. acid or alkaline. Chemical weathering such as carbonation releases calcium from the parent rock which can make the resulting soil pH alkaline. This is common on Rendzina soils formed over limestone.

Chemical weathering of parent material can affect soil texture, e.g. sandy, silty, clay or loam. Hydrolysis of feldspar in granite rocks can release clay particles into the resulting soil giving it a clay texture.

Chemical weathering of soil can affect its colour. In the latosol soil of Brazil, extreme chemical weathering of rocks by oxidation of iron produces red, orange or yellow soils.

Mechanical weathering can affect soil structure, e.g. crumb, platy, blocky or crumb. Freeze-thaw action and exfoliation/onion weathering provides mineral grains that are angular in shape. This can contribute to a blocky texture. The local environment (relief) can affect the rate and type of weathering. Highland soils tend to have a more sandy texture due to increased levels of freeze-thaw action.

Laterisation*

Laterisation is a form of chemical weathering involving oxidation, carbonation and leaching. It occurs in hot, wet, tropical and equatorial climates. Laterisation leads to the formation of zonal soils such as latosols. A zonal soil is a soil that is fully developed in response to the climate and processes that operate upon it.

Laterisation affects soil structure, e.g. blocky, platy, crumb. Latosols lack any well-defined structure. This is partly due to the laterisation of the mineral grains that dissolves them, preventing them from forming permanent shapes that hold together in peds. It is also due to the lack of deep roots in latosol soils, root growth being an important influence on soil structure.

Laterisation affects soil colour. In the latosol soil of Brazil, laterisation of rocks containing iron produces red, orange or yellow soils.

Laterisation affects soil pH. It involves extreme leaching by acidic rainwater. Leaching is the removal of soil minerals by water. In laterisation the soil water is acidic and dissolves all the soluble material out of the soil. This process affects the soil pH by making it slightly acidic.

Soil Profiles

Soil profiles: 2014 Question 17
Soil profiles are the result of the operation of soil-forming processes.
Discuss. **[80 marks]**

> **What You Need To Do:**
> - Explain and describe soil profiles.
> - Describe two soil profiles making sure to link the appearance of the profiles to the soil processes acting upon them.
> - Make sure to name and explain the soil processes that affect the profile.

Answer

Soil Profiles*

A soil profile is a section of soil that runs from the surface down to the bedrock. Soil profiles show different layers called horizons within the soil. These layers form by a combination of processes acting on the soil and its parent rock.

A general soil profile contains four layers. These are: the O (organic) horizon on the surface and three lower horizons called A, B and C.

The O horizon has a high percentage (30%) of organic matter. It contains leaves, dead plants and animal litter which collects on the surface of the soil. The O horizon is rich in micro-organisms such as fungi and bacteria. Humus forms in this layer.

The A horizon is also called the topsoil. It contains organic matter leached from the O horizon mixed with mineral matter in the soil. The A horizon is usually dark in colour and is often mixed up by burrowing animals. Plants send roots into the A horizon as it is usually the most fertile layer of soil.

Below this is the B horizon, also called the subsoil. This layer is rich in mineral grains from the bedrock below and contains minerals leached from the upper layers.

The C horizon is the bedrock or parent material from which the soil originally formed.

Depending on which soil processes are in operation in a soil, different soil profiles form.

Podzol Soil Profiles*

Podzol soil profiles form from the podzolisation process. This is leaching by rainwater that is more acidic than usual. Leaching is a soil-forming process whereby rainwater washes mineral matter down through the soil profile.

Podzol soil profiles form under coniferous forests such as the boreal forests of northern Europe. On the forest floor lays a thick layer of pine needles that are slow to decompose. Rainwater seeps through this layer and becomes acidic due to the absorption of humic acids from the dead vegetation.

As the rainwater seeps through to the soil below, it dissolves all the minerals except quartz. Quartz is resistant to chemical and physical weathering. Quartz is a pale coloured mineral and the quartz grains give the A horizon a pale ash grey colour. The B horizon, below, is enriched with the dissolved minerals and appears dark in colour.

The B horizon may also contain a reddish layer of iron oxide (rust). This is called a hard pan (or iron pan) and forms during podzolisation when the dissolved minerals are deposited together. The hard pan is impermeable and prevents the flow of water down through the soil; podzols may become waterlogged for this reason.

Climate is an important factor affecting the formation of podzol soil profiles. Fully developed podzol profiles are zonal. This means that they have formed in response to a particular climatic zone. In this case podzols form in response to temperate climates, e.g. the cool temperate climate of northern Europe.

Brown Earth Soil Profiles*

Brown earth soil profiles are zonal. They have developed in response to the cool temperate oceanic climate, e.g. Ireland. They developed underneath mixed deciduous forests containing trees such as oak, ash and chestnut.

Brown earth soil profiles have no distinct horizons; they are uniformly dark brown in colour. This is due to the temperate climate. Temperatures range from 6°C in January to 15°C in July. Rain falls throughout the year and amounts to an average of 1,500 mm. This climate has a long growing season and almost year-round earthworm, fungal and bacterial activity. Many other living things occur in brown earth soils, e.g. beetles, spiders, rabbits and badgers. Burrowing animals (such as rabbits and badgers) mix the soil grains up and remove any horizons that may form.

Several processes have combined to form a brown earth soil profile. The two main processes are humification and leaching.

Humification is the method by which dead organic matter is converted into humus by the action of bacteria and fungi. Humus is the black sticky gel that remains in the O horizon when dead things are decomposed. It contains nutrients that are washed into the A and B horizons by rainwater. Humus helps bind soil grains together.

Climate affects the rate of humification. In temperate climates, humification occurs throughout the year but more slowly in winter. In hot humid climates, it occurs rapidly. In dry desert climates, the lack of water inhibits the growth of bacteria and fungi, reducing the amount of humus produced. In Ireland, brown earth soils have a high humus content.

Leaching is the removal of nutrients from the soil by rainwater. Brown earth soils are only lightly leached due to the moderate amounts of rainfall in the temperate climate. Deciduous trees lose their leaves each winter adding more humus to the soil, so there is a constant resupply of nutrients.

All brown earth soils have a well developed crumb structure due to the presence of plant roots and animals.

The brown earth soil profile varies according to local factors such as relief and parent rock. These intrazonal brown earth profiles are slightly different from the standard profile. Acid brown earth soils form in uplands of granite or sandstone rock and are more acidic, e.g. the Comeragh region of Co. Waterford. Shallow brown earth soils are thin, alkaline fertile soils that form on limestone, e.g. north Co. Clare. Podzolised brown earth soils form on glacial drift covering Ireland's lowlands. They are young soils formed since the last Ice Age, 10,000 years ago.

Other processes affect soil profiles across the world. For example, gleying (waterlogging) gives the A and B horizon a mottled blue grey colour due to the lack of oxygen in the soil. Laterisation (extreme leaching by alkaline water in tropical climates) removes all minerals from the soil except iron and aluminum oxides leaving a uniformly red/orange soil profile.

Factors affecting soils

> **NOTE:** Factors affecting soils are climate, relief, organisms, parent material and time.

> **Q** **Soils: 2006 Question 16**
> Examine the factors that influence soil characteristics. **[80 marks]**

> **What You Need To Do:**
> - Choose 3 – 4 soil characteristics to discuss.
> - Discuss how these characteristics are affected by the factors affecting soils.
> - Refer to specific soils in your answer.

Answer: Factors affecting soil characteristics

A In this answer the factors affecting soil characteristics of colour, soil texture and humus content will be discussed.

Factors affecting soil colour – parent material, climate, organisms*

The characteristics of any soil include its colour, texture, structure, pH, humus content and water content. Factors affecting soils are climate, relief, parent material, organisms and time. They affect soil characteristics directly and indirectly by influencing the processes that affect a soil, e.g. leaching.

Parent material, climate and organisms are three factors that affect soil colour.

Soils can have a variety of colours from black to orange. The colour of the soil depends on the soil-forming processes acting upon it, e.g. humification. Climate controls which soil-forming processes occur and therefore its characteristic colour. In cool temperate oceanic climates the temperate and rainfall amounts are moderate throughout the year. The temperature range is about 8°C and about 2,000 mm of rain fall throughout the year. This climate encourages deciduous woodland to grow. These trees provide leaf litter in autumn. Humification occurs in this climate. Humification is the method by which dead organic matter is converted to humus by the action of fungi and bacteria. Humus is a black gel-like substance that is washed into the soil by rainfall, making the soil dark brown in colour. This climate leads to the formation of brown earth soils.

Climate also controls the amount of leaching that can occur and this affects soil colour. Leaching is a soil-forming process that tends to lighten the colour of soils. Leaching occurs when rainwater washes soluble nutrients such as phosphorous down into the lower B horizon of the soil. When leaching has washed most of the nutrients from the soil, it becomes pale and ash coloured. Podzol soils in a cool temperate climate have a pale grey-coloured A horizon for this reason but the lower B horizon is darker due to the build-up of minerals here.

Latosols are orange in colour because of laterisation which is a form of extreme leaching in a wet tropical climate. In tropical climates conditions of heat (27°C), humidity (88%) and rainfall (3,000 – 6,000 mm) mean that all nutrients are leached from the soil very quickly except iron oxides and aluminium oxides. This makes the soil an orange/red colour.

Parent material can also affect soil colour. Pale brown soils often form on sandstone parent material. This is because the sandstone is also pale brown and the soil mineral grains produced from it have that colour too.

Factors affecting soil texture – climate, parent material*

Soil texture is the way a soil feels when rubbed in our hands. Texture is affected by the size of the mineral grains in the soil. Soils can have four types of texture: (a) sandy texture, (b) silty texture, (c) clay texture and (d) loam texture.

The different types of texture are affected by factors such as climate. In cold climates such as the Tundra where the temperature drops below freezing point (0°C), mechanical weathering processes such as freeze-thaw action act on rocks and can produce sandy soils. This is because the mechanical weathering processes produce scree particles that are the size of sand grains (1-5 mm in size).

In wetter and warmer climates such as a cool temperate oceanic climate, granite rocks are chemically weathered by hydrolysis. This is the action of water on feldspar minerals in granite rock. The feldspar is converted to clay particles which produces clay-texture soil. Clay grains are not visible to the naked eye and so clay soils feel smooth to the touch. Clay soils are fertile but are not well drained because the clay grains are so small and hold water easily.

Parent material can also affect soil texture. This is because of the size of the grains in the parent material. Granite rock contains feldspar which produces clay soils as described earlier. Sandstone tends to produce sandy soils and shale tends to produce silty-textured soils.

Factors affecting humus content of soils – climate, organisms, relief*

Climate, organisms and relief affect the humus content of a soil. These factors control the drainage and depth of the soil as well as the presence/absence of living organisms in it and the vegetation growing on it (which in turn affects humus content).

Humus is a black gel-like substance produced by the action of fungi and bacteria on dead organic matter. Anything that reduces the amount of organic matter or the activity of fungi and bacteria will reduce the humus content of the soil. Cold climates, high altitudes and steep slopes reduce the humus content of the soil as the cold slows down the activity of the microorganisms and water washes the humus out of the soil on sloping land. Tundra regions have low temperatures (-20°C in winter) and this prevents humus production in the soils of this region.

In contrast temperate climate regions such as Ireland have mild winters and warm summers (8°C in winter, 16°C in summer). Vegetation grows easily in temperate climates. The mild temperatures promote the action of microorganisms on any dead organic matter and this leads to a high humus content in the brown earth soils that are found in temperate regions.

Relief also affects humus content. Lowland soils tend to have high humus content as dead organic matter builds up in lowland areas. These areas are also warmer so microorganisms convert the matter to humus. Uplands by contrast may have a build-up of dead organic matter but low humus content as uplands are colder, preventing the conversion of the organic matter into humus. Peat soils are therefore common in upland areas.

Soil types: Brown earth, latosol, aridisol

Soil type: 2010 Question 18
Describe and explain the characteristics of any **one** soil type studied by you.
[80 marks]

What You Need To Do:
- Name the soil type you are discussing.
- Describe three or four of its characteristics.
- Explain why the characteristics occur.

Answer 1: Brown earth soils

In this answer the characteristics of the brown earth soil will be examined.

Brown earth soils are zonal soils. This means that they have developed in response to a climatic zone and its natural vegetation. In the case of brown earths they have developed in response to the cool temperate oceanic climate and mixed deciduous woodland.

The influence of climate, parent rock and the presence of living things has given the brown earth soil its main characteristics: texture, humus content, pH, structure and colour.

1. Texture of brown earth soils*

Brown earth soils often have a variety of textures.

The texture of brown earth soils is affected by the type of weathering that occurs. The type of mineral matter in brown earths gives the soil its texture – clay, sand, silt and loam. Mineral matter develops from the parent rock in response to mechanical and chemical weathering. In the cool temperate climate, freeze-thaw action in uplands and sheltered lowlands during winter and frosty weather supplies larger angular sand-sized mineral grains for the soil. Chemical weathering of the rock grains releases nutrients and clay minerals into the soil from the mineral grains. Hydrolysis of granite rocks is a very important process in temperate climates as it provides clay particles for the brown earth soil, thereby influencing its texture.

Most Irish brown earth soils have a loam texture. Loam soils have a roughly equal mix of sand, silt and clay particles. Brown earth soils have this texture because they have developed on a variety of parent rock such as limestone, slate and sandstone. In Ireland most brown earths developed on glacial till deposited at the end of the last Ice Age.

2. Humus content of brown earth soils*
Brown earth soils have a high humus content. This is because of the action of humification. Humification is a soil-forming process that is dominant in cool temperate climates. Humification occurs when dead organic matter is converted into a black gel called humus by the action of fungi and bacteria on dead things. Then rain washes the humus into the soil and raises its fertility.

Because the cool temperate climate is a mild climate, brown earth soils contain lots of living things such as earthworms, fungi, bacteria and insects. These are active for most of the year and provide humus for the soil. Annual autumn leaf-fall from the deciduous trees adds organic matter to the soils and this is also converted to humus and increases the amount of it in brown earth soils.

3. pH of brown earth soils*
The pH of brown earth soils varies from mildly acidic to mildly alkaline. This is due to the moderate rainfall that only mildly leaches the soil, as well as the variation of parent material that can occur in the cool temperate region. Acid brown soils form on acid rocks such as sandstone while more alkaline brown earths form on lime-rich parent material. The pH is also affected by organic matter and living things present in brown earth soils. Because the cool temperate climate is a mild climate, brown earth soils contain lots of living things such as earthworms, fungi, bacteria and insects. These are active for most of the year and they can influence the pH with their droppings and by decomposition when they die.

Acidic brown earth soils develop in upland areas over 500 metres in altitude where the parent rock is acidic crystalline rocks such as granite. The increased rainfall on upland areas also makes these soils more acidic.

Podzolised brown earth soils are also more acidic. They developed where podzolisation occurs on lowland areas. Podzolisation is leaching by acidic water and leads to pale-coloured brown earths. Podzolised brown earths are common in the midlands of Ireland.

4. The colour of brown earth soils*
Brown earth soils in Ireland are usually dark brown in colour. Unlike other soils brown earth soils are usually the same colour down through the profile horizons. This is due to the action of burrowing animals which occurs in large numbers in the cool temperate climate. Because the climate is mild, the animals are active for at least nine months of the year and are able to mix the material in the soil horizons making the colour a uniform dark brown. The dark brown colour is also due to the high humus content. Humus is also dark brown. The parent material influences the colour of brown earth soils. Sandstone makes the soil a more pale brown while limestone parent material gives it a darker colour.

Answer 2: Characteristics of latosols

A In this answer the characteristics of latosol soils will be examined.

Latosols are deep zonal soils. This means that they have developed in response to a climatic zone and its natural vegetation. In the case of latosols they have developed in response to a tropical and equatorial climate and rainforest vegetation.

The influence of climate, parent rock and the presence of living things gives the latosol soil its main characteristics: texture, water content, humus content, pH, structure and colour.

1. Colour of latosols

Latosols are orange, red or yellow in colour. Latosols are orange in colour because of laterisation in the wet tropical climate. Laterisation is an extreme form of chemical weathering involving oxidation, carbonation and leaching of mineral particles. It occurs in hot, wet, tropical and equatorial climates such as Brazil. Leaching is the process by which water dissolves minerals from the soil and washes them deeper into the soil profile where they cannot be reached by plant roots. Leaching tends to make soils pale in colour. In latosols the water leaching through the soil is normal acidic (pH 5.6) rainwater. There is so much water leaching through the soil each day that only iron and aluminium oxides are left in the soil. Oxidation of soils occurs when mineral substances combine with oxygen in the air and water. Oxidation gives the soil its red/orange colour.

In tropical climates conditions of heat (27°C), humidity (88%) and rainfall (3,000 – 6,000 mm) mean that laterisation can reach deep into the soil and so latosols are very deeply weathered to a depth of 50 m in places.

2. pH of latosols*

Latosols are usually acidic in pH. This is due to the considerable amount of rain that falls onto the soil. All rainwater is a weak carbonic acid. It is naturally acidic with a pH of 5.6. This is due to the absorption of carbon dioxide from the air by rainwater. In the tropical and equatorial climates the annual amount of rainfall can reach over 6,000 mm; this amount of rain causes the pH of the soil to be acidic.

The laterisation process that occurs on latosols is a type of extreme leaching. Leaching is the removal of soil minerals by water. In laterisation the soil water is acidic and dissolves all the soluble material out of the soil. This process also makes the soil pH slightly acidic. The pH of latosols is also affected by the parent material on which it develops. Granite is the bedrock in large areas of Brazil which contributes to the acidic pH of the latosol that develops.

3. Structure of latosols*

Latosols lack a well-defined structure, e.g. blocky, platy, crumb. This is due to the process of laterisation which can affect soil structure. Laterisation of the mineral grains dissolves them and prevents them from forming permanent shapes that hold together in peds. However, one of the most important factors affecting soil structure is the presence of plant roots. Plant roots form a web through the soil, holding and shaping the peds together. The more plant roots in the soil, the more likely it is that the soil will have crumb structure. In latosols, most plants have very shallow roots in order to catch the nutrients formed by humification before they are leached away. The lack of deep roots in latosol soils is another reason why they lack a well-defined structure.

4. Humus content of latosols*

Even though a lush jungle vegetation provides organic matter, latosols do not have a high humus content. Ninety per cent of nutrients are found on the surface layer (O Horizon) in the root mats formed by plants or at the very top part of the B horizon.

The humus content in the A and B horizons is low because of the way that plants have adapted to the hot, wet, tropical and equatorial climates.

In the hot (27°C), humid (88% humidity), wet (over 3,000 mm of rainfall per year) conditions, plants grow rapidly and provide plenty of organic matter to the soil. The warm humid conditions encourage billions of microorganisms to decompose the dead material into humus. However the heavy convectional rain that falls each day soon leaches the nutrients from the soil. Plants have adapted by having shallow roots to capture the nutrients from the O horizon almost as soon as they are formed. As a result there is a low humus content in the A and B horizons.

Answer 3: Characteristics of aridisols

In this answer the characteristics of the aridisol soil will be examined.
Aridisols are zonal soils. This means that they have developed in response to a climatic zone and its natural vegetation. In the case of aridisol soils they have developed in response to a hot desert climate and sparse desert vegetation.

The influence of climate, parent rock and the presence of living things have given the aridisol soil its main characteristics: texture, humus content, pH, structure and colour.

1. Humus content of aridisols*

The humus content of aridisols is generally low. They contain little organic matter. This is caused by dry conditions and low plant productivity. Due to a lack of water and plant material, the activity of microorganisms that convert organic matter into humus is restricted. Consequently aridisols are mineral-rich but lack humus.

Vegetation is scarce or almost completely absent, unless it has specifically adapted to this harsh environment. The plants that do thrive are mainly ground-hugging shrubs and short woody trees such as yucca, agaves, cactus and mesquite shrubs which have adapted to the dry conditions by storing water.

There is rapid growth in vegetation after the unpredictable torrential downpours of rain. Plants are closely linked with many animals and insects which use the plants as shelter and food sources. The animals make burrows, leave food and droppings, have babies and die in the shelter of plants. These are the raw materials for humus formation. Humus is produced therefore around existing plants which form islands of fertile soil in the desert.

2. pH of aridisols*

Aridisols are generally alkaline in their pH. They have high calcium carbonate and sodium concentrations which makes them alkaline. During calcification water is drawn up through the soil pores by capillary action driven by evaporation of water. Calcification of aridisols is responsible for the formation of the chalk-rich hard pan or caliche within aridisol soils.

From the surface calcium carbonate is deposited in layers in the soil or near the surface. This hard pan makes the soil hard and it is therefore difficult for plant roots to break through.

The intense evaporation of water from desert soils tends to bring dissolved sodium salts to the surface. This process is called salinisation. The high surface content of sodium and calcium ions can lead to extensive hard surface crusts of salt (saltpans/salinas) where little or nothing can grow because the salt is toxic to plants. Farmers need to break up this hard pan and dilute the salt with irrigation water to get the soil into production. In some countries the salt pans are put into commercial production for table salt.

3. Texture of aridisols*

Aridisols have a coarse sandy or gravelly texture because there is less chemical weathering in desert areas to provide smaller soil grains such as clays. Mechanical weathering, particularly onion weathering, produces particles the size of sand and gravel for the soil. The finer dust and sand particles are blown away, leaving heavier pieces behind. Coarse-textured soils are found on lower mountain slopes and are fairly well drained. In lower-lying basin areas finer particles carried by the wind have built up creating a deep well-drained silty soil cover.

Relief has a major influence on the texture of aridisols. Valleys provide pathways for flash floods which remove soils in the valley floors. Water flowing off mountainsides deposits mud, sand and gravel at the base of the slopes in huge fan-shaped deposits called alluvial fans. These alluvial fan sediments influence the texture and mineral content in soils nearby by providing sand, silt and clay particles. Aridisols far from the source of the fan material are not as sandy as those that develop close to the apex of the fan.

4. Colour of aridisols*

Some aridisols have the same pale, brownish colour from top to bottom, but others may be layered with browns, reds, pinks, and whites. The variation in colour is due to the action of living things, salinisation, weathering and parent material.

Aridisols may contain white/grey layers called calcic horizons. These are accumulations of calcium carbonate – the same material found in chalk, concrete and agricultural lime. They form due to the process of calcification. Calcic horizons may vary from 15 cm to 1 m in thickness and form an impermeable, white/grey cement-like layer or hard pan in the soil known as caliche.

In desert soils parent material has also influenced the colour. In some areas of the South-West USA, parent material is gravelly alluvium derived from old granite rocks. This parent material has influenced the colour of the soil here where it is dark red due to the pink feldspar crystals in the granite rock.

The intense evaporation of water from desert soils tends to bring dissolved salts to the surface by the process of salinisation this gives the O horizons a white colour.

Chapter 36

Human Influence on Soils/Soil Erosion

Q

> **Human influence on soils: 2012 Question 17**
> Discuss how human activities can accelerate soil erosion.
>
> **[80 marks]**

> **What You Need To Do:**
> - Name three human activities that cause soil erosion.
> - Name two examples where these processes occur.
> - Explain how each of the three activities are interrelated and can increase the rate of soil erosion.

A

Answer

Overgrazing*

Overgrazing occurs when farmers stock too many animals such as sheep, cattle or goats on their land. This damages the soil surface and increases the rate of soil erosion. Animals eat the vegetation cover and their hooves dig into the soil in wet areas or compact it into a hard surface in dry regions. This prevents grass growth and prevents water from percolating into the soil. Dry soils are eroded by the wind very easily. Once the soil has been trampled and stripped of plants, its structure is damaged and its ability to hold water and nutrients is reduced. Soil structure is important because plant roots and water are found in the spaces between the soil peds. Peds are the small grains which are held together by humus and water. Peds have different shapes. Rounded peds give the soil a crumb structure. A crumb structure is best for soil aeration, water content and fertility. Overgrazing can change the structure to a platy structure or destroy the structure completely. As a result it can be easily eroded by wind and rain and pasture growth is also reduced.

Too many animals on the land will eat all the plants and strip the soil of its protective vegetation cover. Plants, roots and branches protect soil from wind and rain. Soils that are exposed become drier and are more easily blown or washed away.

This situation had happened in many places around the world such as the Sahel region of Africa where population growth has led to an increase in the numbers of cattle and goats grazed on already dry land. It also occurred in County Mayo in Ireland during the 1990s when EU farm subsidies encouraged farmers to overstock their land with too many sheep. The fragile boglands of West Mayo were soon severely eroded.

Over-cropping*

Over-cropping occurs when the land is under continuous cultivation and not allowed to rest (lie fallow) in between crops. The effect of over-cropping on soils is to reduce its water content and fertility. Infertile soils are more easily eroded by wind and rain. As nutrients are removed its structure is damaged as well. Over-cropped soils become dry and very dusty because the humus content has been reduced. Humus is important for improving the texture and structure of the soil and for keeping it moist. In the Sahel region of Africa, over-cropping and overgrazing often occur together as a result of population increase. More people on the land leads to greater numbers of farmers who keep animals and grow crops. There is also less land to go around so whatever amount of land is available is under stress to produce food for the increased population. Intensive cultivation of land in the soya plantations of South America can also lead to over-cropping. Here the soil is fertilised but the application of chemical fertilisers does not benefit the land as much as applying manure from animal waste. Therefore, over time the soil structure is damaged and erosion increases. The effect of over-cropping can be reduced by the addition of organic matter (cattle dung) to the soil and through irrigation.

Desertification*

Desertification is the spread of desert conditions into new areas. Desertified soils are dry, dusty and lack humus. Their fertility is reduced and they are quickly eroded. Africa is the continent most at risk from desertification although Southern Europe, especially Southern Spain is also at risk. Desertification often occurs as a result of a combination of drought, over-cropping, overgrazing and deforestation. High population growth in countries such as Sudan contributes to desertification due to the increased demand for food and fuel. Drought conditions increase the chance of desertification occurring when the soil is already stressed by over-cropping and overgrazing. In Sahelian countries such as Chad and Niger, cotton and cashew nuts are grown as cash crops on huge plantations as part of economic reforms (structural adjustment programmes) in return for debt relief. People are removed from their land to make way for the plantations and must make a living on poor land at the edge of the plantations. This land is overgrazed and over-cropped and trees are cut down for fuel and building materials. Because so many trees have been cut down, cattle dung is used for fuel instead. This further deprives the soil of valuable nutrients leading to increased soil erosion in the region during drought.

Desertification lowers the water content in soils, and they then become hardened on the surface. This prevents absorption of any rain that might fall. Soil structure is damaged by desertification as the humus content falls. This prevents plant growth leading to further soil erosion.

The introduction of solar cookers in the Sahel could reduce the need for timber as a fuel. Trees are then planted which can help slow desertification and erosion in the region.

Q

Soil Characteristics: 2013 Question 16
Examine how desertification and conservation have impacted on soil characteristics. **[80 marks]**

What You Need To Do:
- Name and explain the general soil characteristics that are affected by desertification and conservation.
- Explain how desertification affects each soil characteristic.
- Explain how conservation affects each soil characteristic.

Answer

A General soil characteristics*

All soils are classed according to their soil characteristics. These are: colour, structure texture, water content, humus content and soil pH.

Soils have a variety of colours, from black to orange. The water content, parent rock and other processes acting on the soil, such as laterisiation or humification, affect soil colour.

Soil structure describes how soil grains are stuck together in small lumps – called peds – by water and humus. Soil structure can be blocky, platy or crumb/granular. The spaces between the peds, called pores, hold air and water. Plants grow best in a crumb-structured soil.

Soil texture describes how the soil feels in the hand. Soil textures may be silt, clay, sand or loam. The size of the soil grains affects texture. Clay particles are too small to be visible to the eye, so clay soils feel like playdough. Clay soils contain 40-100% clay particles. They are cold and become waterlogged easily.

Sandy soils contain over 85% sand grains that are up to 2 mm in size. Sandy soil feels gritty to touch and does not hold water easily.

Silty soil feels powdery to touch and contains silt particles that are barely visible to the eye.

Loam soils contain an equal mix of sand, silt and clay. They are well-drained, fertile soils. They feel slightly gritty to touch.

All soils contain water in the pore spaces. Climate and human activity such as irrigation affects water content.

Humus content is the amount of humus in soils. Humus is a sticky black gel formed when fungi and bacteria in the soil become organic dead matter. Humus adds nutrients to the soil and helps prevent soil erosion by sticking the soil grains together. It also gives soil a dark colour.

The acidity or alkalinity of soil is known as its pH. Humus and parent rock affect the pH of soils. Acid soils tend to form on acid rocks like granite. Alkaline soils tend to form on alkaline rocks such as limestone. Most soil is slightly acidic or slightly alkaline. Human activity also affects soil pH, e.g. farmers add lime to neutralise acid soils.

How desertification affects soil characteristics*

Desertification is the spread of desert conditions into new areas. Desertified soils are dry, dusty and lack humus. Their fertility is reduced and they are quickly eroded.

Africa is the continent most at risk from desertification although Southern Europe, especially Southern Spain, is also at risk. Desertification often occurs as a result of a combination of drought, overcropping, overgrazing and deforestation. High population growth in countries such as Sudan contributes to desertification due to the increased demand for food and fuel. Drought conditions increase the chance of desertification occurring when the soil is already stressed by overcropping and overgrazing. In Sahelian countries such as Chad and Niger, cotton and cashew nuts are grown as cash crops on huge plantations as part of economic reforms (structural adjustment programmes) in return for debt relief. People are removed from their land to make way for the plantations and must make a living on poor land at the edge of the plantations.

This land is over-grazed and over-cropped and trees are cut down for fuel and building materials. This further deprives the soil of valuable nutrients leading to increased soil erosion in the region during drought.

The introduction of solar cookers in the Sahel could reduce the need for timber as a fuel. Trees are then planted which can help slow desertification and erosion in the region.

How conservation affects soil characteristics*

Soil conservation protects soil from erosion by wind and water and protects the soil from harmful farming practices such as over-irrigation, over-grazing and over-cropping. Soil conservation has positive effects on soil characteristics.

The main methods of soil conservation include contour ploughing, terraces, windbreaks and stone walls. In contour ploughing farmers plough around hillsides rather than uphill and downhill. This prevents soil erosion and increases water content and humus content by reducing the loss of soil downhill. Contour ploughing is used in Europe and North America.

Terraces are steps cut into steep ground. They are used to cultivate crops such as rice. Terraces slow the run-off of water downhill and increase the water content of soil. Terraces also prevent the loss of clay particles that would be carried away in run-off, thus increasing soil fertility on sloping land. Terraces are used in mountainous regions such as India.

Windbreaks prevent soil erosion by the wind. Bands of trees or tall crops are planted around the edges of fields. This increases the depth of soil in windy exposed regions. In Africa soil protected by windbreaks is 20% more productive than unprotected soil.

Irrigation can lead to salinisation of soils. In salinisation, water evaporates from soil, leaving crusty layers of salt on the surface. This affects the soil pH and kills micro-organisms in the soil, reducing humus production and preventing seed germination. Better land-use management can improve soils that have been degraded by salinisation. Growing salt-tolerant plants will remove salt from the soil. Improving drainage and flushing the soil with water are common methods to reduce salinisation.

Soil structure regulates water content and seepage through the soil. It helps to control the passage of nutrients from soil to plant. Soil structure also affects the ability of plant roots to grow in the soil and the presence of micro-organisms. Farming practices such as over-cropping and over-grazing as well as desertification can damage soil structure so conserving soil structure is important for farmers. Soil structure is best conserved by adding humus to the soil. Humus helps the development of a crumb structure.

Soil pH is affected by human activities that acidify soils such as burning fossil fuels in cars and power stations, leading to acid rain. Acidified soils are less productive and lose their structure. Farmers conserve soils affected by acidification by adding powdered lime to the soil, e.g. Norway and Sweden.

Chapter 37
Biomes

> **NOTE:** Biomes are a popular topic. Students need to be able to describe and explain the characteristics of climate, soil, plants and animals for one biome. Students should also be able to discuss how plants and animals adapt to soil and climate.

Characteristics of biomes

Q

Biome characteristics: 2011 Question 18
Examine the characteristics of any one biome that you have studied under **three** of the following headings.
- Climate
- Soils
- Flora
- Fauna

What You Need To Do:
- Name the biome you are discussing.
- Describe its main characteristics: climate, flora (plants) and fauna (animals).
- Explain why these characteristics occur.

> **NOTE:** The question requires discussion of **three** characteristics. For additional information, the sample answer below contains **four** characteristics with at least **eight** SRPs in each.

A

Answer 1: The Tropical Rainforest Biome

In this answer the main characteristics of the tropical rainforest biome will be discussed. Rainforest regions include South America (Brazil), Malaysia/Indonesia and the Congo region of Africa.
The tropical rainforest biome has four main characteristics:
1. Climate
2. Vegetation
3. Soils
4. Plants and animals

1. Tropical climate*
The tropical rainforest biome is found between 23° north and south of the equator. It has a tropical climate that is hot and humid all year. The average temperature is about 27° Celsius. Humidity is high (up to 88%). These conditions of heat and humidity are due to

the position of the biome across the equatorial region. The equatorial zone is the region of maximum solar heating on the earth's surface. At these latitudes the sun's rays are directly overhead and hit the earth at a high angle causing intense heating of the surface and high levels of evaporation. The high rate of evaporation causes heavy convectional rain to fall each day resulting in an annual rainfall total of up to 6,600 millimetres per year. Although there are no seasons in the rainforest biome the areas that receive most rain and highest temperatures do change resulting in a slight drying and cooling at the edges of the rainforest biome region in June and December. The conditions of warmth, moisture and sunlight in the tropical climate are perfect for the growth of living things. As a result the climate has led to the high biodiversity in the tropical rainforest biome.

2. Rainforest/Vegetation*

The natural vegetation in the tropical rainforest biome is jungle or rainforest. Rainforests contain highly specialised plants and trees such as mahogany. Every rainforest contains four layers of vegetation. The layering of rainforests is an adaptation by plants to reduce competition for nutrients, water and sunlight.

(a) The forest floor
The forest floor occupies the lowest 2 metres or so of the rainforest. It is very dark as only 1% of the sunlight that falls on the forest actually reaches the ground. As a result few plants grow here unless a tree falls, creating a clearing where sunlight encourages rapid growth of vegetation.

(b) The understorey
This layer of vegetation reaches 2 to 20 metres above the forest floor. It consists of tall, non-flowering shrubs, ferns, small trees and vines. This area is also very shaded but trees receive more sunlight here and have large leaves to trap the sunlight.

(c) The canopy layer
Extending 20 to 40 metres above the forest floor, this layer is full of life. Vines grow on the trees and other tree-living plants called epiphytes (mosses and orchids) grow in this layer. Leaves are large to trap as much light as possible. Canopy trees have shallow buttress roots which capture nutrients in the O horizon of the soil and support the tree.

(d) The emergent layer
The highest layer of forest vegetation is the emergent layer. This contains the tallest trees in the forest, e.g. mahogany which is up to 70 metres high. Because emergent trees are exposed to sunlight and breezes which decrease the humidity, they have smaller leaves.

3. Latosol soil*

The soil associated with this biome is the latosol. This soil has a thin O horizon (humus layer) due to intense bacterial activity which rapidly decomposes dead organic matter. The A horizon contains aluminium and iron oxides. The B horizon is very deep and uniform in texture due to intense leaching in the high temperatures.

This soil is red/orange or yellow. The colour is a result of the laterisation process. Laterisation is a form of intense chemical weathering and leaching that occurs in hot climates. All the soluble minerals are washed out of the soil and only insoluble iron and aluminium oxides remain. These give the soil its colour. Latosols have a low humus content due to the rapid decomposition of dead organic matter which is quickly absorbed by plant roots or washed from the soil by the heavy rain. Consequently little humus gets deeper than the O horizon.

Laterisation can reach many metres into the ground. These soils can be 40 m deep. Plants of the tropical rainforest biome have adapted to this and grow very quickly. If they did not, they would get insufficient light or nutrients to grow. Fast-growing plants rapidly use the humus so that it does not get much chance to be leached into the soil. This short nutrient cycle gives the impression that the latosol is very fertile. But in fact once the forest is removed, the latosol has very little fertility and crops fail after two or three years. Exposed latosols are baked into a hard brick-like laterite soil which is impossible to cultivate.

4. Specialist and camouflaged animals*

Tropical rainforests are unique because they contain a great variety of living things found in different layers of the forest. This is due to the availability of warmth, water, sunlight and therefore plants. One hectare of rainforest may contain 42,000 species.

The variety of life differs between Asian, African and South American rainforest. The orang-utan is found only in Asian forests while gorillas are located in African forests. Such high biodiversity of life is not found in any other biome. In order to avoid competition for food and living space among the many thousands of animal species, animals have become very specialised. They may live in only one forest layer, even just on one species of tree. For example, mammals, such as spider monkeys, as well as snakes and birds, such as parrots, are found in the canopy layer of the rainforest.

Animals may be nocturnal and have very specialist ways of finding food. Some forest animals and plants live in association with each other – they depend on each other for food and reproduction. A good example of this is the Swordbill Hummingbird which feeds only from Datura flowers. Its bill cannot reach nectar from any other plant. In turn the bird passes pollen from one Datura plant to another, ensuring its reproduction.

Many plants and animals have adapted to the rainforest by using camouflage to hide from predators. Insects disguise themselves to look like twigs (stick insects) or leaves. Animals such as the Brazilian tree-living sloth have fur that is covered in moss and algae which helps them to hide while they hang from the canopy.

Answer 2:
Characteristics of the Hot Desert Biome of the South-West USA

A

In this answer the characteristics of the hot desert biome in the South-West USA will be discussed.

Hot desert biomes are found in North Africa, Australia, Arabia, South America, South-West America and Central Asia.

1. Reasons for the hot desert climate*

Hot deserts are located between 15° and 30° north and south of the equator. This area is under the influence of a global high pressure belt. The year-round high pressure means air sinks to the ground and warms up all the time. The moisture in the air evaporates causing the air to be very dry. Hot deserts are also found on the western side of landmasses close to cold sea currents, e.g. the Canaries current which causes rainfall to occur over the cool sea rather than the land. Hot deserts lie in the path of dry trade winds, e.g. North-East Trades, and are influenced by dry descending air in the high pressure belts found at this latitude. So, as a result of its location the climate of the desert biome is hot and dry. Temperatures are very high during the day, typically 30°C. The sun is high in the sky and the cloudless conditions and lack of vegetation mean there is little shade. As a result, the ground is exposed to the full force of the sun. Humidity is low. There is an extreme difference between day and night temperatures. The diurnal range may be 30°C as temperatures may fall below 0°C at night. The dry air above the desert lacks moisture for cloud formation and so heat from the surface radiates rapidly out into space, cooling the desert at night.

Rainfall is infrequent and falls as short but violent showers. Rainfall totals may vary from 0 to 500 mm in wetter areas. Rain falls in either summer or winter depending on the desert location.

2. Lack of vegetation/plant adaptations*

Desert regions have very little vegetation. The plants that do grow are well spread out and have adapted to the hot, dry conditions. Desert plants can be divided into two groups: ephemerals and succulents. Ephemeral plants make up 40% of desert plants. Ephemerals complete their life cycle each year over a 6-week to 8-week period. They take advantage of moisture during the rainy season to quickly germinate, grow and reproduce in just a few weeks. The seeds have a waxy coating to prevent water loss and they can survive desert conditions as seeds for many years if necessary. The Paper Daisy is an ephemeral desert plant.

Succulent plants such as the cactus and Joshua Tree survive desert conditions by storing water in roots, stems and fruits. Succulent plants are often spiny to repel water-seeking animals and birds. Succulent plants have also developed different root systems to capture moisture. The Mesquite bush has deep tap roots that can grow 50 metres to reach water deep underground. Other plants such as the cactus have shallow root systems that cover a large area and trap a lot of water in a short time when rain falls.

Desert soils are also very salty due to the process of salinisation in hot, dry conditions. Plants have evolved to tolerate high levels of salt in the soil. They can either excrete salt compounds from their bodies or even store it in their bodies if necessary.

3. Aridisol soils*

The characteristic soil of the hot desert biome is the aridisol. These are pale grey-coloured soils. Calcification is the main soil-forming process that affects aridisols. Calcification occurs when nutrients that are leached into the soil are drawn back up to the surface by capillary action. This is the movement of water upwards through tiny pore spaces in the soil. Compounds such as calcium are deposited as hard pan on the soil surface. This prevents the growth of plants and makes the soil pH very alkaline. Aridisols lack organic matter because there are so few plants in the desert region to provide it. Humus is found around the roots of plants but is not widely distributed across the soil. Few microorganisms are present to make humus and so the soil is pale in colour.

The parent material of the aridisol is rock particles weathered from nearby uplands that have been washed into the desert area by the infrequent but torrential rains.

Aridisols are often very deep but have no clearly developed horizons due to the lack of organic matter. Aridisols are often pale grey or white due to the presence of caliche, a hard chalky material formed by calcification of the soil.

4. Generalist and opportunist animals*

Desert animals have evolved bodies and ways of living that enable them to survive in the hot, dry conditions. Deserts tend to contain small animals because of the hot, dry conditions. Few large mammals live in desert regions because they cannot store enough water to survive and find it hard to regulate their body temperature in the hot conditions. In order to survive the dry harsh conditions, desert animals tend to be 'generalists' and 'opportunists'. In other words, they eat whatever they can find wherever they can find it. This is an adaptation to the dry conditions and sparse vegetation.

Animals cope with desert conditions in several other ways. For example, the desert tortoise burrows underground to find cool places to rest during the day. They are active only at dawn and dusk. The elf owl is also nocturnal to avoid the high daytime temperatures. Many animals are dormant and hibernate during the summer, e.g. desert squirrels. Snakes conserve water by removing waste from their bodies in the form of uric acid. The Sonoran Toad has a very short reproductive process. Once rain falls, their tadpoles can emerge just two days after the spawn is laid in small pools or streams. The pale brown colour of many desert animals acts as a camouflage to avoid predators.

Adaption of Plant and Animal life in biomes

Plant and animal life in biomes: 2007 Question 18
Describe how plant and animal life adapt to soil and climatic conditions in a biome which you have studied. [80 marks]

What You Need To Do:
- Identify the key words in the question: plant, animal, soil, climate.
- Explain the term adaptation.
- Discuss how plants adapt to soils and climate in your named biome.
- Discuss how animals adapt to soils and climate in your named biome.

Answer 1: The tropical rainforest biome

In this answer the way in which plants and animals have adapted to soil and climatic conditions in the tropical rainforest biome will be discussed.

Plant adaptations to climate and soils in the tropical rainforest biome*

A biome is a region based on the climate, soils, vegetation and animals that are found there. In a biome, plants and animals have adapted to the soil and climate of that region.

Adaptation means that the animals and plants have evolved body structures and ways of living that enable them to survive and reproduce in the biome. The plants and animals that are best adapted to their biome will reproduce most successfully and so pass on their genes to future generations.

In the tropical rainforest the climate is wet and humid all year round. Heavy convectional rain falls each day with over 6,600 millimetres per year. Temperatures are high (average 27° Celsius) and this combined with the heavy rain leads to high humidity levels of up to 88%.

Plants have adapted to the wet and humid conditions in the following ways: many plants have leaves designed to shed water from their surface very quickly. This prevents the branches becoming weighed down with water and breaking. Such designs include elongated leaves with deep grooves on the leaf surface to channel water to the tips. Leaves also have very pointed ends (drip tips) to allow water pour off the leaf easily. Leaf surfaces are also very smooth and hairless to allow water flow easily over the leaf surface. A typical plant with these adaptations is the palm oil tree.

If plants did not have these adaptations to their leaves, the plant would be weighed down with water and prone to fungal attack in the warm and humid conditions.

Leaves are also large in order to capture as much light as possible in the dark understorey layer of the rainforest. Many tree species have saplings that have large leaves when they start to grow in the dark understory but which then produce smaller leaves when they reach the light of the canopy. The emergent layer of trees is also an adaptation as tall trees grow and compete for light in the forest.

The bark of rainforest trees is exceptionally thin – just 1 to 2 millimetres. This prevents the trees overheating in the warm conditions. The bark is also very smooth to prevent parasites attaching themselves to the tree.

Plant adaption to soils in the tropical rainforest biome*

Plants in the rainforest have adapted to grow successfully in the infertile latosol soil of the rainforest. They have adapted by growing very fast and having shallow root systems and buttress roots.

Because of the wet, warm and humid conditions in the tropical climate, dead organic matter is converted to humus very quickly by fungi and bacteria. There are plenty of nutrients available for plants to use. However, the heavy daily convectional rain leaches the nutrients from the soil very rapidly. If plants did not grow fast, they would not be able to use the nutrients in the soil before they are leached out of it by the heavy rains.

Root systems are shallow and spreading in order to capture as many nutrients as possible before they are leached away. Ninety per cent of nutrients in the rainforest soil are in the upper O horizon so there is no need for plants to have deep roots. There are few nutrients in the A and B horizon of latosol soils. However, to help support their great weight and height, the tallest trees (e.g. mahogany) have developed wide structures on their roots called buttress roots which support them. Stilt roots are also used by some trees. These roots grow down from branches to the ground and help to support the tree.

Animal adaptations to climate and soil in the tropical rainforest biome*

Animals have adapted to the climate and soil indirectly by becoming tree living (arboreal). The climate and soil of the tropical region has produced a biome of dense forest which is dark and humid. The forest is layered to reduce competition for light, with the highest trees reaching up to 70 metres while the canopy below is a zone of dense branches connected with vines called lianas which link the canopy trees. Below the canopy is the understorey which is a dark, shaded zone of shrub trees and bushes. The forest floor is covered with the dead leaves and branches that fall from above.

The animals that live in this biome have adapted to survive in the different forest layers. Each layer has different animals some of which live their entire lives without touching the ground. Most animals have evolved excellent camouflage in order to survive in the rainforest. Frogs such as the Giant Leaf Frog have adapted to the leafy environment on the trees and ground by having green skin and a body with an irregularly-shaped outline which makes them look like a leaf. This makes it hard for predators to see them. Other animals such as the jaguar have spotted coats so that they cannot be easily seen in the shady conditions. They are also good climbers so that they can wait in the tree branches before pouncing on animals below.

Trees of each species are spaced far apart in the rain forest. This is to reduce the spread of disease in the hot, humid conditions. Animals have adapted to this by being able to climb or fly from tree to tree in search of their preferred food source. Or, they may be well camouflaged to avoid being seen in their food tree. The Brazilian Tree Sloth moves very slowly and has green moss and lichen growing on its fur to hide it. The Spider Monkey has a prehensile tail that can curl around branches and give extra support as the animal moves amongst the trees. Some animals such as the Sugar Glider (a type of possum) have flaps of skin between their front and back legs that help them glide as they jump from tree to tree.

Answer 2: The hot desert biome

In this answer the way in which plants and animals have adapted to soil and climatic conditions in the hot desert biome will be discussed.

A

Animal adaptations to desert climate*

Most desert animals are generalists and opportunists – animals that eat whatever they find whenever they can find it. Small animals are more common in desert regions, e.g. coyote, jackrabbit, desert toad and kangaroo rats. Small animals can regulate their body temperatures more easily in the high diurnal temperature range (hot day/cold night) of the desert climate.

Animals have long limbs and are pale coloured to help them to keep cool. Some such as the jackrabbit have huge ears fed by a network of blood vessels to help cool their blood. Kangaroo rats can absorb water from the digestion of dry seeds.

Most desert animals are nocturnal to avoid the harsh daytime heat. Many animals conserve water by not sweating. Some live in burrows during the day and come out at night to feed when it is cooler, e.g. desert foxes.

Very few large mammals live in deserts. They cannot cope with the heat and lack of water. Larger animals would die of heat stress in daytime.

Beneath plants, organic materials are buried by the burrowing activities of mammals. Dead plant roots provide abundant organic matter on which many small animals feed. Each plant is a 'fertile island' and encourages higher densities of small animals living on and in the soil.

Very small spiders and microscopic worms live in the soil close to plant roots.

Plant adaptations to desert climate*

Plants in the hot desert biome have adapted to survive the hot dry conditions.

Desert plants have developed ways of storing water in their leaves, stems and roots to survive the dry conditions. These plants are called succulents, e.g. cactus plants.

In order to store water for months on end, succulent plants have developed several ways to reduce the amount of water they lose by evaporation through their skin.

Desert plants have thick waxy leaves and dense hairs that prevent moisture loss and sharp, thorny leaves that prevent birds, insects and animals from biting into the plant to get at their water. A dense coating of hairs (trichomes) slows air moving over the surface of the plant. Since air in the desert is very dry, any air movement tends to increase evaporation. The trichomes create a layer of still, humid air around the plant thus reducing water loss.

Succulent desert plants have the ability to expand when water is available. The plants have thick grooves which direct water to the roots and enable the plant to fill up during rainfall, e.g. the Barrell Cactus.

Many desert plants have evolved to cope with the dry climate by completing their life cycle in just a few weeks after rain has fallen. These plants are called ephemerals, e.g. the desert poppy and Cereus plant (Desert Dandelion).

These plants produce seeds that can survive in a dormant state for many years while they wait for rain to fall and trigger germination into a new plant. When rain falls, the seeds quickly grow into new plants, flower and produce new seeds and then die in the space of three or four weeks.

Plant adaptations to desert soil*

Aridisols are desert soils. They have low moisture content and, due to calcification, they contain impermeable chalk deposits called caliche in the B horizon. The amount of moisture that is available for plants to use is dependent on the soil. Some desert soils have few caliche horizons and allow deep infiltration of water. In some areas desert soils are less permeable and allow water to seep only a few millimetres into the soil.

Perennial plants live for several years and must adapt to the changeable water content of the aridisol. Perennial plants have adapted differently to the contrasting soil moisture conditions. Some plant species are better adapted to soils that allow deep infiltration of moisture by having long tap roots, e.g. the mesquite bush and creosote bush both have long tap roots that reach deep into the soil in order to reach the permanent water table.

Other desert plants such as cacti have relatively shallow fibrous root systems which spread out over large areas to capture as much water as possible when it rains. They are capable of quickly using shallow soil water when it is briefly available and then surviving lengthy periods when it is not.

The location of the creosote bush in deserts is related to the soil type. The creosote bush is found in desert soils that allow deep infiltration of water. It has adapted by evolving a deep root system that enables it to extract water from deep underground. However, the creosote bush also has shallow roots systems to take advantage of shallow soil moisture so it can survive in a variety of desert soil types.

Influence of climate on characteristics of a biome

Q

> **Influence of Climate: 2013 Question 17**
> With reference to one biome that you have studied account for the type of climate experienced in this biome and explain how this climate impacts on soils and vegetation within the biome. **[80 marks]**
>
> **Influence of climate on biomes: 2010 Question 16**
> Examine the influence of climate on the characteristics of one biome that you that have studied. **[80 marks]**

NOTE The answer provided below applies to questions from **2010 and 2013**.

> **What You Need To Do:**
> - Name your biome.
> - Name and explain the climate in the biome.
> - Explain how climate affects soils and vegetation in the biome.

Answer 1: Tropical rainforest biome

A

The Tropical Climate*

The climate of the rainforest biome is the tropical climate.

The tropical climate lies within the Hadley Cell of atmospheric circulation where warm air rises from the equatorial region forming a low-pressure area and sinks at the edges of the tropical zone forming a high-pressure area.

The tropical climate is hot, wet and humid throughout the year. This is because in the tropical zone (23·5°N Tropic of Cancer to 23·5°S Tropic of Capricorn), sunlight strikes the earth at a roughly 90° angle and the region receives 12 hours of sunlight every day. Day length barely changes between summer and winter. This causes intense heat. The average temperature is 27°C and there is a small temperature range. At night, the cloud cover restricts heat loss and minimum temperatures fall no lower than about 22°C.

Due to the intense heat, moisture evaporates from the ground and vegetation (transpiration). Each tree in the rainforest may release 755 litres of water to the air each day. The water vapour rises, cools and condenses to form convectional rain that falls each afternoon during intense thunder storms. Depending on the region, rainfall varies from 1,250 mm – 6,600 mm per year and causes high levels of humidity, between 77%-88%.

The tropical climate has no seasons; there is a slight increase in cloud cover and rainfall when the sun is overhead at midday. This occurs at the summer and winter solstices (June 21st/December 21st).

Influence of tropical climate on vegetation

The tropical climate influences vegetation in the following ways. The high rainfall (up to 6,600 mm per year), warm temperatures (average 27°C) and high humidity (88%) of the tropical climate are perfect conditions for the growth of plants. As a result of the tropical climate the vegetation is lush forest of tall trees, also known as 'jungle'. Typical tree species include mahogany, Brazil nut and palm oil trees. The warm, humid, sunny conditions mean that there are many thousands of plants growing close together. In order to avoid competition with each other for nutrients and sunlight, the forest plants have adapted by growing to different heights. The climate has therefore led to the development of rainforest layers such as the emergent layer, canopy layer and shrub layer. The tallest trees form the emergent layer. They can be up to 70 m high and have small leaves due to exposure to drying winds and the strong sunlight. Plants in the canopy layer below are about 20 – 40 m high and have larger leaves because it is darker. Most life is found in the forest canopy. In the shrub layer and forest floor it is very dark as most sunlight has been absorbed by the canopy plants. Plants in these zones have large leaves to capture as much light as possible.

The humid wet conditions of the tropical climate have also affected the structure of the plants in the biome. Leaves shed water very easily and have drip tips and grooves to allow rainwater run off the leaves. Branches are flexible to avoid snapping under the weight of torrential rain. Leaves are waxy to avoid becoming wet and at risk from fungal attack in the warm conditions.

Influence of tropical climate on soil*

The tropical climate has led to the formation of latosol soils in the rainforest biome. The tropical climate influences the soil-forming processes that can occur. In the tropical climate laterisation is the main process that occurs. Laterisation is a form of intense chemical weathering and leaching that occurs in hot, wet climates. All the soluble minerals are washed out of the soil and only insoluble iron and aluminium oxides remain. These give the soil its red orange colour.

The latosol has a thin O horizon (humus layer) due to intense bacterial activity in the humid climate which rapidly decomposes dead organic matter. The A horizon contains aluminium and iron oxides. The B horizon is very deep and uniform in texture due to intense leaching in the high temperatures. Latosols have low humus content due to the rapid decomposition of dead organic matter which is quickly absorbed by plant roots or washed from the soil by the heavy tropical rain. Consequently little humus gets deeper than the O horizon. Laterisation can reach many metres into the ground. These soils can be 40 m deep.

Influence of tropical climate on animals*

Animals have adapted to the climate indirectly by becoming tree-living (arboreal). The climate and soil of the tropical region has produced a biome of dense forest which is dark and humid. The forest is layered with the highest trees in the emergent layer reaching up to 70 m while the canopy below is a zone of dense branches connected by vines called lianas which link the canopy trees. Below the canopy is the understorey which is a dark, shaded zone of shrub trees and bushes. The forest floor is covered with the dead leaves and branches that fall from above.

The animals that live in this biome have adapted to survive in the different forest layers that result from the climate. Each layer has different animals some of which live their entire lives without touching the ground. Most animals have evolved excellent camouflage in order to survive in the rainforest. Frogs such as the Giant Leaf Frog have adapted to the leafy environment on the trees and ground by having green skin and a body with an irregularly-shaped outline which makes them look like a leaf. This makes it hard for predators to see them. Other animals such as the jaguar have spotted coats so that they cannot easily be seen in the shady conditions. They are also good climbers so that they can wait in the tree branches before pouncing on animals below.

The Brazilian Tree Sloth lives its life completely in the canopy and eats leaves. It has adapted to this life by moving very slowly and having a very slow metabolism which enables it to survive on the low energy content of the leaves it eats. The fur of the Tree Sloth is camouflaged to look green because it lets moss and lichen grow on it. They have large eyes to see in the shady conditions and their paws have long hooked claws to allow them hang easily from the tree branches.

Other animals have also adapted to life in the trees. Animals that live in the canopy are usually able to fly or jump from tree to tree. The Spider Monkey has a prehensile tail that can curl around branches and give extra support as the animal moves amongst the trees. Some animals such as the Sugar Glider (a type of possum) have flaps of skin between their front and back legs that help them glide as they jump from tree to tree.

Answer 2: Hot desert biome

A

The Desert Climate*

The hot desert biome has a hot desert climate.

The hot desert climate has low rainfall, less than 250 mm per year. It has a high rate of evaporation and a wide daily (diurnal) range in temperature of 45°C. Humidity is low.

The large temperature range is caused by the low humidity. The lack of moisture prevents cloud formation. This allows 90% of the solar energy hitting the ground during the day to radiate back to space at night.

Several factors cause the desert climate. First, deserts have a low latitude; they are found between 15°-30° north/south of the equator. This area is under the influence of a global high-pressure belt called the 'subtropical high' that occurs at the junction of the Hadley and Ferrel Cells of the atmospheric circulation system. The year-round high pressure means that air is constantly sinking to the ground, warming up all the time. This causes constant evaporation and prevents clouds and rain forming.

Secondly, deserts lie in the path of dry trade winds (north/east Trades and south/east Trades). These winds blow towards the equator and are, therefore, warming up as they blow across the deserts. These winds absorb moisture so the air is constantly drying out over the deserts.

Finally, hot deserts lie beside cold ocean currents on the western edge of continents. The Sahara and Kalahari Deserts lie beside the cold Canaries Current in the Atlantic Ocean. These currents cool the prevailing winds before they reach land, 'triggering rainfall over the sea.

Due to the combination of these factors, deserts have small amounts of irregular rainfall. It may arrive in short violent storms 3 – 5 times per year.

Influence of climate on vegetation*

The desert climate characteristics are low rainfall (less than 500 mm per year), very high rates of evaporation (7 to 50 times as much as precipitation) and a wide daily (diurnal) range intemperature. Hot desert temperatures range from 0°C at night to 45°C during the day. The climate has influenced the type of plants that are found in the desert biome. Plants in the hot desert biome have adapted to survive in the hot dry conditions.

Desert plants have developed ways of storing water in their leaves, stems and roots to survive the dry conditions. These plants are called succulents, e.g. cactus plants.

In order to store water for months on end, succulent plants have developed several ways to reduce the amount of water they lose by evaporation through their skin.

Desert plants have thick waxy leaves and dense hairs that prevent loss of moisture and sharp, thorny leaves that prevent birds, insects and animals from biting into the plant to get at their water. A dense coating of hairs (trichomes) slows air moving over the surface of the plant. Since air in the desert is very dry, any air movement tends to increase evaporation. The trichomes create a layer of still, humid air around the plant reducing water loss.

Succulent desert plants have the ability to expand when water is available. The plants have thick grooves which direct water to the roots and enable the plant to fill up during rainfall, e.g. the Barrell Cactus.

Many desert plants have evolved to cope with the dry climate by completing their life cycle in just a few weeks after rain has fallen. These plants are called epehemerals, e.g. the desert poppy and Cereus plant (Desert Dandelion).

These plants produce seeds that can survive in a dormant state for many years while they wait for rain to fall and trigger germination into a new plant. When rain falls, the seeds quickly grow into new plants, flower and produce new seeds and then die in the space of three or four weeks.

Influence of climate on soils*

The characteristic soil of the hot desert biome is the aridisol. These soils have been influenced by the hot desert climate. Aridisols are pale grey-coloured soils. Calcification is the main soil-forming process that affects aridisols. This process occurs in desert climates due to high evaporation rates in the dry air. The air is so dry because of the location of hot deserts between 15° and 30° north and south of the equator. This area is under the influence of a global high pressure belt. The year-round high pressure means air sinks to the ground and warms up all the time. The moisture in the air evaporates causing the air to be very dry.

Calcification occurs when nutrients that are leached into the soil are drawn back up to the surface by capillary action. This is the movement of water upwards through tiny pore spaces in the soil. Compounds such as calcium are deposited as hard pan on the soil surface. This prevents the growth of plants and makes the soil pH very alkaline. Aridisols may also contain white/grey layers called calcic horizons. These are accumulations of calcium carbonate, the same material found in chalk, concrete and agricultural lime. They form due to the process of calcification. Calcic horizons may vary from 15 cm to 1 m in thickness and form an impermeable, white/grey cement-like layer or hard pan in the soil known as caliche. The pale grey colour of desert soils is a direct result of the climate-induced calcification.

Aridisols lack organic matter because there are so few plants that can grow in the desert climate to provide it. Humus is found around the roots of plants but is not widely distributed across the soil. Few micro-organisms are present to make humus and so the soil is pale in colour. The parent material of the aridisol is rock particles mechanically weathered from nearby uplands that have been washed into the desert area by the infrequent but torrential rains.

Aridisols are often very deep but have no clearly developed horizons due to the lack of organic matter available in the desert climate.

Influence of climate on animals*

The desert climate has influenced the type of animals found in the desert biome and the way that they live. Most desert animals are generalists and opportunists, animals that eat whatever they find whenever they can find it. Small animals are more common in desert regions, e.g. coyote, jackrabbit, desert toad and kangaroo rats. Small animals can regulate their body temperatures more easily in the high diurnal temperature range (hot day/cold night) of the desert climate.

Animals have long limbs and are pale coloured to help keep cool. Some such as the jackrabbit have huge ears fed by a network of blood vessels to help cool their blood. Many animals conserve water by not sweating. Kangaroo rats can absorb water from the digestion of dry seeds

Most desert animals are nocturnal to avoid the harsh daytime heat. They live in burrows during the day and come out at night to feed when it is cooler, e.g. desert foxes.

Very few large mammals live in deserts. They cannot cope with the heat and lack of water. Larger animals would die of heat stress in daytime.

Beneath plants, organic materials are buried by the burrowing activities of mammals. Dead plant roots provide abundant organic matter on which many small animals feed. Each plant is a 'fertile island' and encourages higher densities of small animals living on and in the soil.

Very small spiders and microscopic worms live in the soil close to plant roots.

Chapter 38

Human Influence on Biomes

> **Human Activities and Biomes: 2011 Question 18**
> The development of economic activities can alter biomes. Discuss this statement with reference to appropriate examples that you have studied. **[80 marks]**

What You Need To Do:
- Name the human activities you will discuss.
- Name the biome(s) that is (are) affected.
- Describe the human activities.
- Discuss how the biome(s) is (are) affected by the activities.

Answer

In this answer the impact of economic activity on the coniferous forest biome of Northern Europe and the impact of deforestation of the tropical rainforest biome will be discussed.

Economic activities affecting biomes: Acid rain and deforestation*

Industrial activity in Europe produces acid rain, which has an impact on the soils and vegetation of the coniferous forest biome of Europe. Acid rain is polluted rainwater that has a pH of less than 5.6. Acid rain occurs when man-made air pollutants such as sulfur dioxide and nitrogen oxides combine with moisture in the atmosphere. These two gases are produced by burning fossil fuels in power stations and vehicles. The sulfur and nitrogen oxides combine with water vapour in the atmosphere to create sulfuric and nitric acid. When it rains, these fall onto the land as acid rain. When acid dust particles fall to the land it is called acid deposition. When particles of sulfur are emitted, it takes about 10 days for them to settle back to earth. In this time they can travel thousands of kilometres and affect countries far from their source. The maximum amount of acid deposition that a biome can receive without damage to the soils and vegetation is called its critical load. It is estimated that in Europe, 20% of forests have acid deposition greater than their critical loads.

Deforestation is the unsustainable removal of trees from a biome. The tropical rainforest biome is the most affected by deforestation. Globally, rainforests are disappearing at about 40 hectares per minute, day and night. Trees are felled in order to extract valuable timber or the forest is burned to clear land for soya bean plantations and cattle ranching. In developing countries such as Brazil, the need to repay international debt has led to the increase in the production of cash crops for export. These cash crops are grown on deforested land. Mining is also responsible for deforestation as is urbanisation and road-building projects such as the Trans Amazon highway.

The impact of acid rain on the vegetation and soil of the coniferous forest biome*

Acid rain damages the vegetation of the coniferous forests in several ways. First, the acid damages the surface of the leaves. This causes uncontrolled water loss from the leaf pores (stomata) and prevents photosynthesis – the process by which plants make their own food. Damage to the leaf therefore damages the trees' health and reproductive ability. This reduces forest growth rates since the seeds from acid-damaged trees have lower germination rates. The damage done by acid rain to the coniferous forest in Europe has had an effect on forest production. In Sweden, it is estimated that the loss of growth amounts to €495 million each year. This is a serious loss to an economy where forests are considered to be 'green gold'.

Second, acid rain depletes the soils of essential nutrients such as calcium and phosphorous. This damages the trees' health. Soils most at risk of acid deposition are those with acidic parent rocks, such as granite and sandstone. Soils under Swedish forests are badly affected by acid rain because most of Sweden is underlain by acidic granite rock.

Third, acid rain can increase the concentration of aluminium in the soil. Aluminium damages the fragile root hairs of a tree, preventing them from absorbing essential nutrients from the soil. So acid rain results in the trees 'starving' since they cannot make or absorb the food they need. In order to neutralise the acid in the soil, it is 'limed'. This involves the spreading of powdered lime onto the soil. In Southern Sweden it takes about 3 tonnes per hectare of lime to protect a field from acid rain for about 20 years.

Impact of deforestation on tropical rainforests*

Once an area of forest is cut, the natural habitat for wildlife is severely reduced and species begin to become extinct. Many animals and insects in the rainforest have not been clearly identified yet and as more of the rainforest is destroyed, the opportunity to study and identify these animals is lost.

The loss of many species of plants is a serious cause for concern as some contain chemicals that could one day lead to cures for serious illnesses such as cancer and AIDS. We already get many common drugs from different species of tree, e.g. aspirin. About one quarter of all the medicines we use come from rainforest plants. Curare comes from a tropical vine and is used as an anaesthetic and to relax muscles during surgery.

When a forest is cleared, the nutrient cycle is destroyed. Cutting the forest removes the source of humus from the O horizon. The heavy daily convectional rain then quickly leaches any remaining nutrients out of the soil making it infertile. The remaining latosol soil can be easily washed away by heavy rain. In addition, as a result of the high temperatures in the tropical region, the exposed soil is baked into a hard, brick-like surface which cannot support plant growth. This is known as a laterite soil, which is useless for farming.

In mountainous areas such as Indonesia soil erosion occurs within days of forest clearance, reducing the productivity of the soil even more.

Deforestation affects rainfall patterns in the forested area and beyond. In the forest water cycle, moisture is transpired by rainforest plants and evaporated into the atmosphere. This moisture forms rain clouds before being precipitated as rain back onto the forest. When the forests are cut down, less moisture is released into the atmosphere resulting in the formation of fewer rain clouds. Subsequently there is a decline in rainfall. The area then experiences drought. Without rainfall the area can become arid within a few years due to the strong tropical sun baking down on the scrub-land. For example, Madagascar is today largely a red, treeless desert due to generations of deforestation.

Notes

Book 2 → Ch 5, 7, 8, 9

Notes

- Footloose pharmaceutical in Cork ✓
- Globalisation Brazil ✓
- Globalisation Ireland ✓
- Energy Sources
- Economic Activities : OS Map
- Ch 9 - Fair Trade etc
- Econ activities and the environment

- Get revise notes on colonialism ✓
- MNC

Notes

Notes
Physical

<u>Usually</u> Q1 • <u>Ordinance Survey Map skills</u> ✓
Q2 • <u>Landform of erosion/deposition</u> ✓
Any • <u>Human interaction with surface processes (Dam)</u> ✓
Any (most ↕) • <u>Specific Rock Type</u> ✓
2 or 3 • <u>Human interaction with rock cycle (Geothermal)</u> ✓
Any • <u>Isostatic Process</u> ✓
3 • Process shaping karst region — To do + Formula
• Weathering ✓
• <u>Earthquakes</u> ✓
• <u>Volcanoes</u> ✓
• <u>Folding</u> ✓

+ Riv patterns

Notes

<u>Regional</u>

- Regions — Climatic, Geomorphological, Cultural, Socio Economic
-

Notes (Biomes)

- Impact of human activities
- Climate and its impact
- Adaptations of plants, animals etc

↳ Economic activity alters...
↳
↳ Characteristics of biome